The Best of NEW YORK archives

The Best of NEW YORK archives

Selections from the Magazine, 2001–2011

New York State Archives Partnership Trust

excelsior editions

AN IMPRINT OF STATE UNIVERSITY OF NEW YORK PRESS

Cover: View of the Niagara River at the American Falls in the summer, ca. 1898–1910. Source: New York State Archives. Education Dept. Division of Visual Instruction. Instructional lantern slides, 1911–1925. Cover Design: 2K Design.

Published by State University of New York Press, Albany

Printed in the United States of America

Excelsior Editions is an imprint of State University of New York Press

For information, contact State University of New York Press, Albany, NY
www.sunypress.edu

Production, Jenn Bennett
Marketing, Fran Keneston

Library of Congress Cataloging-in-Publication Data

Names: New York State Archives Partnership Trust
Title: The best of New York Archives : selections from the magazine, 2001–2011
Description: Albany : State University of New York Press, [2016] | Series: Excelsior Editions | Includes bibliographical references.
Identifiers: ISBN 9781438464473 (hardcover : alk. paper) | ISBN 9781438464497 (e-book)
Further information is available at the Library of Congress.

10 9 8 7 6 5 4 3 2 1

Contents

Foreword

In memoriam

July 19, 1930–August 30, 2014

New York State sits atop a mother lode of history, from the decisive battle of the Revolutionary War at Saratoga to the tragedy of 9/11 in 2001, and much of that history is preserved within the New York State Archives. This repository is so immense, however, that we need a medium to help digest it, to illuminate it, to tell us about the fascinating people and events—and sometimes the forgotten chapters—of New York's rich past. Since 2001, we have been fortunate to have just such a medium, the *New York Archives* magazine, which is now into its second decade as our window into the Empire State's history. In its pages we learn about what preceded us and made us what we are today, from the bustle of New York City to the mountains of the Adirondacks, from the Southern Tier to the Niagara Frontier. We come to know the heroes and the villains, the giants and the ordinary folk, the splendid achievements and the dismal failures, the tragedies and the comedies that make up our heritage.

As a historian and as a cover-to-cover reader of the magazine, the articles are engagingly written, solidly researched, and above all readable. Now we have a special treat: publication by the State University of New York Press of the best from the first ten years of *New York Archives*. We owe a debt of gratitude to those who began the publication of this magazine whose talents, love of history, and love of New York State have repeatedly lifted the past from something too often seen as dusty and musty and instead have made our forebears and the lives they led spring once more to vibrant life.

Congratulations, *New York Archives*, and keep the good reading coming.

—Joseph E. Persico

Acknowledgments

The New York State Archives Partnership Trust wishes to thank the following individuals and organizations:

Richard Andress
Robert Arnold III
Jennifer Betts
Tom Birdsey
Samuel Bogen
Janet Braga
Lisa Buell
Robert Bullock
Joanne Burnside
Jeffrey Cannell
V. Chapman-Smith
Meredith Cherven-Holland
Jennifer Clunie
James Corsaro
CSEA, Civil Service Employees Association
Bruce Dearstyne
The Gladys Krieble Delmas Foundation
Jennifer Dorsey
EYP Architecture & Engineering
Scott Fein
Jeanne Finley
Kris Fitzgerald
James Folts
John Frederick
Furthermore, the publication program of the J. M. Kaplan Fund
Kimberly Gilmore
George Hamell
Hearst Foundations
George R. Hearst III

Judy Hohmann
Maria Holden
Harold Holzer
William Howard
Geof Huth
Carole Huxley
Christine Karpiak
KeyBank National Association
Edward Knoblauch
Paul Lee
Jennifer Lemak
The Lucius N. Littauer Foundation, Inc.
Philip Lord, Jr.
Stephen Madarasz
Josie Madison
Anthony Mattrazzo
Jackson McPeters
Laura Eve Moss
Jeremy Naidus
New York State Archives
New York State Archives Partnership Trust Board of Directors
New York State Library
New York State Museum
New York State Office of Cultural Education
PEF, Public Employees Federation
Renae Rapp
Laurie Roberts
Sam Roberts
Kathleen Roe
Harry Rosenfeld
Tom Ruller
Jill A. Rydberg
SUNY Press
John Suter
HISTORY®
Sonya Tucker
Judith Van Allen
Christine W. Ward
Grazia Yaeger

Early New York, the 1600s and 1700

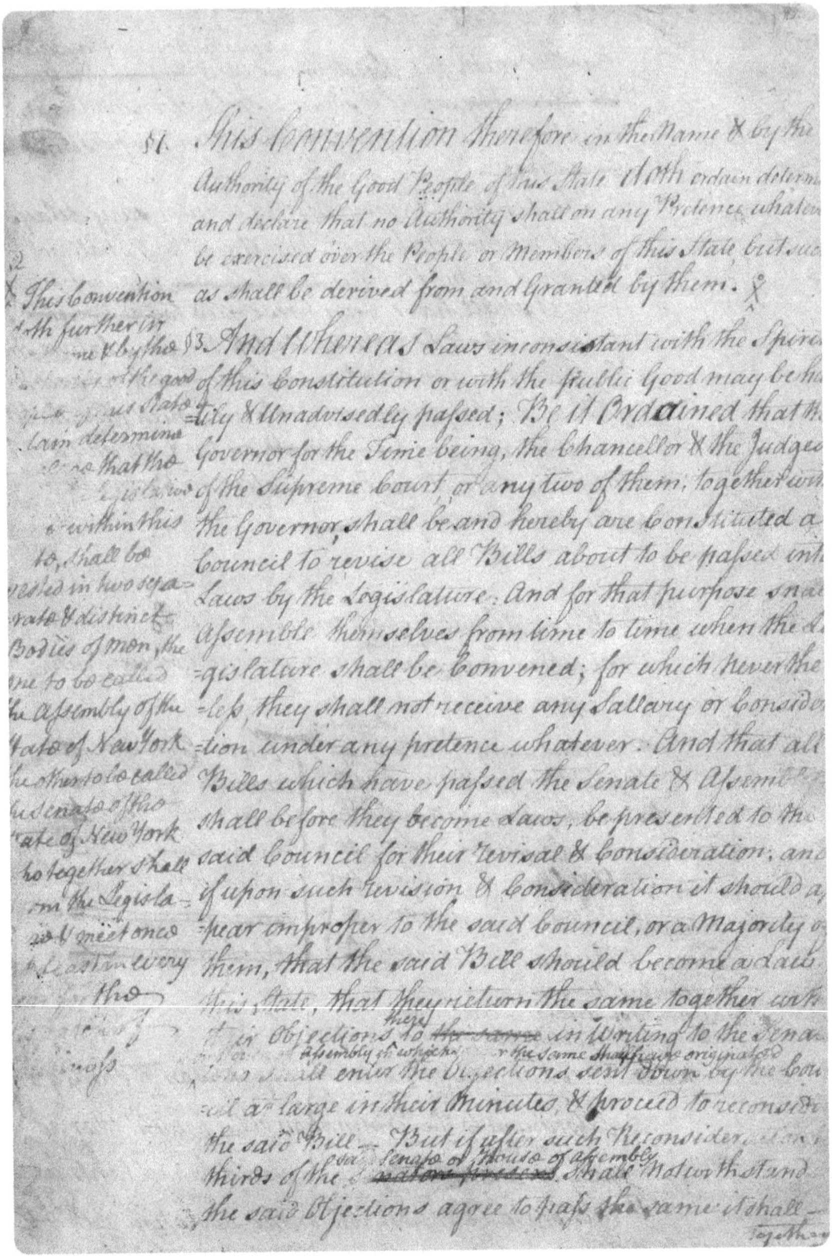
1. This Convention therefore in the Name & by the Authority of the Good People of this State doth ordain determine and declare that no Authority shall on any Pretence whatever be exercised over the People or Members of this State but such as shall be derived from and Granted by them.

3. And Whereas Laws inconsistant with the Spirit of this Constitution or with the Public Good may be hastily & Unadvisedly passed; Be it Ordained that the Governor for the Time being, the Chancellor & the Judges of the Supreme Court or any two of them, together with the Governor, shall be and hereby are Constituted a Council to revise all Bills about to be passed into Laws by the Legislature. And for that purpose shall assemble themselves from time to time when the Legislature shall be Convened; for which nevertheless, they shall not receive any Sallary or Consideration under any pretence whatever. And that all Bills which have passed the Senate & Assembly shall before they become Laws, be presented to the said Council for their revisal & Consideration; and if upon such revision & Consideration it should appear improper to the said Council, or a Majority of them, that the said Bill should become a Law of this State, that they return the same together with their Objections to there [illegible] in Writing to the Senate or Assembly in which the same shall have originated [illegible] shall enter the Objections sent down by the Council at large in their Minutes, & proceed to reconsider the said Bill — But if after such Reconsideration [illegible] thirds of the said Senate or House of Assembly shall Notwithstanding the said Objections agree to pass the same it shall —

The New York State Archives has both the handwritten and typeset copies of the 1777 State Constitution. Credit: New York State Archives, Albany, New York.

1

New York's First Constitution

Sketching a Map for Becoming American

Edward Countryman

In January 1779, London cartographer Claude Joseph Sauthier published an enormous "Chorographical Map of the Province of New York." Dedicating it to "Major General William Tryon, Governor," Sauthier depicted New York as it had existed in 1774, when resistance to specific British policies was starting to yield to independence—the goal of the American Revolution. The map showed Long Island, Staten Island, Manhattan, and the upper Susquehanna and St. Lawrence, Delaware, Hudson, and Mohawk Rivers, as well as the Connecticut River and the mountains between it and the Hudson. The Catskills and Shawangunks were portrayed, but the Adirondacks were barely sketched. Sauthier also showed Wood Creek, almost touching the Mohawk at its headwater, and Oneida Lake with its outflow into Lake Ontario, but he ignored the Finger Lakes, the Genesee Valley, and the headwaters of the Allegheny. These were just white space, the country of the Six Nations.

Wishful Thinking

Sauthier showed nothing of the Empire State's modern shape. Like many New Yorkers, Loyalist and Revolutionary alike, what interested him was not firm borders but the blurry borderland between New York and New England. Though surveyors and politicians had drawn the lines that separated New York from Massachusetts and Connecticut, Sauthier extended a few New York claims beyond those borders and

This essay first appeared in spring 2002, volume 1, number 4.

drew detail all the way to the Connecticut River, as if to suggest that New York had an interest there. The Green Mountains were entirely New York's. But east of the Connecticut, New England was just more white space.

There was no evidence on Sauthier's map of either the Revolution or imminent American independence. But by 1779, the map's year of publication, only Long Island, Staten Island, and Manhattan were still under British military control. A front and a no-man's-land crossed Westchester County. The Mohawk Valley, the upper Delaware and Susquehanna, and the territory of the Six Nations were aflame with civil war. William Tryon was governor only by an empty commission. The Green Mountains had become Vermont.

Sauthier's map was wishful thinking. Ulster County's George Clinton, a former provincial assemblyman and in 1779 a Continental brigadier general, was the true governor of New York State. His military commission was from Congress, not the British king, and he owed his governorship to election, not royal favor. Clinton would have agreed that most of what the map showed belonged to New York, including the British-controlled Southern District and the "pretended State of Vermont." But New York was remaking itself in ways that went beyond independence. If Sauthier's map displayed the memory of an old order, the State Constitution of 1777, which created Clinton's governorship, outlined both possibilities and problems for the state's future.

An Undefined Existence

There was little precedent for New York's constitution-makers to follow. The Dutch mandate of 1614 simply permitted the West India Company to make four trading voyages without competition. The English conquest in 1664 was based on a directive from James Stuart, Duke of York. Though he would become King James II, Stuart's "Duke's Laws" of 1665 were the act of a lord proprietor, not a sovereign. As king, Stuart melded by decree the chartered New England colonies, together with New York and New Jersey, into the abortive Dominion of New England. In 1683, an Act of Assembly established counties, but that was just a local statute, and like previous documents it left New York's outer boundaries undefined. New York did exist, without question. But neither as a well-defined place nor as a set of institutions did colonial New York enjoy the firm legal basis that "charter colonies" like Massachusetts and Connecticut could claim.

The 1777 State Constitution's preface reflects these historical insecurities, suggesting an awareness that old New York had a weak legal foundation and that the nascent state needed a firmer basis for existence. But the language of the preface offers no basis for codifying a system of government other than a call to elect a convention. That body was elected with the specific power to write a constitution. But neither the convention's mandate nor the constitution itself said anything about how it would take effect. After the convention assembled, New York City's "Committee of Mechanicks" demanded that the "elected delegates" submit their work to the public. But the completed State Constitution was proclaimed, not submitted, and no official ratification ever took place.

Both Visionary and Provincial

The state constitutions that predate the federal Constitution of 1787 were experiments in visionary government, addressing the hopes and concerns of their drafters and the political balance within each new state. New York's constitution actually presaged many features of the federal document. Its strong, directly elected governor, who served a multiyear term and had a role in public appointments and in approving or vetoing laws, pointed toward the powers of the presidency. With a state senate whose members served overlapping terms, as well as an independent judiciary, the New York Constitution foreshadowed the structure of Congress and the federal courts. But in other ways it spoke only to "state" issues of the time, the most pressing of which was the state's own existence. The document was written as if the Southern District counties were not still occupied by British forces and could thus send members to the legislature. It could not recognize hostile military occupation, because to do so might amount to renouncing the occupied territory's independence. In fact, the state constitutional convention appointed those counties' first assemblymen and senators, and until 1784 the legislature filled vacancies among them. The State Constitution also granted representation to Cumberland and Gloucester Counties, even though most of their population identified themselves as Vermonters. Not until 1791 would New York acknowledge Vermont as a separate state.

Ignoring these realities was wishful thinking almost to the same degree as Sauthier's map. Clarity prevailed, however, in the document's permission of bills of attainder, which convicted a person by legislative decree rather than by court proceedings, until "the termination of the present war." This made possible the Act of 1779, which named more than seventy Loyalists, confiscated their property, and banished them under penalty of death. The act was harsh, but it also recognized that the Revolution posed fundamental questions of identity and allegiance. To Revolutionaries, the act was both necessary for the state's survival and a just punishment for choosing the crown; to outright Loyalists and to would-be neutrals, it was tyrannical, as were the political police known as "Commissioners for Detecting and Defeating Conspiracies."

Grappling with "the People"

The framers of New York's constitution also tried to address three immediate, fundamental issues that confronted the state. They solved two: survival as an entity through the Revolution and division of power into the modern American triad of bicameral legislature, strong executive, and independent judiciary. But the third problem was what historian Edmund S. Morgan has called "inventing the people": how to invest popular sovereignty as an abstract authority superior to all others. Early state proclamations referred to "subjects of this state" and closed with the incantation "God Save the People," but those phrases were just variations on the language of the royal era. The new constitution did "ORDAIN, DETERMINE and DECLARE, that no authority shall . . . be exercised over the people or members of this State, but such as shall be derived from and granted by them"—but the Massachusetts Constitution of 1780 was the first American document to use the elegant, straightforward, and poetic phrase "we the people."

John Jay's Vision

The Constitutional Convention, first headquartered in White Plains, retreated in 1776 to Kingston, the state's de facto capital. Writing the constitution took nine months; it was drafted primarily by John Jay, whose mixture of militancy about independence and caution about change within America is reflected in the document. Jay and his sons would become prominent critics of slavery. But though neighboring Vermont's constitution flatly abolished slavery, New York's ignored the issue. Many white New Yorkers held slaves with no intention of freeing them, and New York's last slaves would not become free until 1827. On the issue of separation of church and state, however, Jay was firmer. His voice is clear in the long paragraph that condemns the political influence of "wicked priests" and casts off the Church of England's tie to government. But Jay also revered private property, and the constitution makes no mention of Trinity Church's large property in Manhattan.

Yet Jay's was not the only vision represented in the document. Secret ballots were permitted once the "present war" ended, but only as an experiment that the legislature could rescind. Drafting committee chairman Abraham Yates was already moving toward the vision of white male democracy and state autonomy that would underpin his (and George Clinton's) anti-Federalism in 1788. It seems likely that Yates, or a similar thinker, was probably responsible for the secret ballot proposal.

A Matter of Property

New York's constitution did not grant the economic powers that would be given to Congress (and denied to the states) in 1787. In 1779, New York's Confiscation Act declared "the sovereignty of the people of this state in respect of all property within the same." That statute, not the constitution, presaged the active economic role that the state would take in peacetime. But what property the legislature actually meant remains uncertain. Was it Loyalist land, to be seized? Was it Vermont, to be reclaimed? Or did it mean the white spaces that Sauthier's map showed as belonging to the Six Nations, including the short, vitally important portage known as the "Carrying Place" that Sauthier noted between the Mohawk River and Wood Creek? This last possibility seems plausible. The constitution did grant the state government exclusive power over Indian affairs, a matter over which the state and Congress would soon conflict and which is still in litigation today.

Between the constitution's proclamation on April 20, 1777, and its replacement in 1821, New York bootstrapped itself into the Empire State, very different from the province that Sauthier drew. Like Sauthier's map, New York's original constitution was far from complete and showed only a sketch of the enormous changes that were to come. Statutes, rather than the constitution itself, would underpin the state's strong role in economic development, in securing its modern geographic boundaries, and in the destruction of both slavery and the Iroquois' Six Nations. But the map of government outlined in New York's first constitution helped set the public agenda for ceasing to be British and for becoming American.

Artist's recreation of the English merchant slaver, *Henrietta Marie*
Drawing: Peter Copeland

Slave ship *Henrietta Marie*, 1699/1700, F014, as shown on slaveryimages.org. Credit: Compiled by Jerome Handler and Michael Tuite, and sponsored by the Virginia Foundation for the Humanities and University of Virginia Library. Drawing by Peter Copeland, in David Moore, *Site Report: Historical and Archaeological Investigation of the Shipwreck Henrietta Marie*, Key West, Florida.

2

Re-Examining Slavery in New York

A. J. Williams-Myers

The South was not the only area of the United States complicit in slavery. Two hundred years before the Civil War, the North, particularly New York, was also a willing participant in the buying, selling, and enslavement of Africans during slavery's most active era (late 1600s through 1700s). African labor contributed not only to the enormous wealth New York State had accumulated at the start of the Revolutionary War but also to the prosperity that New York merchants and the landed aristocracy enjoyed from business, including slaving. Some of the state's most reputable and politically influential citizens—the Rensselaers, Philipses, Schuylers, Beekmans, Livingstons, and Van Cortlands—owned slaves. These families, possessing huge manor lands, benefited from slave labor for generations—their own and their slaves'.

Under both Dutch (ca. 1609–1664) and English (1664–1776) rule, and even into the early decades of American independence (1783–1808), wealthy New York gentry participated in all aspects of the slavery spectrum: from the Atlantic shipping trade of transporting Africans for future enslavement, to buying and selling slaves, to owning slaves on family land in New York. The Frederick Philipse family of Westchester and New York City, for example, ran ships directly to coastal Africa and the island of Madagascar. A story has it that one of those ships attempted to avoid import duties by disembarking a number of Africans at Rye, New York, and then marching them overland to the family's upper mill at Tarrytown.

Not every free New Yorker owned slaves, but those that did held, on average, between one and three. Although the numbers of slaves never reached those of the South on large plantations, a few of the manor lords owned a significant number. On a trip through the Hudson River valley in the early 1790s, an English visitor remarked

This essay first appeared in winter 2002, volume 1, number 3.

that "many of the old Dutch farmers . . . have 20 to 30 slaves [and] to their care and management every thing is left." New York in 1771 had the largest percentage of slaves in the North, about 10 to 12 percent of the population. In that year, the total population of the province of New York was 168,007, of whom 19,873 were slaves. By 1790, the total enslaved population in New York was over 21,000.

But who were those historically silent ones transported across the Atlantic on the infamous "Middle Passage," who were chained in subhuman conditions in the holds of ships, and who faced a lifetime of servitude at their destinations? In the chilling words of one of the discoverers of the sunken slaver *Henrietta Marie*, "One pair of shackles was extremely small, suitable for a child or perhaps a young woman." The captured were men, women, children of all ages, and very often whole families. Those who, during the Middle Passage, died, suffered from disease, or mutinied—in other words, the economically useless—were thrown overboard.

Although the largest number of enslaved Africans imported into New York were from Caribbean islands such as Jamaica, Barbados, St. Christopher, and Antigua, by the middle of the eighteenth century a significant number were arriving directly from Africa. The ship *Oswego* out of Jamaica, upon arrival in New York in August of 1741, carried a consignment of twelve enslaved Africans for Philip Livingston. Two later slavers, the *Rhode Island* and the *Revenge*, both sailed directly from Africa in 1749 and 1751 and carried consignments of thirty-eight and fifty-two African captives, respectively, for buyers in New York—the latter for William Beekman.

Along the river wharves in New York and up the Hudson to Albany, Africans were bought and sold out of taverns and grog houses or at designated markets. One of the most notorious open-air markets was along the East River at the end of Wall Street. In Albany in 1682, an African male was sold for "the sum of 50 good, whole deliverable beaver skins, but failing of beavers . . . good, marketable winter wheat, or peas." Gerard G. Beekman of New York City wished, in 1748, to purchase "a young negro wench and child of 9 months. If she is likely brisk and no bad quality the two will fetch fifty pounds or more." Cadwallader Colden of New York City and Newburgh sought to purchase a thirteen-year-old female. "My wife desires her chiefly to keep the children and to sow . . . [preferably] one that appears to be good natured."

In both urban and rural cultures, a division of labor existed between male and female, although there were chores that both could do. Women were often cooks, housecleaners, washerwomen, and nannies for their owners' children, as well as integral producers of linens and woolens for home consumption and the colonial markets. Men were waiters, butlers, coachmen, and skilled craftsmen such as carpenters, masons, and wheelwrights. Children were a vital link in this work chain. An English visitor to the homes of Chancellor Robert Livingston and his mother, Margaret Beekman Livingston, in Dutchess County in the early 1790s observed children at work alongside adults:

> Four black boys, eldest about 11 or 12, the youngest about 5 or 6 years old, clean and well dressed but barefooted in a livery green turned up with red, waited about the table [during breakfast]. . . . Three black men in livery waited at dinner and the boys before mentioned, their children. It is not unusual for female blacks to wait.

Preliminary archeological findings from the African Burial Ground in lower Manhattan show that over one-third of the African population during the eighteenth century consisted of children under sixteen. Adulthood for the enslaved was usually defined as beginning at age ten; after 1746, it was sixteen. In 1712, when the total African population of New York City was 975, 34 percent were children; in 1746, with the African population at 2,610, 44 percent were children. By 1771, when the population was 3,137, 36 percent were children.

One nonlabor role that some enslaved children assumed was that of personal companion to slave owners' children. An example of this factotum status is the life of the enslaved African Caesar on the Bethlehem estate of the Rensselaer Nicoll family, eight miles below Albany. At his death in 1852 at the age of 115, Caesar had already outlived three masters in that family. He lived longer than the first to whom he originally belonged, longer than the second with whom he grew to adulthood, and longer than the third—the son of the second—to whom he was a constant companion.

Perhaps the most far-reaching legacy of slavery for the African was the tenuousness of slave families, which at any time, given the nature of the institution, could be broken up or dissolved. Cadwallader Colden did exactly that in 1717. In a letter to a friend on the island of Barbados to whom he sent slaves, Colden wrote:

> I send by this vessel, the *Mary Sloope*, Capt. Edward Harely Commander, a negro woman and child . . . she is a good house negro. . . . Were it not for her allusive tongue, her sullenness . . . I would not have parted with her. . . . I have several of her children I value and I know if she would stay in this country she would spoil them.

Since slavery was a violent act, and as long as one race held another in bondage against its consent, the institution remained highly volatile. Thus interpersonal relations between masters and slaves were unpredictable. One area where the differences remained constant and obvious between masters and their slaves was in the legal relationship of slave parents and their progeny. On the Livingston Manor in upper Dutchess County, a tenant farmer, John Dykeman, was murdered in 1715 by his slave Ben. Coming in the aftermath of the Negro Rebellion of 1712, the act was first thought to be part of another such uprising. But after a preliminary hearing conducted by

Robert Livingston, Sr., and some county magistrates, it was determined that the murder was the sole act of a heartbroken, vengeful father: Dykeman had sold Ben's daughter off the manor to one of Livingston's kin in New York City.

The actions of Ben and of others like him were part of a continuum of African resistance to slavery. Such resistance was fueled in the eighteenth century by the enactment of New York's slave code, the Duke's Laws, first published in 1664 and amended periodically beginning in 1674. These laws were a British attempt to undo, or at least undermine, an air of liberalism that the British felt existed in the colonies and that carried with it an enslaved status of "half-free," at least under Dutch rule. Such laws moved to tighten the parameters of slavery, making an African/black-skinned individual synonymous with a slave. A repercussion seems to have been the Negro Rebellion of 1712, followed by the Negro Plot of 1741 and the Kingston Conspiracy of 1775, all trying to enable African freedom and end the nightmare of slavery.

According to Herbert Aptheker, the author of *American Negro Slave Revolts*, "Discontent and rebelliousness were not only exceedingly common, but, indeed, characteristic of American Negro slaves." In the English colony of New York, this was the driving force behind many Africans who participated in the American Revolution. Their bondage would end, they thought, with victory over the British. But it would not be until July 4, 1827, when New York's emancipation legislation took effect, that the nonparticipants, and those who were reenslaved, would gain their freedom.

For New Yorkers to truly confront the legacy of slavery, we must take "the psychological and spiritual journey . . . back into the past in order to move forward," as historian Tom Feelings writes, by re-examining slavery as an integral part of New York's history. If we can do this, says writer Rosemarie Robotham, "we may at last move beyond terrors and the angry racial conceptions that divide us, toward the deeper connections that can render us whole."

Robert Rogers and his few remaining men make a last stand against the French and Indians. Credit: From the collections of the New York State Library, Manuscripts and Special Collections, Albany, New York.

3

The Battle on Snowshoes

Joseph F. Meany, Jr.

When James Kent, chancellor of the Court of Chancery (1814–1823), called New York "the Flanders of America," he meant that the state was a place condemned by geography to be a repeated battleground. Through the colonial wars, the American Revolution, and the War of 1812, New York was indeed the scene of many hard-fought engagements. None, however, was more bitterly contested than a battle fought at the height of the French and Indian War that became known as the Battle on Snowshoes.

In the winter of 1758, the British sought intelligence about French forces at Fort Carillon (Ticonderoga) and Saint Frederick (Crown Point). The intelligence mission fell to a body of American frontiersmen formally named "His Majesty's Independent Companies of Rangers" but universally called "Rogers' Rangers" after their charismatic commander, Robert Rogers. He and 184 rangers left their camp on Rogers' Island adjacent to Fort Edward on March 10, 1758, and moved north on the frozen surface of Lake George using ice creepers and snowshoes.

Marching the Lake

On the morning of March 13, the fourth day of the patrol, Rogers ordered his men to don snowshoes, push inland, and circle behind Bald Mountain, out of sight of the French outpost there. The rangers moved out at 7 a.m. and marched on snowshoes until 11 when they halted, concealed behind a ridge. The rangers expected a French supply party, but by 3 p.m. Rogers judged that the party had already passed and that

This essay first appeared in winter 2004, volume 3, number 3.

his men had regained their strength after the four-hour snowshoe march. So he ordered the rangers to move down frozen Trout Brook, keeping Bald Mountain to their right and "thinking to lay an Ambush" to the outpost.

The rangers moved in three divisions. Captain Charles Bulkeley commanded the point and Rogers himself commanded the main body, followed by the rear guard.

But unknown to Rogers and his men, Sieur Durantaye of the Compagnies Franche de la Marine, along with thirty French marines and two hundred Indians, had arrived at Fort Carillon the previous evening. According to legend, the Indians' medicine man prophesied that an English war party was out. When Indian scouts reported crossing the trail of two hundred men on snowshoes (where the rangers had struck inland from Lake George), Sieur Durantaye's Indians were eager to attack.

Durantaye, without waiting for reinforcements, rushed out along Trout Brook in search of the invaders. Meanwhile, Sieur Langy, another experienced partisan fighter at Fort Carillon, mustered two hundred French marines, Canadian militia, and Indians and set out fifteen minutes behind the impulsive Durantaye.

Converging into Battle

In the journal account he wrote afterward, Rogers described the battle's first phase:

> We kept close to the mountain, that the advanced guard might better observe the rivulet, on the ice of which I imagined the enemy would travel if out, as the snow was four feet deep, and very bad traveling on snow shoes.
>
> I orderd Ensign McDonald to the command of the advance guard, which, as we faced to the left, made a flanking party to our right. We marched to within a few yards of the bank, which was higher than the ground we occupied; and observing the ground gradually to descend from the bank of the rivulet to the foot of the mountain, we extended our party along the bank for enough to command the whole of the enemies at once.
>
> We waited until their front was nearly opposite to our left wing, when I fired a gun, as a signal for a general discharge upon them; whereupon we gave them the first fire, which killed about forty Indians, the rest retreated. My party pursued them & Scalped about forty Indians in about one quarter of an hour.

It was a classic hasty ambuscade, delivered with devastating surprise. But because Durantaye's and Langy's French and Indian fighters had started out in two parties fifteen minutes apart, the ambushers were about to be ambushed with equally devastating effect.

The Rangers Retreat

The veteran Langy, hearing firing to his front, deployed his two hundred men and advanced in a rough battle line. Within minutes, Langy's force received the fleeing survivors of Durantaye's force, hotly pursued by Ensign MacDonald's flank guard and followed by virtually the whole of Captain Bulkeley's division. The exultant rangers ran straight into Langy's volley, delivered at close range in total surprise. Captain Bulkeley and all his officers were killed or wounded in the fusillade. The survivors fell back in confusion to Rogers' main body of rangers.

Rogers, in turn, was unable to form his remaining men into a line to face the attacking French and Indians. Some rangers were captured as they scalped the dead at the first ambush site, while others scattered through the woods. As the French counterattack came in on his right, Rogers found his flank turned and in danger of being enveloped.

But Rogers, a superb combat leader, was mentally and emotionally resilient. He took in the chaotic situation and made his decision immediately, ordering the rangers to fall back toward the high ground of Bald Mountain. If he could not break contact, he would make his stand there.

The French and Indians, realizing that the destruction of Rogers' hated rangers was within their grasp, pressed their attack so forcefully that the rangers could not manage to break contact. Rogers recorded in his journal that he lost fifty men while scrambling to high ground:

> The remainder I rallied, and drew up in pretty good order, where they fought with such intrepidity and bravery as obliged the enemy to retreat a second time; but we not being in a condition to pursue them, they rallied again, and recovered their ground, and warmly pushed us in front and both wings, while the mountain defended our rear.

Casualties Mount

Rogers had no more than 120 men, many wounded, on his firing line. The rear guard, on the left, were cut off and overwhelmed in the confusion as the remaining rangers retreated. The French and Indians, well handled by Langy and Durantaye and infuriated by the sight of scalped victims of the first ambush, continued to press the rangers on all sides and attempted to envelop the perimeter around both flanks. But the rangers held their position, and the attackers "were so warmly received that their flanking parties soon retreated to their main body with considerable loss."

As his casualties continued to mount, however, Rogers' position became more and more precarious. Later he remembered: "The Enemy pushed So close in the front that the partys were not more than 20 yards apart & oftentimes intermixed with each other." Darkness was approaching and Rogers, having lost over one hundred men, sought only to hang on until nightfall. Langy and Durantaye, in turn, were equally determined to finish the rangers before they could break up and escape into the night. Their final assault came from all sides.

Lieutenant Phillips on the right was the first to be cut off and overwhelmed, although Rogers continued to hold the center. His strength down to twenty men, their right flank cut off from Phillips, and the enemy so close that combat was virtually hand to hand, Rogers, now in the last extremity, ordered his remaining men to scatter and evade capture in the woods: "I thought it most prudent for me to retreat & bring off as many of my people as I possibly could."

A Legendary Escape

Rogers himself made good a legendary escape, supposedly sliding down the smooth, frozen, near-vertical east face of Bald Mountain to the surface of Lake George, over a thousand feet below. It would forever after be known as "Rogers' Slide." Some historians suggest that he only backtracked to the lip of the cliff, to convey the impression to his pursuers that he had actually used "Rogers' Slide." In his journal, Rogers does not mention his own escape, saying only that "the Indians closely pursu[ed] us."

But as the rangers dispersed into the gathering gloom, Rogers threw off his uniform coat, which was, of course, later discovered. In the pocket was his captain's commission, signed by Sir William Shirley. The French were convinced that Rogers was among the dead. One warrior boasted that "he had himself killed him."

The rangers' designated rally point was the shore of Lake George, where they had left their sleds and packs so many hours before. Rogers reached Lake George about 8 p.m. and struck out for the rendezvous. He soon met other survivors, including several wounded. He gathered the survivors at the rally point and immediately sent two rangers on ice skates south to Fort Edward, with requests for a relief force. Four severely wounded men were put on sleighs, with two men each to pull, and also sent south. The remaining handful of survivors he kept in a perimeter around the rally point, where they were able to collect others as they came in, though all nearly froze to death that night without fire or blankets.

"A Vast Cold & Tedious Day"

At daybreak on March 14, the remaining rangers started for Fort Edward. The two advance messengers arrived there at noon and informed the garrison that Rogers "[h]ad a Hot Ingagment Such as Scare Even [*sic*] was Knowed in ye Country & Most of His Party Destroyed." Colonel Haviland immediately ordered three companies of rangers to Rogers' support. These met the survivors at Sloop Island, six miles from the head of Lake George. Rogers spent the night of March 14–15 on Sloop Island, first sending again to Fort Edward for three horse-drawn sleighs to carry the remaining wounded.

The next day, March 15, was described by Ranger Jabez Finch as "a Vast Cold & Tedious Day Espacially for ye Wounded Men." The defeated rangers trickled into Fort Edward in small groups about 3 p.m. Rogers, bringing up the rear, reached the fort about 5 p.m., bringing with him fifty-two survivors, eight of them badly wounded. He had lost 125 men.

Rogers immediately set about reconstructing his shattered force. In April, he was promoted to "Major of the Rangers in His Majesty's Service," a vote of confidence in the partisan leader that subsequent events would more than justify. The rangers continued to undertake many hazardous missions, including the 1759 raid on the Abenaki village of Saint Francis that, almost two hundred years later, would become the historical basis of both the novel and the film *Northwest Passage*, starring Spencer Tracy as Captain Robert Rogers. And a tangible legacy of the Battle on Snowshoes still remains: today's U.S. Army Rangers proudly trace their existence back to Rogers' Rangers, the intrepid eighteenth-century American fighting force.

The oil brought home from whaling voyages was refined into lamp oil or made into candles. Credit: L. F. Tantillo.

4

Navigating the Deep

Margaret B. Schram

Something remarkable occurred 120 miles up the Hudson River in 1783: a whaling port was born. Two brothers, Thomas and Seth Jenkins, arrived at the small Dutch community of Claverack Landing and proceeded to buy the surrounding land from the local inhabitants. The brothers represented a consortium of men from the war-wracked New England coast, particularly Nantucket and Rhode Island. The Revolutionary War had destroyed their businesses, their ships, and, for those from Nantucket, their only industry: whaling.

At the end of the war, Britain, Nantucket's major market, had slapped a heavy tariff on the importation of whale oil into that country, rendering profit impossible. As a result, many American whaling masters and their crews departed for Britain to join the growing British whaling fleet, although others remained steadfast to their homeland. A group of the latter formed an organization founded on equity and called themselves "proprietors." The group originally consisted of eighteen men, later expanding to thirty, the majority of whom were members of the Society of Friends, generally called Quakers. These men determined to locate and establish a commercial settlement on the American mainland that would be suitable as a shipping port and free from the danger of foreign invasion. They sought a location surrounded by land that could supply quantities of timber, grain, and other foodstuffs for trade with southern and Caribbean ports.

These proprietors signed Articles of Agreement promising that they would obey the rules and regulations of the future settlement and guaranteeing that they were all merchants "concerned with navigating the deep." A pooled sum of up to $100,000 was

This essay first appeared in spring 2005, volume 4, number 4.

made available for land purchases and other expenses. All promised to relocate to the new settlement before 1785.

Location, Location, Location

Claverack Landing had many advantages as a shipping port. Deep water ran right up to the land's edge, offering mooring close to shore for vessels of all sizes. The surrounding countryside, extending far into Massachusetts, could furnish an ample supply of forest and farm products. A bonus was the freedom of the Claverack Landing folk to dispose of their properties; the landing was part of the 1664 Van Hoesen grant, which was outside the Van Rensselaers' jurisdiction and thus free of manorial restrictions.

The proprietors—the Jenkins brothers among them—purchased the landing parcel by parcel and soon began to arrive with their families (and, in some instances, the frames of their future homes). The new settlement was named Hudson. Committees were formed to plot the future city, divide it into building lots assigned to a proprietor, and plan and construct roads. Those proprietors who were "concerned with navigating the deep" brought fleets of vessels—schooners, brigs, sloops—that were immediately consigned to the coastal and West Indies trade, and whaling vessels sailed for the South Atlantic whaling grounds.

The waterfront along the western side of Hudson was divided among eighteen proprietors into water lots, each one extending some distance into the river. The first shipyard soon opened, beginning an active shipbuilding industry that would see more than seventy-five new vessels leave Hudson's yards between 1784 and 1827. By 1785, twenty-five vessels were owned by the settlement, making the new port of Hudson second only to New York City in shipping in the state. That year the proprietors also incorporated the settlement with a charter that required a mayor, a common council, and a full set of officers to oversee and manage municipal affairs, although most of those offices were held by the proprietors.

A Vibrant Whaling City

By 1786—just three years from the time the first proprietors set foot on the landing—a vibrant city thrived on the river's edge. Wharves, four large warehouses, a ropewalk, and a ducking factory (which made the material for sails) were among the many enterprises run by the proprietors. As Hudson's fame spread, other businessmen and scores of workers moved in. Many families from other Quaker communities cast their lots with the new city.

The first documented whaling vessel out of Hudson was the *Claverack*, sailing in 1785 for the Brazil Banks. The *Hudson*, built in Hudson's own shipyards, also sailed that year under Master Robert Folger. From 1785 to 1796, sixteen whaling vessels left the port for the whaling grounds. The oil brought home from the whaling voyages was refined into lamp oil or made into candles at local factories. Many of the whalers were also involved in sealing, either exclusively or in combination with whaling. The importance of seal hides to Hudson was indicated by the numerous tanneries located there. Shoe leather was made from seal hides, as well as from cattle hides harvested in the city's slaughterhouses.

In 1795, Hudson was designated a Port of Entry, and a custom house with custom officers was located near the docks. The city had jurisdiction over vessels south to the Catskill Creek and north to Albany.

However, Hudson's remarkable prosperity, achieved in so short a time, would soon falter. When the United States signed the Jay Treaty with Britain, which allowed reciprocal commercial relations between the two nations, France considered it a violation of their own 1778 treaty with the United States, which promised American aid to France in the event of war and was a precondition for French help during the Revolution. In 1797, France turned its warships loose on American vessels. Over three hundred American ships, along with their cargoes and crews, were confiscated, including the Hudson whaler *American Hero*. Known to history as the Quasi-War (because war was never declared), this strictly maritime conflict ended in 1800 with France's commerce in the West Indies destroyed.

More trouble followed. War between France and Britain smoldered and flared, leading to blockades of ports by each country. America declared neutrality, and her ship owners, including those in Hudson, became wealthy carrying food and raw materials to European ports. Britain's heavy-handed impressment of seamen from American ships, however, was a constant irritant. Facing an insupportable situation, President Jefferson imposed the Non-Importation Act in 1806, followed by the Embargo Act in 1807, which prohibited American vessels from sailing to foreign ports and even restricted coastal trade. This was the death knell for Hudson's shipping industry. Both acts were repealed in 1809 and replaced by the Non-Intercourse Act, which limited the constraints on trade to a prohibition on trade with Britain, France, and their possessions, but the damage was done.

The Shipping News

The shipping charts of Hudson bear out this distress. Prior to 1797, countless vessels left Hudson for Europe and the Caribbean. By the start of the nineteenth century, far fewer voyages were logged, and those were confined to other Hudson River ports. Whaling had virtually ceased. No whaling voyages were reported from 1798 until 1802, when only four were listed. The year 1803 saw just four whale ships depart Hudson. Strangely, shipbuilding continued, with twenty-seven ships, seven brigs, and four schooners built between 1798 and 1807.

Yet the city continued to grow. By 1800, the population had reached 4,048. Two 1803 libel trials involving the editor of Hudson's Federalist newspaper, turnpike construction, Robert Fulton's steamboat, and the 1805 relocation of the Columbia County seat from Claverack to Hudson kept residents and the economy energized.

War fever was growing, however, and Hudson's common council ordered a powder house to be built. War was finally declared in 1812, causing further disturbance to the city's seafaring businesses, but there was little respite when the war ended in 1814. In 1815, Hudson lost its designation as a Port of Entry; all vessels from the Hudson River would henceforth register in New York City. The opening of the Erie Canal in 1825, giving access to limitless forest and farm products, further sealed the port's doom: trade now bypassed the city on its way from Albany to New York.

The five whaling voyages from Hudson between 1815 and 1819 marked the end of the city's whaling ventures until 1829, when stocks were sold to form the Hudson Whaling Company. The principals reasoned that, since Hudson had once been a whaling port, the industry could succeed again, even though the city no longer had the ships, the experienced whalemen, or the business to supply and support the vessels. But the company and a few hardy individuals raised funds to purchase ships and convert them into whalers. Shipmasters, mates, and harpooners were hired from coastal whaling ports. Crews could be picked up en route, or local boys could be trained. The whaling company's agent was the firm of Barnard, Curtiss Co., which also operated a whale oil and candle factory located near the present Hudson train station. Soon twelve refitted whalers sailed from Hudson.

At first the voyages were successful. Then misfortunes accumulated. A leaky ship was condemned. A shipmaster was drowned when he was pulled overboard by a fouled line, and the unlucky ship was sold. Another ship sank. Cargoes of oil grew smaller and smaller. The greatest blow was the financial depression of 1838. By 1842, only two whale ships remained active from Hudson, the rest having been sold to New England ports. The last two were sold in 1845.

Like the Tide, Fall, Then Rise

This failed attempt to revive Hudson's whaling industry nearly destroyed the city's economy, which was further shaken by a series of disasters. A financial fiasco with a

Hudson–Berkshire railroad added to fiscal woes. Over 12,000 acres of the city were lost when the Town of Greenport was formed in 1837, leaving Hudson with only 1,600 acres in which to further expand. Two huge fires—one in 1838, another in 1844—destroyed most of the busy southwestern section of the city. When the Hudson River Railroad sought a right-of-way through Hudson in 1850, the citizens opted to have the tracks placed along the riverbank, all but shutting off easy access to the river, the source of the city's early prosperity. By 1850, only an occasional steamboat docked at the once-busy port.

There would be other booms and other busts for Hudson over the next 150 years. The former "miracle city" would several times be declared a "finished city," but it would always rise again from its own ashes, fueled by a new burst of economic activity. Hudson's current incarnation as a vibrant arts and antiques center with soaring real estate values owes no small debt of gratitude to those eighteenth-century proprietors who sailed upriver and, far from the sea, built a seaport on a hill.

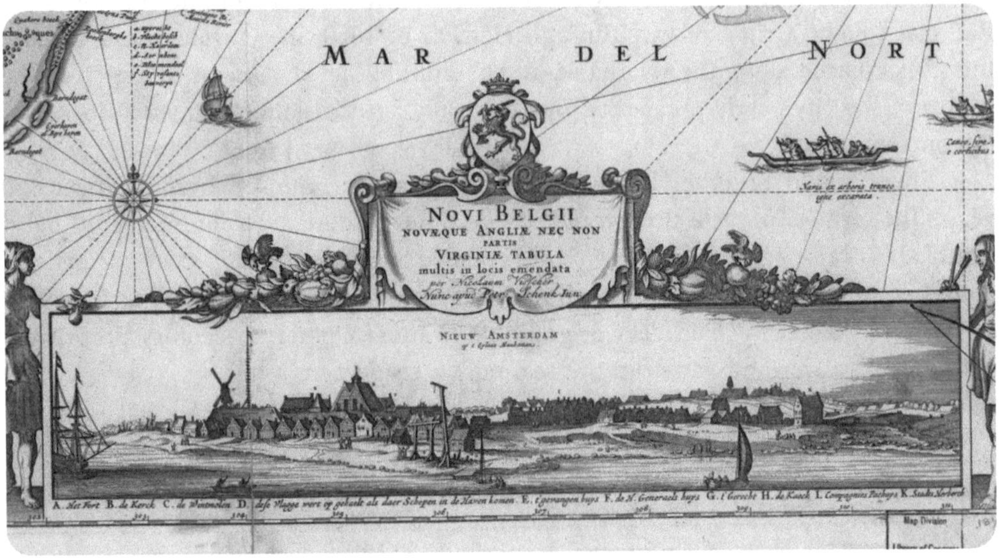

Nieuw (New) Amsterdam. Credit: Library of Congress—Map Division.

5

Citizen vs. Citizen

John Hanna, Jr.

In New Netherland, pig snatching was not uncommon. Pigs, being unfenced, got out and about; what fences there were kept pigs out of gardens and crops instead of penning them in. Thus, to whom a pig belonged was often unclear. Pieter Cornelisz of Breuckelen put the snatch, as Damon Runyon might say, on Dirck Volckertsz's boar. So whose pig was it? Arbitrators in 1655 awarded the snatched boar to Dirck—but Pieter, it seems, did not comply and did not give back the pig. Dirck then applied for enforcement of the award to the "lords high counselors," the judicial authorities of the colony, who issued an order to the *schout* (the equivalent of a combination sheriff and public prosecutor) to return the boar to Dirck with expenses—in other words, to enforce the award. It is important to note that the arbitrators themselves could not enforce the award any more than they could today. Rather, application was made to the judicial authorities (the equivalent of today's courts) to issue an order of enforcement—just as enforcement of a modern arbitration award that is not obeyed follows the same process, with the marshal or sheriff as actual enforcer.

An Old, Peaceable Practice

The ancient practice of arbitration was common in New Netherland during the period of Dutch government, 1630 to 1664. It also had decidedly modern characteristics. For over 250 years after the Dutch period, arbitration in the United States was viewed with suspicion by the courts. That attitude did not change until the 1920s, with the

This essay first appeared in summer 2005, volume 5, number 1.

enactment of state and federal laws supporting arbitration. New York State enacted the first modern arbitration law in the country in 1920, and the Federal Arbitration Act of 1925 "revers[ed] centuries of judicial hostility to arbitration agreements . . . by plac[ing] arbitration agreements 'upon the same footing as other contracts.'" The main features of modern arbitration are: the parties must consent to arbitrate, they are free to determine the arbitrators and/or the process for selecting them, and the courts enforce awards without inquiring about the merits of such awards except in extreme circumstances that might have affected the proceeding, such as not providing one party an opportunity to present its case, corrupt arbitrators, or absence of an agreement to arbitrate. Even this last issue is often left to the arbitrators to decide. One element of modern arbitration not found in New Netherland was any evidence of an agreement to arbitrate future disputes. Today, many commercial and employment agreements, particularly international ones, contain such a provision as an essential element.

Government Support for Arbitration

In February, 1653, Petrus Stuyvesant, director general of New Netherland, and his fellow councilors set out a form of government "in favor [of] this new and growing city of New Amsterdam." Included was an explicit description of arbitration, instructing the burgomasters and *schepens* to meet once or twice a week to determine "whether by judgment or arbitration . . . all civil questions" brought to them. The *schepens*—today's equivalent of magistrates—had both judicial and legislative functions. According to I. N. Phelps Stokes' volume 4 of *The Iconography of Manhattan Island, 1498–1909*:

> [I]f they find the case fit to be arbitrated and the parties disposed thereto, the arbitration shall be conducted completely out of court by both burgomasters and those whom they[,] according to the circumstances of the case[,] may wish to adjoin to themselves from among the schepens or other honest burghers, yes, even, if the burgomasters should find the matter of sufficient importance, from among the council, from which arbitration there shall lie no bill of review or appeal.

Thus, in 1653, it was established in the new municipality that would become New York City that arbitration depended on the consent ("disposed thereto") of the parties, required "honest" men (from which we may infer they were impartial), and provided for an award that was final and not subject to judicial appeal. This is pretty modern. The case of Dirck's pig also has a modern ring to it: he took his award to what amounted to a court, which directed, without reviewing the merits of the award, that the *schout* should seize the pig and return it to him.

A Barrel of Brandy

The U.S. Federal District Courts—trial courts—have established certified mediation and arbitration panels that are available for litigants' use. Sometimes judges exert substantial pressure on disputing parties to use arbitration and mediation, mainly to reduce case overload. Petrus Stuyvesant had the same problem and used the same method to reduce his dockets. Charles T. Gehring, translator of New Netherland's government documents, has noted that

> [t]he increase of population on Manhattan was accompanied by an increase in legal activity: lawsuits, petty squabbles, and other nuisances best handled by arbitrators rather than the full central council. In order to keep the council from being swamped by such cases, a court [we would today call that a panel] of arbitrators, consisting of nine men, was established in 1647. Their function was to decide cases referred to them by the council.

An example involved a suit between Jacob Jansz Huys and Pieter Rudolphus. Huys was the skipper of a vessel, *de Peereboom*, which carried a barrel of brandy belonging to Rudolphus, who claimed that the brandy was destroyed because of poor storage. The suit raised the issue of "average" (a charge by a shipmaster for expenses incurred to save cargo), as well as other technical issues relating to maritime law and customs. The councilors referred the case "to three arbitrators who understand the matter": Jacob Gorter, skipper of the warship *de Waagh*; Pieter Dircksz, skipper on the ship *Nieu Amsterdam*; and Lourens Cornelissen van der Wel, a skipper and a *straetsvaerder* (strait sailor), someone who had sailed through the Straits of Gibraltar.

It is recorded that Rudolphus left the meeting (presumably, he stormed out). Perhaps he regarded the arbitrators as hostile. The arbitrators, in turn, seem to have been exasperated with both parties, because they determined that Huys the shipmaster would get no average and Rudolphus the merchant would not get the value of his brandy. This determination was "conformed" (entered as a judgment) by the council so that each party would bear its own expenses but not those of the arbitrators, which the parties "shall split half and half." This has modern resonance. Today's arbitrators usually have the authority to award the winning party the right to recover all or part of his or her own legal expenses from the loser, and to impose all or part of the costs of arbitration, such as arbitrator's fees, on the loser. In this case, however, each party was sent off to lick his own economic wounds.

The Dog in the Larder

As vividly described by Russell Shorto in his book *The Island at the Center of the World*, Petrus Stuyvesant was passionate about strict control. Unhappily for his choleric temperament, he governed an almost ungovernable community of free spirits. Thus, the New Netherland government had to be far more flexible than Stuyvesant had any desire to be. There was not always a clear line between arbitration and judicial action.

For example, Stuyvesant and his councilors spent considerable time on a master/apprentice dispute. Gelyn Planck was a teenager who had been apprenticed to Allard Antony in his house for four years. Gelyn and Antony's dog were not on good terms. Dogs were not permitted in the attic of a house, since food was stored there. As he was climbing the attic stairs, Gelyn had occasion to kick the dog off the stairs, but the dog climbed back up. Given the damage that a dog could do in a short time to a larder of ham, Gelyn said he "called" to the dog to come down. How he "called" made sufficient ruckus to attract Antony, who cuffed Gelyn on the head and went to get a cane. Gelyn fled to the warehouse. Antony ordered Gelyn to come back to the house. Gelyn declined, saying he would be beaten. Antony is supposed to have said either "Go away" or "Get back to your father now." The dispute ended up in a lawsuit. Gelyn's father demanded full payment for Gelyn's four-year term of apprenticeship, from which he said his son had been dismissed prematurely and without cause, as well as restitution of Gelyn's chattels, or possessions. Antony countersued for his own weekly expenses for two years because he said Gelyn had improperly left his service, although he offered to return Gelyn's chattels if the boy's "book debts" were balanced "in the presence of honest persons."

Lord Director General Stuyvesant and the council considered the matter, but they ended up with a tie vote, whereupon they asked for the "recommendation" of council secretary Cornelius van Ruyven. He opined that Gelyn should serve out his time with Antony. If Gelyn (his father was the actual plaintiff and guardian) refused, he should compensate Antony for the apprenticeship expenses. If Antony refused to take Gelyn back, then Antony should pay Gelyn's father, at the end of the apprenticeship, the full amount that had been promised. And that is what the council ruled. One might conclude that the council "split the difference"—which is considered poor arbitration practice—or speculate that Antony, being a burgomaster and a merchant, was not someone the council wished to rule against. Or it may be that Secretary Van Ruyven was shrewdly suggesting to both Gelyn's father and Antony (and quite possibly to the council) that it was time for everyone to turn to more important matters and get on with things.

The New Netherland government records have survived for over 350 years despite fire, neglect, and unprotected storage in the holds of British ships during the Revolution. Russell Shorto thought that New Netherland made New York unique "and, in time, influenced America in elemental ways." One way New Netherland was unique was that its government before 1665 was more hospitable to arbitration than New York State's—and the rest of the country's—governments were until well into the twentieth century.

The nineteenth-century illustrator Howard Pyle depicted a woman arrested for witchcraft as an old hag. Credit: From the collections of the New York State Library, Manuscripts and Special Collections, Albany, New York.

6

In the Matter of Goody Garlick

George DeWan

In the early spring of 1658, on the far eastern end of Long Island, a married woman of about fifty named Elizabeth Garlick was accused of being a witch. Thus did the wave of social and religious upheaval that had been festering in New England—and would later reach its apogee with multiple hangings in Salem, Massachusetts—spill over into the isolated village of Easthampton (now East Hampton).

It was a time of discontent for Easthampton's thirty-four families, strung out along opposite sides of Main Street near the burial ground and the Presbyterian Church. The village was only ten years old, and its residents were still struggling among themselves to create a sense of community. Whispering, innuendo, and backbiting were common, and charges of slander were adjudicated regularly. Given the temper of the times, what happened to the wife of Joshua Garlick was predictable.

A Sudden Death

The trouble began on a Friday—the date is not certain—in early February 1657/8. (The British did not give up the older Julian calendar for today's Gregorian calendar until 1752. Under the Julian calendar, the new year began on March 25, not January 1.) Across the street from the burial ground, a sixteen-year-old mother, Elizabeth Gardiner Howell, lay feverish and delirious in her bed, having just given up her infant daughter to an attendant after nursing. Elizabeth, also known as Betty, crooned a psalm after her child, then suddenly stiffened and shrieked, "A witch! A witch! Now you are come

This essay first appeared in fall 2005, volume 5, number 2.

to torture me because I spoke two or three words against you! In the morning you will come fawning."

Elizabeth's father, Lion Gardiner, the community's founder and the most important man in town, was duly summoned from his residence across the street. "What did you see?" Gardiner asked his daughter.

"A black thing at the bed's feet," shrieked Elizabeth, stretching forth her hands as if to strike at what she saw.

The next day, Elizabeth's mother, Mary Gardiner, who had herself been sick in bed, was well enough to cross the street. "I went there and presently went to her bed and asked Betty how she did," Mary Gardiner said later. "She put out her hand. 'Oh, mother.' And she cried and I cried and she said, 'Mother, I am bewitched.' I asked her who she saw, and she said, 'Goody Garlick in the further corner and a black thing in the hither corner, both at the feet of the bed."

By Sunday evening, just one day later, Elizabeth Gardiner Howell was dead. Her death set in motion a series of events that consumed Easthampton for the remainder of that spring: charges of witchcraft leveled at Goodwife Elizabeth Garlick, a three-week hearing before three local judges, and a witchcraft trial in Hartford, Connecticut.

Neighbor against Neighbor

Elizabeth Garlick and her husband, Joshua, lived just down the street from Elizabeth Gardiner Howell and her husband, merchant Arthur Howell. Joshua Garlick was a farmer who had once worked for Lion Gardiner on his nearby island, originally called the Isle of Wight but later renamed Gardiner's Island. "Goody" was a shortened form of "Goodwife" and was used for many of the women on Main Street: Goodwife and Goodman were not names but terms of address for a married person who was not of high rank—similar to Mr. or Mrs.—but also not of the lower class.

On February 19, the hearing began before village justices John Mulford, John Hand, and Thomas Baker. In the space of three weeks, thirteen witnesses testified. The justices got an earful, and much of what they heard was bad news for Goody Garlick. Neighbor after neighbor had their say: tales of black cats showing up at odd times, of children getting sick and dying, and of strange and unexplained things happening out on Gardiner's Island. It was implied that Goody Garlick had a hand in all of them: a child that was "taken away in a strange manner," a man who turned up dead, a fat and lusty sow and her piglets that died soon after birth, an ox with a broken leg.

Goodwife Simons said that she was with Elizabeth and her husband Arthur on the second day of Elizabeth's illness when the sick woman asked them, "Send for Goody Garlick! Send for Goody Garlick! . . . I could tear her in pieces! She is a double-tongued woman! Did you not see her last night stand by the bed side ready to pull me in pieces? And she pricked me with pins."

Witch . . . or Scapegoat?

Richard Stratton "said that he heard Goody Davis say that her child died strangely at the Island and she thought it was bewitched and she said she did not know of anyone on the Island that could do it unless it were Goody Garlick." Goody Birdsall related that Goody Davis had once told her of the day that Goody Garlick visited her home:

> Goody Garlick said "The child is not well, for it groaneth," and Goody Davis said her heart did rise, and Goody Davis said when she took the child from Goody Garlick she said she saw death in the face of it and the child sickened presently upon it and lay five days and five nights and never opened the eyes nor cried 'til it died.

Thomas Talmadge, who was also secretary for the hearing, told the judges of an event one day when he was at the house of Goody Davis:

> She [was] there speaking to me about some accidents that had fallen out among them at the Island as concerning the death of her child in what manner it was taken away and of an ox that had his leg broke and having reference in her speech concerning Goody Garlick as if she were a witch.

Jeremiah Vaile, who lived next door to the Garlicks and who had once worked for Lion Gardiner, claimed that Gardiner had challenged Davis' story that Goody Garlick had caused the death of Davis' child. Vaile testified that Gardiner said that "Goody Davis had taken an Indian child to nurse and for lucre of a little wampum had merely starved her own child."

The name Goody Davis keeps coming up in the testimony—and if ever there was anyone who was a community leader in whispering, innuendo, and backbiting, it was she. Oddly enough, she did not testify, but when reading the transcripts, it becomes clear that much of the accusatory, hearsay testimony against Garlick heard by the justices originated in the mind of Davis. Why she focused her bile on Garlick is uncertain.

Brief Trial, Terse Verdict

In the end, however, Goody Garlick stood accused, and the three Easthampton justices sent the case to Hartford, Connecticut, to the Court of Magistrates for a jury trial on the charge of witchcraft. Although all of Long Island had originally been claimed by the Dutch as part of New Netherland, by 1650 its eastern half had been ceded to the British. The East End communities thus had administrative ties to New England, which is why Elizabeth Garlick was sent to Hartford for trial.

The record of the trial—on May 5, 1658, about three months after Elizabeth Gardiner Howell's death—is brief. Recall that when Elizabeth Gardiner Howell died in February, the year was still 1657 (commonly written 1657/8 O.S., or Old Style), and the trial of Elizabeth Garlick three months later was in 1658. Because of this time discrepancy, some writers have mistakenly concluded that Goody Garlick was held in custody for more than a year. The court was headed by Connecticut governor John Winthrop, and the indictment was severe:

> Elizabeth Garlick . . . that not having the fear of God before thine eyes thou hast entertained familiarity with Satan the great enemy of God and mankind, and by his help since the year 1650 have done works above the course of nature to the loss of lives of several persons (with several other sorceries) and in particular the wife of Arthur Howell of East Hampton, for which both according to the laws of God and the established law of this commonwealth thou deserveth to die.

There is apparently no record of testimony or arguments made by either side. The judgment was terse: "The jury doth not find Elizabeth the wife of Joshua Garlick guilty according to the indictment." This verdict was hardly pro forma. At least four hangings for witchcraft had taken place in Connecticut before the Goody Garlick case.

An Execution Averted

It is Salem, Massachusetts, in 1692 that we remember for witchcraft trials in America. In her recent book *In the Devil's Snare*, Cornell University historian Mary Beth Norton enumerates the toll:

> [L]egal action against at least 144 people (38 of them male), most of whom were jailed for long periods; 54 confessions of witchcraft; the hangings of 14

women and 5 men; the pressing to death of another man by heavy stones; and the deaths in custody of 3 women and a man, along with several infants.

The jury in Hartford got it about right, according to Northwestern University historian T. H. Breen in his book *Imagining the Past: East Hampton Histories*:

> The investigation into witchcraft had uncovered no witch. Rather, it had exposed once again a pattern of slander and defamation. Discontented people in East Hampton who had come to this isolated extension of New England culture looking for a fresh start and some possible bettering of their lives had, in their ambition, turned on each other.

Elizabeth Garlick went home to Easthampton and lived for almost another half-century. Not so fortunate was Goody Davis, who appears to have died soon after the Hartford trial.

Thomas Jefferson. Credit: New York State Archives, Albany, New York.

7

The Princes of Queens

Peggy Cornett

In the late eighteenth and early nineteenth centuries, Americans were becoming interested in new and improved methods of agricultural cultivation and animal husbandry and in improvements to seed stock. Specifically, they sought more productive varieties of fruit trees and more ornamental plantings to beautify their lands. In this pragmatic spirit of what can be called the American version of the Enlightenment, President George Washington, as well as three future presidents, came to Queens, New York, to visit the Prince Family Nursery.

Occupying eight acres of land on the north shore of Long Island, it was America's first commercial nursery. Robert Prince established the business in the 1730s in a community of mostly French Huguenot settlers. Initially called the Old American Nursery, it soon became the largest supplier of fruit trees and grapes in the New World, producing most of the grafted apple, pear, and cherry trees found in early Northeastern orchards. In 1771, the nursery's first broadside advertised thirty-three different plum trees, forty-two pear trees, twenty-four apple trees, and twelve varieties of nectarines.

By 1774, the nursery, then owned by Robert Prince's son William, had diversified its stock, advertising in the *New York Mercury* that it offered "Carolina Magnolia flower trees, the most beautiful trees that grow in America, and 50 large Catalpa flower trees," along with other flowering trees and shrubs. William Prince was the first to commercially propagate the native pecan, and the nursery was also among the first

---

Peggy Cornett's essay, originally entitled "Encounters with America's Premier Nursery and Botanic Garden," first appeared in *Twinleaf* (number 16, spring 2004), a publication of the Thomas Jefferson Center for Historic Plants; it was adapted by State Archives staff member Robert W. Arnold III for *New York Archives*, appearing in summer 2006, volume 6, number 1.

to introduce Lombardy poplars; by 1798, it advertised ten thousand trees for sale. It continued to focus on fruits, and, according to agricultural historian U. P. Hedrick, "the first planned attempt to improve fruit on a large scale began in the Prince Nursery" with its work on plum seedlings.

The Politics of Horticulture

In October 1789, the new nation's capitol was located in New York City, and President George Washington, accompanied by Vice President John Adams, "set off from New York, about nine o'clock in [the president's] barge, to visit Mr. Prince's fruit gardens and shrubberies at Flushing." However, Washington was unimpressed with what he saw, noting that "these gardens, except in the number of young fruit trees, did not answer my expectations. The shrubs were trifling and the flowers not numerous," although his assessment would improve upon later visits.

Two years later, in 1791, Secretary of State Thomas Jefferson was consumed by political and personal matters. As his ideological vision for America conflicted with Alexander Hamilton's, Jefferson's political relationships were crumbling and his friendship with Vice President John Adams was deteriorating. Thus, when Jefferson embarked on a four-week "botanizing excursion" through New England with then-congressman James Madison in June, it was the subject of much speculation. Hamilton and others were convinced that this lengthy vacation of two Republican stalwarts through Federalist strongholds in the North had ulterior motives. But the trip was actually innocent of intrigue and incorporated elements of a working vacation, for Jefferson was seeking ways to advance the new nation through alternative domestic industries, and Madison was seeking "health recreation and curiosity." Their trip evidently met both goals: Madison's "bilious attacks" vanished, and Jefferson found a way to promote his most recent idea—the addition "to the products of the U.S. of three such articles as oil, sugar, and upland rice," which he believed would lessen America's reliance on foreign trade, improve the lot of farmers, and ultimately result in the abolition of slavery itself.

Around that time, Quaker activist and philanthropist Dr. Benjamin Rush of Philadelphia, an ardent opponent of slavery, was seeking ways to persuade political leaders and slave owners to create a maple sugar industry in America. Rush was convinced such a native industry would "lessen or destroy the consumption of West Indian sugar, and thus indirectly . . . destroy negro slavery." Thomas Jefferson took up Rush's cause and became a conscientious consumer of maple sugar. Jefferson wrote to a friend, "What a blessing to substitute a sugar which requires only the labour of children, for that which it is said renders the slavery of the blacks necessary."

Monticello's Shopping List

In their quest for productive sugar maples, future presidents Jefferson and Madison visited the Prince Family Nursery on the north shore of Long Island. While there, Jefferson left a note requesting "all you have" of sugar maples and bush cranberries (*Viburnum trilobum*), as well as three balsam poplars, six Venetian "sumachs" (*Cotinus obovatus*), and twelve "Bursé" (Beurré Gris) pears. A month later, while in Philadelphia, he wrote an enormous addendum to that original short list, explaining, "To [my original order] I must now desire you to add the following . . . which I take from your catalogue." The expanded order included Brignole plums, apricots, Red and Yellow Roman nectarines, Green Nutmeg peaches, Yellow October and Lemon Clingstone peaches, Spitzenburg apples, Madeira walnuts (*Juglans regia*), and filberts. The fruits, according to his planting instructions, were to be established "in the vacant places" of his south orchard at Monticello in Virginia, the Madeira walnuts were to be "among the trees on the S.W. slope . . . towards the grove," and the filberts were for the "room of the square of figs."

Jefferson also ordered three each of all ten rose varieties the Prince Family Nursery offered in 1791. This extensive assortment has since proven to be the richest and most comprehensive documentation of Jefferson roses that is presently known. These thirty shrubs were to be planted around the clumps of lilacs at the East Front of Monticello. In addition, he purchased firs, balsams, willow, and spruces, as well as "Carolina kidney bean trees with purple flowers" (native wisteria, *Wisteria frutescens*), rhododendrons, and "monthly honeysuckles" (possibly the native *Lonicera sempervirens*). The quantity and diversity of these trees and shrubs exemplifies the evolution and complexity of Jefferson's long-ranging aspirations for Monticello.

In December, Jefferson received sixty sugar maple trees—Prince Nursery's entire stock—which he planted "in a grove" below the Second Roundabout on the northeast slope of Monticello Mountain. This grove became Jefferson's experiment in sugar production. Unfortunately, the central Virginia climate was not ideally suited for adequate sap flow in the spring, and Jefferson's well-intended project proved unsuccessful.

A Love of Botany

Jefferson's subsequent associations with the Prince Nursery were few and indirect. A notable connection occurred years after the Jefferson-inspired Lewis and Clark Expedition, when the Prince Family Nursery played a leading role in making commercially available one of the expedition's most popular discoveries, the ornamental

Oregon grape holly (*Mahonia aquifolium*). According to Stephen Spongberg's 1995 book *A Reunion of Trees*, the demand for this novel shrub was staggering: "By 1825, when the plant had become widely known up and down the Atlantic seaboard, the Prince Nursery . . . listed plants in their catalogue at twenty-five dollars each, in today's currency doubtless equivalent to several hundreds of dollars!"

As nursery ownership passed from father to son, each generation shared a common, underlying goal: to propagate and make available every known plant of merit, including North American species, less for profit than from a deep love of botany and the discipline of horticulture itself. William Prince subsequently divided the nursery between his sons Benjamin and William. In 1793, the second William Prince began the Linnaean Botanic Garden and Nursery, named for Carolus Linnaeus, the Swedish botanist and naturalist who devised the revolutionary system of binomial nomenclature (genus and species) for naming and identifying plants and animals. Prince's Linnaean Botanic Garden served to educate the public, as well as encourage potential customers, by displaying the richness and diversity of the world's botanical treasures.

William also became an active member of the newly created New York Horticultural Society. Through this prestigious organization, he began a friendship with Dr. David Hosack, who established the Elgin Botanic Garden in 1801. This was New York City's original botanical garden, the site of which is now Rockefeller Center.

Remains of Its Heyday

William's son, William Robert Prince, was the fourth and final generation to oversee the family enterprise, and he operated the nursery mostly as a botanical garden. As a young man, William Robert accompanied Professor John Torrey of Columbia University and Thomas Nuttall of Harvard on botanical trips throughout the Atlantic states, and he later published *A Treatise on the Vine* and *A Pomological Manual*, which became standard references for decades. William Robert's now-rare *Prince's Manual of Roses*, published in 1846, established him as the premier authority on roses of the nineteenth century. This small manual concluded with the Prince Nursery's catalog of over 1,600 rose varieties, which he claimed was the largest collection of roses in America and perhaps the entire world. The nursery's catalogs from 1815 through 1850 also became resources for both professional and amateur horticulturists.

For nearly 140 years, the Prince Family Nursery in Queens was a cornucopia of fruit, trees, and shrubs for the farms, orchards, and gardens of America—especially the gardens at Jefferson's Monticello. Although the Prince Nursery's operations ended after William Robert's death in 1869 (unfortunately, his zealous importation of white mulberry trees and his promotion of the silkworm industry had nearly bankrupted the business), many unusual trees and shrubs continued to flourish on the property and throughout Flushing well into the twentieth century. In her 1901 book *Old Time Gardens Newly Set Forth*, antiquarian Alice Morse Earle described the "oldest Chinese magnolias" and the "finest Cedar of Lebanon in the United States" still standing in the forlorn and forgotten gardens at the Prince homestead. Today, the Prince Nursery no longer exists, and its once-verdant grounds are now a busy commercial area of concrete and blacktop.

Governor George Clinton. Credit: From the collections of the New York State Library, Manuscripts and Special Collections, Albany, New York.

8

Good Peter and the Governor

Alan Taylor

During the American Revolution, the Iroquois Six Nations were divided: the Oneidas and most of the Tuscaroras assisted the Patriots, while the Cayugas, Mohawks, Onondagas, and Senecas supported the British. Yet no matter their alliance, all the Iroquois had suffered devastating raids that had destroyed almost all their villages by 1781. These violent dislocations promoted malnutrition and disease, which reduced Iroquois numbers by a third, from a prewar nine thousand to a postwar six thousand. Whether they had become refugees at Schenectady on the American frontier, or at Montreal or Niagara within the British orbit, the Iroquois left behind a broad and bloody no-man's-land—a vacuum that American settlers and speculators began to fill after the war.

Rivals for the Prize

During the 1780s, settler and speculator pressure was compounded by bitter competition among the Americans over who would win the prize of this Iroquois land. Citing a colonial charter, Massachusetts competed with New York to claim the territory. Nearly bankrupted by the long, hard, expensive Revolution, both states' governments wanted the potential revenues from selling Indian land to speculators for development by farmers; a wary New York congressman worried in June 1784 that "the whole world seems to look on that W[estern] Country with a wishful eye." To strengthen claims and weaken its rival, each state plotted to secure Indian land cessions and rush settlers

This essay first appeared in winter 2007, volume 6, number 3.

into the contested region. The victor would reap public revenues when selling the land, collect taxes on the new farms, and consolidate authority by promoting speculation and settlement.

Measured by population and economic development, New York in the 1780s was relatively weak but possessed of immense potential. Thinly settled, it ranked a mediocre sixth in population and prosperity among the original thirteen states, lagging behind even little Connecticut. New York's political authority and its population remained virtually confined to the long, narrow corridors of the Hudson and Mohawk Valleys; for enhanced strength, the state needed more farms and more people. By expanding westward into Iroquois country, which contained resources that could either permanently endow the state or attract despoilers, New York might develop wealth and power—but only if it could overcome its initial vulnerability to rivals.

Spokesmen for Both Sides

At the end of the Revolution, the most coveted and fertile Iroquois land belonged to the Oneidas, who lived at the head of the Mohawk valley and along the upper reaches of the Susquehanna River—a domain in tempting, valuable proximity to New York's existing settlements. To defend their land, the Oneidas relied on their most perceptive and dignified spokesman, Gwedelhes Agwelondongwas, a serene, gray-haired man in his late sixties. Americans called him "Good Peter" because of his Christian piety and morality; Philip Schuyler extolled him as "a man of sense and sobriety." As an orator, Good Peter impressed Americans, even when they could not understand a word of his Oneida language. The missionary Samuel Kirkland praised him as the most powerful mind and best speaker among the entire Six Nations: "His exhortation far outdid my sermons; I have often thought that if I could speak with as much ease & fluency as he that I would preach every day of my life."

On the American side, New York's politics during the 1780s were dominated by George Clinton. A powerfully built man with bushy eyebrows and a penetrating gaze, Clinton came from a prosperous family of farmers and surveyors in Ulster County. During the 1760s, he had been a country lawyer and an assembly representative. An early critic of British rule, he had embraced the Revolution and performed with courage and zeal as a brigadier general; in 1777, he won a surprising electoral victory to become the state's first governor under the new Republican constitution. His stunned and defeated rival, Philip Schuyler, conceded that Clinton had "played his Cards better than was Expected," although the state's most prestigious and wealthy families—the Livingstons, Morrises, Schuylers, and Van Rensselaers—disdained Clinton's modest origins and limited education as beneath the proper dignity of a governor. Often underestimated by elitists, Clinton repeatedly defeated them in elections and in the legislature, with a cunning and insights unmatched in his generation in New York.

Clinton aggressively promoted the state of New York, which he regarded as embattled by powerful and greedy neighbors. In 1784, he urged the legislature to provide "the utmost encouragement to the speedy settlement of the country. The cultivation of our lands ought to be one of our first cares, since the riches of the state is [*sic*] to be found in the number of its people." This relentless policy expressed both his anxiety and his optimism for New York's future, and with his characteristic persistence Clinton worked to multiply New York's farms and towns by obtaining Indian land.

Faceoff at Fort Herkimer

A quick study, he mastered the traditions of Iroquois diplomatic customs, including the conduct of formal councils—mass gatherings with Indian nations—to renew their relationship with the state. With his bold manner, Governor Clinton commanded attention by his charisma and keen sense of timing and mood. Impressed, the Oneidas named him Aquilanda, which meant "Rising Sun." In pleasing their chiefs, however, Clinton was working to soften their resistance to his agenda: the steady transfer of Iroquois lands into state possession for sale and settlement.

In 1785, Clinton faced off against Good Peter at a council at Fort Herkimer, near German Flatts on the Mohawk River. Missionary Samuel Kirkland was impressed that Good Peter held his own in debating Clinton: "There were some very <u>smart</u>, ingenious & really affecting speeches passed at this treaty between the <u>Governor</u> & <u>Good Peter</u>. Whether they were all put upon the Journals of the Treaty I do not know." For his part, Clinton proposed a radical scheme: that the Oneidas should cede all of their land along the Susquehanna River between its Unadilla and Chenango tributaries. According to Good Peter, Clinton "produced a heap of money & told some of our nation to take up a handful but they could not consent to do this; it was too heavy. He then . . . said all this shall be yours, on condition that you will follow my advice."

The Oneidas countered with an innovative alternative: rather than cede their land, they would lease a buffer zone to the state. Good Peter explained:

> We are however willing and ready to lease one Tier of Farms in the Manner they are done by the White People, along the Boundary Line throughout the Extent of our Country, and that People of Influence might be settled on these Farms to prevent Encroachments, and that a Person might be appointed to collect our Rents annually. Brothers! We shall be happy to find that the

> Proposals We now make will be accepted, as We cannot sell any more of our Lands and this Leasing may be an Income to our Children.

As landlords rather than sellers, the Oneidas would receive an annual income while retaining title to the land, thus preserving their power and enhancing their wealth. But while beneficial to the Oneidas, the lease scheme would hurt New York's chance to beat Massachusetts in the race for additional land.

In blunt reply to Good Peter's "highly disagreeable" proposal, Clinton denounced it as demeaning to New York: "We are sorry that You made an Offer to lease [y]our Lands. We fear You have lost your good Opinion of Us, by making a Proposal which, if accepted, would make the Government of the State tributary to You." Since Clinton considered the Iroquois poor, ignorant, and primitive, he could never accept them as prospering landlords with economic power over the state's citizens.

Trump Card

Ultimately, Clinton held the winning card: 240,000 New Yorkers outnumbered the approximately 600 Oneidas. In addition, without state protection, the Oneidas would fall prey to invading settlers and conniving speculators. Clinton announced that, without a land cession, there would be no such protection, "and that if this is not now done, it is your Fault and not ours." Of course, the Oneidas regarded such protection as their due, given their exertions and suffering as wartime allies, the lands previously bestowed by them on New Yorkers in the upper Mohawk Valley, and the past promises of New York governors. But what could they do if the state demanded more land as the price to renew those promises?

Alarmed, the Oneidas shifted their position overnight. On the morning of June 27, 1785, Good Peter abruptly withdrew as council spokesman in favor of a more pliant chief, Oneyanha, through whom the Oneidas agreed to sell outright to the Americans about 460,000 acres for a single payment of $11,500. The shift apparently registered a swing in Oneida politics away from the warriors, represented by Good Peter, in favor of the chiefs; this meant that the clan mothers had taken initiative away from the warriors and given it to the chiefs. The clan mothers wanted peace and food relief, which hinged upon the state's goodwill, while the warriors cherished the contested tract for deer hunting.

Clinton returned to New York City in triumph, for the Fort Herkimer purchase enabled New York to begin selling land in the region. During the next two years, New York sold 343,594 acres in the cession for $125,955. In addition to making money for the state, those sales spawned new farms and towns inhabited by thousands of settlers loyal to New York—which indeed weakened the claim by rival Massachusetts to the land. Massachusetts governor James Bowdoin begged Clinton to stop the sales, pending a legal resolution of the dispute.

At Hartford, Connecticut, in December 1786, agents for New York and Massachusetts compromised. New York obtained political jurisdiction over the entire contested region, realizing its goal of a western boundary on Lake Erie and the Niagara River. But the two states agreed to split the title to the land—or, more accurately, the "preemption right" to purchase land from the Indians. Massachusetts would obtain this supposed right to purchase six million acres at the far western end of New York beyond the Finger Lakes as far as Lake Erie, as well as 230,400 acres from Clinton's purchase from the Oneidas, but New York would get the right to buy and sell all the rest of the Iroquois land. Thus by outmaneuvering Good Peter at Fort Herkimer, Governor George Clinton ultimately secured an empire in land for the future Empire State.

This early depiction of Margaret Hardenbroeck's Manhattan includes working slaves, detailed period attire for men and women, and a bustling town in the background. Credit: New York Public Library.

9

The She-Merchant of Manhattan

Jean Zimmerman

In 1659, a twenty-two-year-old Amsterdam woman named Margaret Hardenbroeck made the arduous six-week journey across the Atlantic to the harbor of Manhattan and the struggling outpost of New Amsterdam, in the Dutch colony of New Netherland. The only daughter of a merchant family in the trade-besotted climate of Golden Age Holland, Hardenbroeck was the first of their children to venture across the sea to North America. She would sail between New York, Europe, the West Indies, and Africa many times during her lifetime; many of her peers would do the same, crisscrossing for work or family between the Old World and the New.

Hardenbroeck arrived in New Amsterdam bent on finding success as a trader. Her cousin, a successful Amsterdam ship merchant named Wouter Valck, sold straight pins, cooking oil, and other essential domestic goods both in Holland and abroad. Recognizing his young relative's potential, Wouter had hired her to serve as his "factor" or "supercargo," a superintendent of cargo. Margaret would represent his trading business in New Netherland, with the critical responsibility of overseeing the sale of trade goods and the loading of return cargo.

A letter from Hardenbroeck to Valck, dated September 19, 1659, with a return address of "Manatans in Nieu Nederland," indicates the young woman's first assignment in North America. She was to collect payment of thirty-two beaver skins from a Manhattan merchant named Hendrick van der Vin, who seems to have been reneging on an installment plan he had made to purchase two hogsheads of vinegar. "I could not get payment from . . . Van der Vin," Margaret confessed, assuring her cousin that when he next came to New Amsterdam she would make sure he was paid in full, with interest. "I did my best," she signed off.

This first essay first appeared in spring 2007, volume 6, number 4.

Hardenbroeck's five-year apprenticeship with Valck would teach her to handle such transactions successfully and would secure her reputation as an independent trader. Court records in 1664 listed her as a "free agent of New Amsterdam." Over the next thirty years she would become the richest woman in the colony of New York and the first to build her own fortune.

Benefits and Lucre

For the Dutch, the not-inconsiderable risks of ocean travel to the new colony were offset by a host of benefits. The first of these was the potential profit on the velvety, deep-pile pelt of the North American beaver, whose population had already been hunted out in the lower Hudson Valley but still thrived farther north, in the Mohawk Valley. The glossy felt hats made from beaver fur were the impetus for the early European settlement of the northeastern United States. Such hats had been produced with Russian pelts in Holland and Spain since the fourteenth century. But two contemporary developments spurred the North American fur trade. By the mid-1600s, the animal's European breeding grounds had been exhausted. And around the same time, style maven Charles II of England cemented the beaver hat's popularity by sporting a slouchy, ostrich-feather-adorned chapeau. It did not hurt that in this pre-umbrella era, beaver felt offered virtually waterproof protection from the elements.

Another benefit was that the West India Company offered blandishments for colonists, in the form of land tracts and free passage for whole families. A report penned by the West India Company's Cornelius Van Tienhoven extolled Manhattan's "fine maize lands" and its "numerous valleys of sweet and salt meadows." Word of the colony's bounty traveled back over the sea: blue crab virtually climbed into fishing nets, and oysters "fat as butter" were normally served a foot long.

While the majority of colonists were young, single men, unmarried women such as Margaret Hardenbroeck were for the first time crossing the ocean from Amsterdam. More than three hundred years before Harvard unleashed its first cohort of female MBAs on New York's financial district, an earlier breed of businesswoman thrived at the southern tip of Manhattan. Census figures listed 134 female traders residing in New Amsterdam during a sample decade of 1653 to 1663, out of a population of around 2,000.

This trend seems less improbable when one considers the climate for female citizens in the Netherlands. Travelers to Holland frequently noted the role of women there; a comment made by an Italian merchant as early as 1567 captured the prevailing view of the time. Dutch women, he said,

> are in conduct, speech and all things able, hardy and brave; they remain, however, in such liberty very honest and virtuous, and they not only go about in the town to manage their affairs: but also travel without blame in the country to one another, with little company. They are very frugal, busy, and always doing something, not only the housework . . . but also occupy themselves with trade, buying and selling.

The women of Holland exercised such "skill and industry," he said, that in many places "the men suffer the women to manage all."

Thus, the participation of women in mercantile life was not only accepted, it was expected and even nurtured. "She-merchant" was the term frequently applied to the female entrepreneurs, shopkeepers, and ship traders who operated in both Holland and New Amsterdam in the seventeenth century. Women were primed to participate in commerce: unlike any other country in Europe, the Netherlands offered universal elementary-level education for girls alongside boys, as well as social mores that sanctioned independence for women and a legal system that ensured women's marital and inheritance rights.

Marrying Well

Soon after her arrival in New Amsterdam, Hardenbroeck wed a husband more than twice her age, an established merchant named Pieter Rudolphus de Vries. With him, Hardenbroeck entered into trade as an equal, importing casks of wine and prunes. When an epidemic known as the "hot sickness" hit the colony two years after the wedding, she became a wealthy widow: sole owner of two vessels, a clutch of properties in and around Manhattan, and seed money to expand the business. For a second spouse, Hardenbroeck settled upon an equally ambitious ship carpenter, Frederick Philipse, whose resources paled beside hers. She made the most of the union, however, capitalizing on Philipse's knowledge of building and his political contacts.

Between trips up the Hudson River to the fur-rich environs of Albany and passages across the ocean—she still served as factor, but now for her own cargo and on her own ships—Hardenbroeck raised four children who survived to adulthood, itself a feat in an age famous for maternal mortality and epidemics that mercilessly laid waste to children. But commerce remained at the center of her life. Over time, Hardenbroeck and Philipse amassed a fleet of nearly two dozen vessels. They embarked on a land-buying spree and eventually acquired fifty-seven thousand acres in the lower Hudson Valley, piecing together vast parcels of undeveloped land purchased from local Indian tribes to make an estate that comprised most of today's Westchester County. In the wilderness of what would become present-day Yonkers, they erected a stone mansion whose premises doubled as a secure storehouse for goods they shipped between Manhattan and Albany. When they decided to enter other markets, they purchased an estate on the Caribbean island of Barbados, making it their base for exporting sugar to the colonies. When slave-trading emerged as a good business opportunity, Harbenbroeck and Philipse had little compunction about getting into that franchise as well—almost no one in America questioned slavery on moral grounds at the time. Their ships brought Africans to labor on the brutal sugar plantations of the West Indies and to the province of New York, where some toiled in Philipse's wheat fields and gristmills.

But home base for Hardenbroeck and her sister she-merchants was always lower Manhattan, below the wooden wall that would lend its name to today's Wall Street. This was the only precinct of the island that was extensively inhabited during the seventeenth century. Manhattan provided a bustling harbor, thriving trade opportunities, and a perfect setting for a status-conscious woman to impress her peers with a stylish home of imported brick: Hardenbroeck raised her children on Stone Street, the settlement's most elegant thoroughfare.

Precious Cargo

In 1664 the English invaded New Amsterdam and made it New York. After the changeover, a gradual clampdown on women's legal rights drove most she-merchants out of business. Women could no longer represent themselves in court or sign contracts, and they no longer stood to inherit wealth on the same basis as their male siblings. But Hardenbroeck managed to stay in the game anyway. Bills of lading filed in the London Shipping Office reveal the sheer volume of merchandise she customarily shipped out of New York harbor through London to Amsterdam. One record from the mid-1670s for a ship named the *Beaver* carried the following inventory: 1,713 beaver pelts, 502 bear, 1,550 buck, 46 cowhides, 1,250 standard foxes and 53 timber grays, 94 timber minks, 1,100 "catts," 1,100 otters, and 363 "musquashes" (muskrat) and other animal skins. Hardenbroeck's ships also carried a vast array of textiles from Amsterdam to England; grain, Rhenish wine, salted beef, and lumber from New York to the West Indies; sugar and molasses back from the West Indies; casks and muskets from Manhattan to Amsterdam; and African slaves to America. These records give a sense not only of Hardenbroeck's business practices but also the goods that would have filled her own household. For example, she transported 2,636 "iron hatchetts," 682 "pair stockins," and

"30 thousand goose quills" from Holland in 1680 on the *St. Peter*. We can be confident that these products played an integral role in her own household.

We know something further of Hardenbroeck's character from a journal kept in 1679 by a young missionary en route to America from Holland on one of Hardenbroeck's ships. The narrative paints a detailed picture of an ocean journey and affords a warts-and-all view of the vessel's owner and factor. The missionary belonged to a religious sect called the Labadists that did not look kindly on independent women, and he took pains to describe the successful she-merchant's "miserable covetousness" and "terrible parsimony" as a shipowner and supercargo.

Mansion on the Hudson

In 1682, a ship named *Margaret* sailed from Amsterdam laden with building materials for the house that Margaret Hardenbroeck and Frederick Philipse were preparing to build on the east bank of the Hudson River. The cargo included sixty thousand bricks, hand tools and saws, and four millstones. The building site lay at the junction of two rivers, the Hudson and a smaller, faster stream called the Nepperhan ("trap-fishing place" in the language of the Lenape, the Native Americans who occupied the lower Hudson Valley). A natural harbor offered an ideal spot for sloops to anchor en route between Manhattan and Albany, the center of the region's fur trade.

The house became both a workplace and a showpiece. Its two stories made it a highly unusual dwelling for the period. Constructed of coursed rubblestone masonry with granite harvested from surrounding lands, it was visible to all river traffic and a clear statement of wealth and position, embodying the pride and pretensions of its successful owners. It also boasted half a dozen extra-large casement windows squared up with the durable Dutch brick imported from their home country.

Margaret Hardenbroeck died around 1692. The exact date cannot be determined from available records, but the following year Frederick Philipse married a younger woman and continued the family dynasty. The brick and stone house that Margaret and Frederick built, eventually called Philipse Manor Hall, still stands, twenty miles north of lower Manhattan in downtown Yonkers, a lasting reminder of a resourceful, profit-minded, indefatigable she-merchant of the New World.

Sybil Ludington's ride to alert patriots that the British were coming is commemorated by a statue by Anna Hyatt Huntington on the shore of Lake Gleneida on Route 52 in Carmel, New York. Credit: Putnam County Historian's Office, Brewster, New York.

10

New York Patriot

V. T. Dacquino

I first heard of Sybil Ludington in 1997, via one of those yellow and blue historic markers that dot New York's highways: "Sybil Ludington rode horseback over this road the night of April 26, 1777, to call out Colonel Ludington's regiment to repel the British at Danbury, Connecticut." But just who was this heroic woman? I began by reviewing some basic facts in my local library.

Sybil Ludington was just sixteen years old in April of 1777 when General William Tryon, formerly royal governor of New York, landed at Compo Beach in Connecticut with two thousand British troops from twenty transports and six warships. Tryon marched across Connecticut to Danbury to destroy supplies and munitions that had been stored there by the American rebels. Within hours of his arrival, and upon consuming barrels of rum, Tryon's drunken soldiers went on a rampage, burning homes and killing several Danbury residents. When word of the raid got out, American soldiers rushed to settle the score. The Americans sent out warning messengers in every direction, as Generals David Wooster and Benedict Arnold, receiving intelligence at New Haven, gathered escorts and moved westward, picking up various militia companies along the way. Meanwhile, General Gold Selleck Silliman was en route to Danbury with five hundred militiamen, and Colonel Henry Ludington, several miles to the north, was summoned from Fredericksburg in New York (part of which is now known as Ludingtonville, in the town of Kent, Putnam County) to bring four hundred more men.

I found a further account of the incident by Willis Fletcher Johnson in his book *Colonel Henry Ludington: A Memoir*, published in 1907:

This essay first appeared in spring 2007, volume 6, number 4.

> At eight or nine o'clock that evening a jaded horseman reached Colonel Ludington's home with the news . . . But what to do? His regiment was disbanded; its members scattered at their homes, many at considerable distances. [It was April, planting season, and the farmers needed to tend their fields and had been granted leaves to get their work done.] He must stay there to muster all who came in. The messenger from Danbury could ride no more, and there was no neighbor within call. In this emergency he turned to his daughter Sybil, who, a few days before, had passed her sixteenth birthday, and bade her to take a horse, ride for the men, and tell them to be at his house by daybreak. One who even rides now from Carmel to Cold Spring will find rugged and dangerous roads, with lonely stretches. . . . But the child performed her task . . . as she rode through the night, bearing the news of the sack of Danbury. . . . By daybreak, thanks to her daring, nearly the whole regiment was mustered before her father's house at Fredricksburgh, and an hour or two later was on the march for vengeance on the raiders. . . . That night they reached Redding, and joined Arnold, Wooster, and Silliman. The next morning they encountered the British at Ridgefield . . . and made [the British] retreat to their ships at Compo resemble a rout. . . . Arnold had his horse shot from under him as, almost alone, he furiously charged the enemy, and the gallant Wooster received a wound from which he died a few days later. There were far greater operations in the war than this, but there was scarcely one more expeditious, intrepid and successful.

A Prospective Biography

I was immediately taken by Sybil's story. Paul Revere, in his forties, had traveled twelve miles to warn of a British invasion, but sixteen-year-old Sybil had ridden more than forty miles. Paul Revere rode through populated Boston on a clear night, but Sybil rode through woods and brush over mud-laden paths. Paul Revere had two helpers, while Sybil had none. Paul Revere was captured—but Sybil wasn't. There were great differences in their stories and their reasons for riding, but it seemed that Sybil had earned her own place in history, and I set out to write her biography.

I thought the research would simply involve gathering the necessary documents from the many archives and repositories in New York. I picked out a favorite chair at the Putnam County Historian's Office in Brewster—and then discovered that there was little or no biographical information on Sybil's life after her famous ride. There were countless articles, but most of them contained information about her father (the colonel) and the Revolution, and they just repeated the same information about her own ride. Articles from the 1930s to the late 1990s told of the markers erected in 1935 along the route of her ride, a statue of her by Anna Hyatt Huntington in 1961, and a United States commemorative postage stamp in 1975—but the most peculiar item was one paragraph that appeared at the end of each article:

> After her famous ride, Sybil Ludington lived to be seventy-seven years old. She married her childhood sweetheart, Edmond [or Edward, or Henry; the first name varied with the article] Ogden, who was a lawyer in Catskill, New York. Sybil bore six children: four boys and two girls. One of her children was a hero in Kansas. The family later moved to Unadilla, where Sybil died on February 26, 1839.

The paragraph was interesting enough, but it hardly covered more than sixty years of a hero's life. I realized that the way to begin my research was with the six Ogden children. But there were no graves to be found, nor any medical, school, birth, or death records. In fact, there was no mention of their names in any history books, newspapers, or archives. As for Sybil's husband, he not only did not have a grave, there was also no record of his law practice in Catskill. A trace of Sybil's "son" in Kansas was also confusing: Edmund Augustus Ogden, hero of Fort Riley, Kansas, who had remained with women and children stricken with cholera at the cost of his own life, was a graduate of West Point, and his mother's name was Julia, not Sybil.

Breakthrough

After these disappointments, I spent three frustrating years doing research in Washington, D.C., as well as in Albany, Catskill, and Unadilla, New York, and countless libraries and archives. Very quickly I gained respect for New York's archivists and historians. But the answers to Sybil's puzzle began to emerge, with a line here and a document there. A breakthrough came with my discovery of a series of articles written by Mabel Parker Smith, a historian from Catskill. I soon uncovered deeds and did genealogical searches in a Mormon Church basement in Ossining, New York; a second breakthrough required a trip to the National Archives in New York City, where I reviewed a file on "Cibal" Ogden that had remained nearly unnoticed since 1839.

The result of my efforts is my book, *Sybil Ludington: The Call to Arms*, the first birth-to-death account of the young female hero that is documented by primary source research. And it corrects that erroneous paragraph that had been repeated for years.

After her famous ride in 1777, Sybil Ludington remained a member of her mother's household until she was twenty-three years old. At that time, she met Edmond Ogden, whose family had recently moved to New York. They married in 1784, and Sybil gave birth to a child in 1786. They sold the land they lived on in Fredericksburg, New York, in April 1793. On August 23, 1793, Edmond signed a school subscription, donating money to a school his son attended in Catskill, New York. He donated money again in 1795. By 1799, Edmond was dead from yellow fever, and his body was cremated.

In 1803, widow Sybil Ogden bought a tavern on the corner of Green and Main Streets in Catskill. She assisted her son in becoming an attorney. Six years after she purchased the property, she sold it for over three times her purchase price and traveled up the Catskill Turnpike to Unadilla, New York, where she purchased a home for her son and his family. She lived with them for thirty years. Around 1838, her only son, Henry Ogden—who by then was the father of six children, four boys and two girls—died. One of those boys was Major Edmund Augustus Ogden, hero of Fort Riley, Kansas. Sybil applied for a pension from the United States government on September 8, 1838, and provided proof that her husband Edmond had served three terms of military service during the Revolution; one of those terms was with John Paul Jones on the USS *Bonhomme Richard*. But her pension was denied because she produced "insufficient proof of marriage." Sybil Ludington Ogden died in poverty on February 26, 1839, and was buried with her parents behind the Presbyterian Church in Patterson, Putnam County, New York.

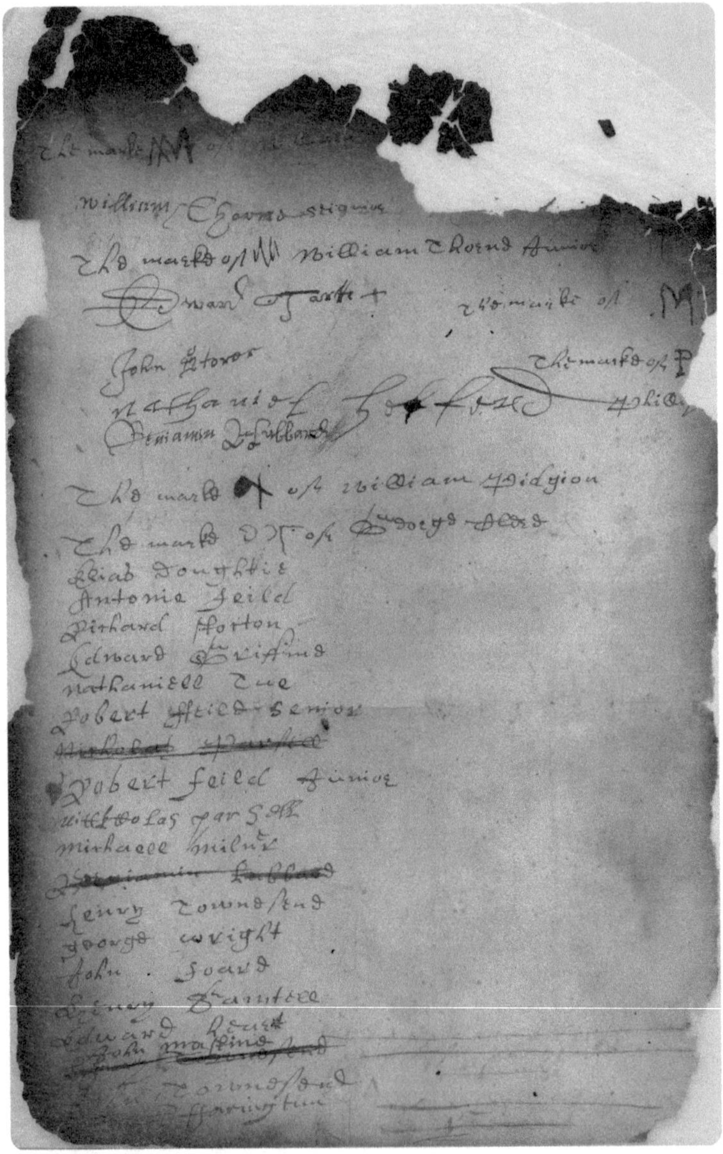
The marke of ...
William Thorne seignior
The marke of William Thorne Junior
Edward Tarne
The marke of
John Store
The marke of
Nathaniel Hefferd
Phil...
Benjamin Hubbard
The marke of William Pidgion
The marke of George Clere
Elias Doughtie
Antonie Feild
Richard Hortor
Edward Griffine
Nathaniell Tue
Robert Ffield senior
Robert Feild Junior
Nickolas Parsell
Michaell Milner
Henry Townsend
George Wright
John Foard
Henry Semtell
Edward Hart
John Mastine
... Townesend
... Farrington

Both the text and the signatures of the Flushing Remonstrance were evidently copied and incorporated into the Dutch Colonial Council minutes, which were signed in the 1911 Capital fire. The signatures on this copy of the remonstrance all appear to be in the same handwriting, a clear indication that the document is a contemporary copy, and not the original. What happened to the original petition is unknown, but it may have been returned to the individual who presented it to Stuyvesant. Credit: New York State Archives, Albany, New York.

11

The Importance of Flushing

Russell Shorto

Considering its significance—considering how foundational it is to American history, to the root idea of a free society that we all take for granted—the Flushing Remonstrance is a document that gets very little respect. It could have something to do with the name: it's an awkward mouthful, is it not? In the first place, we must admit—and forgive us, residents of a certain city in the borough of Queens—that if "Flushing" stirs something in people, it is not especially lofty. As to "remonstrance," it might be interesting to query your coworkers or members of your family to see how many can give you a reasonably close definition of the word. Perhaps calling it The Long Island Protest would have gotten the document bigger play over the centuries. Or something poetically in keeping with its era (only a few decades from that of Shakespeare): say, The Complaint of Conscience.

Let's both put this remarkable piece of paper in context and outline its significance. Flushing—the city in Queens—was originally Vlissingen, after a Dutch city of that name. It was part of the Dutch colony of New Netherland, which stretched across the Middle Atlantic region of what would become the United States. New Netherland is best remembered today for its capital—New Amsterdam—which became New York City, and for its last director, Peter Stuyvesant.

The Dutch brought several things to the region they colonized. Most notable was an idea they more or less invented in the seventeenth century: "tolerance." As everyone knows, the Dutch provinces are mostly below sea level, and this geographical fact meant that they were a relatively easy place to invade or to run to. Thus, throughout the 1500s and 1600s, Europeans fleeing war or seeking freedom to think or write or

This essay first appeared in winter 2008, volume 7, number 3.

worship made their way to the Low Countries. As a consequence, the major Dutch cities—Amsterdam, Rotterdam, The Hague, Utrecht—became multicultural centers. The idea of tolerance developed not through lofty ideals but as a way for these disparate peoples to get along with each other. At the same time, the Dutch found that it *worked*: tolerance allowed a mixed society not only to get by but to do business, to flourish. It became one of the keys to the success of the Dutch Golden Age.

This idea got transferred to the New World colony. One of the principles of Dutch tolerance was freedom of conscience. According to Dutch law, you couldn't be harassed because of your religious beliefs. Naturally, not everyone went along with this. In fact, a goodly portion of Dutch society thought it was exactly the wrong approach. In this, they were only following what was common belief nearly everywhere. The seventeenth century was the age of religious war, when it was almost universally held that in order for a society to be strong, it had to be unified, particularly in matters of religion. Religious intolerance was thus more or less official policy in England, France, Spain, and elsewhere.

Peter Stuyvesant—the son of a Calvinist minister—was among the Dutch who were also of this mind, and to be fair he had good practical reasons for it. He was the ruler of a small, weak colony that was surrounded by would-be enemies: Indians, but most dangerously of all, the English to the north and south. Unlike the English colonies, New Netherland comprised a mixture of nationalities and religions. Stuyvesant believed this weakened it, and no doubt he was right; bickering among different ethnic and religious groups was more or less constant. He tried, therefore, to keep the tolerance in check. When Jews arrived in 1654, seeking asylum, he barred them from settling. The Jews went over his head, however, appealing to the directors of the West India Company, which administered the colony, and to the provision in Dutch law that dictated freedom of conscience. Stuyvesant was overruled and had to allow the Jews to remain. (He managed to make their lives miserable, though, so that most eventually left.)

Then, in 1657, the issue came back in a new form. The Dutch colony had been receiving more and more English settlers, thanks in large part to the fact that the Puritan rule in England (and New England) meant that those of other religious persuasions were unwelcome there. Many of these non-Puritan English pilgrims thus settled in parts of the future boroughs of New York. One such group was the Quakers, whose penchant for spirit-fueled frenzy—quaking—caused some residents discomfort. Stuyvesant in particular seems to have felt they were out of their minds; at any rate, he believed their form of religious belief was a threat to the public order, and in 1657 he barred the town of Vlissingen from allowing them to settle. In response, the English residents crafted a complaint, or remonstrance. The most memorable phrase from the Flushing Remonstrance, to my mind, is the one in which the residents appeal to "[t]he law of love, peace and liberty in the [Dutch] states extending to Jews, Turks, and Egyptians, as they are considered the sonnes of Adam, which is the glory of the outward state of Holland." The inhabitants informed their leader that "our desire is not to offend one of [God's] little ones, in whatsoever form, name or title he appears in, whether Presbyterian, Independent, Baptist or Quaker, but shall be glad to see anything of God in any of them." Therefore, they went on, "if any of these said persons come in love unto us, wee cannot in conscience lay violent hands upon them, but give them free egresse and regresse unto our Town, and houses, as God shall persuade our consciences."

This is an outright statement of religious freedom, and it is a watershed. But let me add something else. It has often been misinterpreted in American history as being an English-versus-Dutch statement. That is, it has been viewed in terms of "the English believe in religious liberty, while the Dutch do not." This is simply wrong. The context was Dutch. The laws to which the residents of Vlissingen/Flushing appealed were Dutch laws. The situation is unique to New Netherland—and thus to New York. Its Dutch character is one reason why New York grew into a vibrantly multiethnic culture: one reason why New York became New York. The English of New England undeniably gave us their language and many aspects of government, but they were at this time in American history very far from enunciating such an ideal of religious freedom. What we see in the Flushing Remonstrance is a fledgling American colony applying hard-won rights from the Old Country to a New World setting, where they would flourish in an entirely new way. The mixed peoples who founded New Netherland would become a wellspring of American religious liberty, and also a source of America's notion of equality.

Many places in the world today still have state religions and bar faiths other than the approved one. When Americans want to tally the things they value most in their society, the things to be proud of and hold close, the Flushing Remonstrance—by whatever name—should be high on their list.

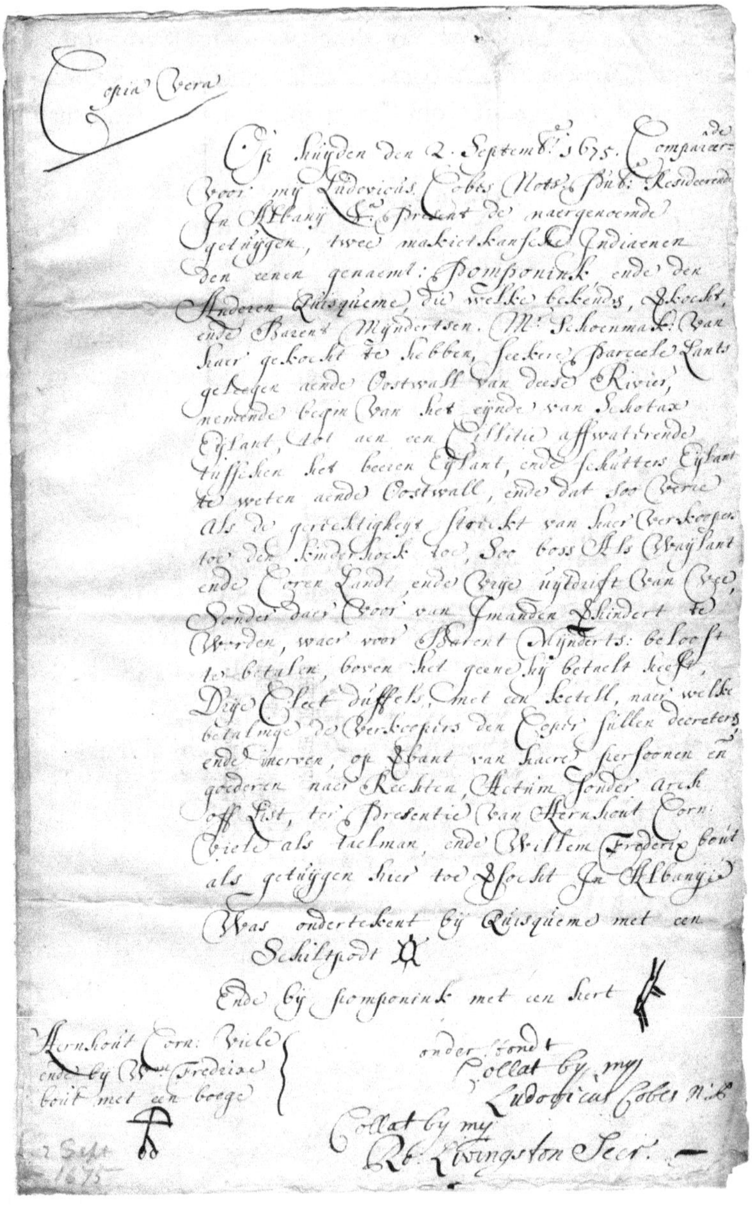

Copia Vera

Op huyden den 2 Septemb: 1675 Compareerde voor my Ludovicus Cobes Nots Pub: Residerende In Albany &c Present de naergenoemde getuygen, twee makiekanse Indiaenen den eenen genaemt: Pomponink ende den Anderen Quisqueme die welke bekende, verkocht, ende Barent Myndertsen Mr Schoenmaker van haer gekocht te hebben, seekere Parceele Lants geleegen aende Oostwall van deese Rivier, nemende begin van het eynde van Schotax Eylant, tot aen een Killitie affwaterende tusschen het beeren Eylant, ende Schutters Eylant te weten aende Oostwall, ende dat soo verre als de gerechtigheyt strekt van haer verkoopers tot den Kinderhoek toe, Soo boss Als Waylant ende Coren Landt, ende vrye uytdrift van vee, Sonder daer voor van Imanden verhindert te worden, waer voor Barent Myndertsz: belooft te betalen, boven het geene hy betaelt heeft, Drye Elen duffels, met een ketell, naer welke betalinge de verkoopers den Coper sullen decreteren ende inerven, op verbant van haere persoonen en goederen naer Rechten, Actum sonder arch off List, ter presentie van Arnhout Corn: Viele als tuelman, ende Willem Frederickx bout als getuygen hier toe versocht In Albanij

Was onderteekent by Quisqueme met een Schiltpadt

Ende by Pomponink met een hert

Arnhout Corn: Viele ende by Wm Frederickx bout met een boege

onderstondt Collat by my Ludovicus Cobes N.P.

Collat by my Rt Livingston Secr.

2 Sept 1675

This 1675 deed in Dutch conveys Mohican land on the east side of the Hudson River at present-day Schodack Landing to Barent Meyndertsen, a master shoemaker. One Mohican Indian signed with a turtle icon; another signed with a deer. The Dutch witness, also illiterate, drew an anchor. Credit: New York State Archives, Albany, New York.

12

A Peaceful Indian Nation

Shirley W. Dunn

"You remember, when you first came over the great waters, I was great and you was very little, very small." This reminder was offered to Dutch and English leaders by chiefs of the Mohican Indian Nation at Indian conferences beginning in the mid-seventeenth century and suggests that New York State owes the Mohicans a historical debt for allowing the settlement of the upper Hudson Valley. While the history is complicated, it is correct to state that without Mohican cooperation, the new fur trade in New York would have been delayed, settlement of the area might have been violent, and the history of land ownership in the Hudson Valley would have been very different.

Peace prevailed along the Hudson River when Henry Hudson's ship, the *Half Moon*, approached the Mohicans' shores in 1609. The Indians were astounded but friendly when they encountered Hudson and his crew near present-day Catskill. A few days later, the *Half Moon* came to a halt south of present-day Albany, where Hudson visited a Mohican village.

Within a few years, the name Mohican appeared prominently on a map attributed to the Dutch ship captain and explorer Adriaen Block, who made yearly trading visits up the Mauritius (Hudson) River from 1610 to 1614. Block spelled the name "Mahican," although today's Hudson Valley descendants use the conventional spelling Mohican that became common in New England, where a mission town, present-day Stockbridge, Massachusetts, was established for them in 1734.

Before the 1650s, some Mohicans lived along the Housatonic River east of the Taconic Hills. A century later, some Mohicans later moved to the Bethlehem,

---

This essay first appeared in winter 2008, volume 7, number 3.

Pennsylvania, area with Moravian ministers. During wars with Canada in the mid-eighteenth century, Mohican fighters and families were encouraged by Sir William Johnson, Indian superintendent for the Northern Region of New York, and the Iroquois to share Mohawk and Cayuga locations along the Susquehanna River in New York. A particularly large Mohican village called Otsiningo (sometimes written Chenango) flourished north of present-day Binghamton on the Chenango Creek in the 1750s; Mohicans were also present at Oquaga on the Susquehanna. At the invitation of the Oneidas in 1784, the Stockbridge Mohicans relocated to a village called New-Stockbridge at present-day Munnsville, Madison County (New York). However, as white farmers slowly took over their land, the Mohicans were removed piecemeal by federal policy in the 1820s to a reservation near Bowler, Wisconsin, to land that had little potential for farming but that remains their official headquarters. The group today is federally recognized as the Stockbridge-Munsee Band of the Mohican Indians.

First in the Valley

The important position of the Mohicans on Block's 1614 map indicates that they were the most notable Native American group in the Hudson Valley. Mohican place-names still dot the area; Coxsackie and Taconic are examples. Besides controlling a large territory, the Mohicans maintained a strong leadership, had a growing population, functioned in a complex society, and lived sustainably in their environment. Mohican lands not only spanned the Hudson but also extended west along the Mohawk River beyond present-day Schenectady, went north around lower Lake Champlain, and continued east to the edges of today's Vermont, Massachusetts, and Connecticut. North of Mohican limits on Lake Champlain's east shore were the Abenaki; to the south in the Catskill Mountains were the Waranawankongs, or Esopus (according to Indian tradition, the dividing line between the two nations was Little Sawyers Creek, north of present-day Saugerties); and on the Hudson's east shore was the Wappinger Nation. Mohicans occupied locations as far south as the Roelof Jansen Kill near Germantown, Columbia County. Of the neighboring Algonquian nations, some were allies of the Mohicans, and all were friends.

However, near the mouth of the Schoharie Creek along the Mohawk River to the west was the main territory of the enemy Mohawks, an Iroquois tribe unwelcome among the Algonquians and potential rivals of the Mohicans for any developing trade relationship with Europeans. Having dealt with the French on the St. Lawrence, the Mohawks were familiar with foreigners, while the Mohicans said they had never before seen visitors from afar. Both Fort Nassau, built in 1614 on an island that underlies today's Port of Albany, and Fort Orange (which became present-day Albany), built in

1624, were erected on Mohican land, and as part of the trading agreement with the newcomers the Mohicans reluctantly agreed that other tribes could come to trade at these stations.

The resulting close contact between the Mohicans and the Mohawks caused conflict, which led to renewed war between the two groups. The Mohicans built a fort opposite Fort Orange but lost crucial battles to the Mohawks in the Albany and Catskill areas. By 1629, the Mohicans sued for peace and conceded domination to the Mohawks for many years. As a result, the Mohawks confiscated Mohican lands at will, especially west of the Hudson, and collected yearly tribute not only from the Mohicans but also from many other Algonquian tribes.

Victims of the Europeans

Unfortunately, in the Hudson Valley as elsewhere, the effect of the arrival of Europeans was a drastic reduction in Native American populations. It is possible that the Mohican losses in battles with the Mohawks in the 1620s resulted in large part from a shortage of warriors due to communicable diseases contracted from foreign sailors. John W. Quinney, a Stockbridge Mohican chief living in Wisconsin, asked rhetorically in an 1845 lecture, "Where are the twenty-five thousand in number, and four thousand warriors, who constituted the power and population of the great Muh-he-con-new Nation in 1604? They have been victims to vice and disease, which the white man imported. The small-pox, measles, and strong waters [alcohol] have done the work of annihilation." Quinney included allied tribes along the Hudson in his numbers.

Kiliaen Van Rensselaer, who in 1630 and 1631 bought land from the Mohicans for farms in order to establish his tract called Rensselaerswyck, located in today's Albany and Rensselaer Counties, suggested a lower but still substantial population. He explained in 1634 that "in their time" the Mohicans were "1,600 strong," the number referring only to warriors available to fight. Van Rensselaer believed that war with the Mohawks was the main reason for the diminished Mohican population, and he considered war losses the reason they were willing to sell land. Another estimate came a century and a half later in the 1790s from Hendrick Aupaumut, a literate Mohican leader who wrote historical notes about his nation's past. He recalled the days "before they began to decay" when the Mohicans could raise one thousand warriors.

The loss of Mohican population in the seventeenth century may have contributed to their willingness to sell land to the Dutch, and later to the English, although selling land was alien to Indian beliefs. While Mohicans knew precisely where their tribal territories ended, within their own boundaries life was communal and land was shared. Farming sites were assigned to families and clan groups only for as long as they were using them. The Dutch idea of taking a tract away permanently in exchange for goods was a new concept, and many Mohicans never accepted the reality of land loss. When land was put to use, they could understand that the land was in the possession of the newcomer, although occasional gifts for continued use were expected. When purchased land stood idle, however, Indians sometimes reoccupied sites as their own.

The Power of Deeds

Some seventeenth-century Mohican leaders were willing to facilitate land sales. They learned that Dutch and English colonial laws governing acquisition of land required written proof, in the form of deeds, that the land had been purchased from the Indian owners. Thus deeds can help us understand the unacknowledged power wielded by Mohican and other Native American nations over colonial development. Nevertheless, by the 1720s protests arose from leading Mohicans that some New York deeds were fraudulent. Later, when lands were occupied without purchase, a few payments were made after the fact. In the meantime, various sales of formerly Mohican lands had been made by the Mohawks, and in 1768 the Mohicans made an official settlement with the Mohawks about land ownership.

Both Indian and colonial wars (such as those with Canada), which interrupted hunting and gardening, contributed to the Indians' need for food and for European products such as blankets, cloth, tools, guns, powder, lead, tobacco, and alcohol. To pay for these goods, or as a result of debt, Indian land was mortgaged or deeded to Europeans. Formal deeds were written in Dutch or English, and the Mohicans signed with symbols. Colonial deeds sometimes offer personal data about Native American people by providing signers' names, clans, status, locations where they lived, lists of goods given in exchange for land, and tribal boundaries. Occasionally, a deed includes invaluable statements about the Indian way of life, such as one from Saugerties that describes what an Esopus Native should do if he strayed over the boundary into the neighboring Mohican Nation and shot a deer in the neighbor's territory (protocol required him to share the deer). Some Mohican deeds preserve the names of successive chief sachems and their wives and children and often list lesser chiefs. The names of grantors are written phonetically, reflecting the sounds of the Mohican language. Fascinating details about the place of women in the Mohican network, lines of inheritance, the burden of debt in Mohican society, the character of individuals, the Indian desire for alcohol, and Mohicans' friendships with certain traders also emerge.

As the years went by, however, the land described in deeds often took in larger territory than the Indians had actually sold. These and other deceptive practices were used by some buyers and traders, but certain Albany traders developed fair relations with the Mohicans and were considered friends who could be relied upon for credit or for desperately needed goods or food.

Hudson Valley Mohicans remained loyal to, and fought for, their American friends when the Revolution forced them to choose sides. Ironically, after the Revolution, land was withheld as a reward for their services, although land was offered in lieu of monetary pensions to many white soldiers who had served. Even more ironic is the fact that these land grants to Revolutionary War soldiers included land that had once belonged to Mohicans.

Benedict Arnold. Credit: New York State Archives, Albany, New York.

13

Spies of the Revolution

John A. Burke and Andrea Meyer

By 1779, the Revolutionary War had reached a stalemate outside New York City. Many states were no longer sending their allotted shares of money, men, and supplies. The British, headquartered in Manhattan, controlled the lower gate to the Hudson, but the American-controlled fortress at West Point kept them from sweeping up the Hudson to accomplish the most important strategic goal of the war for both sides: control of the Hudson Valley. If the British gained it, they could divide the colonies in two, conquering New England and the South separately.

One way to break the stalemate was for one side to gain an intelligence advantage over the other, and the Americans did just that. A group of citizen-spies known as the Culper Spy Ring (from its code name, "Samuel Culper") operated from 1778 to 1780 in an intricate network from New York City to Setauket, Long Island, north to Connecticut, and then back west to George Washington's headquarters at Newburgh, New York, and Morristown, New Jersey. They also uncovered the biggest plot of the Revolution: Major General Benedict Arnold's scheme to "sell" West Point to the British.

Target: Treason

At the beginning of the war, Benedict Arnold was a wealthy, self-made merchant. During the brutal 1775 campaign to attack Québec, and the Battle of Valcour Island in 1776, Arnold built a fleet of boats to escape the British and used his personal fortune to supplement the lack of funds from Congress. But conflicts with members of Congress, and loss of receipts during the heat of battle, combined to deny him

---

This essay first appeared in fall 2009, volume 9, number 2.

reimbursement. By 1776 he was ruined financially, and by 1780 he was still petitioning Congress for repayment—and still being denied. Even his salary was withheld because Congress maintained he was accountable for the expenditure of original funds for which he lacked proof of payment. Ironically, modern historians eventually located Arnold's receipts in Canadian archives and discovered that he had been scrupulous in his record keeping.

By the summer of 1780, Arnold, now a major general, had gained command of West Point—and was also preparing to surrender it to the British Army, commanded by General Sir Henry Clinton, in return for money. This disaster would have occurred if American intelligence had not uncovered the developing plot and reported it to General George Washington.

Arnold's full intentions were worse than previously recognized. He intended to surrender the fort with Washington and the French leadership inside—a blow General Clinton referred to as a *coup manqué*, which he was sure would end the war. Today's history books state that the plot was foiled by a lucky accident, in which three highwaymen strip-searched Arnold's British cohort, Major John André, and discovered incriminating documents about the plot. But information in several archives shows this tale to be a fabrication, possibly intended as a cover story to protect the rest of the Culper spies still in place.

An Elaborate Network

In 1778, Benjamin Tallmadge, a young American officer who was about to become General Washington's new intelligence chief, organized an ingenious top-secret network of spies. Washington ordered that not even he himself should know who they were. For recruits, Tallmadge turned to old friends and acquaintances in his hometown of Setauket, Long Island. One of these, Abraham Woodhull, was chosen as his agent. But Woodhull (code-named "Culper Senior") soon fell under suspicion of British counterintelligence due to his frequent trips to Manhattan. So Woodhull recruited a relative living in his sister's Manhattan boardinghouse, a dry goods merchant and society reporter, Robert Townsend of Oyster Bay. Code-named "Culper Junior" and the ring's central figure, Townsend gathered information on British forces and passed it on to Setauket tavern keeper Austin Roe, who rode the 110 miles into New York ostensibly to buy supplies but who also carried these dispatches (often written in invisible ink and code) from Townsend's New York store back to Setauket.

In Setauket, Caleb Brewster, another ring member and a childhood friend of Tallmadge's, was captain of a whaleboat that raided British shipping on Long Island Sound. Every few weeks he would slip into one of Setauket Harbor's coves to receive dispatches. According to British counterintelligence reports and a report from Brewster to Tallmadge, Anna Strong, who lived nearby on Strong's Neck, would signal Brewster's exact location, probably using her clothesline and a certain number of handkerchiefs hanging out to dry. At the signaled location, Abraham Woodhull would then pass the dispatches to Brewster. Revisionists today challenge these stories as family lore, but careful inspection of letters and ledgers provide evidence to support them.

Important Friends

Robert Townsend's early reports to Tallmadge indicated that he could get good information on the British Navy, but little on the British Army. This situation continued for months until Woodhull mentioned in a letter to Tallmadge that he was on his way to Manhattan to visit a woman of his acquaintance, with whose help he expected to "outwit them all." Within two months, detailed headquarters-level intelligence on the British Army flowed to Washington in Newburgh from Townsend's reports. Who was this woman, and was she recruited by Woodhull as an official member of the Culper Spy Ring? We may never know. We do know, however, that not long before going to meet her, Woodhull had a near miss when British Colonel Simcoe and his Queen's Rangers rode to Setauket to arrest him—and he was not at home. Woodhull subsequently sent a report that he had been saved only by the intervention of a "friend of the Gen'l Aide"—the "aide" being none other than John André, adjutant general of the British Army and head of British intelligence. Evidently, this person's friendship with André was crucial to the spy ring's future success: while they continued to suspect Woodhull of spying, the British never again attempted to arrest him.

Ladies' Man

John André was considered the most eligible bachelor in New York. Handsome and extremely cultured, he was constantly surrounded by beautiful women. But they were also his weak point. In 1777, when the British occupied Philadelphia, André held a secret meeting in the Darragh house where he was quartered. Housewife Lydia Darragh simply sneaked up to the closed door, listened in, and subsequently warned General Washington of an impending surprise attack on his army at White Marsh. When the British Army took to the field, it became obvious that Washington had been warned. During André's investigation of the leak, he questioned everyone in the Darragh house except Lydia—since he believed that eighteenth-century women all held the same political views as their husbands.

The Culpers' secret reports all but ceased when André left New York in December 1779 for the siege of Charleston, and Washington was soon complaining to his aide, Alexander Hamilton, that the ring's information had become useless. However, within a few weeks of André's return to New York in May 1780, the Culper Ring was reporting the biggest scoop of the war: an American general was "in compact with the enemy." Washington's staff warned their other spies, and Benjamin Tallmadge wrote the governor of Connecticut, who was in charge of supplying West Point, to expect "some sudden and unexpected stroke" and that "the enemy would know well American forces and disposition." Tallmadge added, "And for God's sake be guarded against such a movement."

Was Tallmadge's female acquaintance, with whose help he expected to "outwit them all," the friend of John André who intervened on behalf of Woodhull? Since Woodhull did not indicate the gender of "the friend of the Gen'l Aide" (André) who saved him, we cannot be certain. However, if they were the same person, this might explain why the spy ring's reports ceased when André left New York and resumed when he returned.

André as Unwitting Source

Obviously, covert British plans to use an American general to capture the most important fort on the continent were shared only on a need-to-know basis. André himself handled the correspondence-based negotiations with Arnold, originally making contact through Arnold's wife—who happened to be André's old Philadelphia theater friend, Peggy Shippen. Meanwhile, at Washington's headquarters, Benjamin Tallmadge and Alexander Hamilton took charge of tracking the developments. A view of these ongoing machinations can be seen in Hamilton's letter to his best friend, fellow aide, and recently exchanged prisoner John Laurens. Written after the September 1780 arrest of André, the letter shared some aspects of the plot that could never have come to Laurens through public sources. Hamilton wrote that the scheme traced back to June 1780 (coinciding with André's return to New York) and noted that the Americans had intercepted some of the letters between the conspirators. While neither Hamilton nor Tallmadge ever explicitly credited a source, ringleader Robert Townsend's ledgers and other Culper letters show that a pattern of action occurred whenever Arnold and André corresponded. During these same months, the Culper Ring provided enormously important counterintelligence about information that Arnold leaked to the British in his correspondence, including news of the arrival of the vulnerable French fleet at Newport.

Arnold began to suspect that his mail was being intercepted. Soon after, André received a letter from Arnold that no one at British headquarters could decode; it appeared to be gibberish. Then Arnold and André attempted to meet in the dead of night at West Point, but for reasons unknown they missed each other. Another meeting was scheduled, but General Henry Clinton ordered André not to leave the ship that would take him upriver without the company of experienced field agent Colonel Beverley Robinson, and under no circumstances was André to carry documents back or remove his uniform. As history has recorded, despite these instructions all three events transpired: André was captured alone, in civilian dress, with maps of West Point and a pass signed by Arnold in his possession. Benjamin Tallmadge's memoirs reveal that when he heard the news, he immediately recognized both André and the situation. The memoirs also detail a struggle to prevent the news of André's capture from reaching Arnold, who ultimately escaped. André confessed and was hanged as a spy.

The Unknown Spy

General Clinton went into mourning, and Arnold began a hunt for the spies who had obviously warned the Americans of his plans. Since the plot's discovery had been reported as an accidental encounter involving highwaymen who just happened to intercept André on his ride back to headquarters, perhaps details from public reports of André's capture and trial revealed discrepancies that made Arnold suspicious and tipped him off that spies had forewarned the Americans. During this period, Abraham Woodhull's correspondence indicates that Robert Townsend and other Culper ring members fled New York City and went into hiding. After about two weeks, sensing a decline in tempers, they returned. But then disaster struck: Woodhull informed Tallmadge of the arrest of "several of our dear friends," including "one who hath been ever serviceable to this correspondence."

Townsend's powerfully emotional reaction to this news is evident through his own ledgers and in Woodhull's letters. He traveled to Setauket and arrived at Woodhull's home in a state of extreme depression. According to Woodhull, Townsend swore to stop spying, and according to Townsend's own business ledgers, he proceeded to steal large sums of money from every business with which he was connected, including his father's, for a total of over six hundred pounds in ten days—a veritable fortune at the time. No evidence reveals what the money was for, but ring member Anna Strong had ransomed her husband's freedom from a New York prison earlier in the war. Could the now-arrested "one who hath been ever serviceable" be the same "friend of the

Gen'l Aide" who had saved Woodhull from arrest, and the same woman of Tallmadge's acquaintance whom he expected to "outwit them all"? And might Townsend have formed a powerful emotional attachment to her and tried to ransom her freedom? No letter describes the release of this arrested individual. Conditions in New York prisons were so horrific that life expectancy was a few months; recent scholarship suggests that more Americans died in such confinement than were killed in all the battles of the American Revolution combined. Could this have been the fate of the anonymous ring member?

Certainly, the quality of the Culper Ring's intelligence peaked after Woodhull's narrow escape *and* when ladies' man John André was in town. After André's hanging and the unknown ring member's arrest, Culper reports decayed significantly, even after Robert Townsend eventually resumed spying. According to family correspondence, Townsend lived out his days depressed, unmarried, and drinking heavily until his death at age eighty-five.

Because of the nature of espionage, good spies leave little documentary information behind. But enough information remains in archival collections to suggest that the Culper Spy Ring played a significant role during a dark period in Revolutionary War history—and that much more of this role remains to be discovered. Both the evidence and history show, however, that this band of citizen-spies scored one of the most important intelligence coups in American history.

Before the British left, they greased the flagpole flying the Union Jack, making it extremely difficult for the Americans to raise the Stars and Stripes. Veteran John Van Arsdale put on cleats used to ascend a ship's mast and accomplished the task. Only then did Washington enter the city. Credit: Library of Congress.

14

Evacuation Day

Jennifer Steenshorne

Fireworks, parades, squabbling local politicians, marching veterans, crowds, parties: all the familiar elements of a Fourth of July celebration—except that New York's Independence Day was celebrated in November. Evacuation Day, commemorating the November 25, 1783, removal of British troops from New York City, was the state's most important civic holiday until the Civil War. But after the war, with the exception of a brief resurgence in 1883, it waned in public consciousness, disappearing by 1916 to remain, in historian Clifton Hood's words, "A holiday that was dedicated to memory . . . remembered for having been forgotten."

British troops occupied New York City after the Battle of Long Island and the Continental Army's retreat in 1776, and New York became the American Gibraltar, the base of British operations. It also became a mecca for Loyalists and thousands of escaped slaves and free blacks. General Sir Guy Carleton was appointed commander in chief in 1781, but after Cornwallis' defeat at Yorktown in October of that year, Carleton organized the removal (mainly to Canada) of Loyalists of all races who wished to leave.

The British Leave

Word of the signing of the Treaty of Paris reached New York in early November 1783. While the treaty marked the official end of the war, the evacuation of the British troops and the celebrations that followed marked the psychological and emotional end. On November 21, 1783, Carleton ordered his troops to prepare for departure. Major General Henry Knox led eight hundred Continental troops to the northern

This essay first appeared in fall 2010, volume 10, number 2.

boundary of the city, while George Washington and Governor George Clinton waited in a tavern in Harlem. On November 25, the British marched down the Bowery to the East River, jeered by the crowd, many wearing the "union cockade" of black-and-ribbon and laurel sprigs in their hats. A Mrs. Day hoisted her American flag a trifle early, and when confronted by a British officer, she bloodied his nose with a blow from a broomstick—the only violent exchange of the day. In a farewell gesture, the British greased the flagpole at Fort George in the Battery without removing the Union Jack, which was replaced with the American colors only after a young sailor named John Van Arsdale donned cleats and climbed the pole. (His descendants retained the honor of hoisting the flag on Evacuation Day until the end of the nineteenth century.)

At 1 p.m. a cannon fired, signaling the British departure. General Knox and his troops entered the city, followed by Washington and Clinton, representing military and civil authority. The procession of troops, led by Knox, Washington, Clinton, the Common Council, and citizens on horseback and on foot, proceeded down Queen Street and Broadway to Cape's Tavern. The "elegant and efficient disposition which prevailed through the whole event," and the contrast between the arrogant British and the dignified Americans, were much remarked upon.

Many raucous celebrations followed. On the evening of November 25, Governor Clinton held a dinner at Fraunces Tavern for Washington and his officers. In honor of the allies and with hope for the future, thirteen toasts were drunk, such as "May the remembrance of this day be a lesson to princes." On the 28th, "citizens who lately returned from exile" entertained the governor, the Common Council, and Washington and his officers at Cape's Tavern. Again thirteen toasts were drunk, such as "May the Trade of America center with those who have been foremost to defend her liberties." The evening "was spent in great good humour, hilarity and mirth." On December 1, Clinton hosted another dinner at Cape's in honor of the French ambassador, the Chevalier de la Luzerne. Present were Washington, his officers, and "upward of one hundred gentlemen." The revelers "with great conviviality" consumed 135 bottles of Madeira, 36 bottles of port, and 30 bowls of punch. Apparently, glassware was broken.

December 2 saw a great display of fireworks, organized by Captain William Price of the Corps of Artillery. The program consisted of three sets and included rockets; "chinese fountains"; illuminated stars, moons, and suns; an "illuminated Pyramid with Archimedean Screws, a Globe and Vertical Sun"; and it concluded with "Fame descending a Flight of one hundred Rockets." The *Independent New York-Gazette* reported that it was so "splendidly beautiful and so well conducted" that the spectators were rendered mute "unless when they some times manifested their satisfaction by loud huzzas."

Finally, on December 4, at yet another dinner at Fraunces Tavern, an emotional Washington took leave of his officers and embraced his comrades, saying, "With an heart full of love and gratitude, I now take leave of you: I must devoutly wish that your latter days may be as prosperous and happy, as your former ones have been glorious and honourable." This occasion, like all the other events of the week, was reported in papers across the nation.

A Holiday in the Making

In contrast, November 25, 1784, passed without much notice. If New Yorkers commemorated the day, they did so privately. Public celebration did not commence until 1787, when the army brigade garrisoned in the city moved the date of its dress review to November 25, marching in formation and performing the *feu de joi* (fire of joy), the rapid firing of guns in succession that was traditionally used to mark victories and that ended with a thirteen-gun salute.

In the 1790s, the celebration became a regular occurrence, a local "national" holiday. New Yorkers attended the military display and then moved on to private parties or the theater. Theaters played a role in popularizing and commercializing the holiday by presenting historical melodramas and pageants about the Revolution.

With the beginning of the nineteenth century, the "anniversary of the evacuation of the British troops" became commonly known as Evacuation Day. This shift symbolized the change in meaning of the day, from an event experienced by the Revolutionary generation to an event memorialized by their children and grandchildren. Evacuation Day gained new resonance with the War of 1812, as veterans from that war marched alongside and then replaced veterans of the Revolution. Another shift came as New Yorkers began to see Evacuation Day as a day of play. Diarist George Templeton Strong referred to it as "glorious Evacuation Day, glorious in one point, at least . . . that it allows us to kick up our heels all day at our leisure."

In the 1830s and 1840s, the regular military were replaced by elite volunteer units, such as the Washington Grays and the Lafayette Horse Guard. Displays of precision gunnery also disappeared. Evacuation Day was also commercialized through depictions in popular prints by Currier & Ives. Barnum's American Museum, at the corner of Broadway and Ann Street in lower Manhattan, advertised its location as the ideal place to view the parade (in paid seats) and then, of course, to see the exhibitions, which included wandering gypsies, fireworks, mechanical figures, and an albino lady.

National Trauma, Then Decline

As the Civil War approached, Evacuation Day became politicized as an expression of support for the Union. New York's City Council, dominated by Copperhead Tammany

Democrats, refused to take part or provide public funds for the celebration. At war's end, the 1865 celebration was appropriately huge, with eight thousand soldiers and twenty regimental bands participating. But the national trauma of the Civil War played a large part in Evacuation Day's decline. In the postwar years, the holiday became increasingly marginalized as it lost its meaning for most New Yorkers. Instead, the Fourth of July represented a renewal of nationalist spirit, and Thanksgiving, a more inclusive holiday that was traditionally observed in New York the same week as the Fourth, became a national holiday in 1863. The *Brooklyn Eagle* noted that the intense anti-British feeling the citizens inherited from their fathers disappeared, and now New York is more concerned about trading with England than . . . avowing a hatred toward her." The veterans of the War of 1812 were also dying off, "decrepit veterans of battles . . . sad-faced, poverty-stricken shadows of themselves."

The centennial celebration in 1883 was both the most spectacular celebration and the last gasp of popular participation. Organized by patrician John Austin Stevens, secretary of the New-York Historical Society, the celebration included the participation of twenty-five thousand troops, with over a million people, including President Chester A. Arthur, in attendance. A naval pageant, with three hundred warships and private yachts, complemented the celebration. Stevens went on to found the Society of '83, later renamed the Sons of the Revolution, which marginalized Evacuation Day by celebrating it privately through dinners and balls reported in society pages, not news headlines.

The last recorded observation of Evacuation Day was November 25, 1916, when sixty veterans of the Old Guard (the 3rd U.S. Infantry) raised the flag a final time. The same day, forty-five thousand spectators watched army beat navy at the old Polo Grounds in upper Manhattan. Thereafter, the holiday was relegated to newspaper stories about old New York customs. Its bicentennial was celebrated in 1983 with a parade and exhibition at the Fraunces Tavern Museum, but no revivals followed, although in 2008 the National Park Service lit beacons in twelve sites in New York and New Jersey and held a ceremony on the steps of Federal Hall.

Carte de visites of famous people, such as this one of Sojourner Truth, were much in demand as collectibles. A *carte de visite* was a thin paper photograph mounted on a thicker paper card, about 2.5 by 4 inches. Introduced in the United States around 1860, these inexpensive photographs became tremendously popular. Credit: Library of Congress.

15

In Search of Truth

Margaret Washington

Isabella Van Wagenen was forty-six years old in 1843 when she changed her name, left Manhattan, and headed east. She had money in the bank but took only twenty-five cents for the Brooklyn Ferry—enough to "pay Caesar," she said. A woman who once thought of herself as "vain in her clothes," she now carried only a few belongings in a knapsack. Disembarking on Long Island, she met a Quaker woman who criticized her new name, which was "Sojourner." Plodding over the sandy road, she asked God for "a handle" to go with her first name. It came to her "as true as God is true, Sojourner *Truth*." She "leapt for joy."

Thus began the forty-year public career of this remarkable former slave who would become a champion of social justice for both slaves and women, who would be quoted and cited by many cultivated Americans, who would meet famous authors and statesmen, as well as three presidents, and who would speak in twenty-one states and the District of Columbia. Lyceum organizer F. P. Powell recalled that Sojourner Truth "carried the people by storm. . . . Her presence was so powerful, her magnetism so great, her personal appearance so majestic—her eye keen." Standing six feet tall, she would swing out one long arm, gesticulate, and walk back and forth across the platform as she spoke with "eloquence . . . only equaled by her wit." While her "withering sarcasm" could silence menacing hecklers, her true nature was kind, gentle, and sweet.

Bell

At first glance, Sojourner Truth seems an unlikely candidate for the "lasting place in history" that she has been accorded. Yet her life illuminates both her witness of oppression

---

This essay first appeared in fall 2010, volume 10, number 2.

and her desire to change America. Born a slave in 1797 in Hurley, Ulster County, she was named Isabella and called Bell. Her first owner, a Dutch man named Johannes (Hans) Hardenbergh, was the third of his line born in America. His grandfather and others had acquired the contested Great Hardenbergh Patent, two million acres that included the Catskill Mountains. The investors later divided the land, but the Hardenberghs, a prominent Pietist family, retained the lion's share and wielded tremendous power in Ulster County. Hans' domineering father had been instrumental in the founding of Rutgers University, and his younger son, Dominie Jacob Rutsen Hardenbergh, was its first president. Hans, whom Bell called "the Old Colonel," had fought with George Washington during the Revolution in the unsuccessful battle for New York.

Bell's family consisted of her mother, Elizabeth, father James ("Bomefree"), and younger brother Peter. As Hans' "kitchen family," they had certain privileges, such as growing foodstuffs, flax, and tobacco, which they sold or used themselves. But the family lived in a dank cellar with the other slaves, and Bell's many older siblings were sold or presented to white family members as gifts. This was a great source of suffering to Elizabeth, who implanted memories of lost children in her daughter's mind: "Those are the same stars and that is the same moon that look down upon your brothers and sisters, which they see as they look up to them, though they are ever so far away from us, and each other." Later on the lecture circuit, Sojourner would relive these and other painful moments when her mother vicariously attempted to reconnect her family and console herself.

The Old Colonel's son, Charles, inherited Bell's family, but Charles' untimely death in 1806 led to freedom for Bell's parents. While Elizabeth was freed to care for the aged Bomefree, the half-Mohawk giant of a man who had once been the Old Colonel's favorite and was now nearly blind, Bell and Peter were auctioned off. Elizabeth "cried as if her heart would break," while Bell took the corner of her mother's apron and wiped her tears. As Sojourner would relate: "My poor mother would weep and say in Dutch, 'Oh! *Mein Got* (My God), my poor children will be sold into slavery.' "

John Neely, the rough English newcomer who purchased puberty-age Bell, beat her mercilessly because she did not understand English (the Hardenbergh family spoke only Dutch). Her final owner, John Dumont, was a Dutch Huguenot who owned a large farm in New Paltz. There Bell grew to womanhood and had two black "husbands" and five children.

Bell (and later Sojourner) was certainly influenced by Dutch-American culture and customs, particularly those of Dutch women. For example, Bell was never educated—but her reason was that "[t]he Low Dutch were very close and ignorant, and so, naturally, to this day, I can neither read nor write." But they also wielded subtle power behind the men's patriarchal authority. They kept their maiden names, ran taverns, conducted financial transactions, brought lawsuits, and inherited separate property. Capable of signing documents with only an X, they nevertheless had the business acumen to make binding contracts. Sojourner Truth bought property on four different occasions, dictated two narratives, compiled a collection of her experiences (including personal commemorations from famous people), and filed lawsuits—and signed her will with an X.

Rural Dutch women drank ale and smoked publicly. Bell also loved ale and smoked a Dutch pipe—and while as Sojourner she became a temperance advocate, she was seventy-one before abandoning the "filthy weed." She claimed to feel no "bodily or mental inconvenience or depression": "The dear Lord has filled the part that longed [for tobacco] with his own love and Spirit."

Sojourner believed that the "Spirit of Truth" had anointed her life's mission. Yet while enslaved, Bell had received no religious instruction, even though the pious Dutch women of the Dumont household recited prayers and sang psalms. Instead, Bell's spiritual mentor was her mother. "My children," Elizabeth instructed, "there is a God, who hears you and sees you," and God was their hope "when you are beaten, or cruelly treated, or fall into any trouble." Bell embedded this teaching in her consciousness as the cornerstone of her mystical faith. To her, God was a warm personal friend with whom she conversed and from whom she sought counsel. As Sojourner, she said, "I talk to God and God talks to me."

Bell's parents had taught her that obedience, honesty, and faithfulness were possible insurance against abuse and sale. Thus, on John Dumont's farm, she was the best field hand on the place. She adored Dumont, who proudly proclaimed that his "wench" was "better to me than a man." But the traumas of bondage—her mother's early demise, the death of her own firstborn son, a cruel mistress, her partner's whipping, which left him crippled and led to his death, and the fate of her beloved father, Bomefree, who, after serving three generations of Hardenberghs, froze to death in the woods, blind and alone—finally obliterated her loyalty.

In 1826, Bell fled slavery with her infant daughter and sought asylum with an anti-slavery Quaker man who was gravely ill, even though New York's emancipation act would take effect within a year. He suggested several families who might assist her after his death. Bell chose the home of Isaac Van Wagenen, a Dutch man her own age whom she had known since birth and to whom she could explain her predicament: John Dumont had "promised" her freedom a year early, then changed his mind, and she would rather go to jail rather than return. Naturally, a confrontation ensued when Dumont appeared and demanded his slave back. Dumont and Van Wagenen argued, and finally Dumont "sold" Bell and her daughter to Van Wagenen for $25, whereupon Van Wagenen freed them and held an emancipation ceremony. The grateful young mother took the name of her benefactor, thereafter calling herself Isabella Van Wagenen.

Isabella

But Dumont sold Isabella's five-year-old son Peter to his nephew and neighbor, Solomon Gidney, who thereupon sold Peter out of the state—an illegal act, since Peter, if he stayed in New York, would be free upon reaching adulthood. Isabella broadcast the injustice throughout the countryside, although disdainful looks from whites fell upon her "like a heavy weight." Local Quakers explained her legal rights, gave her money for counsel, and contacted the New York Manumission Society in Manhattan.

So Isabella sued to get Peter back. She capitalized on her Hardenbergh connections and became the first black woman to go to court against a white man, and win; Peter was subsequently freed in 1827 by New York statute.

But Isabella insisted that it was not the court; rather, "God only could have made such people hear me." She had attended Methodist camp meetings and experienced a soul-grappling confrontation with the Holy Spirit, claiming sanctification through the fire of Pentecost, which had made her "melt like wax before the flame" and "wilt like a cabbage leaf."

This experience would seal her destiny as a "mouthpiece for God." Local Methodists took her to New York City in 1829, where she became a popular camp meeting preacher and reformer among prostitutes: "even the learned and respectable people were running after her." She followed Methodist Perfectionism, a radical offshoot of the Great Western Revival that began in upstate New York with such scorching conversions that the region was called the Burned-Over District. As Sojourner, she was proud of these New York roots, and although by 1844 she lived in Northampton, Massachusetts, her stops in her myriad travels generally included Rochester, as well as towns, villages, and hamlets in the upstate corridor. Even her final migration to Michigan in 1857 was influenced by a host of progressive transplanted New Yorkers.

Unfortunately, Isabella's Perfectionism and involvement in a cult in 1832 led to false accusations of immorality and implications of criminality. She was undaunted. "I have got the *truth*," she proclaimed against her accusers, "and I will *crush* them with the *truth*." Her stellar reputation, her assertiveness and willingness to employ the legal system, and above all her intuitive sense of justice, saved her from ruin.

The Birth of Sojourner

Yet even New York City could not contain Isabella's expanding sense of mission. After fifteen years in Manhattan, she insisted, "The Lord has directed me to . . . leave this city at once," though her employer and friends said she was crazy. By 1845 she was back in the city, transformed into Sojourner Truth—and it was Sojourner who delivered the most famous speech of the 1851 Ohio Women's Rights Convention in Akron—"Ain't I a Woman?"—which would seal her place in history and become not only a rallying cry for abolitionists but one of the fundamental documents of both the nineteenth-century suffrage and twentieth-century women's movements.

New York in the 1800s

Abraham Lincoln affixes his signature to the Emancipation Proclamation, Secretary of State (and former New York governor) William H. Seward at his side, in this 1865 lithograph by Currier & Ives of New York. Credit: Library of Congress.

16

The Poetry and Prose of the Emancipation Proclamation

Harold Holzer

It is difficult to deny that the reputation of the Emancipation Proclamation has fallen into historical decline. Unenlightened on issues of race, the fashionable arguments go, Lincoln used emancipation as a desperate weapon of war only when it became clear that the Union could not be preserved without depriving the South of "slave power" and without arming blacks in the North to put down the Rebellion. Furthermore, critics suggest, Lincoln's document really had little effect: it freed slaves only where he had no power to free them and left them enslaved where he exercised the authority to break their chains. And finally, detractors assert, so many slaves were in the process of liberating *themselves* by the time it was written, fleeing into Union lines throughout the South, that even if Lincoln had not proclaimed it, black freedom was inevitable. As historian Barbara Fields has argued, "No human being alive could have held back the tide that swept toward freedom."

But is it fair to imply that all Lincoln did was *not hold back* the tide of freedom? Unfortunately, he did little to herald the importance of his own courageous act. The man capable of writing so dazzlingly—who counted Harriet Beecher Stowe, Leo Tolstoy, Karl Marx, and Walt Whitman among his admirers—intentionally checked the power of his pen in writing the document he privately called "the great event of the nineteenth Century." No leader ever cloaked a great act in more intentionally deceptive public relations, or more intensely stultifying prose; Lincoln overexplained and underwrote the Emancipation Proclamation. To understand why is to suggest a new assessment of a document whose importance has been in historical decline.

This essay first appeared in summer 2001, volume 1, number 1.

Lincoln enjoyed the constitutional authority to abolish slavery only in those areas in active rebellion against the federal government. He surely knew from the start that a presidential proclamation would be a paper tiger unless and until Union armies overran the Confederacy and liberated the slave population. To drive the "harpoon into the monster" of slavery forever, as he put it, Lincoln would also make sure that the 1864 Republican Party platform called for a constitutional amendment abolishing slavery *everywhere*—completing the work the Emancipation Proclamation began.

But there is little justification for arguing that Lincoln failed to craft an inspiring document because he was a reluctant emancipator. "I am naturally anti-slavery," he reminded a Kentucky editor in April 1864. "If slavery is not wrong, nothing is wrong. I can not remember when I did not so think and feel." More likely, Lincoln wrote an undistinguished document because he was a deliberate, perhaps even fearful, emancipator. Only when his initial qualms evaporated did he temper the prosaic writing style of his document with some of the most masterful poetry he ever crafted, sublime rhetoric that should really be considered side by side with the document as part of his overall message of liberty.

It is true that many leaders of the day urged prompter action on slavery, but many others cautioned against it, leaving Lincoln whipsawed by the conflicting demands from within the disparate elements of his fragile Union coalition. Abolitionists prodded him. Two generals, John C. Frémont and David Hunter, precipitously issued orders confiscating slave property in their respective military departments, and Lincoln promptly revoked them. From a modern vantage point, Lincoln seems to have impeded liberty. But judged by the public sentiment of his own time, he was merely postponing it until he felt it could be sustained. As Frederick Douglass understood: "While he hated slavery, and really desired its destruction, he always proceeded against it in a manner the least likely to shock or drive from him any who were truly in sympathy with the preservation of the Union." Because if the Union died, Lincoln knew, so did any chance for democratic government *or* equal opportunity, here or throughout the world, then or in the future. With crucial, slave-holding border states teetering on the verge of secession, Lincoln worried that if emancipation propelled them into the Confederacy, the city of Washington would be isolated, the balance of power roiled, and the Union irrevocably lost. He nervously joked that he hoped to keep God on his side. But he simply *had* to keep Kentucky.

So he took small steps. He signed one law that abolished slavery in the federal territories and another that liberated slaves still held in the nation's capital. He implored the border states, although without success, to accept gradual, compensated emancipation; he felt he could not risk further action that might propel them into the Confederate orbit.

Then, on July 17, 1862, Lincoln assembled his cabinet to read them a brief executive order that called emancipation "a fit and necessary war measure" to restore federal authority. Yet no proclamation was issued that day, because Secretary of State Seward counseled delay. The war was going poorly, and the country would likely view a proclamation against slavery as "the last measure of an exhausted government—a cry for help . . . our last *shriek*, on the retreat." Lincoln saw the wisdom in this objection. He put aside his draft and waited.

In August, Horace Greeley, editor of the *New-York Tribune*, published an editorial entitled "The Prayer of Twenty Millions" condemning Lincoln as "strangely and disastrously remiss" for not acting to end slavery. Of course, Lincoln *was* prepared to act—just not prepared to say so. Instead the president seized on Greeley's attack as an opportunity to place a convincing rationale for emancipation before the public.

Lincoln's widely published letter to the editor has often been cited as evidence of his belief that emancipation was a secondary concern. But since he already knew that his course was leading irrevocably to emancipation, the letter should really be viewed as a shrewd advance public relations effort to set the stage for the new initiative—to rally public support for the measure as a military, not a moral, imperative—so more people would accept it. "My paramount object in this struggle *is* to save the Union, and is not either to save or destroy slavery," Lincoln wrote. "If I could save the Union without freeing any slave, I would do it; and if I could save it by freeing all the slaves, I would do it; and if I could save it by freeing some and leaving others alone, I would also do that." Of course, he had already determined precisely what to do. His Greeley letter ingeniously set the stage for the announcement.

Lincoln would not admit the inevitability of emancipation even to a delegation of free black citizens visiting the White House on August 24. Instead he all but told them to move to Haiti or the Caribbean. "It is better for us both . . . to be separated," he said. "There is an unwillingness on the part of our people, harsh as it may be, for you free colored people to remain with us." But this performance, too, was designed specifically for white audiences, who may have been willing to accept a militarily necessary emancipation but not an integrated society.

As late as September 13, Lincoln told a group of religious leaders visiting the White House: "What good would a proclamation of emancipation from me do? . . . would my word free the slaves when I cannot even enforce the Constitution in the rebel states?" Once again he was skillfully provoking false expectations of government inertia on slavery, ending the meeting by admitting: "I have not decided *against* a proclamation of liberty to the slaves, but hold the matter under advisement." If he took any action at all, it would come "as a practical war measure, to be decided upon according to the advantages and disadvantages it may offer to the suppression of the Rebellion."

The military success that Lincoln needed as a prerequisite for emancipation finally came on September 17 at the Battle of Antietam. Five days later, he reassembled his cabinet and read his new Preliminary Proclamation. It was issued publicly, without fanfare, that same day. "It is now for the country and the world to pass judgment on it," Lincoln told a small crowd of serenaders a few days after its release. But he could not have been pleased with the first of those judgments.

A regiment from his own home state of Illinois promptly deserted, defiantly vowing to "lie in the woods until moss grew on their backs rather than help free slaves." One New York soldier wrote home, in a letter preserved in the New York State Archives: "I sware I wish that all the abolissions sons of bitches had to come downe here and take the front . . . and all Git blowd to hell." Illinois political leaders added fuel to the fire by declaring: "We will not render support to the present administration in carrying on its wicked abolition crusade against the South."

There was praise, to be sure, but it came mostly from the abolitionists—and most of them were angry that the document offered an escape clause: one hundred days' notice for the Confederate states to end the Rebellion, in return for which they could keep their slaves after all. Approbation appeared in the Northern press, but plenty of journals assailed the proclamation. Democratic papers charged that the president was "adrift on the current of radical fanaticism." To the *Chicago Times*, the proclamation was a "monstrous usurpation, a criminal wrong, and an act of national suicide." By the time his vice president wrote to him to praise the proclamation as "the great act of the age," Lincoln was distraught. And the worst political aftershock was yet to come: the fall 1862 congressional elections. Lincoln's Republicans took a severe beating.

Yet Lincoln had created a legally sound document that African Americans could later use, "if necessary, to establish judicially their title of freedom," as New York historian La Wanda Cox has argued, since he was not certain, at least not in September 1862, that the courts would even uphold the proclamation and keep slaves "thenceforward and forever free." He had rejected the impulse to place the proclamation on "high moral ground," as the *New York Times* insightfully detected, and framed it instead "as a war measure from the commander-in-chief of the army, not one issuing from the bosom of philanthropy." That was the only way he could defend it to border states, Democrats, even Northern racists vital to the Union coalition. The poetry could wait. It would follow within months—along with celebratory tributes in the graphic arts that decorated American homes for generations, offering mute but powerful visual testimony to Lincoln's achievement.

The final Emancipation Proclamation, issued on January 1, 1863, did not add much to the vocabulary of freedom. Space was devoted to a list of the states and counties exempted from the order. The most inspiring sentence—"I invoke the considerable judgment of mankind, and the gracious favor of Almighty God"—was suggested by someone else. At least Lincoln inserted his belief that it was "sincerely believed to be an act of justice," hastily adding, "warranted by the Constitution, based upon military necessity."

But eventually Lincoln provided the poetic accompaniment he initially resisted. In his annual message to Congress that December, the voice of a genuine liberator could be heard declaring,

> We cannot escape history. . . . The fiery trial through which we pass, will light us down, in honor or dishonor, to the latest generation. . . . In giving freedom to the slave, we assure freedom to the free and honorable alike in what we give and what we preserve. We shall nobly save, or meanly lose the last, best hope of earth.

By the time he rose at Gettysburg to consecrate the soldiers' cemetery the following November, he would declare that "the great task remaining before us" promised nothing less than a "new birth of freedom."

Lincoln's magnificent apology for the sin of slavery, in his Second Inaugural Address on March 4, 1865, is perhaps the most epic of all the "poetry" he produced, not only because of its conciliatory ending that urged "malice toward none" and "charity for all" and its thunderbolt invocation of a vengeful God who "gives to North and South, this terrible war, as the woe due those by whom the offence came"—the "offence" being slavery. Lincoln showed exactly what kind of national apology was required:

> Fondly do we hope—fervently do we pray—that this mighty scourge of war may speedily pass away. Yet, if God wills that it continue, until all the wealth piled up by the bond-man's two hundred and fifty years of unrequited toil shall be sunk, and until every drop of blood drawn with the lash, shall be paid by another drawn with the sword, as was said three thousand years ago, so still it must be said "the judgments of the Lord, are true and righteous altogether.

The day he signed the final proclamation, Lincoln took up his pen, then stopped abruptly and put it down, fingers quivering from hours of handshaking that New Year's morning. "My hand is almost paralyzed," he told the few onlookers gathered in his office. "If my name ever goes down in history, it will be for this act, and my whole soul is in it. If my hand trembles when I sign the proclamation, all who examine the document will say, 'He hesitated.' "

But when it counted, he did not. He took up the pen again, and as one witness remembered, "slowly, firmly wrote that 'Abraham Lincoln' with which the whole world is now familiar. He looked up, smiled, and said: 'That will do.' "

Matilda Joslyn Gage. Credit: Matilda Joslyn Gage Foundation, Fayetteville, New York, matildajoslyngage.org.

17

Writing and "Righting" the History of Woman Suffrage

Mary E. Corey

Through a grand historic irony, one of the women most instrumental in the preservation of woman suffrage history has, herself, been largely overlooked in the histories of this movement. Matilda Joslyn Gage was one of three National Woman Suffrage Association (NWSA) founders known to their contemporaries as the "triumvirate," leaders who organized the work, set the agenda, and, most importantly, preserved the records of the nineteenth-century woman suffrage movement. With Elizabeth Cady Stanton and Susan B. Anthony, Gage determined in 1876 to prepare for publication the *History of Woman Suffrage*. The first three volumes of this work, prepared over the next ten years, are the seminal resource for historians researching this movement. Gage's role in that work alone should have guaranteed her a place of honor in our collective memory of the suffrage past. Instead, it has obscured her part in this and other movement histories.

The first three volumes preserved the work of the National from the beginnings of the movement to about 1883. Gage's contributions to these three volumes cannot be overestimated. Her essays, "Preceding Causes," "Woman, Church and State," and "Woman's Patriotism in the War," begin and end each volume, and fully the first third of volume 3 comes from Gage's newspaper, the *National Citizen and Ballot Box*. These materials are just the beginning of what easily can be traced directly to Gage. Unfortunately, volume 4 prepared after the bitter disagreement between Anthony and Gage over merging the NWSA and the American Woman Suffrage Association

This essay first appeared in fall 2001, volume 1, number 2.

(AWSA), and after Gage's death, covers the NWSA's most active years and those spent writing the *History.* This volume minimized Gage's activism and her contribution to the *History.* For this reason, modern historians who have relied on volume 4's description of her work have also tended to minimize Gage's contribution.

The rift between Gage and Anthony had its roots in the circumstances surrounding the formation of the NWSA in 1869. Immediately following the Civil War, the reform alliance between abolitionists and women's rights advocates crumbled in the fierce infighting over suffrage priorities. For abolitionists and many woman suffragists, including Lucy Stone and Henry Brown Blackwell, it was "the Negro's hour" and woman suffrage would have to wait as they threw their support behind the Reconstruction Amendments. For others, such as Stanton, Anthony, and Gage, waiting would mean losing the reform momentum of Reconstruction. Worse, they felt the insertion of the word "male" into the Constitution through clause 2 of the Fourteenth Amendment would set woman suffrage back a hundred years. Unable to prevail on this issue, Stanton, Anthony, and Gage left the final American Equal Rights Association Convention in May 1869 and held an impromptu evening session where they agreed to concentrate fully on woman suffrage by forming the NWSA. They were soon reviled by the Boston contingent headed by Stone and Blackwell for what was perceived as a purposeful attempt to exclude them from the new suffrage organization. As a result, they formed their own woman suffrage association, the AWSA, the following November. The two associations remained bitter rivals for the next twenty years.

Over the course of those years, however, it would become clear that Anthony had a vision both larger and smaller than Stanton and Gage. Larger, in that she knew implicitly that the NWSA would need broad-based support in order to accomplish its goals. And, smaller, in that, for her, NWSA had only one goal, woman suffrage.

To this end, by the late 1880s she had begun to pursue women's groups that had formerly been anathema to the NWSA, the AWSA and the Women's Christian Temperance Union. These groups supported legislation that was directly opposed to the proclaimed ideals of the NWSA, including inserting God as the founder of nations into the United States Constitution and Sunday "blue laws." The WCTU had actually opposed woman suffrage until Frances Willard convinced them they could use the vote to legislate their peculiar moral order. Anthony also began surrounding herself with younger, more easily manipulated protégés within the NWSA, women like socialites Rachel Foster Avery and May Wright Sewall.

Overtures to merge the NWSA and the AWSA began circulating during the years just prior to the 1889 NWSA Convention, none taken seriously as long as Gage was chair of the Executive Committee. But in 1889 Anthony pleaded reduced resources to deny Gage's travel expenses to the Washington meeting. Anthony did not reveal that she had received a new proposal from AWSA that she was determined to accept on behalf of NWSA. Therefore, she waited to address the merger proposal until the last evening of the convention, after most delegates had already left. She then boldly assumed Gage's office, in order to bring it before the Executive Committee, and argued strenuously against allowing the members to vote on it. It was an outrage! She had argued on behalf of woman suffrage for forty years and now denied its necessity within the suffrage association itself. Gage raised a storm of protest, but the majority of the members accepted the move as a fait accompli. At that, Gage quit the NWSA and formed her own organization. To Anthony, Gage was, according to one contemporary observer, "abandoned . . . cast out, even her name an unclean thing." Anthony considered it treason, "ridiculous, absurd, and too horrible for anything." As for the merged association, the National American Woman Suffrage Association, the old rivals found it an uncomfortable alliance and within months Stanton was privately calling Henry Blackwell an "autocratic hag." For our purposes, one of the more important long-term effects of the merger was the loss of Gage to the historic record, a truly monumental loss.

Therefore, in order to recover Gage's work, we must begin where she always began: in the archival evidence. From her first speech, Gage brought a historian's perspective to bear on the tasks before her. She became and remained the acknowledged historian of the movement for the next half century. Further, her own magnum opus, *Woman, Church and State*, is the only historic monograph to emerge from the nineteenth-century woman suffrage movement. Indeed, it is the first volume in what would later be known as women's studies.

Her story begins on a crisp September afternoon in 1852. The women at the Syracuse Woman's Rights Convention watched as the young newcomer from Fayetteville inched her way toward the podium to deliver her first speech. Although unscheduled to speak and unknown to the assemblage, she approached the podium "when her courage had reached a sufficiently high point. With palpitating heart she ascended the platform, where she was cordially given place by Mrs. Mott." Lucretia Mott later recalled that she was "trembling in every limb."

She began, "This convention has assembled to discuss the subject of woman's rights, and form some settled plan of action for the future. Let Syracuse sustain her name for radicalism!" With these words, Gage launched her life's work in women's rights as a speaker, activist, and historian. In her judgment history offered important insights into the status of women analogous to other previously dependent groups. She argued that in an earlier day "science and learning were in the hands of the priests, and property held by vassalage, . . . education was held to be unfit for the masses [and] kept them in a continual state of dependency." These same kinds of forces conspired to keep women of her day dependent. Implicitly, she empowered women to use the precedents of the past to inform their present and shape their future.

Her historian's eye offered a usable past. Gage insisted that women needed to know their collective past in order to refute the prevailing wisdom that women were unfit for spheres beyond the home and children. For her it wasn't enough to argue speculatively about what women would be able to do in the future. She spoke of governing women "from Semiramis to Victoria, the scientific genius of Helena Lucretia Coran, and Caroline Herschell, and literary giants such as Sappho, Margaret Fuller, and Harriet Beecher Stowe." Women *had* a proud history of achievement in every avenue of learning.

Her analysis of the marriage laws showed that even in woman's designated "sphere" she was powerless. In laws determining inheritance rights, real and personal property, as well as wages, married women were classed with "idiots, persons of unsound mind, and infants. *Well classed, truly!*" (emphasis hers). "Every father," she stormed, "has a right to bind, or give away, any of his children without the consent, or even the knowledge of the mother; and when he dies, she is not considered a competent guardian . . . in his will, or deed, [he can] exclude the mother from participation in guardianship." Gage stressed that women could and must use, manipulate, and interpret the past in their own self-interest. She railed against a republic that made

> great professions in regard to general liberty, yet the right to particular liberty, natural equality, and personal independence of two great portions of this country, is treated, from custom with the greatest contempt . . . color in the one instance and sex in the other are brought as reasons why they should be so derided.

Lucretia Mott was so impressed with her speech that she arranged to have it published with the other convention tracts.

Thirty-four years later Gage was still demanding that the nation live up to its highest ideals. At the dedication of the Statue of Liberty in 1886 she protested, "It is the sarcasm of the nineteenth century to represent liberty as a woman, while not one single woman throughout the length and breadth of the land is as yet in possession of political liberty!" When the official dicta of the organizers stated, "there will be no women in the gathering on the island," she and the members of the New York State Woman's Suffrage Association ignored it, rented a steamship, raised their protest banners, and barged into the official flotilla to deliver their speeches.

Her consuming passion was to make the world a better place for her daughters and her son. Whether that struggle meant arguing with Ezra Cornell to admit women to his college, organizing the women of Fayetteville to elect women to the school board, or hanging funeral crepe from her front porch to protest rather than picnic on the Fourth of July, Gage lived her ideals. Through her activism, her newspaper, her work on the *History of Woman Suffrage*, and her *Woman, Church and State*, she bequeathed a living legacy to the future. That legacy should not be lost.

Maggie, Katie, and Leah Fox. Credit: Department of Rare Books, Special Collections and Preservation, University of Rochester Libraries, Rochester, New York.

18

Speaking with the Dead

The Fox Sisters

Jeanne Mackin

Imagine a cold winter night in Hydesville, a town in upstate New York so small that most maps ignore it. Imagine the wind howling through a rustic cabin, the blackness of night without electric light, the deep quiet of a late winter evening without cars or television or radio. Now imagine in that windy, dark cabin two young farm girls, Maggie and Katie Fox, daughters of an unhappy mother who finds consolation in the ecstasy of evangelical religion and a father who finds his consolation in alcohol, and imagine that on the evening of March 31, 1848, the separation between the world of the living and the world of the dead is not as firm as some might believe—so thin is the veil, in fact, that those two worlds can speak to each other.

Thus began what is known today as the American Spiritualist movement.

On that March night, Maggie, eleven years old, and Katie, eight, were awakened by . . . knockings, they said, except there was nobody at the door, no branches hitting the windows. From their bed, Maggie and Katie watched their father race to and fro, trying to discover the source of the mysterious midnight noises.

Finally, according to chroniclers of the time, the sisters announced, "It's Mr. Splitfoot! See! He answers!" They snapped their fingers, and the sound knocked back in response. Mrs. Fox, convinced that her daughters had found a way to speak with the dead, fell to her knees.

Soon enough, the entire neighborhood gathered in the Fox cabin, and Maggie and Katie knocked out answers to questions posed by astounded friends. According to transcripts of this first Fox séance, the questions were easily answered: How many

This essay first appeared in winter 2002, volume 1, number 3.

children did Mrs. Jones have? What age was Billy when he died? What was the source of Matthew's ailment?—things that neighbors already knew about each other. But soon the sisters grew more adventurous. Using the "Spirit Alphabet" (one knock for "A," two knocks for "B," etc.), they encouraged Mr. Splitfoot to knock out the story of a murder that had taken place earlier in the cabin. A peddler had disappeared, and there had been rumors in town for several years. Maggie and Katie brought those rumors to life with a lurid and painstakingly spelled-out story of a bloody ax and a body in the cellar. Later the cellar was dug out until it flooded, and no body was found. But in one of the many strange twists in the story of the Fox sisters, fifty-four years later human bones and a peddler's tin box *were* found in that cellar, giving belated credence to the story.

For fifty years, skeptics tried to discover the true source of those knockings. Maggie herself revealed, in disillusioned middle age, that the first sounds had been made by tying strings to apples and dropping them out of bed onto the cabin's bare wooden floor. But, she said, she and Katie then devised a system of cracking their toes and other joints to make the rappings, using this system throughout their Spiritualist career. Their many imitators and bandwagoners used showier techniques: "spirits" wrapped in gauze, trumpets dropping from the ceiling, and disembodied hands rising from boxes would become common in séances.

The Hydesville Rappings became an instant national phenomenon, fueled by the growing leisure of the American middle class, the lack of interesting amusements available to a post-Puritan society, the increasing speed of travel and communication, the number of newspapers and the exuberance (some said gullibility) of their editors, and the appeal of the sisters themselves, who were young and pretty and appeared on stage and at private performances with bare feet and loosened hair. Their "advantages" included a grown sister, Leah, who proved to have a keen eye for the theatricality of Spiritualism and its monetary possibilities. Within weeks of the first rappings, Leah had appointed herself Katie and Maggie's manager and arranged public demonstrations. The entrance fee was a quarter a head.

The first public meeting of the Spiritualists was held in the Corinthian Hall in Rochester in 1849. Soon afterward, the Fox sisters toured Albany, Troy, and New York City, where they were sponsored at first by P. T. Barnum and Horace Greeley, who suggested the sisters raise their fee to a dollar a head to keep out the riffraff. The Fox sisters quickly became as famous an attraction as Barnum's Fiji Mermaid (half a monkey and a fish sewn together), or acclaimed songstress Jenny Lind. Maggie, Katie, and Leah had their group portrait painted by Nathaniel Currier and were front-page material in newspapers across the country and eventually in England.

Explanation and History of the Mysterious Communications with Spirits, Etc. by Eliab Capron and Henry D. Barron, a booklet published in 1850 in Auburn, New York, and *The History of the Strange Sounds and Rappings Heard in Rochester* by

D. M. Dewey, which was published in Rochester that same year and sold thirty thousand copies in a few months, were the first of many publications purporting to explain the abilities of the Fox sisters. "Humbug it very possibly is," Dewey wrote of the rappings. "But it will stand severer tests than will many things which pass for sober realities."

The sisters spawned not only an entire industry but also a wave of imitation. "Knocking" tables, with built-in hammers, became a sideline specialty of many industrious cabinetmakers; those who couldn't afford a special table would simply use their legs (hidden under a tablecloth, of course) to tilt the family card table and make the rapping sounds. A decade later, just about every family in the country claimed to have a member (usually a young daughter) who could speak with the dead. Congress briefly considered a special commission to act as liaison between this world and the next. Since money was required for such diplomacy, however, the request was denied.

The Fox sisters' supporters included Sir Arthur Conan Doyle, Harriet Beecher Stowe, James Fenimore Cooper, D. H. Lawrence, Robert Owen, Queen Victoria, Governor Talmadge of Michigan, and, perhaps their most famous clients, President and Mrs. Abraham Lincoln. Spiritualists eventually even claimed that President Lincoln wrote the Gettysburg Address through the guidance of a spirit after having attended a séance.

For a while, the sisters thrived. Leah married a banker (her third husband, after having been abandoned by a first and widowed by a second), and Katie married an English barrister. Maggie's love life was less successful. Her first and only love, the Arctic explorer Elisha Kent Kane, died before he could legalize their union; his family, Philadelphia bluebloods, despised her. By middle age, Katie and Maggie had succumbed to the family weakness for alcohol and found their finances strained both by alcoholism and by a decrease in their own popularity. A feud with Leah progressed into a family split, and in a bizarre twist of events, Maggie, probably motivated more by revenge against Leah than contrition, rented a big hall in New York City and demonstrated to the audience how she "contacted" the spirits with her joints. She confessed that they all had been tricked, and she apologized. Yet—strangest of all—her followers and the many believers in Spiritualism refused to accept her confession, claiming *she* had been tricked by her own spirits!

Once begun, Spiritualism evidently could not be stopped, even by its own founders. Maggie and Katie died within months of each other, alone and impoverished—returning, in a way, to their beginnings.

The Fox sisters were probably the first "media stars" of America. Both Maggie and Leah wrote autobiographies, and many of their visitors recorded séances with the sisters in their diaries and letters. Dozens of newspapers chronicled their career, and the sisters remained a popular print topic throughout the nineteenth and twentieth centuries. The

Rochester Historical Society houses a "knocking" table with built-in hammers for use by those with less flexible joints than Maggie's. But perhaps the most famous artifact of all, the original Fox cabin in Hydesville where the knockings were first heard, has been lost to posterity. It was moved to the nearby Spiritualist colony in Lily Dale, where it promptly burned down. It was rebuilt. It burned again. It was not rebuilt.

Congress Park (shown here in 1916), took its name from Congress Spring, which was named to honor a member of the Continental Congress, John Taylor Gilman, who was part of a hunting party that discovered the spring in 1792. Credit: New York State Archives, Albany, New York.

19

Saratoga Springs

Evolution of a Resort

Field Horne

For two centuries, Saratoga Springs has been one of America's best-loved resort towns. True, it reached its zenith from 1870 to 1900—the most familiar images of Saratoga are those from the Gilded Age, following the Civil War—but those three decades are only part of the story. Archival documents, written by Saratoga's visitors, tourists, and vacationers from the 1700s on, reveal Saratoga's evolution from a spa to a playground for the rich to a resort rich with history.

Frontier Springs Cure the Afflicted

The first European American to visit the springs was probably Sir William Johnson. In 1771, seeking relief from an old wound, he was guided by Mohawk friends to the High Rock Spring, whose mineral-laden water overflowed from a hole atop a curious haystack-shaped rock.

When the Revolution ended, the doughty visitors who followed Johnson to Saratoga were motivated either by curiosity or by the need for those healing waters. In 1784, General Otho Williams wrote to Washington about his visit:

> One motive for extending my tour so far . . . was to visit the springs in the vicinity of Saratoga which I recollect you once recommended to me as a remedy for the Rheumatism. They are now much frequented by the

This essay first appeared in summer 2002, volume 2, number 1.

> uncivilised people of the back country, but very few others resort to them, as there is but one small hutt within several miles of the place.

In 1787, *Columbian* magazine published a view of the springs with an analysis of their mineral content, the first of many scientific reports. Yet Saratoga was still the frontier when William Strickland investigated the springs in 1794: "[T]hey are resorted to by people chiefly of the lower order, afflicted with sores and humours of the blood, but no tolerable accommodations are yet to be met with at the place."

The Beginnings of a Health Resort

However, taverns providing lodging and meals were built in the 1790s, and by 1802, when Gideon Putnam built the first real hotel, Saratoga was already known as a health resort. Alexander Coventry, a physician from Deerfield (Oneida County), stayed at "Putnam's Tavern" in September of its first year and reported that the hotel keeper kindled a fire in his chamber with "boards," probably scraps from construction. Coventry said less about the waters than about the cost; after his one-night stay, he noted, "Paid Putnam a bill of 12/–. Foolishly I did not inquire the items. He charges only 3$ a week for board, and how he got my bill up to 12/– I do not know."

As Saratoga's reputation grew, the roads were improved, and stagecoaches ran north from Albany. Invalids, drawn by both scientific reports and anecdotal information, visited in increasing numbers. In 1813, William Lord of Wilmington, North Carolina, wrote to his wife with humor regarding the most common course of treatment:

> You would be amused & disgusted to see the vast crowd at the Spring in the morning among whom are the first Ladies of company drinking the water, when the object is known by all the men, but even this is not the worst, for after drinking the necessary quart of Water, in order to aid the operation, the Ladies go directly to the House and walk the piazza (which is 200 feet long) among 20 or 30 men and when they feel the effects they pop out of sight for a short time, return, walk, be off, and return again, so on untill all that is required is over.

The Fashionable Arrive

Those who had the leisure for what became known as the "Fashionable Tour" of Saratoga, Niagara Falls, Montreal, and places between joined the health-seekers after the War of 1812. But Ballston Spa, seven miles away, had an even more fashionable reputation. Robert G. Shaw of Boston wrote his mother in 1813 that "Balltown for the dashers carries the bell & while we have a humble collection of about thirty who really come to the Springs for the benefit of the waters, at Ballston they have more than five hundred of the giddy throng."

As the decade went on, Saratoga businessmen added amusements to lure the "giddy throng." Dancing was introduced by 1816, and soon balls were held three times a week. Billiards and bowling were already present, and fishing resorts, at what is now Yaddo and at Saratoga Lake, developed for those who enjoyed the sport, as well as for those who fancied a country drive or perhaps a fish dinner overlooking the water. Lavish hotel meals were an integral part of the Saratoga experience, served in vast dining rooms. Waiters carried dish after dish to the long tables, where guests shared food but not conversation, if they had not been introduced. Wealthy, sophisticated city dwellers put up with chaotic meals, small rooms—"about the size and temperature as an ordinary oven"—and dusty streets, simply because fashion increasingly dictated that fashionable people were in Saratoga simply to be seen.

Railroads Open Saratoga to the Less Wealthy

But the dominance of patricians was short-lived. In 1832, the Schenectady and Saratoga Rail Road began operations, with trains pulled by horses its first summer and by steam engines thereafter. Philip Hone, the New York City diarist, wrote, "This is a pleasant mode of traveling, not very rapid but free from fatigue or inconvenience of any sort." No longer was the enjoyable steamboat trip up the Hudson followed by long hours in a stagecoach, jolting over bad roads. Thus, the less-affluent public became more willing—and more able—to undertake the journey by train. Saratoga's popularity grew by leaps and bounds, and the refined atmosphere of the spa faded; in 1843, Henry McCall, Jr., of Philadelphia wrote to a relative, "Heaven help me for coming here for aristocracy!"

Gambling and Horse Racing

The introduction of gambling was another factor in Saratoga's allure. Andrew Reed, an English minister, wrote in 1835, "There is certainly gambling going on here, but . . . it must be sought for." The first scheduled horse racing, both harness and thoroughbred, took place at Horse Haven, Saratoga's first racetrack, in 1847; bets were most likely placed on these contests. The next year, a visitor recorded in detail the availability of faro, roulette, and other games of chance.

Visitors still drank the waters for their health, but they demanded novel amusements. In the 1840s and 1850s, summer Saratogians could divert themselves with menageries and circuses, concerts, plays, magic lantern lectures, bowling, billiards, cards, an Indian encampment that offered crafts, and even the "circular railroad," on which a small train was propelled by a hand crank.

Southerners were always a large part of Saratoga's summer population—until 1861, when the Civil War prevented them from coming north. According to Englishman Hilary Skinner (and many others), Southerners were the leaders of fashion in every sense. He recalled his 1860 visit: "We had prominent men from both sections of the country staying in the house, and one evening in particular, when some strolling musicians performed before a group of laughing guests, there were citizens standing side by side convulsed with merriment, who have since been deadly enemies." By the summer of 1865, the so-called "shoddy and petroleum aristocracy"—the new rich whose fortunes were made in war contracts—dominated the scene. Most of the Southerners were financially ruined—or dead.

But the war years gave birth to Saratoga's most enduring pastime. In 1863 the old race track, Horse Haven, which had been in use sporadically since 1847, hosted the first formal thoroughbred race meeting. A year later the present thoroughbred track was constructed, and despite a temporary loss of cachet in the 1890s (because of its sale to a somewhat coarse German immigrant gambler from New York City), Saratoga's became known as the finest racetrack in America.

Resort Grows to Host Thousands

All that new "war" money, along with the growth of a culture of leisure, resulted in a vast expansion of Saratoga from 1866 to 1874. The town had not only the racetrack, beautiful shops, and varied amusements, but three of the largest and most sumptuous hotels in America: the Grand Union, the United States, and Congress Hall, which between them could accommodate thousands. The truly rich, like the Vanderbilts, tended to stay in small private cottages on hotel grounds, but by the 1890s, seeking greater privacy, they rented—or in some cases, bought—mansions on North Broadway or Union Avenue.

Yet Saratoga was no longer a resort dominated by the elite. Through the 1870s and 1880s, conventions filled its hotels; day excursions brought farm families like the fictional Josiah Allen's wife, immortalized by Marietta Holley in *Samantha at Saratoga* (1887); and the burgeoning middle class sought Saratoga's entertainment, fashion, and even the benefits of its mineral waters. By the late 1880s, the resort had become a "spa" for all Americans, rich, middling, and poor. It offered high-quality accommodations, a plethora of diversions, and a very public stage for social leaders and celebrities.

Despite demographic changes, auto touring, the suppression of gambling, and a nearly complete eclipse in the 1950s, Saratoga's racetrack has remained a constant attraction, maintaining its historic reputation to the present day. And in the last forty years, America's greatest spa has once again reinvented itself, becoming one of New York State's most attractive places to play—and to live.

A company of cadets forming for infantry drill at the United States Military Academy at West Point in September 1911. Credit: New York State Archives, Albany, New York.

20

West Point

The "Key to America"

Joseph P. Franklin, Major General, U.S. Army (Retired)

In 1775, New Yorkers Christopher Tappan and James Clinton visited and surveyed the Hudson River valley after the Continental Congress charged the New York Assembly with defense of the Hudson River against British forces in the colonies. Fifty miles above New York City, Tappan and Clinton discovered that the wide, tranquil river suddenly narrowed into a sharp, S-shaped bend with steep cliffs rising to rocky terrain on either side. The swift water and limited space forced ships to slow down so they could negotiate the dangerous passage. Maps taken from Tappan and Clinton's surveys named the promontory on the western bank of the river "West Point."

Recognizing the strategic value of this terrain in controlling navigation on the Hudson, local militia began to build forts on the surrounding hills south of West Point, near Bear Mountain. Inexplicably, West Point itself was not fortified. The intent of these defenses was to prevent the British from using the waterway as a means to isolate New England, considered the heart of the rebellious colonies. To further impede British navigation, an iron chain was forged and stretched bank to bank across the river. Called the "Great Chain," or the "West Point Chain," the links were attached to log booms, since the huge chain would have sunk without these floating supports.

Foreign Aid at West Point

However, the American rebellion was confronting an experienced and numerically superior force, and in 1777 British troops captured and destroyed the forts and the

This essay first appeared in fall 2002, volume 2, number 2.

Great Chain. Fortunately, the American victory at the Battle of Saratoga persuaded the British to withdraw to New York City. But as the opposing armies went into winter quarters at the end of 1777, the outcome of their conflict was far from certain.

Then a series of events centering on West Point set the stage for the eventual triumph of the fledgling United States. In January 1778, General Samuel Parsons marched a garrison of troops from Peekskill across the frozen Hudson to occupy the ground that today is the site of the United States Military Academy. Thaddeus Kosciuszko, the Polish nobleman who had come to America in 1776 to design the fortifications at Saratoga and to help plan the defenses of the Continental Congress in Philadelphia, was given the rank of colonel and traveled to West Point in 1778 to complete its defenses, which had been designed by the French engineer Lieutenant Colonel Louis de la Radiére. Captain Frederick von Steuben, the Prussian Army officer who had journeyed to America to join the rebellion in 1777, arrived at West Point in 1779 to begin drilling and disciplining America's untrained Continental Army troops in the manner he had begun the previous winter at Valley Forge. These technical skills brought to the battlefield by foreign friends made a difference for the American army. To keep an eye on British attempts to move up the river, in 1779 George Washington established his headquarters at West Point, calling it the "key to America."

A Traitor in Their Midst

But the road ahead was not without perils. Major General Benedict Arnold persuaded Washington to give him command of West Point. Arnold had earned his rank by courageous service in many major battles, including Saratoga. He was reputed to be one of Washington's best commanders, and West Point was seen at the time as America's strongest military post. However, Arnold's second wife was from a Philadelphia family loyal to the British Crown, and he may have begun to plot his treason as early as 1778, when he commanded the defenses of that city. In addition, many grievances were shared by the officers of the Continental Army, among them low pay and lack of political support, which undoubtedly contributed to Arnold's traitorous behavior.

By 1780, Arnold had found a British officer, Major John André, to help him carry out his scheme: turn West Point over to the British, and profit personally in the bargain. But André was caught in civilian clothes with the plans of West Point's fortifications—in Arnold's handwriting—hidden in his stocking. André was hanged as a spy at Tappan, New York, but Arnold escaped on a British ship and lived out the rest of his life with his family in England. The British did not ultimately test the defenses of "America's strongest military post," Washington eventually marched south to victory at Yorktown in 1781, and the new United States found a temporary peace with its fractious trading partners in Europe.

No Support for an Academy

Historians, poets, and philosophers have recorded since time immemorial that the end of war quickly erodes support for all things military. For America, it meant the fading from memory of Washington's Continental Army, the trained and disciplined units that had ultimately been victorious. With so many other pressing matters to address, the people and their political representatives soon came to believe that the militia—the "Minute Men" who had won the battle of Bunker Hill so brilliantly in 1775—could be the guarantors of America's military defense. This opinion fit conveniently with the lingering fear that a standing army would become an elite force that supported exactly the sort of dictatorial regime Americans had risked their lives to escape. None of this bode well for the establishment of a military academy, so from 1785 until 1790, with New York City serving as the United States' capital and Washington elected its first president in 1789, there was faint support for any sort of regular army.

As commander of the Continental Army, General Washington had envisioned the creation of an academy to train the nation's military leaders in the art of war. As president, he continued to press for an academy, citing the risky and unsatisfactory alternative of depending on foreign professionals to provide the expertise for modern warfare. Critical among the technical skills needed were gunnery; aiming and adjusting artillery fire; and engineering, situating, and building fortifications. Nonetheless, reflecting the politics of the day, Thomas Jefferson, Washington's secretary of state, argued that the Constitution did not grant power to the government to provide for a national academy of any sort. Jefferson was also opposed to the creation of an elite class of military professionals commanding the power that a standing army could wield.

The Need for Education

World events would eventually bring changing attitudes. In addition to the threats posed by hostile foreign interests, education in America became a central concern for the country's future prosperity. While major institutions of higher learning had been educating a small portion of the populace for over a century, their curricula were focused on scholarship, philosophy, and religion. There were no universities for scientists, engineers, or builders. In recognition of the need to impart some technical skills to the country's small army, Congress in 1794 authorized the grade of cadet, and a military school was finally built at West Point. The army's tiny Corps of Artillerists and Engineers was moved there, and Colonel Henry Burbeck, chief of artillery, set up a school in rudimentary gunnery and engineering for cadets and junior officers.

Unfortunately, the school burned down in 1796, and the idea of a military academy languished. In 1799, one of Washington's last earthly acts was to write a letter to Alexander Hamilton, then commanding general of the army, seeking to endorse a previous correspondence from Hamilton to the secretary of war that laid out plans for establishing a military academy at West Point. President John Adams was a strong supporter of the navy, since he felt that plying the seas for trade was the lifeblood of the colonies and that using resources to support the nation's merchant and warships was sound policy, unhampered by sensitive domestic issues. But Adams harbored grave doubts about a standing army. Like many of the Founding Fathers, he perceived the threat such an army could pose to the hard-fought liberties they had created and protected; thus, the idea of a military academy did not move President Adams to action.

It remained—until Thomas Jefferson became president in 1801—for the coincidence of military threats against the nation's interests to point out the need for a standing army and a military academy to train their leaders. Congress was moved to draw up a bill creating a Corps of Engineers that "shall be stationed at West Point . . . and shall constitute a Military Academy." In that same year, the secretary of war directed that all cadets training to be artillerists should report to West Point. A school opened in the final days of 1801, and four officers and one civilian were assigned to West Point as instructors and administrators.

A Change of Heart for Jefferson

Although originally opposed to the idea of a military academy, Jefferson had undergone a change of heart as president, motivated in part by the possibility of putting the new academy in Virginia, where cadets could be drawn from families supportive of his own policies and politics. However, prevailing sentiment favored the more remote location at West Point, since any mischief that the professional army officer corps might foment could be more easily isolated and dealt with if kept away from the capital, which by then had moved to Washington.

President Jefferson finally signed the academy bill into law on March 16, 1802. Thus two Virginians, George Washington and Thomas Jefferson, became the founders of the United States Military Academy at West Point (Sylvanus Thayer, army officer and educator, is known as the "father" of West Point). Coincidentally, Washington and Jefferson had also established the first engineering school in America, the first institution of higher learning in America not founded by a religious order, and the oldest continuously occupied military post in the United States. And from the very beginning, it has been New York State that has hosted this great and unique institution.

Major General John E. Wool. Credit: Library of Congress.

21

Reclaiming a Reputation

Laurence M. Hauptman

High on a hill in Oakwood Cemetery in Troy, New York, stands a huge obelisk, visible for miles around. The structure marks the graves of one of the greatest American military officers of the nineteenth century, Major General John Ellis Wool, and his wife Sarah. But the monument was also erected to counter history: as a tribute to the leadership of this lifelong resident of the Hudson Valley in one of the Civil War's ugliest episodes, New York City's draft riots of 1863.

Born in Newburgh, New York, on February 29, 1784, John Ellis Wool had a long career that spanned three major wars and over a half century of vital military service to the nation. He first distinguished himself at the Battles of Queenston Heights and Plattsburgh during the War of 1812. Probably his greatest military achievement came during the Mexican War in 1846, when he trained, supplied, and commanded raw recruits, subsequently leading them out of San Antonio to join General Zachary Taylor's forces at the Battle of Buena Vista where they decisively defeated the Mexican Army.

A Knack for "Dirty Assignments"

Wool proved himself to be an honest, intelligent, and efficient officer, with keen military acumen and an ability to get things done. Because of these qualities, he was often given extremely difficult assignments. Despite his role in the inevitable controversies that followed, the numerous political debts owed him by the military brass over the years for taking such "dirty" assignments allowed him to advance in the military

This essay first appeared in winter 2003, volume 2, number 3.

hierarchy. For example, after the War of 1812, he served for twenty-five years as the inspector general of the United States Army. In order to ensure honest and efficient procurement of military supplies, however, he exposed frauds in contracts. In 1836, he was placed in command of the Cherokee Indian removal from the southeastern states, but he soon fell into disfavor with the governors of both Alabama and Georgia because he would not entirely accede to their insistence on forcing the Cherokees out as quickly and ruthlessly as possible. Although he was court-martialed for this, Wool was unanimously acquitted by a military court headed by General Winfield Scott.

In the 1850s, Wool served as head of the Department of the Pacific—another contentious post, and a true "hot seat." In the wake of the California Gold Rush, he had to contend with increasing frontier tensions that resulted in further wars with the Indians, their dispossession from tribal lands, and their placement in a defenseless state on newly created reservations.

Waning Fortune

By the start of the Civil War, Wool was ranked fourth in the Union Army and was second only to Winfield Scott in seniority. But his fortunes began to wane when, with the retirement of General Scott in 1861, he was bypassed for the top post in the Union Army and younger men were promoted ahead of him for other key positions. He also found himself contending with officers whom he considered military upstarts, such as General George B. McClellan, the commander of the Army of the Potomac. During the Peninsula Campaign of 1862, Wool was peeved at having to report to the young general, who he thought was too deliberate and possessed of an unrealistic view of the enemy.

In June 1862, Wool was assigned to head the Union Army's headquarters at Baltimore. His appointment quickly drew criticism. Detractors mocked him for being too old—he was seventy-eight at the time—and incompetent. But he turned out to be remarkably evenhanded in his command. With Lee preparing to invade Maryland, Wool sent additional troops and arms to Washington. Having no troops to spare, and suspicious that Lee would seize Harper's Ferry, Wool refused to send home the three-month enlistees who guarded the federal arsenal there, even placing his own troops under his rival McClellan's command before Harper's Ferry fell. A military commission subsequently blamed Wool for the loss of Harper's Ferry, despite McClellan's overall command of the debacle. Yet once again, Wool's steadfastness in the midst of controversy won out: the commission's conclusions were rejected by both General-in-Chief Henry Halleck and President Lincoln, and Wool was subsequently exonerated.

As the war progressed, Wool received commendations for his role in the capture of Norfolk in 1862 and for his command of Fort Monroe in Virginia during the Peninsula Campaign. He was ultimately placed in charge of the Department of the East in New York City from January through mid-July 1863. But it was this assignment that would finally prove to be his undoing.

Wool immediately took charge of operations in New York City, cooperating with the city's leading citizens to help mobilize the war effort. Operating under emergency status, and expecting a major role in the Union Army, Wool issued orders for arms without getting approval in advance from Washington—which brought a reprimand from Secretary of War Cameron for this unauthorized action. It would also indirectly bring unprecedented violence to New York's streets: the ensuing draft riots cost at least 119 lives, polarized the black and white population of the North's largest city, and remains to date the largest civil disturbance in American history.

Riots in the Streets

The violence was largely—but not completely—fueled by efforts to enforce federal conscription, and by the battlefield casualties of Irish immigrants. A loophole in the conscription process allowed drafted men to buy a waiver for $300; of course, poor men could not purchase such a waiver, and so a disproportionate number of them were drafted and subsequently killed. Many of these poor were Irish. Tensions in the city increased steadily through the first week of July 1863, aggravated in large part by criticism of the draft from New York governor Horatio Seymour and by a major longshoremen's strike that resulted in strong anti-black attitudes in the city, since African Americans were employed to take the place of the striking longshoremen. News of the heavy losses of Union troops at Gettysburg, including significant numbers of Irish Americans, precisely coincided with the scheduled drawing of New York's new draft lottery. Wool could not rely on Governor Seymour—who actually impeded Wool's efforts at every turn—to quell the increasing unrest, since Seymour was a leading critic of conscription. And despite Wool's frequent warnings to both Washington and Albany about the city's deteriorating situation and the lack of federal and state troops to serve as a home guard, he was ignored by both cities' officials.

Inevitably, an armed and enraged populace exploded. Riots erupted on July 13 and continued unabated for four days and nights. Despite the governor's irresponsibility and inaction, much of the blame for the riots was soon leveled at Major General Wool, who was portrayed as a bumbling old fool incapable of leadership. He was unceremoniously removed from his command on July 17. The embittered old officer went home to Troy, where he spent the last years of his life longing for new campaigns and military assignments, while his *bête noir*, Governor Seymour, aimed for the White House, nearly achieving it in 1868.

"Righting" History

Although history has recorded New York City's draft riots as a "civil war within a civil war," history has also been unfair to Wool. Because historians have largely depended on the opinions of his critics and have not fully explored the rich archive of Wool's own papers and writings from the months before the riots (April to July 1863), Wool's abilities as a military commander and logician have been judged primarily on the basis of his advanced age. Yet his many warnings about anti-Lincoln and -Union sympathies in the Empire State went largely unheeded, his descriptions of the unrest caused by the Conscription Act of March 1863 were ignored, and his predictions about the consequences of the lack of military forces to defend New York City sadly came true.

After his death in 1869, Wool's neighbors, the citizens of New York's Capital District, paid homage to this Trojan warrior who had spent his life serving his state and country. They raised enough money to erect the obelisk in Oakwood Cemetery—silent but eloquent testimony that has helped subsequent generations reclaim the reputation of one of New York's outstanding war heroes.

Postscript

Tucked away in the New York State Library is Major General John E. Wool's collection of correspondence, military order books, scrapbooks, broadsides, and memorabilia. This historically important collection contains one of the finest extant records of United States military affairs from the War of 1812 through the Civil War. These items shed light on several diverse and controversial subjects: military campaigns spanning over half of the eighteenth century, federal policies affecting the Cherokee Indians and their removal from the South, Indians and their removal from the Pacific Coast during the Gold Rush, the origins and evolution of the United States Army and its command structure, the Civil War draft riots in New York City in 1863, and the travails of an army wife, Sarah Wool, who had to adjust her marriage and family life to her husband's military duties and frequent absences.

Hall of Famer Hughie Jennings. Credit: National Baseball Hall of Fame Library, Cooperstown, New York.

22

The Ongoing Fable of Baseball

Mark McGuire

The National Baseball Hall of Fame and Museum in Cooperstown, New York, contains:

- 2.6 million library documents
- 30,000 "three-dimensional" artifacts, including 6,251 balls, 447 gloves, Babe Ruth's bowling ball, and Christy Mathewson's piano
- half a million photographs
- more than 15,000 files on every Major Leaguer who ever played
- 12,000 hours of recordings
- 135,000 baseball cards
- one pervasive, massive, enduring myth

For in this mecca of the sport, history and historical fancy coexist. Undoubtedly, the village that's synonymous with baseball's glory is the home of baseball.

It's just not baseball's hometown.

Many kids first learning about the game's lore hear that baseball was invented by Abner Doubleday in Cooperstown. But most historians—and even the Hall—acknowledge that the Doubleday tale is a myth concocted with the thinnest of evidence early in the twentieth century, a yarn promoted by a sporting goods magnate determined to prove that the game was a uniquely American invention.

This essay first appeared in spring 2003, volume 2, number 4.

And Doubleday was truly a unique American. A West Point graduate, he fought in the Mexican War in 1846–1848. He is credited with firing the first Union shot of the Civil War, at Fort Sumter, South Carolina. He was a brigadier general commanding volunteers in charge of defending Washington, D.C. In 1862, he was promoted to major general, later fought at Gettysburg, and served until his retirement in 1873. Thousands saw him lie in state after his death in 1893.

In short, this pious Ballston Spa, New York, native deserves to be exalted and remembered, since he did it all.

Except invent baseball.

Maybe if history had gotten it right the first time, Hoboken, New Jersey, would now be widely hailed as the birthplace of baseball. And if anyone deserves to be called the Father of Baseball, it's Alexander Cartwright, not Abner Doubleday.

But in all likelihood, no one person can take complete credit for evolving the sport from the primordial ooze of a dozen bat-and-ball games that were played at the time. The Hall's library director, Jim Gates, calls any endeavor to identify a single birthplace "quixotic."

So the Baseball Hall of Fame, which embraces both scholarship and legend, deftly balances competing interests. As the Hall's own 2001 yearbook states:

> Whatever may or may not be proved in the future concerning Baseball's true origin is in many respects irrelevant at this time. If baseball was not actually first played here in Cooperstown by Doubleday in 1839, it undoubtedly originated about that time in a similar rural atmosphere. The Hall of Fame is in Cooperstown to stay; and at the very least, the village is certainly an acceptable symbolic site for the game's origin.

But make no mistake: for all the romance surrounding the Cooperstown fable, the Hall is a repository of research. If you doubt it, consider this:

Cartwright is enshrined in the Baseball Hall of Fame.

Doubleday isn't.

Origins of the Game

People have probably been hitting round items with sticks since the Stone Age. The British played two well-known games based on the concept: cricket, the sport of men, and rounders, a children's game. In America, various derivations of these games arose, including town ball, trap ball, and barn ball, to name just a few.

A critical rung in the game's evolutionary ladder can be traced to New York City, where in the first half of 1842 men gathered to play a bat-and-ball game. They first played at Madison Avenue and 27th Street, and later at the foot of Murray Hill.

On September 23, 1845, Alexander Cartwright, a tall, twenty-five-year-old shipping clerk, corralled twenty-eight men to establish the Knickerbocker Base Ball Club of New York City, baseball's first organized club. The name came from a volunteer fire company to which Cartwright and several other players belonged.

Again from the Hall of Fame's own yearbook:

> ALEXANDER CARTWRIGHT Born April 17, 1820 at New York, N.Y. Died July 12, 1892 at Honolulu, HI. Elected to the Hall of Fame in 1938 . . . often referred to as "The Father of Modern Baseball." Though the appellation may be an overstatement . . . Cartwright likely played a key role in formalizing the first published rules of the game, including the concept of foul territory, the distance between bases, the three-out innings, and the elimination of retiring base runners by throwing batted baseballs at them.

Cartwright and the Knickerbockers' rules and concepts posited that the infield was a diamond instead of a square. First and third bases were forty-two paces apart. Foul lines were implemented. Pitchers threw underhand from forty-five feet, elbow and wrist straight. Batters got three missed swings. The balk was defined and outlawed. Runners could either be tagged or thrown out. Soaking (hitting a runner with a throw to retire him) was banned. A schedule of fines for ungentlemanly conduct was imposed.

Open space was hard to find in a city absorbing a flotilla of immigrants, so the Knickerbockers found a new home a ferry ride away at Hoboken's Elysian Fields, a grassy picnic area with a view of downtown. "People began to take an interest in the game, and sometimes we had as many as a hundred spectators watching," wrote Doc Adams, president of the Knickerbockers and a New Hampshire physician.

On June 19, 1846, Elysian Fields was the site of the first prearranged game, pitting the Knickerbockers against the New York Club (formerly identified by historians as the New York Nine). The latter team won, 23 to 1. Historians, using the scorebook as a guide, believe the Knickerbockers did not play their first string: Cartwright umpired and, in fact, levied a six-cent fine against a player for profanity.

But even these historically documented events leave doubt as to whether that Knickerbocker–New York game was really the first. As noted by novelist and baseball historian David Nemec in his book *Great Baseball Feats, Facts & Firsts*:

> [H]ow did the Knickerbockers, purportedly the first club ever to organize mainly for the purpose of playing baseball, manage to lose so egregiously?

> Who were the New York Nine? When and where did they assemble and start mastering the intricacies of the new sport? How sure are we that they didn't secretly play a slew of games to prepare for Cartwright's bunch and that those games were the first ones? Well, the unhappy truth is that we're not at all sure; nor, probably, will we ever be.

In 1849, Cartwright left for California in a quest for gold and riches, taking with him a bat, ball, and the Knickerbocker rule book. He was the Johnny Appleseed of the sport, playing it all along his transcontinental trek. "It's comical to see mountain men and Indians playing the new game," he wrote in his diary in Independence, Missouri.

Cartwright would not find his riches in California; instead, he became a wealthy merchant in Hawaii. He lived long enough to see his game become a national craze before the Civil War, then grow into the National Pastime.

All of which begs the question:

Where did Abner Doubleday come in?

Who Really Invented Baseball?

Henry Chadwick, an English-born newspaperman, was a convert from cricket to baseball. Possibly even more than Cartwright, he nurtured the game from the cradle, convincing the *New York Times* and other dailies to run game scores. He later became the first newspaper baseball editor (for the *New York Clipper*) and worked for more than forty years at the *Brooklyn Eagle*. In addition to writing baseball guides and yearbooks, Chadwick perfected baseball's shorthand, the box score.

In 1905, Albert Spalding was a fifty-five-year-old former pitcher, manager, club owner, and executive. For years he and Chadwick had waged a friendly feud over the game's beginnings. But when Chadwick wrote that the sport had evolved from the British games of cricket and rounders, Spalding had enough.

He (of Spalding Sporting Goods fame) was convinced that the game had been concocted by "some ingenious American lad" and appointed a commission to investigate that claim. The Mills Commission was named after Colonel A. G. Mills, a New Yorker and past president of the National League (1882–1884). Former ballplayers, a pair of U.S. senators, and the president of the Amateur Athletic Union (AAU) rounded out the panel.

In April 1905 came a letter from Abner Graves, a mining engineer from Denver and a "reputable gentleman," who told of his Cooperstown classmate Abner Doubleday designing and naming baseball by abandoning the rules of the old game of town ball. The story went that in 1839, kids from the Otsego Academy were playing Green's Select School in a game of town ball. One Otsego player—Doubleday—sat down and at that moment drew up the rules for a new game, to be called baseball, although first he and the others had to chase the cows out of Elihu Phinney's pasture to play it.

Spalding pleaded for Graves' letter to be given serious consideration. "It certainly appeals to an American's pride to have the great national game of baseball created and named by a major general in the United States Army," he said. (The Hall's Jim Gates has a personal unproven theory that Spalding did not want to antagonize the Irish—many of whom played baseball and bought his sporting goods—by claiming that their beloved game came from the British.) So on December 30, 1907, the commission declared: "The first scheme for playing baseball, according to the best evidence obtainable to date, was devised by Abner Doubleday at Cooperstown, New York, in 1839."

Some of the evidence available at the time (or later unearthed) would ultimately debunk the Doubleday genesis:

- Doubleday was at West Point during the entire summer of 1839, a time when cadets were not allowed off campus. There were plenty of Doubledays living in Cooperstown, including another Abner Doubleday.
- Graves was five years old at the time he was supposed to have witnessed the historic birth of the game.
- "Reputable gentleman" Graves was later declared criminally insane and died in a sanitarium after fatally shooting his wife.
- After his death in 1893, Doubleday left behind more than twenty journals. Not one mentioned baseball.

But twenty-seven years after the Mills Commission's ruling, there was a find in Fly Creek, New York, just outside Cooperstown. A trunk that had once belonged to Graves was found in an attic. Inside was a baseball—gnarled, undersized, misshapen—but a baseball nonetheless. Stuffed with cloth, with a crisscross-stitched cover, it was dubbed the "Doubleday Baseball." For Cooperstown advocates, it was the smoking gun.

The ball was purchased by a local philanthropist who promulgated the idea of displaying it and other baseball memorabilia in a museum that would also enshrine the game's greats. In 1936, the Hall's legendary "first class" was elected: Ty Cobb (the high vote-getter), Babe Ruth, Honus Wagner, Christy Mathewson, and Walter Johnson. The National Baseball Hall of Fame and Museum was officially dedicated on June 12, 1939.

More than sixty-three years later, Cooperstown's Main Street accommodates nearly four hundred thousand pilgrims a year. They come for the displays, the gift shops, the nostalgia scented with wisps of their youth. They come for the artifacts, including a brown gnarled ball in a glass case. They come to be players in the ongoing fable of baseball.

C. D. Walcott, 1850–1927. Credit: Smithsonian Institution Traveling Exhibition Service (SITES), Washington, DC.

23

Self-Taught American Scientist

Ed Landing

Charles Doolittle Walcott was one of the most distinguished scientists America has produced. Born in Utica, New York, in 1850, he was president of the National Academy of Science, director of the U.S. Geological Survey, and secretary of the Smithsonian Institution. Among scientists, he is best known for making one of the most significant discoveries in paleontology, the Burgess Shale fossils in British Columbia. This 505-million-year-old deposit in the Canadian Rockies contains the ancestors of virtually all modern animals, most unknown before their discovery by Walcott, who collected and described more than fifty thousand animal and plant fossils from the spectacular site. The Burgess' astonishing diversity of ancient life, and Walcott's genius in taxonomic description, have contributed greatly to our knowledge of early life on earth.

Walcott's long and busy life (1850–1927) mirrored several stages in the country's relationship to and participation in scientific discovery and understanding. He was a late-blooming autodidact, but he lived in a time when accomplishment, not academic credentials, could be the basis for professional success—truly the Horatio Alger of American science. His work bridged the transition from Victorian-era fascination with science as a way to explain the history and workings of the world, to the current popular view of science as a synonym for technology, health issues, and esoteric research.

Poor Relations

The Walcotts were a distinguished and wealthy family who owned textile mills on the Sauquoit Creek at New York Mills, west of Utica. Yet Charles' life had few of the

This essay first appeared in spring 2003, volume 2, number 4.

privileges commonly associated with a prominent family. His father died when Charles was two years old. Charles, his mother, sister, and two older brothers lived as poor relations of their relatives.

At times, they resided in Utica hotels, and Charles worked summers on the Rust family farm near Trenton Falls north of Utica. He collected butterflies, bird eggs, and minerals, and by age thirteen focused on geology and fossils. A mentor was Colonel E. Jewett, a local resident and geologist who had been the curator of the New York State Cabinet, the predecessor of the New York State Museum in Albany.

Self-Taught Scientist

Walcott's teenage years were characterized by poor health, gritty desperation, and hard work. There was no history of higher education in the Walcott family, and Charles ended his schooling by age eighteen. He spent eight years working in a hardware store in Utica and as a laborer on the Rust farm. One of the activities on the farm was fossil collecting from small quarries on the property; the exquisite trilobite fossils (extinct marine arthropods, many of which look like sow bugs) found there were sold to tourists who came to Trenton Falls.

Walcott worked ten hours a day; made daily entries to his diary; read Darwin, scientific reports from state geological surveys, and the Bible (he was a lifelong observant Presbyterian) at night; and corresponded with geology professors across North America. At age twenty-five, he authored two publications on trilobites. The first described new trilobites from Trenton Falls, and the second was an interesting biomechanical study of features on the trilobite exoskeleton (the hard external skeleton common to all arthropods) that allowed the animal to roll into a ball for protection. At the same time, he discovered the first evidence for trilobite legs and gills and began a study of how these marine animals moved and breathed.

The Albany Interlude

Walcott's entrance to professional science began in the personally devastating year of 1876, when his first wife, Laura Rust Walcott, died. Later in the year he was hired as an assistant to James Hall, the New York State Paleontologist, in Albany.

Albany was the center of American theoretical and applied geology because of the nearly fanatical work of James Hall (1811–1898), founder of the New York State Museum. Hall surrounded himself with talented assistants like Walcott, who had corresponded with Hall and conducted him to sites in the Utica area. Walcott owned a superlative fossil collection, which Hall had been trying since 1873 to convince the state legislature to buy (state purchase of natural history specimens was a common practice in those days). Hall would typically acquire important collections following a brief hiring of their owners, and Walcott was another such candidate.

As Hall's assistant, Walcott labeled specimens for exhibits and continued his own trilobite research. He traveled to Indiana, the Falls of the Ohio River, and southern Ontario to collect fossils for comparison with New York's. Today, these Walcott collections are some of the most frequently loaned and studied materials of the State Museum's Paleontology Collection.

In Albany, Walcott also learned political skills that later served him well in Washington: he served as Hall's lobbyist in helping move appropriations through the Ways and Means Committee. But he worked in Albany for just two years. He had the temerity to publish on trilobites from the Saratoga, New York, area without including Hall as a coauthor, and Hall did not renew his appointment at the end of 1878. Walcott thus joined an increasing number of Hall's ex-employees who had either lost jobs during state budget crises or had crossed their old mentor. Walcott was in dire financial straits and pressed hard for the state to purchase his Utica-area fossils. However, New York governor Robinson again vetoed the allocation of $4,000 for purchase of the collection, and this treasure of the state's heritage was immediately bought by Harvard University.

Unparalleled Prominence

Walcott's rise to unparalleled prominence in American science began with his 1879 hiring as the twentieth employee of the newly formed U.S. Geological Survey. He did early field mapping of the Grand Canyon region and the Eureka, Nevada, mining district, and then he served as the survey's director from 1893 to 1906. His service as secretary of the Smithsonian Institution, from 1906 to 1927, accompanied membership in almost every important scientific group, from the American Academy of Sciences to a committee on airplane design and procurement for the War Department.

Walcott discovered the Burgess Shale in 1909, late in his career. He spent five seasons in British Columbia, meticulously splitting slabs of rock to collect the specimens that would ultimately reveal the basic design and evolutionary relationships of many modern animals and would give their discoverer permanent status as one of America's most important paleontologists.

ATTENTION! ANTI-RENTERS!

AWAKE! AROUSE!

A Meeting of the friends of Equal Rights will be held on

in the Town of at O'clock.

Let the opponents of Patroonry rally in their strength. A great crisis is approaching. Now is the time to strike. The minions of Patroonry are at work. No time is to be lost. Awake! Arouse! and

Strike 'till the last armed foe expires,
Strike for your altars and your fires—
Strike for the green graves of your sires,
God and your happy homes!

☞ The Meeting will be addressed by PETER FINKLE and other Speakers.

Farmers are urged to rise up against wealthy, aristocratic landlords who keep them impoverished. Credit: From the collections of the New York State Library, Manuscripts and Special Collections, Albany, New York.

24

Rebellion in the Catskills

Dorothy Kubik

On a fateful day in August, 1845, the quiet farming communities in eastern Delaware County, New York, were caught in a vortex of circumstances and events larger than their own small world. For on that day the steady, reassuring, ritual cycle of plowing, planting, mowing, and harvesting took a back seat to Anti-Rent protest.

Tenant farmers were already rebelling in 1839 in the Helderberg Mountains of Albany County, against oppressive leases under which they labored as little more than serfs of wealthy landlords, without opportunity to ever own the land. They had also begun to question the legality of the landlords' titles to the land. The outbreak was triggered by the demand of landlord Stephen Van Rensselaer IV for back rents, which his father had not collected during economic hard times.

In protest, the farmers refused to pay the rents. When a sheriff's sale of a farmer's property, mainly livestock, was held to collect the rent, armed protesters appeared in calico dresses and grotesque masks, calling themselves "Indians" in the spirit of the patriots of the Boston Tea Party.

The conflict soon spread to Rensselaer, Columbia, and Schoharie Counties, then to Delaware County, especially the communities of Andes, Bovina, Middletown, and Roxbury, where the protest was most intense.

"Shoot the Horses!"

Activities of the Delaware County Anti-Renters infuriated Undersheriff Osman N. Steele, who had resolved to personally root them out. In turn, the Anti-Renters hated

This essay first appeared in fall 2003, volume 3, number 2.

him as an arrogant bully. Their fateful encounter occurred after he and the landlord's agent showed up at Moses Earle's pasture in Andes, as Steele and the so-called Indians were discussing the sale of Earle's livestock for rent. Ignoring the Indians' orders to keep out, Steele prepared to jump the pasture bars. Someone shouted, "Shoot the horses!" The Indians fired and Steele fell, mortally wounded. It was August 7, 1845.

The Indians fled. In the turmoil that followed, over two hundred men were arrested, under suspicion for Steele's murder.

The Anti-Renters Speak

A grand jury was subsequently convened. Afraid they would be hanged, most of the Anti-Renters who testified before this grand jury abandoned their oath of secrecy and fidelity to each other and, in their own words, revealed the inner workings of the Delaware County Anti-Rent Association. The association, they said, had been organized in the spring of 1844 at the Andes Presbyterian Church. It had a tightly knit network of officers, committeemen, and committees to coordinate activities, and it met often, either in small "town" groups or as a whole organization. Of meeting places, the association had no lack: churches, taverns, private homes, barns, even outdoors on a hill.

Not all Anti-Renters were Indians. Some sympathized with the protest but were not involved in any activities. Others joined the organization and sometimes served in leadership positions. The most active members—the Indians—wore disguises and appeared armed at sheriff's sales, "to intimidate foreign bidders & so they would not come." They were also prepared to shoot any animal on which a successful bid had been made.

The Indians belonged to tribes, as local groups were called, and were led by a "chief" and several subordinate chiefs. Sometimes they referred to themselves as "Natives" or "Rocky Mountain Boys." When they rode out in their masks and calico dresses, they also wore new identities: Black Hawk, Big Lion, Pompey, Thunderbolt, Red Wing, Jumbo. John S. Davis, a leader in Bovina, admitted, "It was said my name was Rainbow."

A special committee recruited new members. Barbour Stafford, a twenty-year-old farmhand, related how, in the summer of 1844 at Peleg Hilton's hotel in Andes,

> Robert Scott came to me . . . and wanted me to join . . . after I signed the pledge H. Scott asked me if I did not want to become a rockey mountain boy I asked him if there was any danger in it He told me no it was nothing but fun and almost every boy was joining it— . . . He then administered the oath to me by the uplifted hand by the ever living God.

The text of the oath varied in the accounts given by the Anti-Renters, but essentially the members swore to support the Anti-Rent cause and not reveal the secrets of the association. This reinforced their seriousness of purpose, bound them together with powerful ties, and secured their protection.

Codes and Disguises

Although the oath was probably their strongest defense, the Anti-Renters, especially the Indians, devised other safeguards as well. When discussing their activities, they used certain code expressions. For example, when questioned about his son's activities the day Steele was shot, Jotham W. Scudder, father of Warren Scudder, replied that his son had said he was "going fishing."

In order to avoid revealing themselves to an unfriendly person, the Anti-Renters also devised "countersigns," as they called them, by which they could identify their colleagues or supporters. William Scudder said, "We had a countersign, the word was 'liberty'—we also had a motion by which we recognized each other—we put our hands to our face."

When going out in disguise, they used great care to preserve secrecy even among themselves. Often they would meet at a certain agreed-upon place on the way to a gathering or sale, where each man would then go off by himself to dress. The Bovina Indians who met on McFarland's hill to plan for the trip to Earle's sale "came to the resolution not to see each other dress in disguise—They were to dress after they got there."

Funds for "Entertainment" and Weapons

Payment of dues of two cents an acre helped support the activities of the association. When the Anti-Rent movement began in 1839, this assessment was intended to help pay for litigation to challenge the landlords' titles. The Delaware County Anti-Renters also initially had the same intention for their funds. Whether or not they pursued this plan, they found plenty of immediate uses for the money. If the Indians shot a farmer's animals at a sale, the association would reimburse him for them. Zadoc Northrup, speaking of Earle's sale, said it was decided to "[l]et the sheriff sell and then shoot the property down."

References to the "entertainment" of the Indians occur often in the grand jury transcripts. One Anti-Renter stated that "when the Indians were called out, their refreshments were paid for out of the funds of the Society." Early in June 1844, James

Blish served dinner for 250 to 300 Indians who met at his house. He added: "The Association paid me."

Money seems to have been generously expended to supply the Indians with both disguises and weapons. Under orders from the committee, James Blish said he spent $30 to $40 for calico and $5 to $6 for sheepskin. For these purchases and a pair of pistols, he estimated that he spent $100. Daniel Squires also admitted to spending $25 for calico, which his wife and daughters turned into dresses for the Indians. Daniel Northrup added that, besides disguises and weapons, the Indians were "to be paid for services if there were funds enough in the treasury." Whether this was ever done is not known.

The Indians had a motley collection of weapons: fowling pieces, muskets, rifles, pistols, swords. At Earle's sale, Warren Scudder, chief of the Indians, had a sword and a pistol. According to one man's testimony, "It was a crooked sword, silver plaited I saw Scudder present his sword at Wright [agent for the landlord, who accompanied Steele] and Scudder then drew a pistol."

The Cause Gains Political Support

One icon of the rebellion was the Anti-Rent flag. Dr. Stephen Forman related that "at the day of the Sale there was an Anti rent flag raised on the pole." The flag must have been part of the spirit of many gatherings, too. Jotham Scudder said, "On the 4th of July I went to an Anti rent meeting in my own waggon with an Anti rent flag over us."

Nelson K. Dart, who admitted creating flags, testified,

> Wickham, Preston & Scudder came this spring with a piece of cloth to paint another flag—they wanted me to put a picture of the possee & the indians. I painted one side as they requested. I told them if they would permit me to put on the other what I was a mind to I would finish it and I put on "Victory by the ballot."

In the end, two men were sentenced to hang for the murder of Steele, though no proof was found to link them to the fatal shots. Four others were sentenced to life in Clinton State Prison, and the rest to terms from two to ten years. After an outcry from the public, however, Governor Silas Wright commuted the death sentences to life in prison. In 1847, Governor John Young pardoned the prisoners, and they returned home in triumph, though the wounds from the whole ordeal would remain with the communities involved for generations.

The real winner was the Anti-Rent cause. The Anti-Renters gained political support and power, achieving several victories at the State Constitutional Convention in 1846. In Delaware County, the Anti-Rent Party became the dominant political party. Though the old leases remained, the power of the landlords had been broken.

Sadly, other than the grand jury transcripts, which are still accessible to the public at the Delaware County Clerk's office, little else remains to tell the story of the Anti-Renters in Delaware County. In the confusion and fear following the death of Steele, many valuable sources probably went the way of treasurer James Blish's books. "Some of my family burnt them up," he said. "I knew they were going to burn them up. I did not object to it." The Anti-Renters' testimonies before the grand jury, however, as close as anyone could come to interviewing the Anti-Renters themselves, provide insight into who they were and how hard they struggled for the simple right to own their property.

"Kansas Charley" was about 5 feet 4 inches tall and 120 pounds, with blonde hair and blue eyes. His execution was the first for the new state of Wyoming. Credit: *New York Herald*, April 23, 1892.

25

The Boy Murderer

Rachel Dickinson

Joan Jacobs Brumberg, a social historian and professor at Cornell University, has always been fascinated with the history of childhood. Author of two books about girls (*Fasting Girls: The History of Anorexia Nervosa* and *The Body Project: An Intimate History of American Girls*), Brumberg knew she wanted to tackle a "boy" topic for her next book, but she needed an angle. She found it in a provocative question. "It was the day after the Jonesboro schoolyard shooting and one of my students asked if there were examples of boy killers in the past," says Brumberg. "That got me thinking, but outside of the Leopold and Loeb case [teenage boys convicted of murder in 1924 but not executed], I couldn't come up with any others."

For the next two years, she and her students built a data set of 125 boys who had committed homicide between 1865 and 1917. Combing major newspapers for names, crimes, and trials, Brumberg decided to focus on an adolescent killer who had wrestled with the classic issues of poverty, family breakup, and abuse, eliminating obvious psychopaths who were serial killers or sexual predators. She chose Charley Miller.

A Brief, Murderous Life

Charley Miller was born to German immigrant parents in New York City in 1874. Orphaned by age six, Charlie, along with his siblings, was raised in the New York Orphan Asylum. He was then "placed out" at age twelve and sent west on an orphan

This essay first appeared in winter 2004, volume 3, number 3.

train, the invention of Charles Loring Brace, founder of the Children's Aid Society in New York City. At age fourteen, Charley began tramping and riding the rails on his own, and a year later, while heading for Wyoming, he murdered two young men in a boxcar. The trial of "Kansas Charley"—the name he liked to be called, in imitation of popular dime novels and his hero, Jesse James—was sensational, covered in newspapers coast to coast. Charley was found guilty of the murders and hanged in April 1892, at the age of seventeen.

When Brumberg found the Miller case, she was intrigued: here was a juvenile murder that had been committed in Wyoming, a brand-new frontier state, and yet the trial had made national news. Brumberg knew that if she could put the pieces of Charley's life and trial together, she would have a story that would resonate with contemporary readers and might stimulate people to think about the continuing use of the juvenile death penalty in the United States.

"Being a historian is a bit like being a detective," says Brumberg. She lucked out with Charley Miller because of the availability of documentary evidence. Charley's "voice" survived because of the poetry and songs he wrote, and the fact that he liked to grant interviews to the press. These interviews provided Brumberg with descriptions of Charley; his crime; his cell and diet in the Cheyenne, Wyoming, jail; and key people in his life after the murders. A transcript of the trial also existed, and this, in combination with the newspaper accounts, gave Brumberg a way to reconstruct a sound chronology of the last two years of Charley's life, as well as his psychological development as he faced death on the gallows.

Reconstructing a Child

But what took legwork was reconstructing his first fifteen years. In New York, Brumberg had to struggle with the fact that Charley's documentary trail was very slim: "Although there are published annual reports of the New York Orphan Asylum, there are no surviving records of individual children, and there's no explanation of the disappearance of these records." As a result, she had to read the annual reports very carefully to get a sense of who the trustees were and what the asylum routine might have been like for Charley and his siblings in the 1880s: "The reports are a telling commentary of what the trustees thought about the future of the kids they had in custodial care."

In the still-preserved ledgers of the Children's Aid Society (CAS), Brumberg found reports on Charley and his brother and clippings about the murders. "Their individual histories were mapped out," she says, "including some affectionate commentary by the adoptive parents of the oldest Miller boy." The CAS records also identified what had happened to Carrie Miller, Charley's sister, leading Brumberg to Ilion, New York, and its local newspaper. In 1882, twelve-year-old Carrie had been selected from among the age-appropriate girls at the New York Orphan Asylum to become a domestic servant in the home of George Weaver, then editor of the *Ilion Citizen*. Weaver and his growing family had moved to Rochester in 1889, so Brumberg visited the Rochester Public Library and the University of Rochester's Rush Rhees Library in search of local materials, such as city directories, census records, maps, and photographs. Then, she says,

> I went from George Weaver the newspaper editor to George Weaver the inventor, who gets stolen away from the Ilion paper to become a publisher of law books in a successful Rochester firm. The connection becomes important because when I looked at the clemency files in the Wyoming State Archives, there was George Weaver, organizer of the most powerful legal appeal for clemency for Charley Miller.

Without the archival sleuthing that took her to four states, Joan Brumberg could not have unraveled the complexities of Kansas Charley's short but historically significant life. And through her book about him, *Kansas Charley: The Story of a 19th-Century Boy Murderer* (Viking 2003), Brumberg has been able to address the efficacy of the death penalty for juveniles—a complicated moral and legal issue that is as relevant today as it was in the nineteenth century.

Survivors comfort the dying two-year-old George Van Nest; a wounded Cornelius Van Arsdale sits nearby as the murderer peers into the room. Credit: The Farmers' Museum, Cooperstown, New York. Museum purchase, F0108.1954.

26

A Case of Trouble

Andrew W. Arpey

At around nine o'clock on a clear, moonlit night in March of 1846, John Van Nest heard a knock on the front door of his farmhouse in the central New York town of Fleming, west of Owasco Lake. When Van Nest opened the door, he recognized a young African American man who had come by several days earlier looking for work. The young man asked if he could step inside for a moment and get warm.

Van Nest let him in. It would be his last act. The man promptly pulled out a knife and stabbed Van Nest in the heart. He collapsed and died instantly. When his wife Sarah rushed into the room, the killer slashed her in the abdomen, mortally wounding her—an agony she endured just long enough to alert her sleeping daughter, Julia, and her own elderly mother, Phoebe Wyckoff, who lived with the family. However, Sarah was unable to save her two-year-old son George; the killer brutally stabbed the sleeping child, tearing open the entire left side of his abdomen and ripping the bedding beneath him. The killer then ran upstairs, where the Van Nests' hired helper, Cornelius Van Arsdale, had been roused by the commotion. The two began to scuffle and the killer stabbed Van Arsdale in the chest, gravely injuring one of his lungs. Nevertheless, Van Arsdale, with the fortitude and bravery borne of desperation, was able to drive the attacker from the house.

There would be one final victim. After being awakened by her daughter's screams, Phoebe Wyckoff tried to flee to a neighbor's house for help and ran through the Van Nests' front yard just as the killer exited the house. He and Wyckoff engaged in a violent struggle that left her terribly wounded, but she was able to stab her attacker in the hand, temporarily disabling him. In spite of her injuries, she reached the neighbor's house; meanwhile, the killer stole a horse from the Van Nests' barn and fled in the

This essay first appeared in spring 2004, volume 3, number 4.

direction of Auburn. Phoebe would die two days later from her wounds, but had it not been for the strength and courage of both her and Van Arsdale, the Van Nests' eldest son Peter, daughter Julia, and a young houseguest might also have been murdered.

The Killer Confesses

Based on the accounts of the survivors, authorities quickly established that the likely attacker was William Freeman, a twenty-one-year-old man of mixed African and Native American heritage. Freeman was pursued and apprehended the following day in Phoenix, Oswego County. He confessed to the violent attack and also divulged his intention to kill the entire family had he not been disabled in the scuffle with Phoebe Wyckoff. While Freeman was being transported to the Van Nest house to be identified by the survivors and then to the Cayuga County jail in Auburn, an angry mob attempted to overwhelm the escorting officers, seize Freeman, and lynch him.

William Freeman's motive for the brutal killings remained a matter of intense controversy for the rest of his short life—and beyond. Yet looking at the case now from the perspective of history reveals far more than his possible motive; it is a window into the world of mental illness, criminal punishment, law, religion, race, and politics in nineteenth-century America. William Freeman's was a classic "case of trouble"—a phrase used to describe deeply controversial legal cases in which long-accepted beliefs, practices, or institutions are challenged or threatened. "Cases of trouble" do more than just illustrate prevailing legal trends and practices. They also tell us why such practices have endured over time.

"Moral Insanity"

The Van Nest killings came just weeks after the conclusion of an intensely controversial murder trial in nearby Auburn. Henry Wyatt, a convict in Auburn State Prison, had stood trial for the murder of fellow inmate James Gordon. Former governor William Henry Seward, representing Wyatt, had entered a plea of not guilty, saying that Wyatt was insane when he killed Gordon. Seward had tried to persuade the jury to consider new theories regarding mental illness. These theories, known collectively as moral insanity, asserted that some individuals were intellectually able to understand that certain acts were crimes yet were unable to control their own impulses to commit such acts. Other individuals became so emotionally disturbed on a particular subject that they could no longer apply abstract notions of right and wrong to their own approach to that subject.

For most Americans in the mid-nineteenth century, the word "insanity" conjured up images of human beasts and incoherent, babbling idiots. Most American criminal courts followed Britain's lead and equated legal insanity with the inability to appreciate the wrongful nature of one's actions. In Wyatt's trial, Seward had drawn upon recent cases in Boston and New York City in which judges had invited juries to consider moral insanity as part of the definition of legal insanity. Judge Bowen Whiting likewise addressed moral insanity in his instructions to the Wyatt jury, although ultimately that jury had been unable to reach a verdict, resulting in a mistrial.

The Van Nest killings were immediately attributed to what many observers perceived as denial of justice in the Wyatt trial. Thus, the ongoing debate between proponents of the death penalty and reformers intensified. Supporters of the gallows blamed anti-gallows reformers for polluting the minds of potential jurors with "misguided philanthropic" notions regarding the inhumanity of capital punishment. They employed biblical defenses of such punishment and touted the death penalty as the only recourse that deterred violent crime and protected the populace. They attacked the new psychiatric theories that had been used to defend Wyatt, dubbing the insanity defense a "clever dodge" and a means by which cold-blooded killers would be spared instead of punished. William Freeman, they said, demonstrated the menace created by a justice system that gave killers every reason to believe they could commit murder without fear of the price of their own lives.

Reasons for Evil

When Freeman's behavior after his arrest cast doubt upon his mental well-being, however, local anti-gallows reformers asked Seward to represent him. Freeman had been convicted of grand larceny and imprisoned at age sixteen, and he now voiced confused notions about wrongful imprisonment and being owed "pay" for the five years he lost while in Auburn State Prison. Reformers, most notably *New York Daily Tribune* editor Horace Greeley, charged that the community's neglect of black children, combined with a racially biased criminal justice system and the harsh conditions at Auburn Prison, trained Freeman for a life of immorality and violence. Gallows supporters replied that evil was evil, regardless of race, and that excusing an entire race from responsibility for heinous acts would invite even more crime and place the community in great danger. Several newspaper commentators used Freeman's racial background to intensify his association with depravity and thereby emphasize the importance of swift and severe justice.

In the courtroom, Seward and his colleague David Wright once again attempted to give credibility to the theory of moral insanity and to convince the jury that William

Freeman exhibited its symptoms. New York State Lunatic Asylum superintendent Amariah Brigham, New York State Medical Society president John McCall, and numerous other experts in the developing field of psychiatry testified on Freeman's behalf. Seward contended that Freeman's sense of morality and self-control had been perverted due to lack of education and religious training. His conviction and incarceration, which in his mind were unjust, had left him dispirited, bitter, and determined to seek compensation for his suffering. Unable to satisfy this need in any other way or to control his emotions, he decided upon random killing and had chosen the Van Nests, who had done him no harm, simply because they resided in a convenient and familiar location. Freeman knew in the abstract sense that murder was wrong, Seward maintained, but felt that in his case it was justified.

The "Security of Law"

Prosecutors, led by New York State attorney general John Van Buren, son of the former president, attempted to dismantle the defense piece by piece. Although Freeman had only been indicted for the murder of John Van Nest, prosecutors signaled that Freeman would face indictments for the other murders if he was acquitted in this trial. They introduced possible motives, including the contention that Freeman had specifically targeted John Van Nest and his family based on the mistaken belief that Van Nest had been a witness against him in the grand larceny case. A constant undercurrent, however, was the "tried experience and security of law." Prosecutors repeatedly warned jurors of the dangers inherent in complicated new psychiatric theories that offered criminals greater means of escaping punishment, saying that the common practice of evaluating defendants based on their ability to distinguish right from wrong guaranteed that only the most severe cases of mental illness resulted in acquittal. Prosecutors also warned that acceptance of new psychiatric theories would make courts completely dependent on the diagnoses of medical experts. Experience had shown, they argued, that juries acted fairly and in the best interest of society when legal insanity was defined in terms they could easily apply.

In the end, William Freeman was convicted of the murder of John Van Nest and sentenced to death by hanging. Seward immediately filed an appeal and obtained a stay of execution until the New York State Supreme Court was able to hear the case. The court ultimately overturned Freeman's conviction on several technical issues and ordered a new trial. It also ruled, however, that knowledge of the wrongful nature of one's actions was the proper legal definition of sanity; no mention was made of the psychiatric theories that Seward had advocated during the trial.

Crime and Punishment

William Freeman was never retried. His health deteriorated rapidly after the court's decision, and he died of tuberculosis in August 1847. Henry Wyatt, on the other hand, was convicted of the murder of James Gordon and executed.

From "cases of trouble" like William Freeman's we can learn a great deal about nineteenth-century American values. Among the most cherished was the desire to feel safe in one's own home and community. Antebellum New Yorkers were also extremely resistant to change when it came to challenging established methods of determining guilt and punishing the guilty—values and attitudes not all that different from ours today.

Alexander Hamilton. Credit: New York State Archives, Albany, New York.

27

"Why, Soldiers, Why?"

Thomas Fleming

On July 11, 1804, Colonel Aaron Burr, vice president of the United States, and General Alexander Hamilton, former secretary of the treasury under President George Washington, journeyed to the west bank of the Hudson River in the vicinity of the village of Weehawken, New Jersey, to fight a duel. Colonel Burr's first shot struck General Hamilton just above the hip, tore through his liver, and lodged in his backbone. Hamilton died in agony some thirty hours later.

Why did these two men, among the four or five best-known politicians in America at the time, choose to settle their differences in this deadly way? The question has exercised historians, novelists, and playwrights for the past two hundred years.

A substantial number of novelists and playwrights have portrayed Burr as a sinister murderer who cold-bloodedly forced a reluctant Hamilton to fight. Others have seen Hamilton as a crafty dissembler who hoped to kill Burr by using a secret hair trigger on his pistol. Some psychohistorians have argued that the duel was a thinly disguised suicide for Hamilton, while others have explained the clash as an example of the popularity of the political duel in the first decade of American national politics. The most common explanation, stated in dozens of textbooks and histories, maintains that Hamilton vigorously opposed and criticized Burr when he ran for governor of New York in 1804. When Burr lost, he supposedly sought revenge by challenging Hamilton.

Refuting History

The claim that Hamilton plotted to kill Burr by using a secret hair trigger on his pistol is best refuted by the actual exchange between Hamilton and his second, Colonel

This essay first appeared in summer 2004, volume 4, number 1.

Nathaniel Pendleton, as the latter handed Hamilton his pistol. "Do you want the hair spring set?" Pendleton asked.

"Not this time," Hamilton said.

There was nothing secret about hair triggers. They were regularly advertised in New York newspapers as an attractive feature of some pistols. Few knowledgeable duelists used them, however, because there was a possibly fatal tradeoff in getting the first quick shot: no time to aim the gun.

Backers of the covert suicide theory point to the indubitable fact that Hamilton's political career as leader of the Federalist Party (forerunner of today's Republicans) was in ruins. Enemies in the Democratic-Republican Party led by Thomas Jefferson had forced him to publicly confess to an affair with a Philadelphia woman, Maria Reynolds. In 1802, Hamilton's oldest son, Philip, deepened his father's melancholy by dying in a political duel with one of the general's Jeffersonian foes—a tragedy that destroyed the sanity of Hamilton's oldest daughter, Angelica. But Hamilton had five other children who badly needed his fathering and care. Though he was discouraged by President Jefferson's popularity, he had by no means abandoned his hope of achieving power.

As for arguing that the spread of the political duel was a sort of psychological "disease" that lured these two gifted men to their appointment in Weehawken, this is true only as far as it goes—which is not very far. The political duel was the background, not the foreground, of the clash between General Hamilton and Colonel Burr.

The most common explanation—Hamilton's supposedly vigorous opposition to Burr in the race for New York's governorship—has a rather large hole in it. After giving one relatively bland speech, in which he urged the members of the New York Federalist Party not to support Burr, Hamilton never said another public word on the subject. The reason was simple: almost every Federalist in New York State dismissed Hamilton's advice as envy and backed Burr with money and votes. Hamilton had virtually nothing to do with Burr's defeat.

Ordeal by Slander

The man who destroyed the vice president's run for governor of the Empire State was President Thomas Jefferson. He and Burr had had a calamitous falling out after they won power in 1800. In the balloting at the Democratic-Republican congressional caucus that nominated Jefferson for another term early in 1804, Burr did not receive a single vote for vice president. Instead, Jefferson chose New York's aging governor, George Clinton, as his running mate—thus giving his tacit approval for one of the most vicious assaults on a major politician in the nation's history.

The director of this smear campaign was Governor Clinton's nephew, DeWitt Clinton, the mayor of New York City, and his conduit was the *American Citizen*, New York's Democratic-Republican newspaper. In print, Burr was called a sadist who had lashed militiamen for the fun of it during the American Revolution and a "cowardly bastard" for failing to challenge Hamilton after the *Citizen* published a critical letter Hamilton had written about him in 1801. Burr was also accused of embezzling his clients' estates (he was a lawyer), denounced as an atheist, and pilloried as a man who seduced innocent virgins and ruined the reputations of married women. Worst of all, according to the *Citizen*, he consorted with Negroes to get their vote.

Few researchers who have portrayed Burr as evil have read this ordeal by slander—or are aware that the vice president refused to respond in kind.

The terrific abuse, climaxed by a crushing defeat at the polls, left Burr a bitter, deeply depressed man. After a month of lonely brooding, he came across a letter in a newspaper that described some caustic remarks Hamilton had made about him at an Albany dinner party a few days after Hamilton's speech to the Federalists. This letter became the ostensible reason for Burr's challenge to Hamilton.

Old Soldiers

Beneath the surface was a far more potent reason. Colonel Burr knew that there was another route to power—military glory—and that General Hamilton was his chief competitor.

Few historians have noted how obsessively Hamilton clung to the title he won when George Washington appointed him commander of the American army in 1798 during the "quasi-war" with Revolutionary France. He was listed in the New York City directory as "General Hamilton." Burr was equally fond of his Revolutionary War title of colonel. One of his close friends said he had a lifelong "ardent love of military glory."

Reinforcing Burr's perception was the presence of Napoleon Bonaparte on the world scene, a soldier whose military prowess had restored order to France, another nation that had undergone a decade of revolutionary chaos. Napoleon's career was followed in obsessive detail by American newspapers. Both Hamilton and Burr publicly expressed their admiration for this "man of destiny," as his French followers liked to call him. And both men were privy to information that made them think a similar chaotic situation might develop in postrevolutionary America.

In 1803, President Jefferson had purchased the Louisiana Territory from Napoleon, which had doubled the size of the American continental domain. The Federalists of New England angrily denounced this acquisition as unconstitutional and unnecessary, claiming that the United States already had more open land than its population could utilize. More to the point, the Yankees found intolerable a future in which the South would be the dominant force in the emerging nation. Led by Senator Timothy Pickering of Massachusetts, who had been secretary of state under President John Adams, the New Englanders began discussing secession. Their spokesmen in Washington asked Vice President Burr what he thought of the idea. He gave them the distinct impression that if he were elected governor of New York, he was prepared to take the Empire State into the new confederacy.

Hamilton, too, was aware of this bubbling conspiracy. In his lone speech opposing the vice president's run for governor, the general dwelt at length on the danger of Burr winning control of this new nation.

The Threat of Secession

Even without New York, the possibility of New England's secession remained strong. Senator Pickering talked of negotiating a treaty with Great Britain that would unite New England and Canada in a new nation. This was the chief reason Burr challenged Hamilton to the duel: Hamilton was the one man who could compete with him for command of a New England army if civil war broke out. If Hamilton refused Burr's challenge, he would forfeit his claim as a military leader.

A second reason for the challenge was the way Napoleon was spending the $15 million that Jefferson had paid him for Louisiana. The "Man of Destiny" had gathered an army of two hundred thousand men and a huge flotilla of shallow draft gunboats to invade England and end its struggle for world supremacy by dictating peace in London's ruins. Many thought that if Napoleon succeeded, he would dismiss the Louisiana Purchase as a scrap of paper and find reasons to start a war with the United States to restore France's colonial empire in North America. In one of the last letters Hamilton wrote, he explained his acceptance of Burr's challenge as a wish "to be in the future useful . . . in these crises of our affairs which seem likely to happen." Previously, he had instructed the editor of the *New York Evening Post*, the newspaper he had helped found, to issue a statement that he would never again accept public office "unless called upon in the event of a foreign or a civil war."

Showdown

At a Fourth of July dinner attended by both Hamilton and Burr seven days before the duel, General Hamilton sprang up on the table and sang his favorite song, "Why, Soldiers, Why?":

Why, soldiers, why
Should we be melancholy, boys?
Why, soldiers, why
Whose business is to die!

Colonel Burr's reaction to this bravado was a saturnine glare.

The duel, then, was a calculated risk, as well as an expression of the long-running mix of envy and animosity between these two old soldiers. They were ready to gamble a few more bullets, betting on their previous record of survival. After all, only one in five duelists died. The smooth-bore pistols were very inaccurate, even at a duel's standard ten paces.

The antagonists confronted each other in glaring sunlight about 7 a.m. on July 11. The shelf of rock on which they fought has long since vanished, dynamited by railroad builders. Hamilton's second, Colonel Pendleton, won the toss and chose to position the general with his back to the steep cliff. Silhouetted against the sun and the shining river, Burr would be an excellent target.

Hamilton, still mourning his dead son, had told Pendleton and other friends that a revulsion against dueling had led him to decide to throw away his first "fire." But his remark to Pendleton that he would not set the hair trigger "this time" suggests that he planned to aim at Burr with his second shot.

Hamilton's decision to fire in the air, called a "delope" in dueling terminology, was not entirely altruistic. It would make Burr look like someone who Hamilton did not think was worth killing. It was a kind of insult, as well as a way of belittling the seriousness of Burr's claim of wounded reputation.

Burr's first shot struck Hamilton as he was raising his gun. The impact caused him to convulsively pull the trigger, sending his bullet into an overhanging tree limb.

When the physician who had been waiting at the water's edge reached the general's side, Hamilton gasped, "This is a mortal wound, Doctor."

Contingency Thinking

Is there a modern lesson to be learned from this tragic collision? Even the best-informed men, insiders such as General Hamilton and Colonel Burr, found it difficult to predict what would happen next in an era of turbulent politics. It explains why many contemporary historians have made contingency an important term in their thinking about history—another way of saying that politicians often make large decisions about the future illuminated chiefly by their hopes and fears.

Robert R. Livingston (1746–1813), oil on canvas by Gilbert Stuart CL.1974.56. Credit: Clermont State Historic Site, Clermont, New York/New York State Office of Parks, Recreation, and Historic Preservation, Albany, New York.

28

The Man Who Won the West

Travis M. Bowman

When President Thomas Jefferson took office in March 1800, he turned to some of his most qualified Republican friends to populate his new administration. Robert R. Livingston of New York was one. Jefferson offered Livingston the position of minister plenipotentiary (ambassador) to France, and in December the president wrote to him, "It is essential to assemble in the outset persons to compose our administration, whose talents, integrity, and revolutionary name and principles may inspire the nation . . . with unbounded confidence, and impose an awful silence on all the maligners of republicanism."

This was more than just flattery; Livingston possessed truly outstanding credentials. He had served with Jefferson on the select committee that had drafted the Declaration of Independence, although he was unable to sign the declaration because he was called away to serve on the committee that wrote New York State's constitution. Later, his 1777 election to the position of New York's chancellor, considered second in prominence only to the governor, made him the state's highest appellate judge and gave him the honor of swearing in George Washington as the nation's first president in 1789. But Livingston's experience was not limited to domestic matters. The Continental Congress elected him minister of foreign affairs in 1781, an office that subsequently became U.S. secretary of state. Even today, the State Department's website lists Robert Livingston as its first leader.

The President's Diplomat

Livingston also had social credentials few in America could match. Royal Governor Thomas Dongan had granted Livingston's great-grandfather the 167,000-acre Livingston

This essay first appeared in summer 2004, volume 4, number 1.

Manor in 1686, an immense piece of land that gave the family control of roughly one-third of modern-day Columbia County, New York. His grandfather and father had added another 750,000 acres through land speculation, political maneuvering, and astute marriages. Contemporary and modern writers have both admired and derided the Livingstons as American aristocrats, but none have denied their power and influence.

Thus, Jefferson's appointment of Livingston as ambassador to France was shrewd. The French nobility were infamous for their opulence and refinement, and as a member of the Hudson River landed gentry, Livingston probably felt he was their equal. The burning of their home, Clermont, in October 1777 had given the Livingstons a strong hatred of the British, and Robert became an avowed Francophile during the Revolution. However, Jefferson's Federalist political enemies had been aloof to France since the French Revolution, and the XYZ Affair during President John Adams' administration had increased resentment against America's biggest ally. In 1797–1798, French foreign minister Charles Maurice de Talleyrand had refused to negotiate with America over the French seizure of American ships until he was paid $250,000 and France got a $10 million loan. (The three agents Talleyrand dispatched with this demand were referred to as "X," "Y," and "Z.")

Reckoning with Napoleon

Livingston's appointment also coincided with a particularly tumultuous time in history—the rise of Napoleon Bonaparte. Territorial aggrandizement was at the heart of Napoleon's rule of France; even a coalition of the old European powers had not been able to defeat him. By virtue of geography, the United States had nothing to fear from France's expansionist policies, since America's western and southern borders had been bounded by the benign Spanish Empire since the end of the French and Indian War in 1763. In 1800, the western border of the United States was the Mississippi River, and most of the territory west of the river belonged to Spain—or so the United States thought.

Shortly before Livingston left for France, rumors began to circulate that France wanted her Louisiana Territory back from Spain. This was both confusing and alarming. Commerce on the Mississippi River was too important to the United States' economy to risk a potential aggressor on the North American mainland. And what claim did the French still have on Spain's territory?

It turned out that neither France nor Spain would admit to their secret Treaty of San Ildefonso of 1800, which gave Louisiana back to France. This treaty was kept hidden—especially from the British and Americans—because the French feared a possible British attack on New Orleans once the British learned that their old enemy owned Louisiana again after thirty-seven years of Spanish rule.

So Jefferson and Secretary of State James Madison gave Livingston his difficult mission: ascertain who was the true owner of at least the city of New Orleans, and then close a deal that would allow America to purchase the city. This would be a tricky diplomatic task, since it would force both France and Spain to disclose the actual owner of Louisiana.

Cloak and Dagger Intrigue

Two days after arriving in Paris in 1801, Ambassador Livingston met France's minister of foreign affairs—the same Charles Maurice de Talleyrand of the XYZ scandal. For seventeen months, even though Livingston and the U.S. administration suspected it, Talleyrand would not reveal that France actually owned Louisiana; it would take Charles Pinckney, the U.S. ambassador to Spain, to finally make public that Spain no longer owned it. This revelation gave Livingston both the information and the impetus he needed to write a lengthy tract entitled "Is It Advantageous for France to Possess Louisiana?," which suggested that America should buy *all* of Louisiana, not just New Orleans. Yet France would still not admit to Louisiana's ownership.

Livingston personally handed out twenty copies of his treatise to Napoleon's advisors, including the latter's brother Joseph. But when his arguments failed to win support, Livingston concluded that only Napoleon himself could decide to sell Louisiana and protested to Secretary of State Madison, "Never was there a government in which less could be done by negotiation than here—There is no people, no legislature, no councillors [*sic*]—one man is everything."

Livingston Seizes the Day

Fortunately, the occurrence of two political events gave Napoleon a compelling motive to stray from his grand plans of conquest and to sell Louisiana. A twelve-year slave rebellion in Santo Domingo (Haiti) that had begun in 1791 subsequently overthrew French rule on the island, costing Napoleon a base of operations from which to establish a French colonial empire in America and in effect rendering Louisiana valueless to him. Then a diplomatic blunder by the Spanish intendant Juan Morales at New Orleans inflamed the Americans. To keep up the pretense that Spain still "controlled" Louisiana,

Morales closed the port of New Orleans to American shipping, causing the western states of Kentucky, Tennessee, Virginia, and Ohio to call for a militia to take New Orleans by force.

President Jefferson used the states' indignation to his political advantage. First he appointed James Monroe, a favorite son of western Virginia, as a "special" ambassador to France in order to placate the westerners. Then he requested appropriate funds from Congress for the purchase of New Orleans, knowing Napoleon would be more receptive to an offer in light of losing Haiti.

Meanwhile, Livingston had not been idle but had intensified his efforts to convince the French to sell all of Louisiana. According to Barbé-Marbois, French minister of the treasury, Napoleon finally acquiesced on April 11, 1803, saying, "I renounce Louisiana. It is not only New Orleans that I cede; it is the whole colony without reserve. I direct you to negotiate this affair. Do not even wait for the arrival of Mr. Monroe; have an interview this very day with Mr. Livingston."

Glory Won and Lost

Monroe arrived in Paris that "very day" and the three men commenced negotiations, taking less than three weeks to write the agreement. The treaty that sold Louisiana to the United States was signed on May 2, 1803, backdated to April 30, when the three had agreed on a price. News of the purchase spread quickly and was hailed as a stunning success, especially for Livingston, whose friends and political allies assured him he would be given the vice presidential nomination in the upcoming 1804 election. But what should have been the crowning achievement of his political career instead turned into a political nightmare.

Three weeks was simply not enough time to negotiate such a crucial purchase. Famous Americans like General Horatio Gates rejoiced that the United States had "bought Louisiana for a song"—512 million acres at three cents each—but ordinary Americans were upset with the second component of the treaty: that America would assume French debts owed to American merchants whose ships had been attacked after the XYZ Affair. Livingston woefully underestimated the amount of damages claimed by the merchants, and naïvely allowed corrupt French officials to disperse the funds to claimants. Monroe claimed that he had been sick during that portion of the negotiations, leaving Livingston to bear the full brunt of public anger over the resulting scandal.

Praise for the treaty soon disappeared, and Livingston feared he would lose all the glory from the deal. To shore up his reputation, he privately remarked to friends that Napoleon had offered to sell Louisiana days *before* Monroe had arrived.

Secretary of State James Madison quickly rallied to Monroe's defense and leaked to the press Livingston's official correspondence showing the actual date of the offer, further discrediting Livingston in the public's eyes. With this loss of party support, his political star burned out.

Elusive Fame

Livingston made one more grasp at fame before he retired from public life. While still in France, he met and formed a partnership with Robert Fulton, and in 1807 the two men invented the first practical working steamboat (known to history as the *Clermont* or *North River Steamboat*), ushering in the "transportation revolution" in America.

A noted nineteenth-century historian, Henry Adams, wrote that "Robert R. Livingston invented the steamboat, and gave immortality to Fulton." Adams' words can also apply to Livingston's inability to achieve the fame he pursued all his life. Livingston managed to secure the greatest real estate deal in history—and three of the four Americans involved in the Louisiana Purchase used its glory to become president. Livingston never achieved that kind of long-lasting veneration. He left politics for his estate at Clermont—the forgotten diplomat who had won the West.

Elizabeth Cady Stanton (seated) and Susan B. Anthony. Credit: Library of Congress.

29

"Failure Is Impossible"

Kimberly Troisi-Paton

Did the Civil War help the United States move toward racial equality but hinder progress toward gender equality? New York's two most famous women's rights suffragists, Elizabeth Cady Stanton and Susan B. Anthony, thought the answer to that question was yes.

Prior to the Civil War, suffragists had struggled for over a decade to secure the right to vote for women. Following the Seneca Falls Woman's Rights Convention of 1848, annual conventions were held to direct the focus of the suffrage effort. However, when Confederate forces fired shots on Fort Sumter in April 1861, the suffragists set aside their own political agenda to support the Union's war efforts.

Lincoln's Emancipation Proclamation of January 1863 officially made abolition one of the goals of the Civil War. In response, suffragists, particularly Stanton and Anthony, mobilized to create the Woman's National Loyal League to help the abolitionist cause, which first met in New York City on May 14, 1863. Its primary goal was to obtain one million signatures in support of a Thirteenth Amendment that would outlaw slavery. At the meeting, the participants also debated "Resolution 5," which included a concern for women's rights in the League's platform.

Rancorous Debate

Transcripts of the debate proceedings reveal that some participants at the convention believed the slavery issue was a far more important matter to address and would only be clouded by involving women's rights issues. One speaker went so far as to say, "It

This essay first appeared in fall 2004, volume 4, number 2.

may possibly be woman's place to suffer. At any rate, let her suffer, if, by that means, mankind may suffer less." Other women indicated that although outlawing slavery was a worthy cause, women should also be pursuing their own interests: "[Resolution 5] simply states a fact, that in a republic based upon freedom, woman, as well as the negro, should be recognized as an equal with the whole human race."

In response to the heated debate between the women, a man in the audience indicated that the very existence of the Woman's Loyal League was an endorsement of women's rights. Several female participants shouted him down by declaring, "I believe this is a woman's meeting. Men have no right to speak here. . . . You are not a woman, sit down." Yet Susan B. Anthony urged the crowd to let him speak:

> Some of us who sit upon this platform have many a time been clamored down, and told that we had no right to speak, and that we were out of our place in public meetings; far be it from us, when women assemble, and a man has a thought in his soul, burning for utterance, to retaliate upon him.

The record of the meeting reflects, however, that although men were granted the privilege of speaking, when the vote was taken to decide whether or not to adopt the controversial resolution, men were not permitted to vote.

In the end, Resolution 5 passed. It read, in part, "There never can be a true peace in this Republic until the civil and political rights of all citizens of African descent and all women are practically established"—language that effectively revived the suffrage movement.

Success at Least for Slaves' Rights . . .

The league promptly commenced its abolition efforts, and hundreds of thousands of petitions urging adoption of a Thirteenth Amendment were, in Elizabeth Cady Stanton's words, "scattered like snowflakes from Maine to Texas." By 1864, after the Loyal League had collected four hundred thousand signatures on these petitions, it disbanded. The Thirteenth Amendment was ratified in 1865, and the league was largely credited with its success.

In 1868, the Fourteenth Amendment was ratified, granting citizenship to all former slaves and protecting the rights of all citizens. However, "citizens," particularly "voters," were carefully described in the amendment as "male." Soon thereafter, former slaves' right to vote became a specific issue before Congress in the form of the proposed Fifteenth Amendment. That amendment provided that the right to vote would not be denied to any United States citizen "on account of race, color, or previous condition of servitude." The suffragists parted ways on whether to support this last of the Civil War–related constitutional amendments, since it addressed voting rights but did not address or acknowledge gender equality.

Deeply wounded by what she considered a lack of appreciation for the suffragists' willingness to abandon their own political struggle in order to support the war effort and the antislavery agenda, Elizabeth Cady Stanton wrote,

> During the six years [the suffragists] held their own claim in abeyance to those of the slaves of the South, and labored to inspire the people with enthusiasm . . . they were highly esteemed as "wise, loyal, and clear-sighted." But when the slaves were emancipated, and these women asked that they should be recognized in the reconstruction as citizens of the Republic, equal before the law, all these transcendent virtues vanished like dew before the morning sun.

. . . but Women's Suffrage Is Elusive

The women's suffrage movement was never the same after the leaders' bitter disparity over the Fifteenth Amendment, which was ratified in 1870. Stanton and Anthony had refused to support the amendment, while many other prominent suffragists had worked to ensure its passage. Eventually, the two women formed the National Woman Suffrage Association to fight for a Sixteenth Amendment that would guarantee women the right to vote. Unlike their efforts in support of the Thirteenth Amendment, however, Stanton and Anthony's campaign for "equal rights" was unsuccessful.

Despite their disappointment, the Civil War–era efforts of New York's longtime suffragists were not in vain. Not only were the slaves freed, granted citizenship, and accorded equal voting rights, but eventually, in 1920, the Nineteenth Amendment (named the "Susan B. Anthony Amendment") assured equal voting rights to all citizens, regardless of sex. In her last public speech in 1906, Anthony proclaimed, "Failure is impossible." She was right.

Hetty Green. Credit: Library of Congress.

30

The World's Greatest Miser

Charles Slack

Some historical figures are so immediately compelling that you never have to ask twice why they capture people's hearts and minds. But Hetty Green takes a little warming up to.

Hetty (1834–1916) built a fortune conservatively estimated at $100 million (close to $2 billion today), and she did so at a time when women were all but absent from Wall Street and didn't even have the right to vote. Her fame during her own time was such that her death after a stroke in 1916 at age eighty-one commanded front-page attention in virtually every major newspaper in the country. But she has since lapsed into relative obscurity, in part because she left no public monuments to herself, and because both of her children married late and left no heirs to perpetuate (or, as in the case of some Gilded Age millionaires, rehabilitate) the family name. Upon the death of her second child, Sylvia, in 1951, Hetty's great fortune was scattered to the wind.

The "Witch of Wall Street"

The public image of Hetty that survives is neatly encompassed in an entry that ran for years in the *Guinness Book of World Records* under the heading "World's Greatest Miser." It contained some of the more enduring stories about her, the most famous being that she stood by while her son's leg was amputated because she had been too stingy to pay for medical care. To this day, every city or town in which she lived or worked retains its own cottage industry of Hetty stories.

This essay first appeared in fall 2005, volume 5, number 2.

In Bellows Falls, Vermont (her husband's hometown), we see Hetty, already worth millions, haggling over the price of day-old bread and spending the evening frantically searching for a two-cent postage stamp. In Hoboken, New Jersey, where she lived in modest, rented flats, we find her squabbling over a $2 license for her dog, with whom she shared a third-floor flat. In Manhattan, she haunts the streets in old black garments, earning the moniker the "Witch of Wall Street."

But a string of miser stories, however colorful, hardly makes for an entire book. I decided early on that I wouldn't pursue her story unless I found her to be a character as notable for her accomplishments as for her oddities.

A Fearless Financial Genius

Happily, a closer look at Hetty Green reveals a woman, for all of her undeniable flaws, not just of wealth but of substance and courage. She possessed a quick wit and was, in her younger years, strikingly pretty. Above all, she was fearless. She never backed down from an adversary, no matter how powerful or intimidating he or she might be. Among her many memorable quotes is this one: "I always try to deal justly with everybody, but if anyone wants to fight me I'll give him all the fight he wants."

She was unquestionably a financial genius, if the term can be used to define financial prowess. Largely through her own shrewdness, tenacity, and cunning, she built one of Wall Street's great fortunes, investing mainly in government bonds, mines, railroads, and other blue chip stocks and becoming a prodigious lender of money. She bought mortgages and through foreclosures became a major property owner in many cities. In their 1996 book *The Wealthy 100*, Michael Klepper and Robert Gunther ranked one hundred rich Americans by the percentage of the American gross national product their fortunes represented at the time of their deaths. Hetty, the only woman on the list, placed thirty-sixth, three places ahead of modern-day billionaire investor Warren Buffett.

She was born Hetty Howland Robinson in Quaker-dominated New Bedford, Massachusetts, into the most successful whaling family in the whaling capital of America. Her father, Edward "Black Hawk" Robinson, was an outsider, a stern, cold, calculating man who had married into the Howland family and proceeded to assume control of the business. While most daughters of privilege stayed amid the large homes on the hill, Hetty's favorite place was down by the docks, padding along at the heels of her father when he would permit it.

Hetty read the financial papers to her father and maternal grandfather, soaked up the language of trade and finance, and by her own reckoning knew more about finance at age fifteen than most men actively engaged in the profession. After the death of an infant brother, Hetty, an only child, made it her mission in life to protect and increase the family fortune. Her life in some ways can be seen as a quest to prove to her forbidding father that she could handle money as well as, if not better than, any man.

A Most Unconventional Billionaire

In 1867 she married Edward Green, a financier and trader. They lived in England for several years, then returned with their two young children, Ned and Sylvia, to Bellows Falls, Vermont, Edward's hometown. To the extent that anything about Hetty's life could be called conventional, she lived a fairly standard life in Bellows Falls for a number of years, spending much of her time in Vermont while Edward traveled to New York to look after his financial affairs.

She burst onto the national scene in 1885 with the collapse of John J. Cisco & Son, the bank where she kept her millions. Edward had made bad investments with the Cisco partners. When it came to light that Edward owed some $700,000, the bank's assignee, Lewis May, demanded that Hetty make good on her husband's debts. After great protest and wrangling, she did indeed pay the $700,000. But to her, Edward had committed the ultimate betrayal; from then on, she would handle everything herself, in her own way. Although she and Edward were never divorced, she left him, and they lived together only sporadically for the rest of their lives.

She left Bellows Falls for New York. Although she owned swaths of real estate in Manhattan, including mortgages on Fifth Avenue mansions, for her own accommodations Hetty preferred the more modest confines of rooming houses and apartments in Brooklyn and Hoboken, all the better to avoid the expense of the city and nosy tax collectors. It was during these years that she became one of the most visible women in America, as well as one of its most celebrated characters. She bought and sold railroads, bailed out the City of New York when it couldn't pay city workers, and acquired large chunks of property in Chicago and other large cities. When she established interest rates for her loans, they were reported as news in the financial pages.

As for that famous story about son Ned's leg being amputated, like most urban legends this one contains a kernel of truth wrapped in layers of myth. Ned had injured his leg in a sledding accident when he was a boy. The condition worsened over time as he grew into a large young man. By the time he was nineteen, his leg had deteriorated to the point that doctors were forced to remove it at the knee. He wore a prosthetic leg for the rest of his life.

True, Hetty's conduct with regard to Ned's leg was at times shockingly unattractive. She hated and mistrusted doctors almost as much as lawyers and was known to appear, dressed in old clothes, with her son at free clinics, in order to avoid charges for medical care. But she did not ignore Ned's injury nor take it lightly. Over the years she often sought care for him and tried any number of home remedies. Ned was in many ways the great love of her life, and it is unimaginable that she would have stood stubbornly by as he lost his leg.

The Heirs Let It Go

When Hetty died in 1916, she left her great fortune in equal parts to Ned and Sylvia, neither of whom subscribed to Hetty's penchant for modest living. Ned, by far the more flamboyant of the two, built great mansions, bought a yacht, and satisfied his large, if unfocused, scientific curiosity by building, on his Massachusetts estate, a technologically advanced radio station, a fully equipped airport, and a laboratory for a scientist from the Massachusetts Institute of Technology.

When Ned died childless in 1936, he left his half of the fortune to his sister. Sylvia, also childless, lived in quiet luxury, dividing her time between Fifth Avenue and a large home in Greenwich, Connecticut, until her death in 1951. Sylvia's will dispersed her half of the fortune, as well as Ned's part, to myriad public institutions and private individuals. And so Hetty's greatest fear—that the fortune would find its way into the hands of strangers—was realized. Within a few years, about all that was left of Hetty Green was the legend. And yet for all of her personal oddities and shortcomings, a new generation may recognize that she was also, in her own way, a pioneer and an American original.

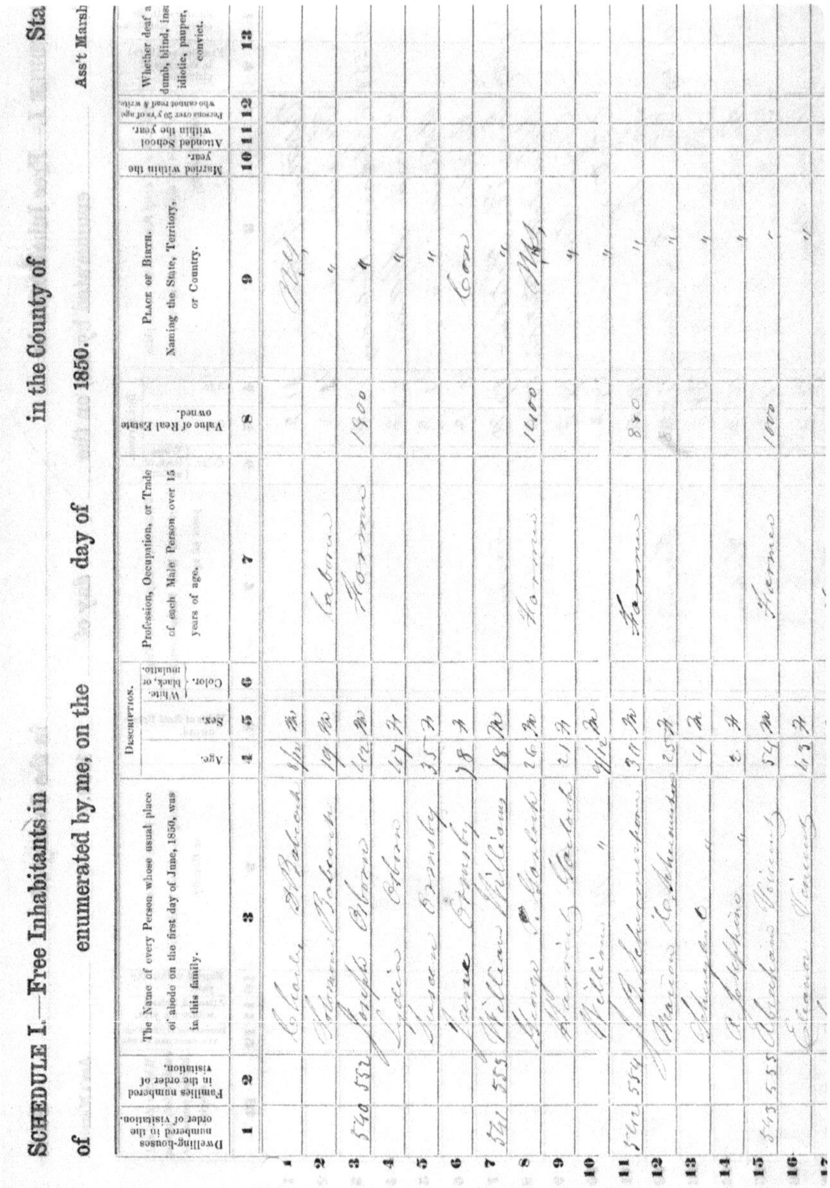
SCHEDULE I.—Free Inhabitants in in the County of State

of enumerated by me, on the day of 1850. Ass't Marsh

State census records and old maps provide evidence of Jefferson County women's ages, their husbands, and where they lived, but little else. Credit: Jefferson County Historical Society, Watertown, New York.

31

The Untidy Origins of Women's Rights

Lori D. Ginzberg

The traditional story of the nineteenth-century movement for women's rights is simple and dramatic. In July of 1848 a women's rights convention in Seneca Falls, New York, presented the first public demand for suffrage. It was the personal revelations of several extraordinary women—Lucretia Mott, her sister Martha Coffin Wright, and Elizabeth Cady Stanton—that inspired the subsequent movement for political and legal rights for women, as well as the right to education, fair employment, and self-respect. It is a triumphant, as well as a triumphalist, narrative; until Seneca Falls, the story implies, women's rights were out of the question. It was true that women had been involved in temperance, charity, moral reform, and antislavery work that drew them into political life, where they appealed for funds, lobbied politicians, and submitted thousands of petitions to legislatures. But women did not demand full equality or the right to vote. Indeed, antebellum politicians, ministers, and writers declared with great conviction that the notion of women's rights was unthinkable, and that any woman who might suggest it was unrespectable and unwomanly.

"A Self-Evident Truth"

But two years before Seneca Falls, six women did protest their legal inequality—and did it publicly. On an August Saturday in 1846, Alpheus S. Greene, a Democrat from Watertown, presented a petition to the New York State Constitutional Convention from "six ladies in Jefferson county." The petition asserted "[t]hat the present government of this state has widely departed from the true democratic principles upon which all just

This essay first appeared in fall 2005, volume 5, number 2

governments must be based by denying the female portion of community the right of suffrage and any participation in forming the government and laws under which they live." The women—Eleanor (O'Connor) Vincent, Susan Ormsby, Amy (Eldridge) Ormsby, Anna (Carter) Bishop, Lydia A. Williams, and Lydia (Ormsby) Osborn—went on to demand "equal, and civil and political rights with men."

The petition is stunning. It is not the deferential and tentative plea that we associate with the disenfranchised, nor did these women adopt the stance of supplicants, quasi-citizens—or, for that matter—"ladies." They did not fortify their plea with the rhetorical arsenal of motherhood, as those familiar with the language of antebellum activism might expect. And they did not use the honorifics "Mrs." or "Miss," as was customary for non-Quakers. On the contrary, they simply confronted their exclusion as full citizens and demanded their "rights, which they as citizens of the state of New York may reasonably and rightfully claim." They closed by noting (perhaps with a touch of impatience) that the points in favor of their demands were "numerous and decisive," but that they were confident "a self evident truth is sufficiently plain without argument."

Radical words indeed in 1846: unpopular at best, outside the boundaries of public discourse at worst. And yet the women considered themselves well within the mainstream traditions of American political thought: that people who were "amenable" to the "government and laws under which they live[d]" were entitled to be included in making them. There is no sense in the petition itself that the Jefferson County women worried much about provoking outrage or derision. Rather, they asserted that they sought "no new right but only . . . those which they originally inherited, but which have ungenerously been withheld from them." Their words force us to rethink our historical assumptions about what ideas were possible and which were "unthinkable," how radical ideas became commonplace, and why a few women believed that, politicians and pundits aside, they had a right to speak out as full members of the nation.

From the Evidence, Ordinary Women

Both the petition and its creators present numerous mysteries, many of which remain unsolved. The fact that the petition was printed in the Constitutional Convention debates at all was unusual, since virtually every other petition was simply noted as having been presented to the convention, with no mention made of the numbers who signed or the specifics of their demands. But *published* is not, of course, the same as *publicized*, and the petition's signers have remained elusive.

The evidence that has survived about these six women and their families is slim. Ordinary, middle-aged farm wives for the most part, they were linked by family, friendship, and conviction. Census records offer little personal data before 1850, but they indicate that most of the women lived on adjoining or nearby farms in the village of Depauville in the town of Clayton, Jefferson County, on remote land near the St. Lawrence River. Settled sparsely and late, the county itself is barely mentioned in old accounts of New York's population and mobility, lists of churches, records of roads, or surveys of agricultural production. Thus much of what I could uncover about the women underscored their *absence* from historical records.

Their families were not the town's leading families, nor were they well connected politically. Neither the women's fathers nor husbands appear in the entries of local biographies that counted men as "notable"; at least some of them were squatters before they gained legal title to their land. None of the women attended the Seneca Falls convention in 1848, and not one of them is mentioned in the seminal book *History of Woman Suffrage*. But if we know little about them as individuals, we do know that it was as a group that these women made sense historically, for it was as members of a community that they settled new farms, raised their families, nurtured their ideas, participated in the antislavery Liberty Party, and expressed their political identities.

A Political Sisterhood

However, buried in maps, records of renamings of towns, deeds, and wills is evidence that more than proximity bound the petitioners together. For example, Susan Ormsby and Lydia Osborn were sisters, Amy Ormsby was their brother Hiram's wife, and details from the few surviving wills suggest that they sustained close relationships with each other's children. A significant number of the women's families, as well as others among their neighbors, had migrated to Depauville from Russia township in Herkimer County between 1817 and 1820. The numbers and timing suggest that the families had known each other for some time and had undertaken this new move together.

The women's fathers, husbands, and brothers were as closely connected as the women were to their farms, their families, and each other. Deeds show that they bought land from one another, cutting and pasting, as it were, to compose a coherent and profitable farm. Their names appear as witnesses on each other's legal transactions, and they traveled together to Watertown to swear out purchases, wills, or claims. As in other rural communities, they likely provided one another with mortgages and short-term loans. The women were clearly involved in these transactions. For example, in the list of debts that Lydia Williams paid from her husband Nahum's estate, the single largest amount was to S. Ormsby; interestingly, Nahum also owed money to Lydia herself. Although they were "pioneers" in the sense of having settled in Depauville in its early decades, they were not isolated. Having migrated and grown old together, they helped with the final work of settling each other's estates after a death. At a time when cheaper western land was a constant temptation, most of them remained very much rooted in the community they had helped establish.

At least some of these families also shared a commitment to antislavery politics, which historians have long associated with the rise of women's rights. Again, Jefferson County records offer little evidence of the fairs, societies, pamphlets, and speakers that signaled abolitionist organizing elsewhere. Clues to these families' political allegiances—a Liberty Party activist who was named executor of Bailey Ormsby's estate; Joseph Osborn, Lydia's husband, singing "liberty songs" at an antislavery gathering that drew some two thousand people to Perch River; a single letter by Joseph Osborn that chided Liberty Party leaders for neglecting to include "the enfranchisement of females" among the party's goals—emerge mostly by chance, although they point to the women's connection to a political community characterized by conviction and purpose. In striking contrast to the town of Clayton, the county, and New York State as a whole, the petitioners' immediate neighborhood was strongly committed to African American men's political rights, voting overwhelmingly in 1846 to eliminate the state's racial restriction on voting from the state constitution.

A Conversation about Rights

Perhaps it seems odd to look to sources such as deeds, wills, and censuses when exploring the history of ideas. But ideas never have a single origin in time or place. If intellectual life is expressed and shared in convention halls, pulpits, and newspapers, it emerges in other places as well, among people living ordinary lives.

When I imagine these six women at work on their petition, the prospect of "kitchen-table conversation" intrigues me. Who first mentioned it? Who put pen to paper? Which of their husbands and brothers—Abraham, Hiram, Luther, Nahum, Bailey, Joseph—supported it, or laughed at it, or dismissed the effort? What did their fathers and mothers think, and what about the sisters and daughters who didn't sign? Most of this we will never know. We know that Susan Ormsby owned both a "Fall leaf table" that was "old & poor" and one that was "better," but not what actually happened around those and other tables. In the absence of supporting records, the petition from six female "citizens of the state of New York," and the exploration of the community and political identities behind it, offers a way to listen in on a conversation about which rights and privileges were not on the table in 1846 and which were "sufficiently plain without argument."

A monument commemorating the 1851 rescue of fugitive slave William "Jerry" Henry stands in Syracuse's Clinton Square today. Credit: John Dowling.

32

Freedom for a Stranger

Dennis J. Connors

Syracuse University Library's Special Collections holds the papers of central New York resident Gerrit Smith, a nationally known nineteenth-century abolitionist, reformer, and philanthropist. Smith corresponded with many well-known individuals involved in antislavery efforts. His notoriety and generosity also drew several strangers to seek his help and counsel—including James M. Clapp, one of the leaders of a dramatic rescue in Syracuse of former slave William "Jerry" Henry. Clapp's name barely exists in the historical record. But his January 3, 1852, letter to Gerrit Smith illuminates the heroism of this otherwise unknown citizen, as well as the commitment and passion of the abolitionists who stood against slavery and the risks and sacrifices they faced in liberating Jerry Henry.

Two Fugitives

Jerry was arrested on October 1, 1851, by federal marshals under authority of the contentious 1850 Fugitive Slave Law. After an unsuccessful individual escape attempt—a violent flight through the streets of Syracuse—Jerry was locked up for the evening in the offices of the police justice. Within a short time, a crowd of organized sympathizers broke in, forced the armed guards to release him, hid him for several days, and then spirited him to freedom in Canada. Nothing else is known about Jerry, since he disappears from the records.

But the story doesn't end there.

This essay first appeared in winter 2006, volume 5, number 3.

The Fugitive Slave Law was part of the Compromise of 1850, federal legislation crafted to keep the country from literally coming apart over the issue of slavery. Federal authorities knew that Jerry's rescue not only freed him but also challenged the government's ability to enforce the statute. Thus, while the authorities couldn't recapture Jerry in Canada, they could prosecute the rescuers in Syracuse. The penalties for breaking the law were harsh, with the potential for both substantial fines and jail time, either one of which could cripple the financial health and personal reputations of those involved. Within days, several arrests were made, indictments followed, and ultimately four men were brought to trial. These judicial proceedings stretched out over two years, severely disrupting the lives of several Syracusans—including James Clapp's.

Rather than face possible arrest and indictment, Clapp fled—ironically, like many fugitive slaves—to St. Catharines, Ontario, Canada, where there were also many residents sympathetic to America's abolitionist cause (Harriet Tubman used it as a base for her activities in the 1850s). Clapp wrote his letter to Gerrit Smith from there, stating that he knew Smith by reputation only but noting they were not strangers in principle. He then asked for Smith's "kind and benevolent counsel under my trying circumstances, driven as I was from home unexpectedly without an hours preparation" and saying that he was "not a little uneasy," since he was having a house built that he'd had to leave half-finished. He owed money on it and hoped that his creditor would be understanding.

A Letter Home

Clapp reminded Smith that he'd also had to abandon his job as a "furnaceman" in the Syracuse iron foundry of C. C. Bradley, effectively halting any steady source of income. He lamented, "My absence has already proved a great sacrifice in time and money," and he worried that he had essentially deserted his family in Syracuse (the 1850 federal census lists Clapp as forty years old with a wife, Rhoda, and a one-year-old child, Ellen).

He then told Smith, "The cause of my leaving so suddenly was the advice of my esteemed friend, Mr. C. A. Wheaton, on the night of the 3rd of Oct following the memorable first of Oct 1851 which as in all probability you well know the part that I am charged with." Smith did indeed know: he had been with Clapp in Syracuse that evening, at a meeting where Jerry's rescue was being planned. Charles Wheaton was another abolitionist present at the meeting.

Afterward, some participants had gone to make the necessary arrangements that would follow the planned rescue, such as transportation, sites for concealment, and connections into Canada. But others had taken on the dangerous task of forcing their way into the building where Jerry was jailed—and a good deal of that responsibility was shouldered by Clapp. Notes from testimony in an Auburn courtroom two weeks later by John W. Jones, who had been deputized and had been inside the police justice's rooms that night, state, "James M. Clapp was the first man I saw come into the room. Had a tussle with him . . . Clapp had a club . . . he also said he would have the negro or die." Jones, who had also been armed with a club, later testified that Clapp had led the crowd of rescuers into the building by climbing through a window: "Clapp seized my club and I caught him by the throat; I told him I would keep him, and he might scratch and bite if he chose." Jones had wrestled with Clapp for a few minutes, but the number of rescuers forced the marshals to relent, although at least one marshal fired his pistol during the commotion.

Clapp was not indicted, since the authorities likely couldn't find him—because, along with some other participants, he had fled. His letter to Gerrit Smith documents his flight:

> When I left, I started for Pennsylvania, thinking of making my parents a visit, but thinking it not advisable, I turned my course to NY City. . . . And deeming it not exactly the place for me under the advise of friends, I left for Mass where I took counsil from Mr. W. Phillips, Sewel, Jackson and others in Boston.

This refers to Wendell Phillips and probably Amasa Soule and Francis Jackson, all active abolitionists. Despite Boston's distance from Syracuse and its reputation as a center for antislavery activity, Clapp was still a fugitive on the run from federal authorities. His Boston friends advised him to head for Canada.

A Plea for Advice

Clapp's letter continued: "So I went up into new hampshire and worked a few weeks, then left for canada by the way of the vermont central road to Ogdensburgh." He then had to travel an additional three hundred miles to reach St. Catharines. The letter concludes with Clapp questioning Smith about whether he should return to Syracuse, "and run the risk of consequences," or remain in Canada. Clapp realized that he might be jailed if he returned, but he probably knew that Smith and others had raised bail for those arrested and had organized a defense fund for the pending legal cases. Clapp expressed hope that Smith and others might "sustain" him should he return.

We have no record of Smith's response, but he may have encouraged Clapp to remain in Canada, since a May 1854 sale of Syracuse property owned by James and

Rhoda Clapp documents a continued exile. The transaction was handled for the absent Clapp by his "attorney." The deed noted that James M. Clapp, the seller, was "formerly of Syracuse."

But by 1854, the cases against Jerry's rescuers had been resolved. One man had been found guilty but died in jail before his appeal was heard; the three others who had been brought to trial were either acquitted or their cases ended with hung juries. All remaining legal charges concerning the incident were then dropped. By 1857, according to the Syracuse city directory, James Clapp was back in Syracuse.

Despite considerable evidence that continuing aid was being given to fugitives in Syracuse, no serious attempts to enforce the Fugitive Slave Law were ever again undertaken there. James Clapp had sacrificed his own freedom and risked much for a few crucial moments that gave a stranger back his freedom.

Family Pride, *Mightier Than Pride*, and *Lucy Harding* are just three of the thirty-one novels written by the prolific Mary Jane Holmes. Her books earned royalties second only to Harriet Beecher Stowe's. Credit: Special Collections Research Center, Syracuse University Library, Syracuse, New York.

33

"A Good, Pure, and Natural Story"

William G. Andrews

Mary Jane Holmes from Brockport, New York, was undoubtedly the most popular—and prolific—American woman novelist in the second half of the nineteenth century. Yet she is virtually forgotten today. During her lifetime, her books sold perhaps three million copies and earned royalties second only to Harriet Beecher Stowe's. Holmes' booklist is staggering: between 1854 and 1907, she published thirty-one novels, at least twenty short stories, three separate short story collections, and over seventy serialized novels and stories in at least nine magazines, which attracted hundreds of thousands of additional readers. At least nine movies and six stage plays were based on her novels; the theatrical production presented in Edna Ferber's 1926 novel *Showboat* is based on Holmes' first novel from 1854, *Tempest and Sunshine*.

Mass Appeal

To understand the reasons for Holmes' appeal, one must understand the popular culture of the time. Holmes wrote in a way that was accessible to typical American housewives, many of whom were barely literate. One critic commented that her work required "no literary qualifications on the part of her readers." But accessibility was not enough: she was also *acceptable* to that audience, because her writings expressed traditional moral values. Holmes' obituary in *The Nation* attributed her success to the fact that the "moral tone [of her books] is as unimpeachable as that of the popular drama." She herself once said, "I mean always to write a good, pure, and natural story,

This essay first appeared in winter 2006, volume 5, number 3.

such as mothers are willing their daughters should read, and such as will do good instead of harm."

But the other half of Holmes' appeal was the character of her heroines. According to one critic, her writings were "freer from the middle-class conventions [of the time] than the works of any of the other women authors"; she depicted "a modern woman who rises in the world much as a man does, by self-betterment and looking to the main chance," needing only "education, experience, and sophistication" to succeed as men did. Literary historians note that, alone among women novelists, Holmes portrayed ordinary people in everyday situations. She abjured the sensationalism of many of her contemporaries: her novels lacked murders, robberies, fallen women, Gothic horrors, violent action, or exotic types. Unlike her rivals, she described conflicts that arose "out of a genuine difference in personality, culture, social, or economic status," and only she among those women novelists used irony and humor. By reaching the widest possible female audience and by providing them with enlightened role models, Holmes both echoed and foreshadowed the freedom that the suffragist, feminist, and women's liberation movements would demand for women.

A Natural Storyteller

She was born Mary Jane Hawes in Brookfield, Massachusetts, on April 5, 1825, into a family of nine children, and even as a youngster she was an accomplished storyteller. Her precocity led to her appointment as a schoolteacher at age thirteen, but the experience ended badly after two months. After moving to Richmond, Ontario County, New York, at age fifteen to live with an uncle, she taught school for seven more years and founded Laurel Hill Seminary for girls in Allen's Hill. There she also met Daniel Holmes, Jr., a teacher and graduate of the Brockport Normal School and Yale University. After their 1849 marriage, both taught for two years in Kentucky and one year in Canandaigua. But in 1852 they moved to Brockport, and both changed careers: Daniel became a lawyer, and Mary Jane began to write. They had no children.

Tempest and Sunshine (1854), Mary Jane's first novel, was an instant success. *Moore's Rural New Yorker* published six of her stories in 1857, and in 1859 the *New York Weekly* signed her to an exclusive contract and began to serialize her work. She became their most popular woman author, attracting so many fans that the magazine nearly quadrupled its circulation in three years. This expansion formed much of the basis of the Street & Smith publishing empire, perhaps the largest such enterprise in American history. A measure of Holmes' importance to Street & Smith was indicated by the $4,000 to $6,000 fee they paid for each of her serialized novels, compared to their usual rate of $40 to $60 per short story.

Her success in the magazines continued to grow. *Ladies Home Journal* published *Mildred's Ambition* in 1889; every year from 1893 through 1909, *People's Home Journal* published a serial; *Good Literature* published three stories in 1905.

Good Citizens, Too

Both Mary Jane and Daniel were prominent citizens in Brockport, active in the civic and community affairs of the small city. World travelers, the Holmeses visited Europe, Russia, the Mediterranean, and the Orient and maintained a summer home on Martha's Vineyard. It was on a return trip from there that Mary Jane fell ill and died in Brockport on October 7, 1907.

Her work was so popular that unpublished novels were still being serialized in magazines until January 1910. But then her reputation lapsed. Two publishers reissued most of her titles in the 1920s, but today, although many of her books can be found in antiquarian book shops or on eBay, she is regarded largely as a literary curiosity, a nineteenth-century Barbara Cartland. Yet the grandmothers and great-grandmothers of many of today's women were the beneficiaries of the early "consciousness-raising" that Mary Jane Holmes' tales produced in their imaginations.

Charles Wood. Credit: New York Public Library.

34

The President's Benefactor

Warren F. Broderick

Between June and July of 1885, Ulysses S. Grant, eighteenth president of the United States, spent the final five weeks of his life in a hospice-like setting at Drexel Cottage (later known as "Grant's Cottage," and now operated as a State Historic Site) on Mount McGregor in the town of Wilton in Saratoga County, New York. Most Americans were aware of the former general's terminal illness, throat cancer. His condition was widely publicized in the press, and while thousands of citizens felt sympathy for the dying national hero, relatively few could be extended the honor of an actual visit, since his strength diminished daily and his family desired to save him from the "common run of visitors." Grant also devoted as much time as he could to the completion of his *Personal Memoirs*, aided mainly by his stenographer and his new publisher, Samuel Clemens (aka Mark Twain), who had persuaded Grant to let his two-person imprint, Charles L. Webster & Company (co-owned by Clemens and his niece's husband), publish the memoir.

Grant desperately needed the money; his well-publicized financial collapse in 1884—about the same time he learned that he was ill—had left him and his family nearly penniless. In 1883 he had joined the firm of Grant and Ward, established two years previously by his son, Ulysses S. "Buck" Grant, Jr., and two financial partners, Ferdinand Ward and James D. Fish. But neither father nor son was aware of the partners' poor judgment, risky investments, and dangerous land speculation. Once Ward and Fish failed to cover their loans, both the firm and the associated Marine Bank went under swiftly. Most Americans realized that the Grants had been well meaning

This essay first appeared in summer 2006, volume 6, number 1. A longer version appeared in *The Hudson River Valley Review*, fall 2005, volume 22, number 1.

and had allowed this "firm of swindlers" to use the family's good name and reputation to secure the trust of unwitting investors. Now Grant was dying, and concern for his family's financial security after his death compelled him to complete his memoirs.

Two Visitors

But on July 9, 1885, the newspapers reported that Grant received two visitors. One was expected. The other was not. It is unclear whether the scheduling of their visits was intentional or merely coincidental. The first visitor was Robert Johnson, associate editor of *Century Magazine*, who had overseen the publication of some articles Grant had written for the publication. The income from these articles had enabled the impoverished former president to repay some of his more pressing debts.

Grant's second and less well-known visitor was Charles Wood, owner of a modest brush factory located in Lansingburgh (presently part of the city of Troy) in Rensselaer County, New York. The newspapers reported only his name, with no description or explanation for his visit. But Grant's principal physician, Dr. John H. Douglas, wrote about Wood's visit in his journal:

> Among the notable visitors to-day was Mr. Charles Wood . . . who, when the disaster of May 1884 came upon Genl. Grant, sent him a sum of money for his immediate use . . . to be returned without interest, when convenient. . . . He lunched with the family today and the General received him with marked kindness.

Charles Wood's family business had been operating for over sixty years in Lansingburgh, which was for many years known as the "Brush Capital of the United States." Wood was well known as a successful brush manufacturer, a respected family patriarch, and the author of several articles in both local newspapers and trade journals on the history and development of the highly specialized brush-making industry. Wood had not fought in the Civil War, but two younger brothers had served in the New York 21st Cavalry. Neither of them had served directly under General Grant in the Army of the Potomac, but this did not lessen Wood's patriotism and deep appreciation of Grant's wartime leadership.

"For Appomattox"

On May 10, 1884, when news of Grant's financial scandal and disgrace broke, Wood had immediately written a personal check for a loan of $500 and mailed it to Grant, offering to loan him an additional $1,000 to be repaid one year hence without interest or security. Wood noted that his check was being sent "on account of my share for services ending April, 1865"—an obvious reference to Grant's securing Lee's surrender. "I owe you this for Appomattox," Wood added.

Grant had responded two days later, writing that "the money at this time would be of exceeding use to me, having not enough to pay one month's servant hire, or room, if I were to leave my house." Upon receipt of Grant's response, Wood immediately sent Grant the additional $1,000, whereupon Grant responded,

> You have conferred an obligation more than I can ever repay. The money, of course, I do not doubt that I can return. But, being caught without $100 in my pocket, and nothing coming in until August, it became a serious question what to do. You, in the generosity of your heart, have relieved that anxiety.

Ulysses Grant repaid Wood's $1,000 on January 5, 1885, and expressed his heartfelt appreciation in another letter:

> I wish to state to you how great was the relief afforded by your timely loan. At the time of the failure of Grant and Ward . . . I had paid my bills for the previous months with checks on the firm. Most of them were not presented until after the failure. Your checks enabled me to meet the second call, and gave me something to go upon until another turn could be made. Mrs. Grant was fortunate enough to [sell] a couple of small houses in Washington . . . since which we have been comfortable in means to live upon, but with nothing to pay past debts. I return you with the greatest pleasure $1000 of the $1500 which you so kindly, and without solicitation or claim upon you, sent me. It affords me greater pleasure from the fact that I have earned this by my own work.

"A Grandeur of Soul"

The connection, then, between Grant's two visitors on July 9, 1885, was that of benefactors: Robert Johnson had learned about Charles Wood's generosity the previous year directly from Grant, and Wood was certainly aware of Johnson's role in convincing Grant to become an author. Grant's income from his articles on the Civil War that appeared in Johnson's *Century Magazine* beginning in February 1885 enabled him to repay the loan from Charles Wood.

The impoverished ex-president had vented to Johnson about his financial woes when Johnson had visited Grant's seaside New Jersey cottage the previous June. The apocryphal story of Grant pointing to the empty vase on the mantelpiece that had once held his wife's prized collection of gold coins that the couple had received from various dignitaries—coins that had been sold to satisfy debts—dates from this visit. Grant had also told Johnson about the loan from Wood, and about another loan for $1,000 from the Mexican ambassador Matias Romero. Wood and Romero were apparently the only people who had loaned Grant money during his financial crisis.

On July 9, Johnson was already present when Charles Wood arrived at noon. Perhaps the two visitors met for the first time. Grant was in great discomfort and could barely speak. His final communication to Wood was written on four little slips of note paper in pencil "in a trembling hand":

> I am very sorry that I am unable to converse even in a whisper. I am reclining in bed as long as it rests me this morning, because yesterday I had a very trying day. My worst hours, most painful ones, are from 4 to 7 in the afternoon. Yesterday we had a number of particular friends call and stay through those hours. I had to converse incessantly with my pencil. About the close the Mexican editors called in a body and delivered a speech . . . I replied . . . then there was a second speech and reply. By this time I was nearly exhausted. I am badly off this minute, because the doctor has been dressing my mouth, and that is always painful. I feel very thankful to you for the kindness you did me last year. I am glad to say that while there is much unblushing wickedness in the world there is a compensating grandeur of soul. In my case I have not found that republics are ungrateful, nor are the people.

Debt Paid

Ulysses Grant died on July 23, 1885. But the public story of Charles Wood's personal generosity would not become known until August 5, 1892, when an article entitled "Some Letters from General Grant" appeared in the *New York Times*. A reporter for the *Times* interviewed Wood, who showed him the four notes from Grant—prized possessions, which Wood had framed. At a reception in his honor, Wood recalled his meeting with Grant and remarked that the letters "show, as do all the other records of the dead hero, that he was a simple, unaffected man, entirely free from overvaluation of his own work and touched by the kindly sympathy of others." The reporter also noted that Wood had been paid the final $500 of his loan following Grant's death, and that Wood's generosity continued: he donated that $500 to charity.

Marietta Holley lived long enough to see women obtain the right to vote. Credit: Jefferson County Historical Society, Watertown, New York.

35

The Female Mark Twain

Kate Winter

In 1872, just up the Salt Road that ran from Syracuse to Canada, Marietta Holley boldly set out from her father's farmhouse to mail a book manuscript—her first—to Mark Twain's publisher, Elisha Bliss. She had a contract to expand one of her stories, written in the dialect of New York's North Country, into a novel written by "Samantha," also known as "Josiah Allen's Wife"—and thus her identity could be obscured by her pseudonym, just as the village of Bear Creek in southern Jefferson County, New York (near the village of Adams, where Holley lived), had been renamed Pierrepont Manor, thereby attaining a small measure of gentility. But renaming alone could not erase the region's history of frontier settlement and farming culture—nor could it hide those influences in Holley's stories.

Art Embellishes Life

A village where a notice in the local paper read "It's only a girl at the Holley house" was a village that did not expect much from, or encourage adventure in, a young woman. Indeed, local folk were likely to censure Marietta for not marrying, or for not attending to chores or to "duty." So, supported by her own innate tendency to solitude and privacy, when she began to write Holley withheld her own name from the world and instead let "Samantha" persuade anyone who would listen that the "inalienable rights" of the Declaration of Independence included, among other things, a woman's right to vote.

This essay first appeared in summer 2006, volume 6, number 1.

Holley's family was already different from other farm families nearby; in many ways the Holley clan broke the pattern of rural North Country life. Her oldest sister was "odd": she stayed at home and never liked to be seen. Her brothers had gone off to chase California gold. Marietta, the youngest, born July 16, 1836, grew up to run the farm with her mother and write poetry and little stories for publication in the Adams newspaper. She also left the Episcopal Church of her family and followed Baptist practice, which allowed her to participate more fully in church life.

Thus, Samantha could not have been more different from her creator. Samantha was large and vocal, assailing Horace Greeley on the subject of "biled vittles and wimmen's rights" while coping with the excessive ignorance of her lightweight husband, Josiah; Holley herself never married. Samantha was an intrepid traveler, not only to the 1876 Philadelphia Centennial, the St. Louis Exposition, and Chicago World's Fair but also around the world; Holley feared travel and never left Jefferson County until midlife. Samantha was quick to buttonhole any politician she saw and turn the encounter into an argument on the evils of drink, the rights of women, the direction America was headed, or the foibles of fashion; Holley almost never spoke in public because of a speech impediment. Samantha insisted on the rule of common sense and on plain speaking, though she loved a good story and would embellish her arguments with allegory in the homely metaphors of rural New York; Holley preferred the modest gentility of late nineteenth-century culture, manifested in the Victorian "cottage" she built for herself on the site of her parents' farm, the laces and velvets that replaced the calico of her youth, and the company of a very few friends, including Clara Barton.

Queen of the Bestsellers

Over the course of her writing life, New York's "female Mark Twain" would, in the personae of Samantha and other female creations, endear herself to the American reading public through twenty-one books and uncounted magazine stories. Between 1873 and 1914, Holley wrote more books than Mark Twain—and sold about ten million of them. Betsey Bobbet, the spinster poet of *My Opinions and Betsey Bobbet's* (1872), became a popular culture hero; Betsey Bobbet Clubs in the East and Midwest provided a venue for readers to recite and act out the comic adventures of Samantha, Betsey, and Josiah. In 1885, *Samantha at Saratoga* was a bestseller, wherein Samantha and Josiah dipped into the whirl of racing season in Saratoga Springs—giving the indomitable farm wife plenty to comment on with regard to the fashions and manners of a health resort "gone to the horses."

These characters found their way to the stage in New York and Boston in 1883, and there was occasional talk of a film thereafter. While Samantha's dialect and politics ultimately did not translate to a movie screen, Holley's life did; in 2005, PBS produced the award-winning TV documentary *The Marietta Holley Story*. As entertaining as Samantha's adventures were, Holley's contributions to American literature, as well as to civil rights and feminist history, make a far more interesting story for film audiences today.

Rooted in New York

Marietta Holley died at her home between Pierrepont Manor and Adams in a March snowstorm in 1926, just shy of her ninetieth birthday. She had lived to vote—and to celebrate that American women finally could. Most of her life she had kept to the comforts of Bonnie View, her grand home in Jefferson County, maintaining her genteel lifestyle on the property her family had claimed and cleared from a wilderness where bears and panthers had once haunted creeks and meadows. It was her wish that her gardens would gambol over their neat fences as intrepidly as Samantha made the rest of the country laugh.

Picking hops was hard work but also a "good time" for young people to get together. One man's lightheartedness is reflected in the hops decorating his hat. Credit: New York State Archives, Albany, New York.

36

When Hops Were King

G. William Beardslee

In the nineteenth century, hop houses were so common it was said that "every other farm and farmer had one." So there is no small irony in the urgency to preserve central New York's surviving hop houses. Alternately called hop kilns or hop barns, they were the specialized structures used to dry, bleach, cure, package, and store the hop flower, or cone, used in the brewing of beer. Hops add stabilizing and preservative qualities to beer: not only is beer improved by the hops' distinctive aroma and bitterness, but hops allow beer to be stored and preserved for longer periods. A further irony is that today it is the hop houses themselves that need preservation. Once numbering in the hundreds, only a few score remain today as relics of a once-dominant agricultural activity in central New York.

Constructed between the early 1800s and 1900 in New York's "hop belt" (Otsego, Chenango, Madison, Montgomery, Oneida, and Schoharie Counties), the hop houses' unique architectural styles remain distinctive despite the passage of time. During these decades, the traditional appearance of central New York's family farms changed as hundreds of hop houses were built. The earliest designs were usually low barns with some ventilation. Later they evolved into narrower and taller structures, topped with a cupola directly above the drying kiln area. As farmers focused on the efficient cultivation and drying of hops, distinctive pyramid-shaped kilns were constructed. In time, multiple pyramid hop house complexes were common.

This essay first appeared in fall 2006, volume 6, number 2.

Fruit of the Vine

The hop (*Humulus lupulus*), first grown by the Greeks and Romans, is a twining, climbing vine closely related to hemp and marijuana that grows prodigiously during the summer months. But hops have not always been part of the beer-making recipe. Historically, beer was made from barley, water, and yeast, and flavored—perhaps to disguise its taste—with a variety of spices and herbs, including rosemary, thyme, spruce bark, sassafras, honey, bog myrtle, yarrow, alecost, and many others. Herbs were chosen not only for their flavor but also for their reputed medicinal properties. In this early form, beer was called gruit. Unless greater quantities of grain were used to increase the alcohol content and thereby reduce spoilage, gruit had a relatively short shelf life.

In the later Middle Ages, brewers (mostly monks) added hops to the beer-making formula. Hopped beer slowly gained popularity for its aroma and bitter taste—and for its ability to stabilize and preserve the wort/mash. Hops helped clarify the beer, provided a good head, and dramatically improved its keeping power. Thus, beer no longer required a high alcohol content to prevent spoilage, which meant that the brewers needed less grain, which translated to higher profits.

Beer and hops were among the first products of New England. A journal kept by one of the *Mayflower* Pilgrims indicated that one of the reasons their voyage terminated in Massachusetts instead of Virginia was a shortage of beer. At that time, most hops were imported from England, where a significant hops industry had developed as early as the fourteenth century. The English conical-pyramidal hop-drying houses, made of stone and called "oasts," are still commonly seen in southern England, particularly in the traditional hop-growing region of Sussex and Kent.

Cash Crop

In New England, the commercial growing of hops began in Massachusetts in the late 1700s. Until 1850, Vermont cultivated significant quantities, but it was the transplanted Yankees of central New York who perfected large-scale hop cultivation. In 1808, Madison County's John Cooledge established a "hop yard," but most farmers ignored the crop until Solomon Root sold two tons of hops for $1,000 in 1815. Within a decade, a hops industry developed. At first the harvests were modest, but after a series of English crop failures in the early 1820s the increased demand for hops, combined with the construction of the Great Western Turnpikes and the new Erie Canal (which allowed for cheaper east to west transportation), made hop cultivation explode. By 1840, forty-three New York State counties reported having at least one hop yard.

By mid-century, due to excellent yields and good market prices, central New York hop production assumed major proportions. By 1849, New York had attained national leadership in the production of hops, and by 1855 the region was raising millions of pounds annually. On the eve of the Civil War, most of the hop crop in the United States was raised in New York; over one-third of New York's production came from Otsego County. By 1879, central New York's hop fields covered over forty thousand acres and produced over twenty million pounds of hops. At its peak in the last quarter of the nineteenth century, the American brewing industry consumed more than thirty million pounds of dried hops each year—the majority grown domestically, and most of it in central New York.

Summer's Work and Play

In late summer, the hop-picking season began. In an era in which women and children were traditionally protected, it was considered appropriate for young women and men to go hop picking together. In the region's hop yards, thousands of men, women, and children were hired for the various field jobs: pickers, box tenders, kiln workers. Although many pickers were local residents, many others were transported in from nearby urban centers, and as part of their wages they were provided room and board for the season. Women and young adults were assigned the "particular work" of picking the hop flowers/cones from the vines, while men performed the heavier tasks of pole lifting, box tending, and carting.

Hop picking was considered pleasant work and was often described as a "good time." For a few weeks each summer, mostly young men and women worked closely together in the fresh air, ate good country food, and attended nightly dinners and "hops"—informal social occasions where participants would dance to music. Correspondence from the time indicates many hop pickers thought an important part of their experience was the chance of meeting "someone special" at a "hop."

Equally as important as the cultivation and picking of hops was the drying and storage of the crop. Picked from the vine in late summer, the hop's flower-like petals contain lupulin, which resembles large yellow pollen grains. Sticky to the touch, lupulin is a stiff oily resin whose complicated chemistry is found in no other plant. Its volatile oils flavor the beer, and its resins contain alpha acids that confer bitterness and natural preservatives.

After picking, the hops were packed, taken to the hop house, and placed on a cloth-covered, slatted drying floor directly above the kiln room's large furnace. Over a period of about eighteen hours, the kiln master—usually the owner of the hop yard—circulated a steady current of hot air (160 degrees Fahrenheit) through the hops; this lowered their moisture content to a straw-like 12 percent. At a critical moment in the process, sulfur was ignited, which bleached the hops to the desired color. Once dried and bleached, the hops were moved to the adjacent cooling room where, after a few hours of "sweating," they were dropped down a chute into the pressing room's hopsacking-lined press, compacted into bales, and stored. Like many agricultural commodities, hops were bought and sold by middlemen and brokers as futures or as a spot commodity. The best prices usually occurred around Christmas.

But by 1900, central New York's golden age of hops was over. A few hardy growers survived into the middle of the twentieth century, but a combination of events caused the industry's demise: competition from more efficient hop producers in Oregon, California, and Washington; the appearance of crop-specific insects and a "blue mold" that attacked and destroyed the hop flower; the emergence of the more reliable dairy industry; and the growing intolerance of many Americans toward alcohol. Prohibition in the 1920s and 1930s resulted in the final collapse of what had been central New York's most successful crop.

Preserving History

Today, aside from a few stalwart farmers trying to reintroduce the crop and a demonstration plot at the Farmers' Museum in Cooperstown, hop growing is nearly nonexistent in central New York. What remain are the few extant hop houses, although each year a few more disappear. Many are in a state of serious neglect and in danger of imminent collapse. The need to preserve these remnants of the area's agricultural history is obvious, and some individuals, groups, and institutions have risen to the challenge.

For example, in Otsego County, the Farmer's Museum in Cooperstown has restored an 1840 hop barn once owned by Samuel Pierce Pope. In the town of Pittsfield, not far from New Berlin, a classic pyramid-shaped hop barn has been privately restored to its 1860 appearance. Madison County's local historians, with the assistance of the Preservation League of New York State, have succeeded in adding seven local hop houses to the League's yearly list of threatened historic resources as "Seven to Save in 2006." But the League's president, Jill DiLorenzo, summarized the need for immediate action:

> The . . . League calls on local and state organizations and agencies to work together . . . to identify, document, stabilize and preserve our remaining hop kilns . . . The work of the Madison County Historical Society and the

New York State Legislature provide important resources for encouraging an appreciation of hop resources. But more must be done to ensure that the tangible legacy of New York's proud agricultural history can endure.

Water rushes through a break in the Forestport Feeder canal levee, 1899. Credit: New York State Archives, Albany, New York.

37

The Forestport Breaks

Michael Doyle

Darkness fell, and the ruffians gathered like ghosts.

The town of Forestport was distracted with its customary frolics on the evening of May 23, 1898. Surrounded by six sawmills, the Erie Canal–side town in upstate New York's upper Oneida County scared the faint of heart. Its bars and pleasuring establishments pulsed with the rowdy river drivers down from the Big Moose River, the wizened and de-fingered sawyers, the canawlers still clinging to their dying trade.

"The citizens are a hardy class of men, honest in the main," the *Brooklyn Eagle* would observe in January 1900, "but having among them . . . the reckless daredevil class which makes its living away from humanity and modern civilization in general."

Prosecutors would make the Forestport case more bluntly. "They've got more saloons than houses," one law enforcement official would state in May 1900, "and that is the way the town is ruled." True enough: the town of 1,500 souls boasted half a dozen saloons, whose owners pulled the strings. There was Walt Bynon's place, and big Dick Manahan's Getman House, and Jimmy Rudolph's dangerous pool hall, and the lumberjack's hotel known as Doyle's. Forestport was a town on the edge, where civilization merged with the North Country wilderness.

Remsen was a rather more placid town, twenty minutes away by the New York Central Railroad line. When the detectives from the Pinkerton National Detective Agency started coming, they transited Remsen. But that would be later, after the Forestport canal levees had collapsed once too often and suspicions could no longer be suppressed.

"There is no law," people whispered, "north of Remsen."

This essay first appeared in summer 2007, volume 7, number 1.

How the Deed Was Done

Erie Canal authorities may have grown accustomed to breaks; by the late nineteenth century, the whole system was as dilapidated as an old man with brittle bones. But when the Forestport levees broke in 1897, and again in 1898, and once more in 1899, the coincidence would provoke Governor Roosevelt's team of investigators. What they subsequently found, one prosecutor would thunder in 1900, amounted to "one of the most gigantic conspiracies that was ever concocted in New York State."

On the night of May 23, 1898, four men gathered unnoticed amid Forestport's customary mayhem. They snuck away from River Street and crossed the bridge spanning the Black River, the sounds of saloon revelry subsiding as they walked up a hill toward the Forestport Feeder canal. The Feeder connected Forestport to Boonville and the Black River Canal eleven miles away, but the men were not going that far. Instead, they struck off down the towpath for several hundred yards, lugging picks and shovels and a bottle. Two of them separated to stand watch. The other two, pool hall owner James Rudolph and a local hard case named John Root, took a warming pull of whiskey and readied their tools. "And Root and I," Rudolph would later testify, "went to digging."

"There was a regular hole worked into the bottom of the canal 30 or 40 feet deep, and that was working back towards the berm bank and up and down the canal in both directions," a local man named Charley Pratt would testify in 1900. "Dirt was caving into the bottom of the canal and big chunks of earth were dropping into this hole as the water undermined it."

Pratt's testimony was recorded in a trial transcript found at the Oneida County Courthouse, as well as in microfilmed editions of the *Boonville Herald*, *Rome Daily Sentinel*, and *Utica Observer*. In fact, all of the Oneida County newspapers were enraptured by the frequent Forestport breaks, which unraveled over the course of several years. By the time a series of criminal trials began in Rome in April 1900, reporters were swarming over the story of a rough-and-tumble town and its ill-fated canal levees.

Walking through History

It's 108 years later, September 30, 2006. Saloon girls sashay before Scooter's bar, a rugged but warmhearted place that a newly painted sign identifies as Forestport's old Hotel Doyle. Nickel beers have been poured since ten in the morning, enlivening spirits for the first-ever Old Forestport Days. A parade forms: a mounted posse, buggies, and impeccably restored antique cars depart River Street at a ceremonious pace. The parade crosses the Black River bridge and moves uphill toward the Forestport Feeder. At the garlanded head of the canal towpath, Scooter's co-owner, Jeannie Wolcott, dedicates the newest section of what's called the North Country Scenic Trail, a 4,600-mile braid of trails connecting North Dakota to Lake Champlain.

Celebrants stroll down the towpath to the place where, 108 years earlier, John Root, James Rudolph, and their cronies had dug all night. Some clues of physical rupture and reclamation endure, and a sepia-toned image forms in the mind's eye: the diggers slivering away the towpath until the canal water starts sluicing through, carrying chunks of levee downhill toward the Black River. One imagines the wound confronting canal men on the fog-bound morning of May 24, 1898.

I came upon the crime scene by accident.

While researching my family history, I learned that my great-grandfather and namesake, a certain Michael Doyle of Forestport, New York, had owned a saloon and lumberjack's hotel. How colorful, I thought. Growing up in California and working as a newspaper correspondent in Washington, D.C., I knew (and cared) nothing about Forestport—until I began digging too.

Census records at the National Archives, and birth and death records in Oneida County, got me started. Turn-of-the-century county histories fleshed out names and faces. At the State Library in Albany, annual reports from the New York State engineer and surveyor recorded the Erie Canal's rise and fall. Canal depredations proved to be well documented; the archives' shelves were thick with reports from canal investigating commissions established in 1846, 1876, and 1898. "If the state's waterways are used as means of favoritism, bad appointments, corrupt contracts or extravagance and mismanagement to promote partisan ends at the expense of public service . . . there ought to be exposure," the *New York Times* reasoned in September 1890.

The Forestport breaks had been sketchily described in works like Noble E. Whitford's 1906 opus *History of the Canal System of the State of New York*, but the breaks were never explored in depth. So that's what I set out to do when I began the research that led to my book, *The Forestport Breaks: A Nineteenth-Century Conspiracy Along the Black River Canal*, published by Syracuse University Press in 2004.

For Money—and Memory

I learned that for decades, well-connected men had plundered the Erie Canal. Businessmen had soaked it with costly contracts, politicians had padded it with patronage jobs, and it had provided dark inspiration for the saloonkeepers and hotel owners of Forestport, who had banded together to hire Jimmy Rudolph's gang. Whenever the canal levees broke, the state would hire hundreds of workers and spend tens of thousands of dollars on repairs, making Forestport flush—for a while.

"The Forestport men," the *Brooklyn Eagle* declared in January 1900, "did not have the position that enabled them to make the raid on the treasury in a polite and genteel manner, and so they went at it brutally."

And Michael Doyle? He had been in the middle of it all. Pinkerton detectives peeled away the Forestport layers until they understood how—and why—the breaks occurred.

"I would give $25 if there was another break," Doyle had told Rudolph in the spring of 1898.

Good old great-granddad! He inspired the 1898 plotting, and similar commercial considerations brought about the breaks in 1897 and 1899. Ultimately, thirteen Forestport men were arrested—the first time anyone was charged with conspiring to destroy Erie Canal property. Several went to Auburn State Prison, but Michael Doyle escaped prosecution by dying before the Pinkertons arrived.

But today his place still stands, as Scooter's bar; the Forestport Feeder still flows; and the towpath still beckons, all of them found through digging up the archives this time, a refurbished trail of ghosts and memory.

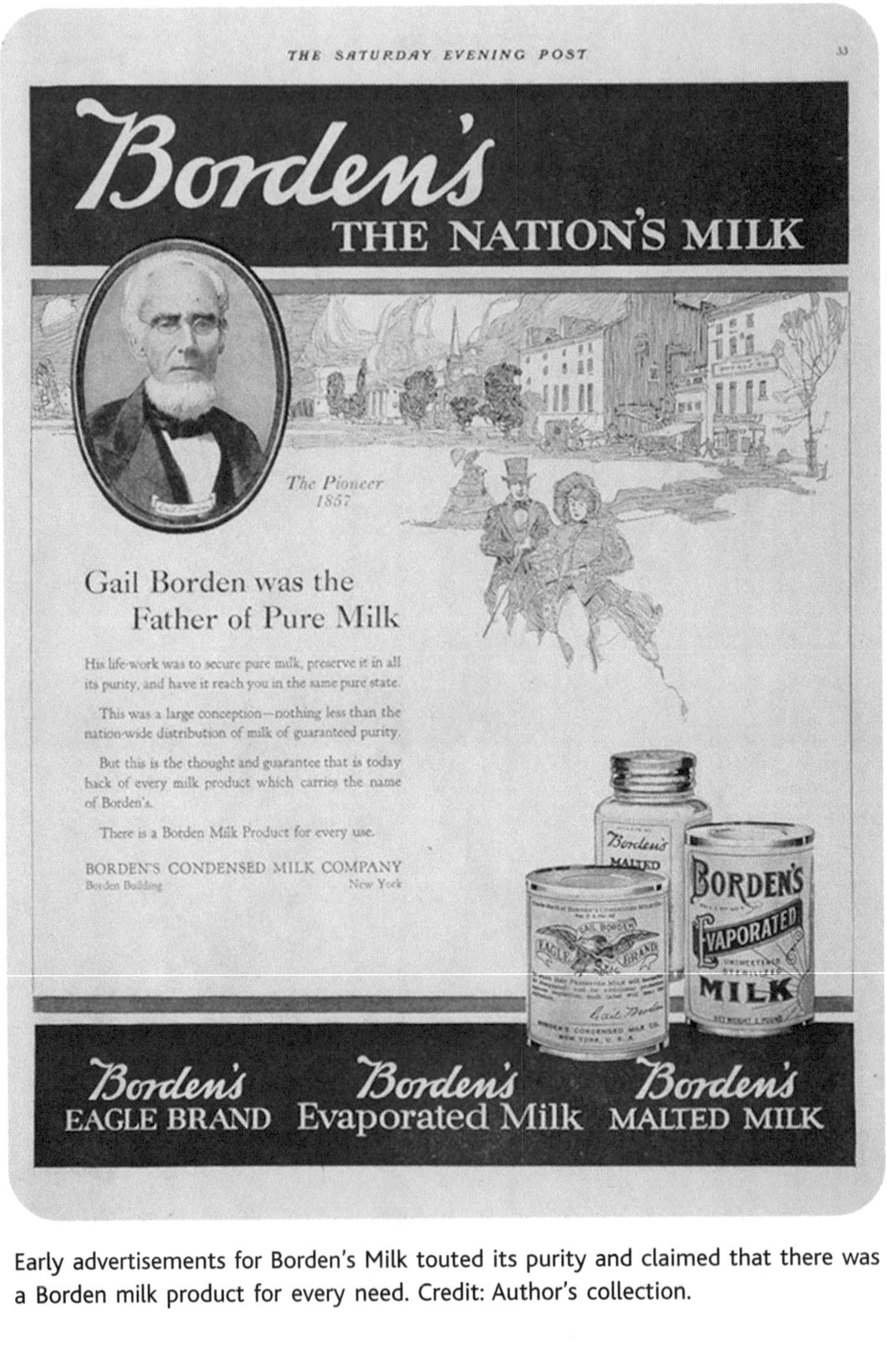

Early advertisements for Borden's Milk touted its purity and claimed that there was a Borden milk product for every need. Credit: Author's collection.

38

"Adversity's Sweet Milk"

G. William Beardslee

I Tried And Failed.
I Tried Again And Again
And Succeeded.

Even Gail Borden's epitaph in Woodlawn Cemetery in the Bronx shows the determination of the nineteenth-century inventor, publisher, and surveyor who is today best known as the founder of the Borden Company. Borden's, a corporate giant of America's food industry, first introduced its pioneering product, condensed milk, after Gail developed a milk preservation process that immediately revolutionized American diets, nutrition, and food safety, particularly during the Civil War. Though he failed several times with his other inventions, by the time of his death in 1874 Borden was internationally renowned as a businessman, inventor, and philanthropist—and as a man whose early legendary failures ultimately contributed to his success.

Gail Borden, Jr., was born in Norwich, Chenango County, New York, in 1801. His family moved first to Kentucky in 1814, then to Indiana, and later to Amite County, Mississippi. By the late 1820s, Borden was married and working as a surveyor. But like many other Americans and central New Yorkers, Borden and his first wife, Penelope Mercer Borden, joined those who were "gone to Texas." There he initially worked as a farmer, stockman, and blacksmith; later he was appointed successor to his brother Thomas as an official surveyor and platted the towns of Galveston and Houston. He also found time in 1835 to establish the first newspaper in Texas, the *Telegraph and Texas Land Register*, and during the conflict between Texas and Mexico, he allegedly

This essay first appeared in fall 2007, volume 7, number 2.

penned the phrase "Remember the Alamo." He was also active in the establishment of the Texas state government.

In 1837, Borden was appointed collector of customs at Galveston by Texas governor Sam Houston. Despite the inherent difficulties of the job, he was extremely popular and was reappointed from 1841 to 1843. Throughout the 1840s, he also continued his development of Galveston real estate and eventually sold over 2,500 lots. He was a trustee of the Texas Baptist Education Society, which founded Baylor University; an officer in the local temperance society; and deacon and clerk of the local Baptist church.

An Inventor Is Born

Then Borden turned his considerable talents to inventing. Having lost his wife Penelope to a yellow fever epidemic in 1844, and with seven children to support, he invented a massive ether refrigeration machine that was designed to "chill" the fever out of the afflicted. It was an immediate failure. Only slightly less disappointing was his "locomotive bath house," invented for Galveston women who wished to bathe in the Gulf of Mexico without being seen. Then came something called the "terraqueous machine," a sort of prairie schooner that would move on either land or water; this too never quite caught on.

But Borden was also fascinated by the potential for food preservation and storage. His initial experiments in this field were designed to preserve meat and bread through water removal and the concentration of nutrients, and they culminated in a "meat biscuit," made of dehydrated meat compounded with flour, that was stored in a sealed can. After spending $100,000 on the process, and having been divorced by his second wife, in 1851 he obtained a patent for his "potable desiccated soup bread." Although the meat biscuit won numerous awards and international recognition, and was considered to be as important as McCormick's mechanical reaper and Goodyear's "India rubber," it was a significant commercial failure.

So Borden abruptly abandoned the project in order to devote time to another idea: the preservation of milk. In 1851 he returned to New York and continued his water removal/condensation experiments, this time on raw milk, allegedly observing processes used at the Shaker community at New Lebanon. Raw milk had historically posed considerable health risks. Loaded with naturally occurring bacteria, it spoiled rapidly, particularly during the summer. It also caused a multitude of sicknesses, including "milksick, milk poison, milk trembles, the slows," and "the milk evil," not to mention death from contamination. Unaware of what would one day be known as the "germ theory" of disease, Borden repeated aspects of his prior desiccation processes and learned that a key to preserving raw milk was preventing the initiation of milk decomposition. Unlike other workers in food preservation who experimented with the removal of certain milk solids or butterfat, Borden's method centered on two processes: removing the water from milk, and preventing introduction of foreign contaminants into it, from the time it was drawn from the cow until completion of the condensation process.

A Milk Revolution

His early efforts to condense milk were failures. But after much experimentation, effort, and expense, Borden discovered that the evaporation-condensation process was enhanced when it was performed under heat in a vacuum kettle and when sugar was added as a preservative. His "vacuum process" was granted the first of several patents in 1856. Instead of a perishable product that decomposed within a day or two, canned condensed milk could be kept pure without refrigeration, had a shelf life of as much as twenty-four months, and was transportable over great distances.

Nearly destitute from the expense of procuring patents, Borden had little capital with which to finance the large-scale manufacture of his condensed milk. But in 1858, with the backing of Wall Street financier Jeremiah Milbank, he began the New York Condensed Milk Company, later renamed the Borden Company. At first slowly, and then in a flood after the 1861 outbreak of the Civil War with its immediate need for field rations for Union soldiers, Borden opened milk condenseries in Wassaic and Brewster, New York; Elgin, Illinois; Livermore, Maine; and Burrville, Connecticut. At the height of Civil War production, the Union Army was buying twenty-five thousand quarts a day from the company; the Elgin condensery alone was producing three hundred thousand gallons annually. Many other companies eventually produced condensed milk under Borden's licensed patents, but the most successful was his own "Eagle Brand Sweetened Condensed Milk." In the mid-1880s, the Borden Company would successfully develop a process that packaged this product in the small cans in which it is still sold today.

Finally flush with his successes, Borden returned with his third wife to Texas after the Civil War and opened several more businesses, including a meat-packing plant, a sawmill, and a copperware factory. He also invented processes for condensing fruit juices, beef extract, and coffee. His community energy undiminished, in 1873 he built schools for both freedmen's and white children, organized a day and a Sunday school for black children, aided in constructing five churches, maintained two missionaries, and partially supported numerous poorly paid teachers, ministers, and students. He died in 1874 in Borden, Texas; his body was shipped by private car to New York for burial in Woodlawn Cemetery.

Got Milk?

Several aspects of American life were permanently modified by Borden's invention, beginning with the economy of rural central New York. The region had long produced significant quantities of milk, primarily for the production of cheese and butter, but between 1865 and 1920 at least several dozen Borden condenseries and milk plants were constructed in scores of central New York's cities, towns, and villages. For example, within a relatively small area of Otsego and Chenango Counties, condenseries were built along the Unadilla and Chenango Rivers, and later along nearby railroad routes in Mt. Upton, Schenevus, Norwich, Edmeston, Oxford, and Pittsfield (New Berlin). The result was an increase in the number of family farms whose single product was raw milk destined for one of these condenseries. As time went on, the farms expanded into even larger entities.

Condenseries were necessarily built near the source of the raw milk, not unlike modern beef-processing plants, which are similarly located near western cattle operations.

The Borden condensery that was built in the town of Pittsfield near New Berlin was converted in 1899 from a cotton factory, which had been built in 1832. Until its sale to the Nestle Company in 1920, this factory (which produced Eagle Brand Condensed Milk) was the world's largest milk condensery. Although no production records are known to exist, other Borden condensery records suggest that the New Berlin plant employed more than 100 workers who produced and packed 25,000 tin cans daily. About 300 barrels of refined white sugar were used each week. The factory's daily consumption of locally produced raw milk was at least 15,000 gallons, supplied by some 7,500 cows from approximately 150 nearby dairy farms.

Gail Borden's legacy also includes important improvements to food safety measures. His insistence on dairy sanitation and cleanliness was well known and became codified into business procedures. Local farmers who sold their milk to Borden's condenseries were required to meet "Borden's Standards" via contractual obligations, which included specific details and techniques for how cows should be milked. The contracts further stipulated that farmers "agreed not to feed cows on turnips, ensilage, wet or dry barley sprouts, falo feed, or any feed which will impart a disagreeable flavor to the milk, or which will not produce milk of standard richness."

Two Centuries of Success

There were social consequences, too. After condensation, the milk was canned, which required the placement of a small soldered top. Scores of young local women, known as "Borden's Girls," were hired to perform this deft and delicate maneuver on the assembly line. A story passed down within a Columbus, New York, family relates that, in the milk season of 1899, one such girl who worked at Borden's condensery in Hoboken, New Jersey, earned the standard nine cents for each hundred of the soldered cans she produced. During one month, she earned over $24 by working ten hours a day and six days a week. Her earnings were more than many young men earned in a month—and her fiancé, a prominent local dairy farmer, publicly considered this "scandalous wage" for a woman an outrage.

The Borden Company's promotion and marketing of the product was also revolutionary. Openly playing to the public's historic fears of contaminated and disease-ridden raw milk, Borden's advertisements featured images of happy, healthy babies drinking safe and sanitary Borden's condensed milk. Gail Borden's own Eagle Brand Condensed Milk is said to be the oldest food product brand name in continuous use.

With the introduction of refrigeration, pasteurization, and homogenization in the twentieth century, the market share of condensed milk within the United States declined. Today, condensed milk (and its close cousin, evaporated milk) accounts for less than 2 percent of all American milk production. But it is still highly popular for dessert items and is still consumed wherever refrigeration is unavailable—evidence that Gail Borden's remarkable invention changed dairy farming from a haphazard small business/family operation into a major industry that has succeeded even into the twenty-first century.

Roscoe Conkling was first elected mayor of Utica, then a U.S. congressman, and finally a U.S. senator. Credit: Library of Congress.

39

Gang of Brothers

E. Fuller Torrey

The story of the Loomis Gang is a rich piece of central New York history. This well-educated family of thieves pitted itself against local law enforcement officers and powerful U.S. Senator Roscoe Conkling, who took on the Loomises in a personal vendetta. Much of the action took place with the drums of the Civil War in the background and culminated in a fire and near-hanging. Ultimately, the good guys beat the bad guys—just like in the movies.

George Loomis, the gang's patriarch, was from the Connecticut Loomis family, which had founded the Loomis Chaffee School. The clan had many distinguished descendants. George's wife, Rhoda Mallot, was a schoolteacher. Of their twelve children, ten were systematically trained as thieves. By the 1840s, the family, headquartered at its farm near Waterville and Sangerfield in Oneida County just south of U.S. Route 20, was thriving through horse stealing and petty theft.

In the 1850s, as the Loomis boys achieved full maturity, their operations expanded into a full criminal enterprise. At its peak, the Loomis Gang numbered perhaps two hundred accomplices, in an area extending from the Finger Lakes to the Vermont border and from southern Ontario to northeastern Pennsylvania. Typically, a gang member might pilfer clothing from a store in Auburn, or steal a horse and bring it to the Loomis farm, where he would be paid. The Loomises would then take the stolen property to Amsterdam, Elmira, or Watertown to sell it at a handsome profit. Some of the proceeds were used to bribe local sheriffs and, it was rumored, members of the New York State Legislature, so that charges against the Loomises—when they were brought at all—never seemed to stick.

This essay first appeared in summer 2008, volume 8, number 1.

The Battle Is Joined

The Loomis family's temerity was perhaps best illustrated in 1864 in Morrisville, Madison County, where the courthouse mysteriously burned to the ground the night before three of the Loomis brothers were scheduled for trial. When the pumper was dragged from the firehouse, water poured from holes that had been cut in its hose, rendering it useless. Another Loomis brother was at the scene and, according to one account, "seemed to be utterly astonished when someone told him that the hose had been cut." All evidence against the family was lost with the courthouse.

However, Roscoe Conkling had taken on the Loomis family when he was a young Oneida County district attorney in 1850 by jailing one of the brothers. In retaliation, the Loomises delivered sufficient votes to Conkling's opponent in the next election to vote Conkling out of office. Given the Loomises' fiscal control of law enforcement officials and political influence over elected officials, they seemed invincible.

Enter Jim Filkins, a young blacksmith from North Brookfield, a village close to the Loomis farm. Filkins had an antipathy for the Loomis family; in 1858 he offered to become the local constable, since no one else wanted the job. Almost immediately he began serving warrants on members of the family and searching their farm. Meanwhile, in Utica, Roscoe Conkling had just been elected mayor, and he vowed to assist Filkins. The battle was now joined.

The fight between Constable Filkins and the Loomis family raged for the next seven years. The Loomises became increasingly bold and lawless, on one occasion even stealing indictments against them directly from the district attorney's office. In 1861, a young woman—the mistress of one of the brothers—was murdered at the Loomis home, although the family said it was an accident. In 1863, another Loomis brother was accused of rape and fled to Canada to avoid prosecution. Later that year, unknown persons (thought to be Loomis accomplices) shot Filkins at his home, but he survived.

Roscoe Conkling was elected to the U.S. House of Representatives in 1859, but he didn't forget the Loomises. In 1861 he took time out from his Washington duties to successfully defend Jim Filkins, who had been indicted for assault and battery against the Loomises by a Madison County judge on the Loomis payroll.

A Changed Landscape

With the end of the Civil War, Union Army veterans returned to home Waterville, Sangerfield, and other Oneida County villages. They had experienced great hardship, while the Loomises—none of whom had enlisted—had plundered the countryside and grown rich selling stolen horses to the Union Army. So a small group of veterans began meeting in a loft over a store in Waterville to discuss the Loomis problem.

At 2 a.m. on October 31, 1865, four figures moved silently through the night to the Loomis farm, where seventeen people were asleep. They called out for Wash Loomis, the leader of the brothers, and when he came out, they beat him to death. Next they called for Grove Loomis, the second in command, and beat him and set him on fire (although he survived). Two weeks later, Jim Filkins was indicted on charges of assault with intent to kill, arson, and murder. Since everyone knew that he had led the group against the Loomises, nobody gave him much chance of eluding conviction—but Roscoe Conkling immediately came to Filkins' defense and got him released on bail, which many local citizens offered to put up. By this time, the exploits of the Loomis Gang were known throughout the eastern United States. The *New York Tribune*, for example, carried the story of the raid under the headline "Mob Law in Oneida County." Even the *London Quarterly Review* published a long article on the Loomises under the headline "Crime in the State of New York."

The Loomis family and their accomplices thought Filkins was neutralized by the charges against him, and so they resumed their criminal activity. In December 1865 they committed another murder during the robbery of a farmer in Leonardsville and six months later shot Jim Filkins again during a raid he led on their farm.

Their Time Is Up

That was the final straw. At dawn on June 17, 1866, a mob of more than a hundred men from nearby villages surrounded the Loomis home. Everyone was ordered out of the house, which was set afire. A rope was thrown over the branch of a maple tree in the front yard and one of the gang members was brought forward. After hanging there for a few seconds, he became very talkative and disclosed everything he knew. The rope was next placed around the neck of Plumb Loomis, who was hung three separate times before he confessed. Grove Loomis, remembering his recent beating and burning, agreed to cease criminal activities even before the rope was placed around his neck.

This mob raid was effectively the end of the Loomis Gang, except for one outstanding item: the charges against Jim Filkins. Roscoe Conkling had the trial postponed twice, during which time he became a U.S. senator and one of the most powerful politicians in New York State. Filkins' trial eventually took place on June 3, 1867, amid great publicity. Despite Filkins' overwhelming evidence of guilt, Conkling argued that, for technical reasons, the "indictment was improperly and illegally found." A three-judge panel deliberated upon this for two hours and finally returned a verdict that agreed with Conkling. The *Utica Morning Herald* noted that this decision was followed by "loud applause in the courtroom."

The indictment against Filkins was never brought again. Senator Conkling would twice be offered a seat on the U.S. Supreme Court, which he refused, and would run unsuccessfully as a Republican presidential candidate in 1876. It is probable that none of the remaining Loomis Gang voted for him.

A woman leaves a baby in a basket at the New York Foundling Asylum. Credit: *Frank Leslie's Illustrated Newspaper*, December 25, 1869, collection of the New-York Historical Society, New York, New York.

40

"Poor Little Innocents"

Julie Miller

On the evening of June 28, 1838, a butcher named Ayres was walking along Manhattan's John Street when he saw a tall Irish woman in a calico dress lay a baby boy on the pavement and run away. Ayres, who had a stall in nearby Fulton Market, scooped the baby up and carried him to the offices of the city's almshouse, or poorhouse, located a few blocks north in City Hall Park. There he told his story to the clerk on duty. The clerk, practiced in the intake of foundlings, determined the baby's age (about five months) and assigned him a name, John Cliff, commemorating his discovery by Mr. Ayres at the intersection of Cliff and John Streets.

John was the eighteenth foundling collected by the almshouse since May 1 of that year. By May 1, 1839 (the almshouse year ran from May to May), the almshouse had taken in a total of eighty abandoned babies.

Economic Causes

How can we understand what happened that June evening? Why would a woman abandon her baby on the street? Why would so many other women do the same? The diary of Philip Hone, which documents life in antebellum New York, reveals some answers. In early 1837, a series of business collapses known as the Panic of 1837 led the country into a depression that lasted several years. Even before the Panic, prices in New York had become ruinously high. Hone was a wealthy man who had retired on the fortune he'd made in the auction business, but even he was affected by the turmoil. As he shopped for his family at the same Fulton Market where butcher Ayres

This essay first appeared in fall 2008, volume 8, number 2.

had his stall, Hone marveled at the cost of food. He empathized in his diary, "What is to become of the laboring classes?"

Poverty, especially the poverty of single women, was behind most instances of infant abandonment in Europe and the United States in the nineteenth century. During the first half of the century, America's economy expanded rapidly; New York, connected to Europe through its Atlantic seaport and to the center of the continent by the Erie Canal, was at the busy heart of the commercial effervescence that characterized this era. The economy drew immigrants to the city; John Cliff's mother may have been among them. At the same time, economic collapses like the Panic of 1837 occurred at intervals of approximately twenty years. In the depressions that followed, women were disproportionately affected.

Young men who came to New York to make their fortunes found many doors open to them. They could work as clerks in businesses that thrived on goods moving in and out of the seaport. They might apprentice at skilled trades, as butchers like Ayres did, or work in one of the new factories. They could train in lawyers' offices or attend college, medical school, or seminary. If they had only their strong backs to offer, they could work on the docks or at the building sites, waterworks, railways, and roads that were transforming the landscape during this period. These opportunities were often determined by connections and social class. But even men without class advantages could choose among a wider and better array of opportunities than women could. Women were limited to very few occupations. Most working women were servants, an occupation that contributed directly to infant abandonment, since few employers allowed their servants to keep their babies with them. Many others worked as seamstresses in the small workshops of the city's garment industry, or carried bundles of piecework home. Whatever they did, they earned less than men. Virginia Penny, a social investigator who surveyed women's occupations in New York and other cities between 1859 and 1861, found that men working in industry earned $1.50 or $2 per day, while women in comparable occupations earned only 50¢ to $1. Seamstresses earned notoriously low wages. "Our hearts sicken within us," Penny wrote, "as we read the prices paid needlewomen."

The story of the fifty-first baby abandoned in 1838 demonstrates the economic burden faced by mothers who had to cope on their own. When Eliza Pride's husband left her, poverty forced her into the almshouse where her daughter, Mary Jane, was born. Pride left the almshouse to work as a servant, paying a woman to care for her daughter out of the $5 she earned each month. It was the caretaker who brought six-month-old Mary Jane back to the almshouse when Pride did not keep up with her payments. When the almshouse official on duty told the caretaker he could not take the child until the following day, she simply left Mary Jane outside the office on her way out. The almshouse had no choice but to take the baby in.

Social Stigma

For unmarried mothers, the financial burden was compounded by another: shame. Once again, Philip Hone is illuminating. In December 1838 Hone was dining with friends at his home near Washington Square when the doorbell rang. A servant dispatched to answer it returned with a baby in a basket that had been left on the doorstep. Whoever had deposited the week-old boy was gone, but a note inside the basket implored, "Have compassion upon my poor orphan child . . . I am a poor friendless widow in a strange city." But Hone did not believe her. He subscribed to the widely held view that a foundling was the child of an unmarried mother who had abandoned her baby to preserve her honor by ridding herself of the evidence of her sexual misdeed. This was a simple reading of a complex problem, but it was true that most foundlings were born to single women.

"Poor little innocent," Hone commiserated in his diary, "—abandoned by its natural protector, and thrown at its entrance into life upon the sympathy of a selfish world, to be exposed, if it should live, to the sneers and taunts of uncharitable illegitimacy!" Hone's compassion, however, was limited. He had the baby repacked in his basket and sent to the almshouse office, where the clerk assigned him number fifty-five.

In 1838 Hone and many others believed that foundlings were a sad but normal part of urban life, products of the ineradicable social ills of poverty and illegitimacy. In the 1850s, however, New Yorkers' complacency about foundlings began to crack. One reason was the reform spirit of the age, which increasingly refused to tolerate the mistreatment of the vulnerable and downtrodden. Another was a rise in the number of foundlings. Between 1849 and 1859 the almshouse received approximately 322 foundlings each year. Compared to the numbers received by foundling asylums in European cities, this was not very many. Historian Rachel Fuchs determined that the Paris foundling asylum accepted an average of 3,704 foundlings yearly during the same decade. But New York had more foundlings than any other American city, and more than it had seen before. In 1851 one almshouse official reported that "the number of children abandoned by their parents at a very tender age is increasing yearly, and calls for prompt and energetic measures."

Civic Efforts

New Yorkers acted. Before the Civil War, only the almshouse cared for foundlings, but in 1857 the city began planning its first foundling asylum. Within a decade of the close of the war, New York had four asylums: the public Infant Hospital, built by the city on Randall's Island in the East River; the New York Foundling Asylum, run by the Catholic Sisters of Charity; the Protestant New York Infant Asylum, which also served as a home for unmarried mothers; and a foundling asylum and home for unwed mothers associated with the Nursery and Child's Hospital, a Protestant-run institution for poor and sick children. To varying degrees, and in keeping with the values of the time, each of these institutions saw its job as the moral reform of unwed mothers. But none succeeded in changing the circumstances or behavior of poor women, and, more seriously, none succeeded in keeping very many of its infant inmates alive. Hidden pregnancies, secret deliveries, and the dangers of exposure on the street all threatened foundlings' lives. Once inside the asylums, they were further weakened by infections passed from one infant to another (at a time when infection was little understood) and by an inadequate supply of wet nurses. By the first half of the 1880s, the four asylums struggled to maintain the 2,041 babies they received each year, both from outside and from mothers giving birth within their institutions. During the first decades of the twentieth century, all but the New York Foundling Asylum had closed its doors.

Social Reform

Yet despite these failures, the problem of New York's foundlings has resolved more positively than the experience of the nineteenth century would seem to predict. Today newspapers report the occasional discoveries of abandoned babies, and within the last decade most states, including New York, have passed "safe haven" laws that allow mothers to abandon infants at designated sites anonymously and without penalty. These laws are a response to a perception that infant abandonment is on the rise. A longer historical view shows that it is actually in precipitous decline. In 2006, just six babies were picked up on the streets of New York City.

The reasons for the decline lie in the broad social changes of the twentieth century that resulted in the improvement of women's lives. The devastating poverty that single working women experienced in the nineteenth century was significantly ameliorated as women gained access to educational and occupational opportunities previously unavailable to them. Poor mothers were assisted by the social safety net implemented by the federal government, in particular the Social Security Act of 1935. Birth control, abortion, and adoption all created important alternatives to abandonment. And the destigmatization of unmarried motherhood, particularly since the 1960s, has removed a significant factor behind infant abandonment. The result is that today most New Yorkers know foundlings only as fictional characters and have forgotten that they were once all too real.

Captured Africans bound for slavery are led into the hold of a ship. Credit: Photographs and Prints Division, Schomburg Center for Research in Black Culture, New York Public Library—Astor, Lenox, and Tilden Foundations.

41

"These Pimps of Piracy"

Ron Soodalter

Of all the cities in America, none was as invested in the Atlantic slave trade as New York. Whether in the Caribbean, West African, or Madagascar trade, New York financed, fitted out, and sent forth more slaving expeditions than any other port city, North or South. Although New York State voted to abolish slavery in 1827, the slave traders of New York City and the ports of New England continued to supply slaves—first to the South, then to Brazil and Cuba—right up to and during the Civil War.

However, there were laws that prohibited slave trafficking. Beginning just five years after George Washington's inauguration, Congress passed a series of laws specifically designed to curb the slave trade; these laws culminated in the Piracy Act of 1820, which specified the death penalty for slavers. Nonetheless, despite imposing penalties of fine, forfeiture, imprisonment, and death for violations, the trade grew as slavers came to realize that the laws were without teeth and that the government did virtually nothing to enforce them.

As late as 1857, the *New York Journal of Commerce* wrote,

> Few of our readers are aware . . . of the extent to which this infernal traffic is carried on, by vessels clearing from New York, and in close allegiance with our legitimate trade; and that down-town merchants of wealth and respectability are extensively engaged in buying and selling African Negroes, and have been, with comparative little interruption, for an indefinite number of years.

This essay first appeared in summer 2009, volume 9, number 1.

Although the money behind the expeditions may have been provided secretly by many of those respected merchants, the slave traders themselves were well known to the business community; some ranked among the city's most prominent members of society.

Corruption and Complicity

By 1860, New York City's reputation for official corruption and leniency toward slavers was unrivaled. It was home to an alarming number of Southern sympathizers, as well as a near-traitorous mayor, a thoroughly corrupt administration, a crooked, proslavery U.S. marshal, a less-than-aggressive district attorney, and a level of slave trade activity that reached gigantic proportions. In the year and a half ending in August 1860, New York City sent out nearly one hundred slaving expeditions. Many of these ships were New York–built steamers whose cargo capacity far exceeded that of earlier sailing ships. Although it was generally known that many of the city's wealthier merchants put a lot of money into the trade, there was no way to prove it. And whenever an attempt was made to impose controls on the traffic, New York's businessmen were among the most vocal opponents. In May, a resolution condemning the slave trade had been shouted down at a meeting of the American Tract Society of New York. Why make waves, these men of commerce reasoned, "simply because somebody takes a few niggers from the jungles of Africa to Cuba?"

Arrests at sea were rare due to the gross inefficiency of the navy's tiny, antiquated, and unmotivated African Squadron. During a six-year period in which its British counterpart seized over five hundred slave ships containing some forty thousand captives, the American squadron captured six vessels—one per year. And on the infrequent occasions when slavers were arrested and brought to trial in federal court, they were almost invariably released or given a token slap on the wrist. In New York City, where most of the Northern prosecutions took place, only one-sixth of those indicted were convicted. From 1837 to 1861, around one hundred and twenty-five accused slave traders—officers and crewmen—were prosecuted, but only twenty were given prison sentences, averaging two years apiece. Of those twenty men, ten received presidential pardons, and three more—indicted for capital crimes under the Piracy Act of 1820—were allowed to plead to lesser charges. One was briefly convicted of piracy, but the conviction was overturned on a technicality. Clearly no one in power wanted to hang a man for trafficking in slaves.

Skilled attorneys were employed by New York's established slave traders to defend accused captains and their crews. Ironically, a number of these lawyers were former U.S. and assistant U.S. attorneys, whose job it had been to prosecute the very men they were now paid to get off. Their defense arguments were transparent and absurd; nonetheless, New York's justices, judges, and juries regularly allowed slavers to walk out of court scot-free.

But attorneys did not rely on their arguments alone; payoffs and violence also helped. A June 1860 editorial in Horace Greeley's *New York Daily Tribune* described the state of "The Slave Trade in New York":

> It is a remarkable fact that the slave traders in this city have matured their arrangements so thoroughly that they almost invariably manage to elude the meshes of the law. Now they bribe a jury, another time their counsel or agents spirit away a vital witness . . . The truth is, the United States offices in Chambers Street, under the influences which have been brought to bear there, have become thoroughly corrupt. . . . To break up the African slave trade . . . it will be necessary to purge the courts and offices of these pimps of piracy, who are well known and at the proper time will receive their "just desserts."

Cohorts in Chicanery

However, these consequences would not occur as long as James J. Roosevelt was United States district attorney for the Southern District of New York. He had been a member of the state assembly, a congressman, and a justice of the New York Supreme Court. He also shared President James Buchanan's avowed refusal to hang a man for slave trading despite what the law stipulated.

The U.S. marshal—the man into whose sympathetic custody accused slavers were placed—was Isaiah Rynders. If any one man embodied the chicanery, bigotry, racism, corruption, and violence that infected New York City politics in the mid-1800s, he did. A Southern-born gambler and brawler, Rynders made his way to New York, and within a short time became boss of the city's gang-ridden Sixth Ward and the main "fixer" for the corrupt Democratic political machine known as the Tammany Ring. While elections were sometimes bought, they were almost always "directed" by the presence at the polls of Rynders' force of "head bangers," "shoulder hitters," and "repeaters."

Rynders and his gangs served three-time mayor Fernando Wood. Born a Philadelphia Quaker, Wood served a term in Congress, during which he was accused (but not convicted) of fraud. He won his first term as New York's mayor in 1854 by garnering four hundred more votes than there were voters in the Sixth Ward, and with the help of the Dead Rabbits Gang's ballot-box-smashing tactics, he carried the election by 9,651 votes. It was later claimed by his opponents that ten thousand of his votes were fraudulent. Corrupt to the bone, Mayor Wood bribed the police, sold public offices, and arranged for immediate naturalization of immigrants—conditional on their voting for him at election time. An article in *Harper's Weekly* in the 1850s asserted that New York under Wood was "a huge semi-barbarous metropolis . . . not well-governed nor ill-governed, but simply not governed at all." "Fernandy" Wood owed much of his success to Isaiah Rynders, who shared his boss' opposition to the liberation of African Americans, declaring them racially inferior and viewing slavery as a "divine institution."

The editor of the *New York Evening Post* observed that "New York belongs almost as much to the South as to the North." In addition to marketing the South's cotton crop, the city was the major supplier of factory-made cheap clothing and other articles for the outfitting and maintenance of slaves. In his 1858 campaign, Mayor Wood stated, "[T]he South is our best customer. She pays the best prices, and pays promptly." Wood's appeal to New York's Southern sympathizers, interlaced with his racist fear-mongering, won him the vote from the city's gentry and its businessmen who benefited from the slave industry, and from its working class who feared free blacks would take their jobs. After his reelection, Wood declared that "the profits, luxuries, the necessities—nay, even the physical existence [of the city] depend upon . . . continuance of slave labor and the prosperity of the slave master!"

Shortly after the 1860 election of Abraham Lincoln, South Carolina seceded from the Union, foreshadowing a series of events that threatened to plunge New York City into a severe economic crisis. Mayor Wood was quick to act. He proposed to the Common Council that New York City follow South Carolina's example and become an independent commonwealth, the Free City of Tri-insula ("Three islands" in Latin, referring to Long, Staten, and Manhattan Islands). As such, it would "make common cause with the South" and refuse to allow passage of Union troops through the city. The Common Council, whose habitual chicanery had earned them the epithet "The Forty Thieves," actually approved the plan, rescinding their approval only after the attack on Fort Sumter three months later would have made their actions treasonous.

Change and War in the Wind

Before the election, a young Maine sea captain named Nathaniel Gordon had been arrested at sea with nearly a thousand Africans confined in his ship's hold. He was taken to New York City and indicted under the Piracy Act of 1820. Marshal Rynders, for a bribe of $50 per night, allowed Gordon to roam the city at will and to entertain guests in his large minimum-security cell. A team of lawyers experienced in defending accused slavers took his case; so sure were they of an acquittal or a presidential pardon that they turned down a deal offered by Roosevelt to charge Gordon on a lesser count in exchange for the names of his backers.

But change was in the wind in 1860. The newly elected Republican administration swept "Fernandy" Wood, Roosevelt, and Rynders from office, replacing them with two honest and dedicated men: Marshal Robert Murray and U.S. Attorney E. Delafield Smith. Attorney Smith set out to eradicate the slave trade from New York City, and he made Nathaniel Gordon his personal demon. After two trials—the first ended in a hung jury, probably due to bribery—Smith got his conviction, and Gordon was sentenced to hang. After considering an appeal from the slaver's lawyer, President Lincoln withheld his customary mercy owing to the severe nature of the offense and allowed the execution to proceed; Nathaniel Gordon was hanged on February 21, 1862, in the courtyard of the Tombs, New York City's prison.

The slave traders were stunned; New York's newspapers exulted. The *Times*' response was typical: [T]he majesty of the law has been vindicated, and the stamp of the gallows . . . set upon the crime of slave-trading. . . . And it was time." In a letter to Interior Secretary Caleb Smith, U.S. Marshal Murray wrote,

> Since entering upon the duties of this office, I have made an earnest effort . . . to check the Slave Trade from the Port [of New York]. This City had become the principal depot for vessels in this traffic, and I felt that here the attempt must be made to arrest [it]. . . . I am satisfied that the parties interested have removed their operations from New York to the ports of New London, New Bedford, and Portland. Allow me to draw your attention to this, so that steps may be taken to prevent the clearance of slavers from the New England waters.

Slavers continued to operate—just not out of New York.

Although Gordon's execution shocked New York's slaving community, it did not have the hoped-for global impact. In fact, the slave trade actually took a brief upturn in the spring of 1862. With the price of slaves in the Congo at rock bottom and the Union Navy busy blockading Southern ports, the temptation was too great for many to resist; despite the presence of British patrol vessels, some American slavers still attempted the run to Cuba. Operating with virtually no American assistance, the British African Squadron captured sixteen American slavers between March and October 1862. But by 1863, the flow had become a trickle, and the following year the Spanish government reported that not a single slave had landed in Cuba. The African slave trade under the American flag had finally ended.

Tenement dwellers slept on roofs to escape the heat. Credit: Library of Congress.

42

The Scourge of Summer

Edward P. Kohn

On August 15, 1896, Theodore Roosevelt, then thirty-seven and president of the Board of Police Commissioners, wrote to his sister Anna about the horrible heat that had plagued New York City for the past ten days. "The heated term was the worst and most fatal we have ever known," Roosevelt noted. "The death-rate trebled until it approached the ratio of a cholera epidemic; the horses died by the hundreds, so that it was impossible to remove their carcasses, and they added a genuine flavor of pestilence." By comparing the number of deaths in Manhattan and Brooklyn during the same ten days, August 4 to 14 in 1895 and 1896, it is evident that the heat wave caused as many as 1,500 fatalities in New York City. It also affected a good portion of the central and eastern United States, from the Plains through St. Louis and Chicago to the cities of the East Coast. So it was a national phenomenon that August, and it was probably the worst urban heat wave disaster in American history.

Yet because of the nature of heat waves—killing slowly, with no physical manifestation, no property damage, and no single event that marks them as a disaster—the 1896 New York heat wave remains one of the least chronicled urban natural disasters in America, even though it took more lives than the New York City draft riots of 1863 or the Great Chicago Fire of 1871. With day after day of temperatures in the 90s, high humidity, and nighttime temperatures never below 70 degrees, the heat wave wore New Yorkers down and killed old and young, rich and poor. It took a particular toll on the urban poor, especially laborers who literally worked themselves to death. And for the most part, city officials stood by and did nothing, with the mayor only calling an emergency meeting of department heads more than a week into the crisis, when the heat wave was nearly over.

This essay first appeared in summer 2008, volume 8, number 1.

The Youngest and Oldest Victims

On Tuesday, August 4, after a fairly mild beginning to the month, temperatures in the high 80s arrived, accompanied by 90 percent humidity. According to the United States Weather Bureau, the high for New York City that day was 87 degrees. Yet as with virtually every day of the subsequent heat wave, the official temperature was recorded high above street level, at an elevation free of much of the radiation heat from brick, concrete, and asphalt and able to catch at least some breeze. Down at street level, thermometers regularly recorded temperatures several degrees higher than the official reading, while temperatures inside the brick tenements of the Lower East Side easily reached 120 degrees.

According to death certificates filed in Manhattan on August 4, the first victim of the heat wave may have been fifteen-month-old Hyman Goldman. Hyman had arrived from Russia with his family only nine months before. For three weeks he had been suffering from what nineteenth-century doctors called "cholera infantium," a common diarrhea that afflicted children during the summer months and often proved fatal. Already weakened, Hyman had little reserve strength when the heat settled upon his family's tenement apartment at 55 Broome Street. According to the doctor, the direct cause of his death was "Exhaustion." Irma O'Brien, age four months and eighteen days, also died on August 4, from "Tubercular meningitis," although the doctor listed "Heat" as the indirect cause of death. Over the next ten days, doctors in Manhattan alone filled out over 2,200 death certificates—almost double the number during the same period in 1895—using various euphemisms for describing victims of the heat. Many infant deaths were caused by "Summer diarrhea" or "Convulsions," while adults died from "Asthemia," "Exhaustion," "Thermic fever," "Heatstroke," "Sunstroke," and "Insolation."

Like the very young, the elderly were also most at risk. Perhaps the heat wave's oldest victim was Catherine Clark, age 103, a widowed housewife who had emigrated from Ireland sixty-three years before. Living in a rear tenement at 430 East 13th Street, Catherine had long suffered from chronic bronchitis, another common ailment among the poor of the Lower East Side. Yet her doctor made a point of noting on her death certificate that her "Hearing & Sight & Cheerfulness Were Fine" when he had last attended to her. Her cause of death, he wrote, was "Bronchitis & Heat." The contributing cause: "Old Age."

Workers Die, Survivors Are Desperate

In the end, it was New York's workers who suffered the most. Working through the hellish heat killed hundreds. John Singer was typical of the young and healthy laborers who literally worked to death. Forty-five years old, married, and living in a tenement on Avenue B, Singer was a silver molder—already a hot occupation—and fell ill on August 11, struggling for life during the hottest night of the heat wave. The official temperature on August 11 never dropped below 76 degrees, although it was probably much warmer inside Singer's brick tenement. When he succumbed the next morning, the doctor listed the cause of death as "Heat Stroke," with the indirect cause "Summer Heat."

For most New Yorkers, there was simply no relief available. Even ice was a precious commodity. Home refrigerators did not achieve widespread use until World War I; before that, Americans relied on large wooden iceboxes, usually lined with tin or zinc, to keep food cool and fresh. Ice was purchased from commercial producers or ice harvesters, who cut it from the rivers during winter and stored it in large blocks insulated with sawdust to reduce melting. Yet it remained expensive. This inspired Theodore Roosevelt to suggest that the city purchase and distribute ice to the poor.

"I had to be in town several nights," Roosevelt wrote his sister, "and I saw some strange and pathetic scenes when the ice was distributed." On August 13, Roosevelt supervised the distribution of one hundred tons of ice in ten-pound blocks from the police precinct houses. Two hundred thousand pounds of ice meant that about twenty thousand blocks were distributed (which cost the city $325), but still it was not enough. The police stations were mobbed. With the ice gone, Roosevelt recommended that two hundred tons be given away the next day, a number that eventually rose to three hundred and fifty tons. Roosevelt noted some fraud in the process, with ice being resold and wealthy parents sending their children for free ice. The police took to asking the children what their fathers did for a living. When one girl was asked where her father was, she replied, "I don't know, sir, we haven't seen him for six months and mother is sick and can't work." The *New York Times* described the sad scene: "Half-fed children, barely able to drag themselves about, were sent by their parents to carry away ten pounds of ice." Some children waited in line two hours. At the busy Madison Street precinct house, which distributed ice to about 1,500 people on August 14, the ice was late in arriving, so hundreds of impatient children, armed with pots and pans, started banging them together, creating a "deafening din."

"The Days of Death Continue"

On August 11 the heat wave reached its height, with an official high temperature of 94 degrees (although much hotter on the street) and high humidity. The *New York Times* wrote, "The days of death continue. The sun is still unwearied of scourging." That day the heat contributed to as many as two hundred and fifty deaths in Manhattan, with another one hundred in Brooklyn, and almost three hundred people were admitted to hospitals. New Yorkers seemed to go mad, killing each other and themselves. Because the city did not lift its ban on sleeping in parks, people took refuge on their tenement roofs or down on the piers, and inevitably some fell to their deaths or drowned. Every salivating dog on the street was labeled "mad" and was gunned down by a police officer. The SPCA reported that five hundred horses had died in the previous five days due to heat. Residents of 96th Street complained that sixteen horses belonging to the Second Avenue Railroad Company had died and were still lying in the street, while in a short walk one reporter counted more than a dozen dead horses. In his *Autobiography* (1913), Roosevelt would later recount the story of a shopkeeper who complained of a dead horse that had laid in front of his business for several days. When the city finally sent a giant cart containing eleven other dead horses to take the carcass away, the cart broke down. The man, Roosevelt remembered, sent "a final pathetic letter in which he requested us to remove either the horses or his shop, he didn't care which."

The heat wave finally broke on August 14: the high temperature was only 80 degrees, and the nighttime temperature fell to 70 degrees for the first time in ten days. With the official response limited to the initiative of individuals like Roosevelt, and some private charities already giving away free ice, it is not surprising that the city only opened "ice stations" for the poor beginning in 1919. Still, the heat wave may have contributed to the debate over tenement conditions among the poor and to the subsequent passage of the Tenement House Law of 1901 that mandated better ventilation for urban housing.

Portent of the Future?

Today, heat remains the country's biggest natural disaster killer, claiming on average more lives than earthquakes, floods, tornadoes, and hurricanes combined. Recent heat waves around the world reinforce heat's ability to kill: 1,700 were killed in the 1980 U.S. heat wave; more than 700 people died in Chicago in 1995; and the European heat wave of 2003 contributed to an estimated 52,000 deaths, 15,000 in France alone. Most scientists agree that the number of extreme heat waves will increase, and the World Meteorological Organization estimates that the number of heat-related fatalities could double in less than twenty years. Yet people died in 2003 and 1995 for the same reasons they died in 1896: heat sources in the city, particulate matter in the air, and the very architecture of cities; employers who took no precautions for their workers, who literally worked themselves to death; no access to air conditioning or cool water; and nothing done to aid the most vulnerable, the very young and the very old. Thus, the 1896 New York heat wave can still give us clues as to how cities should and shouldn't respond to future heat waves, so lives can be saved.

Samuel Clemens, also known as Mark Twain. Credit: Library of Congress.

43

Mark Twain and Elmira

Mark Woodhouse

For most people, the pen name Mark Twain conjures up visions of the American heartland: steamboats on the Mississippi River, Tom Sawyer, Huck Finn, and the idyllic fictional village of St. Petersburg, based on Samuel Clemens' boyhood home, Hannibal, Missouri.

Clemens, however, was a citizen of the world. He traveled widely, and many places can lay claim to him by virtue of his having visited, lived, and worked in them. People are often surprised to learn, then, that his art and life are most deeply entwined with New York State, particularly Elmira, where much of his best-known work took shape.

The Siege of Olivia

Clemens' connection with Elmira began when, as a young reporter from the West, he was commissioned in 1867 by a California newspaper to accompany and report on a group of travelers to Europe and the Holy Land on board the steamship *Quaker City*. One of the travelers with whom Clemens struck up an acquaintance was Charles Langdon of Elmira.

As legend has it, while anchored in the Bay of Smyrna, Langdon showed Clemens a picture of his sister, Olivia, and Clemens immediately fell in love. How true you find this story to be depends on the degree of the romantic in you, but at least there is evidence that Clemens was made aware of Olivia while on the voyage and that his interest in her was piqued. In the months after the journey, at a lecture by Charles Dickens in New York City, Clemens met Olivia Langdon and her parents for the first

This essay first appeared in winter 2011, volume 10, number 3.

time. Shortly after this, he took the Langdons up on their invitation to visit Elmira. By this time, he was most certainly in love, and he began his courtship of Olivia.

Olivia's father, Jervis Langdon, was a prominent Elmira businessman who had made his fortune primarily in lumber and coal. A member of the Congregationalist Park Church that had formed from a split with the Presbyterians over the question of slavery, Jervis had also been active in the Underground Railroad and had served as a founding member of the board of trustees of Elmira Female College, the first college to grant degrees to women equal to those awarded to men at the time. Into this upper-class and progressive society came Sam Clemens, the self-educated, rough-hewn Westerner who, in relatively short order, was asking for the hand of Jervis' daughter.

For his part, Clemens was in demand as a lecturer, and his book based on the *Quaker City* voyage, *The Innocents Abroad*, was about to make him well known as a writer. But he was by no means regarded as the perfect suitor. Nonetheless, after some encounters in which Jervis Langdon took careful measure of the man, consent was granted, and Sam and Olivia were married in February 1870 at the Langdon home. Two ministers presided: Reverend Joseph Twichell of Hartford, and Elmira's Reverend Thomas K. Beecher, pastor of Park Church and a member of the prominent family that included Harriet Beecher Stowe, Henry Ward Beecher, and the feminist Catherine Beecher.

"Rest and Be Thankful"

As a wedding present, Jervis Langdon surprised the newlyweds with a home on Delaware Avenue in Buffalo, since Clemens had recently acquired part interest in the newspaper *Buffalo Express*. Sam and Livy remained in Buffalo only a little over a year before moving to Hartford, Connecticut, which would remain their primary residence for the next twenty years. But beginning in 1870 and continuing until 1889, their summer months were spent in Elmira, where they stayed with Olivia's adopted sister, Susan Crane, and her husband, Theodore, at their home, Quarry Farm. It was on East Hill overlooking the Chemung River and the town of Elmira, a place Clemens called "Rest and Be Thankful."

During these summers, Clemens settled in to work. By his own admission, life in Hartford offered many distractions, while the relatively quiet life at Quarry Farm allowed him to "pile up manuscripts" at a more satisfying rate. Susan Crane had a small octagonal study built for him farther up the hill above the farm. In one letter of 1883, he wrote, "[I]t's like old times to step right into the study and sail right in and sail right on, the whole day long, without thought of running short of stuff or words."

In his time at Quarry Farm, Clemens wrote major portions of his best-known works, including *The Adventures of Tom Sawyer*, *The Adventures of Huckleberry Finn*,

Life on the Mississippi, and *A Connecticut Yankee at King Arthur's Court*. In an interview with a *Chicago Tribune* reporter in 1886, he remarked that "this may be called the home of *Huckleberry Finn* and other books of mine, for they were written here."

In addition, Clemens' first piece for the *Atlantic Monthly* in November 1874, entitled "A True Story, Repeated Word for Word as I Heard It," recounts an evening on the porch during which Auntie Cord, the cook at Quarry Farm and an ex-slave, tells the story of the painful separation from her children and serendipitous reunion with her son. This was the most overt appearance of Quarry Farm in Mark Twain's work, but other references to Clemens' time and work there are abundant in his letters and notebooks.

One notable letter to William Dean Howells in 1877 tells of John Lewis, a black man who owned land near Quarry Farm. Lewis figured as the hero in a harrowing incident in which a runaway horse and buggy bearing Charles Langdon's wife, their daughter Julia, and a nursemaid sped down the steep East Hill and was stopped by Lewis, who blocked the road with his own wagon and grabbed the bridle of the runaway, at great risk to his own life. Clemens' vivid depiction of the incident shows the warm regard he had for Lewis.

The relationships revealed in both of these episodes are useful as part of the complicated conversation regarding Clemens' attitude toward race. Evidence from the farm has also contributed to a more complete picture of Clemens' other complexities as a man and as an artist. Some of this material was only discovered and made available to scholars in 1982, after the generous gift of Quarry Farm to Elmira College by Jervis Langdon, Jr.

Discoveries in Elmira

For instance, many books at the farm were found to contain marginalia by Clemens. These annotations, and the books themselves, speak to his wide-ranging interests and intellectual curiosity. The casual reader, exposed only to the carefully contrived public persona of Mark Twain as a self-taught, simple humorist, might not be prepared for his insightful remarks in such titles as Carlyle's *French Revolution* and William Edward Hartpole Lecky's *History of European Morals*. Similarly, those who have noted Mark Twain's casually intimate conversational style on the lecture platform might be fascinated by Livy's copy of the poems of Robert Browning, which Clemens marked extensively with stress marks and stage directions for the readings he gave in Elmira homes, revealing his meticulous attention to preparation and presentation.

Another unusual artifact is the "Sermon in Stones," a stone split into three slices. On the flat surfaces, Clemens wrote a verse in response to a friendly argument with

Mrs. Thomas Beecher over the question of life after death. Mrs. Beecher, the wife of a minister, predictably argued for an afterlife, while Clemens came down with characteristic humor on the side of there being nothing at all after this life. The stones and the subject of the verse, besides giving further evidence of Clemens' many friendships with clergy, offer a glimpse of his interest in theology and philosophical matters.

Among Clemens' other acquaintances in Elmira were prominent progressives of the time. Zebulon Brockway, the superintendent of the Elmira Reformatory and a pioneer in methods of rehabilitation for prisoners, was a friend; Clemens spoke to the reformatory's inmates on more than one occasion. Rachel Brooks Gleason and her husband, Silas, ran Watercure Sanitarium; she was a respected physician at a time when the profession was not always welcoming to women. She cared for Livy and attended the births of the Clemens children.

Continuing Connections

After 1889, financial difficulties and business setbacks forced Clemens to live abroad for a number of years, but in July 1895 the family gathered at Quarry Farm once again prior to embarking on an around-the-world lecture tour designed to free Clemens from his money worries. Daughters Susy and Jean stayed behind at Quarry Farm, while Sam, Livy, and daughter Clara made the long trip that was eventually chronicled in *Following the Equator*. Tragically, Susy, who had returned to the Hartford home in the interim, died of spinal meningitis while her parents were still abroad.

After her death, the Clemenses never lived in the Hartford home again. They returned to the United States in 1900, living first in Manhattan and then in Riverdale on the Hudson. In 1903, Sam and Livy returned to Quarry Farm for a brief visit before moving to Florence, Italy, where Livy died in 1904; afterward, Sam lived in a leased home on Fifth Avenue in New York City until 1908. He built his final residence, Stormfield, in Redding, Connecticut, where he died in 1910. His final visit to Elmira was in 1907, for the dedication of a new organ at Park Church. He is buried in the Langdon plot in Woodlawn Cemetery in Elmira alongside Olivia, his three daughters, and one son, all but one of whom preceded him in death.

The connection with Elmira College, where Olivia had been enrolled as a student in 1858 and 1859 and where her father was a trustee, continued with Ida Langdon, Charles' daughter, who taught English at the college from 1920 to 1942. Ida spoke at the dedication of the Mark Twain Study, which was moved from its East Hill location to the Elmira College campus in 1952, thirty years before her nephew, Jervis Jr., gave Quarry Farm to the college and the Center for Mark Twain Studies was established.

John Surratt as a papal guard. Credit: Library of Congress.

44

The Conspirator Who Got Away

G. William Beardslee

On November 26, 1866, the *New York Times* excitedly announced the imminent arrival in the United States of the last Lincoln "conspirator," John Surratt, Jr., who had finally been found living under an alias in Rome, Italy. After escaping from Italy, he was captured in Egypt; now he was on his way to the United States aboard a specially chartered ship.

Surratt was rightly seen as the key to the great unanswered question surrounding Lincoln's assassination: did John Wilkes Booth act independently, or was he the instrument of a larger and as-yet-unidentified conspiracy? By fall 1866, Booth and those directly connected to him—George Atzerodt, David Herold, Lewis Powell (aka Payne), Samuel Arnold, Edman Spangler, Michael O'Laughlen, Dr. Samuel Mudd, and John Surratt's mother, Mary Surratt—had either been executed or imprisoned on a remote island in the Gulf of Mexico. It was hoped that Surratt's capture, arrest, and subsequent trial would lift the veil and "obtain from his lips the information which will shed the light of day upon the most difficult as well as interesting criminal mystery of our time."

Over a century and a half, at least seven conspiracy theories have each had their moments of popularity and historical significance. From the moment of Lincoln's death, coming almost immediately after the end of the Civil War, speculation about conspiracy began. The simultaneous attacks on Lincoln and Secretary of State William Seward, and the later failed attack on Vice President Andrew Johnson, all suggested a coordinated plot of some sophistication. One theory centered not only on John Wilkes Booth but also on John Surratt as Booth's alleged coconspirator—especially Surratt's activities, mission, and escape from central New York in April 1865, where he had

This essay first appeared in spring 2011, volume 10, number 4.

been sent by Confederate authorities to obtain information and hopefully launch chaos and civil unrest.

Southern Spy

In 1852, eight-year-old John Surratt was living with his parents, John Sr. and Mary Jenkins Surratt, and his two siblings on a twenty-eight-acre tract of land in rural Maryland. Unlike many other women of her era, Mary was educated; she had attended the well-regarded Roman Catholic Winifred Martin's School in Alexandria, Virginia. The Surratt property soon featured a tavern and post office and was designated an official polling site. "Surratt's Hotel" or "Surrattsville" soon became a popular local community center where travelers stopped for food, drink, rest, and inevitable political discussions.

In 1862, John Sr. died suddenly, and the family's financial circumstances dramatically changed. Mary rented out the Surrattsville tavern and moved to a Washington, D.C., townhouse at 541 H Street that she converted into a boardinghouse. She also enrolled eighteen-year-old John Jr. at a seminary at the nearby Catholic St. Charles College in Maryland. At about the same time, John began serving the Confederacy as a courier and occasional spy. During the next several years, he smuggled information (probably related to prisoners of war) out of Washington and traveled between Richmond and Montreal, where a branch of the Confederate secret service operated freely. In an 1870 speech, Surratt commented on his spying activities:

> We had a regular established line from Washington [down] to the Potomac, and I being the only unmarried man on the route . . . had most of the hard riding to do. I devised various ways to carry the dispatches—sometimes in the heel of my boots, sometimes between planks of the buggy.

It is thought that Surratt obtained much of this sensitive information from his friend Louis J. Weichmann, a fellow seminarian at St. Charles College who was also a clerk in the Union War Department and a boarder at his mother's H Street boardinghouse. In the course of these clandestine activities, Surratt met John Wilkes Booth in December 1864 and invited him to the boardinghouse, where the famous actor was already a regular visitor.

Fateful Involvement

Booth's initial plans did not include the assassination of Lincoln. Rather, his objective was to capture the president, transport him to Richmond, and exchange him for

Confederate prisoners of war held in Northern camps such as "Hellmira" in Elmira, New York, which between summer 1864 and April 1865 held over twelve thousand captives (of those, about three thousand died) in wretched and inhumane conditions. On at least one occasion in early 1865, Surratt participated with Booth and others in an unsuccessful attempt to abduct Lincoln as he traveled from the White House to the Old Soldier's Home on North Capitol Street. But the conspirators discovered someone other than the president—perhaps Treasury Secretary Samuel Chase—in the carriage. There is also evidence of another equally unsuccessful attempt to kidnap Lincoln as he attended Ford's Theatre.

When the Confederacy collapsed in spring 1865, many Confederates believed that rather than surrender, Southerners should engage in a protracted guerilla war for independence, emulating the tactics of another Virginian, George Washington, during the Revolution. General Edwin Gray Lee, a cousin of Robert E. Lee and the chief representative of the Confederacy in Canada, was a proponent of this plan. In response to his cousin's surrender on April 9, he stated, "I cannot and will not believe that because General Lee was compelled to surrender 22,000 men, we therefore have no more armies, and can wage war no more."

The day before the evacuation of Richmond by Confederate forces on April 3, John Surratt left Richmond for Montreal with secret intelligence dispatches from the Confederacy's secretary of state, Judah P. Benjamin, to General Edwin Lee. Surratt carried these in a book—ironically, the autobiography of abolitionist John Brown. Traveling north via Baltimore, New York City, and Albany, Surratt arrived in Montreal only to learn that Richmond had surrendered. After meeting with General Lee, Surratt was sent on a secret mission to the small central New York city Elmira. Surratt was to obtain detailed information about "Hellmira," including its dimensions, internal diagrams, exterior drawings, the number of guards and cannon, and availability of small arms.

The real purpose of Surratt's mission to Elmira was preliminary reconnaissance for a planned Confederate liberation of the camp's prisoners, who would then supposedly wage guerrilla warfare against the Union in central New York. As Surratt later said, "General Edwin Lee came to my room, and told me he had a plan . . . to release the Confederate prisoners in Elmira. . . . He said he had sent many there, but they always got frightened, and only half executed their orders."

On the Run

Surratt arrived in Elmira on April 13 and registered at the Brainard Hotel as "John Harrison." After covertly observing and sketching the prison on April 14, he allegedly learned of Lincoln's assassination and Booth's involvement in it on the morning of April

15. Panicked by his relationship with Booth, Surratt's subsequent escape route relied almost exclusively on sanctuaries provided by a variety of Roman Catholic priests and institutions—until his capture in Alexandria, Egypt, in November 1866.

Surratt fled Elmira on April 15 and went to Canandaigua, New York; perhaps he hoped to transfer to the Baltimore train and return to Richmond. Unfortunately—or fortunately, as this delay provided a persuasive alibi later at his trial—there was no train to Baltimore until the following Monday, April 18. So Surratt registered at a local hotel, and, after learning he had been mistakenly identified as William Seward's attacker, changed plans and traveled directly to Canada via Albany and St. Albans, Vermont.

In disguise, Surratt successfully crossed the border and registered at Montreal's St. Lawrence Hotel. Almost immediately he was taken to the home of John Porterfield, a well-known Confederate agent and former Nashville banker who had attempted to sabotage Northern currency. Four days later, Surratt, now known as "Charles Armstrong," was taken from Montreal to the small village of St. Liboire, where he lived in the rectory of Father Charles Boucher, the local Roman Catholic priest.

Approximately three months later, Surratt was moved again, under the protection of a second Roman Catholic priest, Father La Pierre, to the latter's relative's house in Montreal. During this period, Surratt learned of his mother's arrest and military tribunal trial in connection with Lincoln's murder; the trial commenced on May 9, 1865, and concluded in late June. Curiously, the tribunal sentenced her to hang but signed a letter recommending clemency. Later Surratt claimed he had been assured by his Confederate contacts that Mary's case was meritless—thereby at least partially explaining why he never asserted his mother's innocence. Mary Surratt was hanged on July 7, 1865.

In September, Fathers Boucher and La Pierre delivered Surratt to the SS *Peruvian* bound for Liverpool. Once he arrived, Surratt became "John McCarty" and was lodged in the oratory of the Roman Catholic Church of the Holy Cross. He stayed in Liverpool long enough to collect money and then departed for Rome via London and Paris. In Rome he was concealed in the English College, a Roman Catholic institution, and in April 1866, having become "Giovanni Watson," he enlisted in the Papal Zouaves, part of the army of Pope Pius IX.

However, Surratt's true identity was soon discovered by a fellow Zouave, and after his arrest by Papal authorities he somehow "escaped" prior to his planned transfer to American authorities. Traveling to Naples, he adopted a third alias, "John Agostina," and boarded the SS *Tripoli* bound for Alexandria. But, detained by an unexpected and lengthy port quarantine, Surratt was finally arrested aboard the USS *Swatara* in Alexandria and taken to Washington for trial.

Life after Lincoln

Unlike the military tribunal trial of his mother and the other conspirators, Surratt's trial was held before a civil jury in a federal district court. After sixty-two days and hundreds of witnesses, the jury was unable to reach a unanimous verdict. A second set of charges—conspiracy and treason—was brought, but these were ultimately dismissed under the statute of limitations.

Released from federal custody, John Surratt eventually moved to Baltimore, where he worked as a clerk/auditor for the Baltimore Steam Packet Company for nearly five decades, married Mary Victorine Hunter, a second cousin of Francis Scott Key, and raised seven children. At his death on April 21, 1916, he was the last surviving person associated with the Lincoln assassination "conspiracy"—and was generally considered to be "the one who got away."

Shaker community in Watervliet, New York, ca. 1870. Photographed by James Irving. Credit: Shaker Museum and Library, Old Chatham and New Lebanon, New York.

45

Divorce Decreed

Ilyon Woo

One freezing February night in 1815, three young children, George, Susan, and Julia Chapman, disappeared from a Shaker village in Watervliet, just outside Albany, New York. This was not the first time the Chapman children had gone missing, nor would it be the last. During the course of an epic, five-year ordeal that would rock the state and beyond, they would be "taken captive" a total of three times: once stolen from their home, once whisked away from Shaker grounds, and once thrown into a runaway carriage by the glare of torchlight. Their case would go down in history, thanks to the energies of their remarkable mother, Eunice Hawley Chapman, who stopped at nothing in her quest to recover them.

A Troubled Household

Eunice Chapman's difficulties began long before her children first went missing. She had been miserably married for years when her troubled, alcoholic husband, James Chapman, abandoned her in Durham (Greene County), southwest of Albany. He sold their home and most of their possessions before departing, leaving Eunice and the children, who were just six, five, and two years old, to fend for themselves. It was July 1811, and the nation was on the brink of war.

Eunice endured severe trials as she struggled to support her family, but these were nothing compared to what she suffered when her husband suddenly returned to

This essay first appeared in spring 2011, volume 10, number 4.

Durham more than a year later. During his sabbatical from husbandly duties, James Chapman had followed a dissolute course, allegedly carousing in the vice dens of New York City. In the fall of 1812, however, he had encountered the Shaker community in Watervliet.

The Shakers are famous today for the quality of their durable craft items and their unadorned, functional furniture. In the early nineteenth century, however, they were known as a radical and ascetic religious sect, extreme in their promises and demands. They guaranteed salvation, and their gleaming villages and rich larders seemed to assure their promise of creating a heaven on earth. Yet their heaven also exacted a great price, requiring converts to renounce all earthly bonds, including those of family, property—and sexuality. The Shakers demanded celibacy of all their members, even married couples, who became "Brothers and Sisters" in the eyes of God.

Ann Lee, the charismatic, eighteenth-century English visionary who had first brought the Shakers to America, was a woman for whom sexuality was synonymous with misery. According to Shaker lore, Lee had been traumatized by witnessing her mother's repeated struggles in childbirth; later, Lee herself suffered through an excruciating series of labors. None of her children lived past infancy, and she was reborn as a different kind of mother: Mother of the Shakers.

The Shakers' Allure

The sect and its demands might seem to have been an unlikely fit for a man of appetites such as James Chapman, who was known for his philandering as well as his drinking. But among these unusual people, James experienced a sudden spiritual awakening, which inspired him to give up all that he had in the world and join them. Urged by the Shakers to make things right with his kin, James abruptly returned to Durham—after the Shakers had made it clear that they would not admit him unless he made arrangements for his wife and children. It was James' hope that Eunice might embrace salvation as well.

Though the Shakers were known for their generosity and equitable views toward women, Eunice wanted nothing to do with them. Soon the conflict between James and Eunice spiraled out of control, until Eunice returned home to Durham one October day and found that her children were missing. As she recalled in her personal narrative, *Account of the Conduct of the People Called Shakers*:

> [M]y house was desolate! No sound of my babes' footsteps was heard running to meet me and welcome my return. My sister, with difficulty, assisted

> me to again enter those dismal apartments, and when I did, they echoed with my groans! In vain my friends and neighbors came in to soothe my distracted mind! All my troubles which I had thought were insurmountable fled before this; and I said I never knew grief till now! Those who have had their friends taken captive by the savage, can better realize my feelings than I can describe!

Eunice quickly learned that James had come for the children while she was away, that he had chased them down one by one over the protests of her sister, and that he had driven off with them to the Watervliet Shaker community. This was what might be called the children's first "captivity."

Determined to reclaim them, Eunice traveled to Watervliet, where she had a disastrous confrontation with her husband and the Shakers. Eventually, she encountered even worse news. In February 1815, she learned that James and the children had vanished, and no one would say where they had gone. Eunice was sure that the Shakers had secreted them away in another one of their villages—there were Shaker communities across the nation, as far north as Maine and as far south as Kentucky—but she had no proof. The Shakers maintained their innocence, insisting that the children had not been taken captive a second time, as their mother suggested, but that they had simply left the village with their father.

Asserting Her Rights

Eunice Chapman was in no position to fight back. As a married woman, she could not own property, earn wages, or sign contracts on her own. She had few, if any, rights as a mother: if her husband wanted to take the children to the Shakers, that was his prerogative. A father could not be considered a captor of his children, since they belonged to him, and his wife's duty was to follow his lead, not to question it—much less make her private troubles public.

Eunice did fight back, however, in a sensational bid for her children that would result in historic changes to New York law and special rights for herself, at least, that would make her a woman nearly two hundred years ahead of her time. Although paternal prerogative was presumed, and nothing in state law indicated how a woman might obtain custody of her children, Eunice went to Albany and lobbied the New York State Legislature for her maternal rights. At a time when divorces were granted exclusively for the cause of adultery, Eunice demanded a release from her marital bonds on the grounds that her husband's abandonment of his family for the Shakers, her deprivation by him of her children, and the larger threat to the institution of marriage posed by the Shakers, required legal action.

Not everyone in Albany was sympathetic to Eunice's cause. Though her champions praised her as an "ornament to her sex," others derided her as a "modern enchantress," suggesting that she was a dangerous creature who capitalized on her personal charms to wreak havoc on an innocent faith. In 1818, Assemblyman Nathan Williams was quoted in the *Albany Gazette and Daily Advertiser* as saying:

> Sirs, this Eunice Chapman is not one of those modest, retiring, deserving women, for whom we should entertain a sympathy. She has been boldly courting public opinion for years, instead of concealing her griefs, if she has any. No modest woman would conduct herself thus. No modest and virtuous woman would be harassing the legislature year after year, and barely and avowedly for the purpose of obtaining the liberty of marrying another man. Such a female can only be an object of disgust—if nothing else, for her impudence.

But Eunice remained undeterred by such commentary and instead focused her energies on using the popular media for her cause in her unique way. In an era when "respectable" women were not welcome in the public sphere, Eunice crafted a dazzling persona as a vulnerable, wronged heroine who was making her pleas to save not just herself and her children but many other women experiencing the same fate. Stunning, charismatic, and notoriously seductive, Eunice combined personal appeal with writerly skills to powerful effect. As she told her tragic tale to "the ladies" and lawmakers, she pumped out thrilling narratives of Shaker captivity that preyed upon public anxieties and enchanted an early American readership. Published to acclaim decades before the advent of the "penny press," which popularized such writings, these moving literary tell-alls were also ahead of their time.

The Albany public responded in kind. At the height of the debates about her case, the assembly was crowded beyond capacity, with spectators taking up every available seat and even pouring into the aisles. The case generated an unprecedented degree of heat and sexual commentary, which was deemed so inappropriate at times that many people walked out. It was said that lawmakers lost their heads over Eunice Chapman, overcome with both folly and lust. There was even a play in circulation—called *Indoctum Parliamentum*, or the "unschooled parliament"—that satirized Eunice's hold on the Capitol, a three-act farce that climaxed with hundreds of wiseacres rolling barrels of whiskey into the legislature and Eunice dancing promiscuously with each one.

Stunning Victory

There were no hogsheads of whiskey, but there was a genuine furor when Eunice triumphed in the legislature in 1818. After a three-year battle, she achieved the unthinkable: unprecedented access to custody, and the only legislative divorce ever granted in the history of New York. During the process, her actions also led to the first-ever custody law in New York State in 1815. Her victory in the legislature was a legal milestone that cast a long shadow on the laws of New York: it is still remarkable that Eunice Chapman obtained an instant release from her marital bonds on exceptional grounds—and without a trial—in a state where, until 1966, adultery was the sole criterion for ending a marriage and unilateral no-fault divorce was signed into law only in August 2010.

But the legal drama was only part of Eunice's story: Eunice still did not know where her children were. Her tale would come to a close not in the orderly halls of justice but in a faraway Shaker village at midnight, where vigilante justice trumped the law. In a final act of captivity, and with the help of a mob, Eunice herself forcibly removed her eldest child from a Shaker village in Enfield, New Hampshire. She reclaimed her other two children more peaceably in 1819, achieving a perfect Hollywood ending.

New York in the 1900s

Nelson Rockefeller. Credit: New York State Archives, Albany, New York.

46

Rockefeller in Retrospect

Joseph E. Persico

Memory is fallible. When Simon and Schuster asked if I were interested in doing a book about Nelson Rockefeller, I thought I could write it off the top of my head. I had been, after all, his chief speechwriter for eleven years, while he served as New York's governor and as Gerald Ford's vice president. My intention was to write a highly personal memoir of those years. I soon discovered, however, that memory was not enough.

Fortunately, I had kept copies of every memorandum that had passed between the governor and me, as well as copies of all his speech drafts with his handwritten notations. I had also retained transcripts of his numerous press conferences. But I found that I could not complete the book without consulting the Rockefeller material housed in the New York State Archives and Library. Not only were these depositories invaluable for the information they contained, but they helped jog my memory about other personal incidents.

For example, one of the last speeches filed in the Rockefeller public papers before he resigned as governor in late 1973 was his dedication of the Empire State Plaza. The records of that event reminded me of a day when that massive undertaking was still half-finished, and the governor stood looking out over the construction site from his office on the second floor of the State Capitol. Some workmen had painted "Rocky's Pyramid" in giant letters on the tallest structure. I watched for his reaction. A faint smile crept over his face and he smiled contentedly. That moment spoke volumes. Nelson Rockefeller loved to build, as he put it, "to see the dirt fly." As a young man he had been closely involved in his father's Depression-era gamble, building Rockefeller

This essay first appeared in summer 2001, volume 1, number 1.

Center. And now the son was constructing what seemed to be, in a sense, Rockefeller Center North.

On another occasion, I had worked with the governor on remarks he would make at the newly built campus of the State University at Albany. Rereading those words reminded me of his original impetus for creating the modern state university system. He was alarmed by what amounted to a "brain drain" from New York. The state had some fine private colleges, but unlike so many other states it lacked an adequate system of public higher education; New York merely had what amounted to a chain of teachers' colleges. The state's high school graduates bent on college had a choice of attending a private in-state college (if they could afford it), going to a teachers' college, or leaving New York. With his previously noted propensity for seeing the dirt fly, Rockefeller launched a state university complex that today boasts over sixty campuses and over a quarter of a million students—the largest public system of higher education in the world.

Access to the public records recalled for me other personal moments. Preparation of the State of the State Message was an annual marathon that left the governor's staff near collapse. After he had delivered one such message to the legislature, he invited a half-dozen weary subordinates who had worked on the speech to lunch at the Executive Mansion. It was one of those rare moments when Nelson Rockefeller was not immediately charging off to the next barricade. I took advantage of the respite to say, "Governor, I read somewhere that you had something to do with making the movie *Citizen Kane*. What's that all about?" He looked faintly amused and recounted a story of a young aspiring moviemaker, Orson Welles, coming into his office on bended knee and begging for money to help underwrite a film. The governor found the man's emotionalism so discomforting that he offered to help just to get rid of him. I then said, "And so you had a role in what many people regard as the finest movie ever made. What did you think of it?" He responded with a shrug, "I never saw it."

I read in the *New York Times* a few years ago an editorial lauding the federal grant program to combat water pollution. No mention was made of Nelson Rockefeller's pioneering work in this area. I went back and checked the public papers and sure enough, well before Washington had acted, Governor Rockefeller had won the voters' approval for a $1 billion Pure Waters Bond Issue, the first time I had ever seen this ten-figure sum used in connection with any state government program. This bond issue underwrote the construction of sewage treatment plants to clean up New York's polluted rivers and lakes before the federal government ever came up with a dime. Scoring firsts was a trademark of that energetic man, including the nation's first state laws against racial discrimination, state aid to the arts, and an agency to rebuild crumbling inner cities.

Nelson Rockefeller was not perfect. He made the usual quota of human errors and miscalculations. He became so frustrated by the failure of rehabilitation and education programs to curb the drug problem during the seventies that he pushed through the harshest antidrug laws in America, penalties that many believe are disproportionate compared to sentences for other serious crimes.

While he was a get-things-done state leader, Rockefeller proved not to be a particularly adept performer on the national political stage, failing three times in his bid for his ultimate goal, the presidency. Ironically, it was his immersion in leading New York that may have diminished his presidential prospects. He seemed to believe that by running a superior state administration, he could earn the credentials for running the nation. It does not necessarily work that way. While he was managing New York, his archrival, Richard Nixon, who was not even in office, was out on the hustings lining up delegates, getting nominated and eventually elected.

Still, in a state that has produced great figures as governors—Theodore Roosevelt, Franklin D. Roosevelt, Al Smith, and Tom Dewey among them—Nelson Rockefeller, in his fifteen years in office, was certainly the greatest. His mark is everywhere, in those areas already mentioned and in miles of new highways, dozens of new state parks, and at least one hundred other Rockefeller initiatives. Neil Peirce, an authority on state governments, has judged the Rockefeller administration as "the most complex, fascinating, and socially advanced in U.S. history." Professors Robert H. Connery and Gerald Benjamin in their landmark book on the governor, *Rockefeller of New York: Executive Power in the Statehouse*, did not disagree, demurring only in that "he achieved mightily, but he tried to achieve too much too fast."

Nelson Rockefeller would have loved that verdict.

Polish Blue Army volunteers in France, 1918. Credit: Polish Army Veterans Association of America, Inc., New York, New York.

47

Freedom Fighters from Buffalo

Glenn T. Johnston

They were neither the first Americans nor the last ones to serve in a foreign cause on foreign soil. During World War I, Americans formed the well-known Lafayette Escadrille, valiant and romantic fliers against the Germans. Others served in the British or Canadian armies and some enlisted in the French Foreign Legion. Far less well known are the four thousand Polish Americans from New York who played an important role in World War I and the Polish civil war that followed.

The New Yorkers were part of a twenty-two-thousand-man force of American and Canadian volunteers trained in British tactics by Canadians in Canada. They were so unexpectedly numerous that they overflowed the tents and barracks allotted them and were quartered in canneries, local hotels, and private homes. By December 1917 they were also training at Fort Niagara in Youngstown, New York.

They arrived in France in mid-1918 and served under French command. Because they wore the *bleu horizon* uniforms of the French *poilu*,* they were called "the Polish Blue Army." On September 28, they became an independent Allied army and, on October 4, came under the command of the Polish general Joseph Haller. Their participation in the final, victorious Allied offensive earned Poland a place at the peace table and helped ensure that the Versailles Treaty would establish an independent Poland.

That did not, however, guarantee peace in their homeland. The Bolsheviks had seized power in Russia and attempted to export Communism to their neighbor. In

---

This essay first appeared in fall 2001, volume 1, number 2.

*Literally meaning hairy or shaggy, it was the nickname the French gave to their common foot soldiers, the equivalent of the American "doughboy."

January 1919, the Blue Army was transported to Poland and its ranks swelled by some twenty-five thousand released Polish prisoners of war. This enlarged force was crucial in expelling the Russian invaders and, therefore, to the survival of independent Poland. By 1920, the Blue Army began demobilizing.

Few of the veterans opted to stay in Poland, which was not the romantic agrarian state of their hopes. The Polish government offered them each $10 and a train ticket home once they reached the United States. The Polish National Department added another fifteen dollars and a clean American uniform. Returning to America, these veterans were on their own.

Among the returning veterans was Stefan Ryszkowski, who before the war had been commercial editor of Buffalo's Polish newspaper, *Poles in America*. After serving as a Blue Army recruiter, he went to France as an artillery officer and later was decorated for valor during the Russo-Polish War. Demobilized in 1922, he went back to Buffalo, where he found occasional employment as a painter but never again worked steadily. Perhaps Ryszkowski was a casualty of what was called "shell-shock" in World War I, "combat fatigue" in World War II, and "posttraumatic stress disorder" after the Vietnam War. He joined the PAVA, Buffalo's Polish Army Veteran's Association Post #1, and gave much of his time to improving the lives of his fellow veterans.

His friend Anastazja Hanna Kamienska was born Annette Wiechniarek in 1897. In 1916, she was in France and then Poland with the Polish White Cross organization. In Poland, she was involved in establishing the first Polish veterans' convalescent home, working alongside Helena Paderewska, founder of the White Cross and wife of the famous Polish pianist Ignazcy Paderewski. She became Paderewska's personal secretary and in 1921 married Captain Bronislaw Kamienski, thirty-four years her elder, returning to Buffalo with him.

In Buffalo, Hanna Kamienska became a leader of the Polish Falcons and the Polish Women's Alliance. With Ryszkowski and Katherine Hodkiewicz, she established a Ladies' Auxiliary for the PAVA, which helped to find jobs, housing, and medical assistance for Blue Army veterans.

Ryszkowski, meanwhile, was evidently a man unable to help himself as he helped others, and in 1931, he was still unemployed and living alone in a rented room, eking out his life with charity from the PAVA. In April of 1931, his friend Katherine Hodkiewicz died and Hanna Kamienska was diagnosed with tuberculosis. The day after Pulaski Day that year, Stefan Ryszkowski went to Veteran's Hall and with a pistol shot himself to death. He was buried shortly after in the Polish soldiers' plot in St. Stanislaus Cemetery in Cheektowaga, New York. Kamienska would die of tuberculosis in 1933, at age thirty-six. She was given an elaborate military funeral, befitting a woman decorated for her valor and leadership by several countries and organizations.

In St. Stanislaus Cemetery a nondescript monument testifies to forgotten veterans of a foreign war. It's a patch of ground with no tombstones—only the monument telling of a Polish American army that fought to gain Poland's freedom. The monument reads that it is dedicated to the memory "of the Polish America armoured operation of the Azured Army . . . who fought for the freedom of Poland in . . . France 1918 . . . and against Bolsheviks in 1920–1921." It tersely lists the names of thirty-six men and one woman. In incidental irony, two of these people, Stefan Ryszkowski and Anastazja H. Kamienska, achieved their Polish dream while unable to achieve an American one.

García Rivera, in a white suit surrounded by his supporters, drafted the Unemployment Insurance Act of 1939, which required all employers to contribute to the Unemployment Insurance Fund. Credit: Archives of the Puerto Rican Diaspora, Centro De Estudios Puertorriquenos, Hunter College, City University of New York.

48

Oscar García Rivera, Political Pioneer

Félix V. Matos Rodríguez

Earlier this fall, New Yorkers faced the possibility of having two Puerto Ricans—Herman Badillo, a Republican, and Fernando Ferrer, a Democrat—running for mayor of New York City. Interest in the role that Puerto Rican and Latino politics might play in the election forced many people to look at how political parties have interacted with these groups throughout the twentieth century. Although the definitive history of Latino politics in both New York City and New York State remains to be written, many political pundits have been surprised by the fact that the first Puerto Rican and Latino elected to public office in New York was a Republican. Oscar García Rivera served as an assemblyman in Spanish Harlem in the late 1930s and was also the first Puerto Rican elected to public office in the continental United States.

García Rivera was born in the city of Mayaguez in western Puerto Rico on November 6, 1900. His parents were descendants of early nineteenth-century immigrant families who had fled Venezuela during the turmoil caused by the wars for independence fought against Spain throughout South America. In Mayaguez, García Rivera was a talented student: valedictorian of his junior high school class and president of his high school class of 1925. He was active, along with his family, in the local pro-statehood Republican Party; in Mayaguez, this party had strong support among the families connected with the sugar and coffee industries. In the 1920s, the party formed an uneasy electoral coalition with the Socialist Party in order to debunk the Union Party; almost two decades later, a Republican-Labor coalition would serve as García Rivera's electoral power base in Harlem.

After García Rivera finished high school, he decided to go to New York to study law, combining his desire to travel to the "land of opportunity" with his dream to

---

This essay first appeared in winter 2002, volume 1, number 3.

acquire a first-rate legal education. Although many people associate Puerto Rican migration to New York City as a post–World War II phenomenon, a significant and vibrant Puerto Rican community already existed in various parts of the city: the Navy Yard in Brooklyn, the Lower East Side, and of course Harlem. Since he needed a full-time job, García Rivera began working in a factory. He later took and passed a civil service exam that led to a position as a clerk at the City Hall Post Office, where he encouraged Puerto Ricans and other Hispanics to join the Postal Clerks' Union as a way to advocate for higher wages and better working conditions. His contacts with union leaders and organized labor date from this experience.

During this time, García Rivera began to attend night school to pursue his dream of becoming a lawyer. He studied at St. John's University and completed his degree in 1930. That same year he returned to Puerto Rico and proposed marriage to Eloísa Rivera, his high school sweetheart and a distant cousin. They were married in New York at La Milagrosa Church in the Upper West Side in 1931. Eloísa Rivera would become an important intellectual figure in New York's Puerto Rican and Hispanic community in the mid-twentieth century, particularly in its literary and cultural circles. She completed her doctorate in literature at Columbia University in the 1950s and became an expert on the history of Puerto Rican poetry and literature. She was one of the founders of the Instituto de Puerto Rico in 1954, an organization that still promotes Puerto Rican history, culture, and art in New York City.

After Puerto Ricans were made American citizens in 1917, community leaders in New York decided that they could participate in and benefit from the political party system as citizens, not as immigrants. In the late 1920s, many Puerto Ricans felt that it was necessary to get involved in city politics so they could draw more attention to their problems. Hispanic leaders began to encourage political parties to nominate Puerto Rican and Hispanic candidates for both city council and state assembly positions, particularly in the Seventeenth District in Harlem. The first Latino candidates in that district were Rafael Bosch and Victor Fiol Ramos, from the Liberal Republican Party. Frank Torres, a lawyer and good friend of García Rivera, made an unsuccessful run as a Republican for assemblyman in 1932. Prior to 1937, twelve Puerto Rican and Latino candidates ran for different positions representing Spanish Harlem but were not elected.

In the early thirties, García Rivera set up a law practice in his own apartment on West 110th Street. Later he would relocate to 113th Street and Fifth Avenue, serving mostly Puerto Rican and Latino clients and specializing in criminal law. (Only after his years as an assemblyman would he move his very successful practice to Wall Street.) He was a staunch Republican, and in 1937 he was nominated by the Republican Party to run for assemblyman in the Seventeenth District, which encompassed Spanish Harlem. He was such a consensus candidate among Spanish Harlem's Puerto Rican community that another potential candidate, José Santiago (who espoused a more leftist ideology), decided not to run and instead supported García Rivera. The race, however, was an uphill battle, since García Rivera was challenging an incumbent, Mayer Alterman, a Democrat supported by the corrupt Tammany Hall machine and a protégé of Governor Lehman. But García Rivera benefited from a coalition of independent Democrats, leftists, fusionists, labor unions, and Republicans to propel his candidacy. After a brutal campaign, which included his being stabbed at a political rally, he won the election, receiving 8,806 votes to Alterman's 6,220. At the age of thirty-seven, García Rivera became the first Puerto Rican ever to win elected office in the continental United States.

Prior to 1938, assembly elections were held annually. Yet even though García Rivera was productive in the assembly, he appeared to be too independent for the Republican Party's liking, and his contacts with labor organizations caused suspicion in its more conservative wing. The party decided not to support García Rivera for reelection in 1939 and instead nominated John Ross, an African American. This withdrawal of support did not paralyze García Rivera; instead, he ran on the American Labor Party ticket and won by a narrow margin.

In his three years as an assemblyman, García Rivera sponsored numerous bills. He was particularly proud of drafting the Unemployment Insurance Act of 1939, which, among other measures, made all employers liable for contributions to the Unemployment Insurance Fund and reduced the requisite unemployment period for benefits from five to two weeks. He also drafted a bill that provided Civil Service employees the right to organize and negotiate on grievances. He sponsored legislation that prevented the deportation of social relief clients and that made it a criminal offense to discriminate against any religion or race in employment, housing, social relief, or the Works Progress Administration (WPA). He also championed several antidiscrimination bills, tried to strengthen child labor laws, and advocated for better working conditions and salaries for workers.

The year 1940 was García Rivera's last in the assembly. He ran for reelection as a Republican but became one of the many casualties of the "Roosevelt coattails" that swept many Democrats into office that year. He lost his assembly seat to Hulan E. Jack, an African American Democrat who later became Manhattan Borough president. After García Rivera's defeat, it took thirteen years until another Puerto Rican, Felipe Torres, was elected to political office, as an assemblyman from the Bronx in 1953.

García Rivera remained active in both Republican and Puerto Rican politics. He ran one more time for public office, in an unsuccessful attempt to become a city court judge in 1956. Yet even that defeat was a victory: he was the first Puerto Rican ever nominated by the Republican Party for a judgeship in New York State. Later he became president of the Puerto Rican Bar Association. Throughout his life, he continued to speak about social issues and to maintain ties with the labor movement.

García Rivera moved back to Puerto Rico in the 1960s and died in Mayaguez in 1969. The papers of this pioneer of New York City politics were donated to the Center for Puerto Rican Studies at Hunter College in 1998, where they are currently being processed and cataloged through a grant from the National Historical Publications and Records Commission. The collection opened for public use in fall 2002.

Thomas E. Dewey, New York's forty-seventh governor, addresses the state legislature. Credit: New York State Archives, Albany, New York.

49

Gangbuster in the Governor's Office

Richard Norton Smith

> It is our solemn duty . . . to show that government can have both a head and a heart, that it can be both progressive and solvent, that it can serve people without becoming their master.
>
> —Thomas E. Dewey

On the centenary of his birth, New York's forty-seventh governor is chiefly remembered as America's putative thirty-fourth president, The Man Who Might Have Been, snatcher of defeat from the jaws of victory. All but forgotten is the Depression-era gangbuster, whose crime-fighting exploits inspired radio serials (*Mr. District Attorney*) and prompted Hollywood to crank out dozens of formulaic gangster films. Equally obscured is the internationalist Republican who waged a generation-long battle with Midwestern conservatives led by Robert A. Taft for the soul of the GOP, the champion of bipartisan foreign policy, the engineer of Dwight Eisenhower's 1952 presidential nomination, and Richard Nixon's political godfather.

With an archivist's files and a historian's imagination, it is possible to conjure a time when Dewey dominated the Empire State as he had once held Manhattan courtrooms spellbound. Just thirty-six years old when he was narrowly defeated for the governorship by Herbert Lehman in 1938, Dewey scored the first of three landslide victories four years later among New Yorkers by no means disenchanted with the state's costly tradition of political activism. Inevitably this lent Dewey's governorship its pragmatic, problem-solving cast. Repeatedly he told audiences that before there was

This essay first appeared in spring 2002, volume 1, number 4.

government, there was man, and that government arose to meet man's needs. In the modern age, he contended, these needs included as much economic security as was consistent with individual freedom.

Critics called it "me-tooism," aping the New Deal in a vain attempt to outbid Franklin Roosevelt and his heirs. Dewey reached back for his response to Abraham Lincoln and Theodore Roosevelt, Henry Stimson and Elihu Root. He reminded detractors that it was conservative reforms like antitrust laws and federal regulation of railroads, enacted under Republican presidents, that had retained popular allegiance for a capitalist system combining private incentive and public conscience. To couple individual initiative with social justice, to recapture the very word "liberal" for the party of Lincoln and TR—this was the daunting challenge posed to the first Republican governor since Nathan Miller surrendered the gloomy Executive Mansion on Eagle Street to Al Smith in 1923.

Pugnaciously blue-collar, his new home was "not the sprightliest of cities," Dewey deadpanned to a friend early in 1943. The oxblood-red walls of the Tilden-era governor's residence struck its newest occupant as an invitation to suicide. While the Dewey boys, Tom and John, thoughtfully offered bottles of catsup to dinner guests—with enough catsup, they said, almost anything served at the Mansion could be made palatable—their mother struggled with her role as First Lady. One winter afternoon, gazing out a window at a frozen tableau of swirling flakes, Frances Dewey murmured, "How I love it here when it snows." Asked why, she replied sweetly, "Because it covers up Albany."

For all its aesthetic shortcomings, New York's capital was an exciting place to be in the 1940s, an outpost of political and intellectual ferment. Dewey wasted no time in modernizing the rococo governor's office or dusting the cobwebs from a creaking bureaucracy. He quickly abolished Form 76-A, after learning that it took twenty-nine state employees to order seventy cents' worth of glue. Similarly dispatched was the Milk Publicity Board, a $300,000-a-year nest of patronage jobs, howls of protest from dairy farmers notwithstanding. No man should be in public life, Dewey maintained, who couldn't earn more in private employment. Put another way, "My job," he said, "is to get $50,000-a-year men to take $12,000-a-year salaries." By most accounts, he succeeded admirably.

A natural administrator, Dewey sat behind a desk as orderly as his mind, its surface unbroken save for a brown Morocco folder, a thermos jug of cold water, miniatures of an elephant or two, and four pencils sharpened to precisely the same length. Hating telephones—he claimed they disturbed his thought process—he reluctantly agreed to hide one in a desk drawer. Callers were whisked through the office at fifteen-minute intervals, with lunch taken at the desk Dewey himself designed with four sliding shelves, the better to facilitate informal skull sessions.

These conversations ranged from the latest roadblock athwart the governor's cherished Thruway—an unprecedented high-speed, four-lane highway without stop signs or traffic lights that would connect New York City with Buffalo, 486 miles away—to the controversial idea of a state university, embraced by the Dewey administration following two years of painstaking study. Observers couldn't decide whether Lehman's successor was a conservative innovator or a pay-as-you-go liberal. Certainly progressives applauded when Dewey placed New York in the vanguard of states that outlawed racial and religious discrimination in employment and education. To ensure that his law granting equal pay for equal work was more than an admirable, futile gesture, the governor created a state Women's Council. By 1948, state aid to education had doubled. Teachers and state employees received hefty raises.

"There's only one thing wrong with that fellow in there," said Al Smith after visiting Dewey in his newly streamlined Capitol office. "He's a Republican." Indeed, for all the patina of generosity on his administration, there was an unmistakably conservative tint to Dewey's economics. "I hate debt," snapped the governor. Everything, it seemed, went up in his budget, except the amount allocated to debt service. During his first six years in office, Dewey amassed $623 million in black ink, while simultaneously reducing tax rates 50 percent. The surplus, made possible by wartime restraints on construction, was salted away in a Postwar Reconstruction Fund. In time, the PRF made possible fourteen thousand new beds in the state's mental health system, public housing for thirty thousand families, reforestation of thirty-four million trees, and a model veterans' program.

What it *wouldn't* fund was a $360 bonus for returning veterans. Having discovered early on that residents of the Bronx would be paying for a long-disused plank road called Central Avenue until the year 2147, Dewey was adamant in opposing "the pickpocket scheme of government." A generation that wanted benefits must be willing to pay for them. This meant legislative and voter approval of *short*-term bonds to offset the cost of the bonus. (Years later, Dewey half-jokingly told Nelson Rockefeller, "I like you, Nelson. I just don't know whether I can afford you.")

On being confronted with a new idea, Dewey habitually put two favorite questions before advisors: "Is it right?" he demanded, and "Will it work?" From another mouth, his often-repeated axiom, "Good government is good politics," would have been a spineless platitude. What gave it weight was Dewey's instinctive belief that politics, like government, was not an art but a science. He innovated to reduce risks, to narrow what he called "that great gray imponderable area in the electorate." The first presidential candidate to have his own polling unit, Dewey pioneered the use of advance men, was an early practitioner of televised persuasion, and nearly made 1948 the first national campaign conducted by airplane instead of the traditional whistle-stop.

Not surprisingly, he was a demanding taskmaster. Dewey's perfectionism led his Pawling neighbor and friend Elliott Bell to establish the Brave Twisted Smile

Club, whose members labored long hours on gubernatorial speeches only to see their contributions hacked down to a stray sentence or two by an orator determined to rid his texts of "eighty-five-cent words." The governor's notion of meritocratic teamwork, equaled only by his disdain for "crawling locusts of special interests," left scant room for New York's legislature, a body he saw as a shabby peerage of job-hungry provincials. Early in his administration he imposed a reapportionment plan friendlier to Queens apartment dwellers than to underpopulated, overrepresented GOP bastions upstate. Dewey then forced lawmakers to reform their comfortable ways of payroll padding by requiring legislative workers to justify in writing at regular intervals what they had done to earn their salaries. Some assemblymen quit in protest. Others were denied renomination by Dewey's formidable political organization.

The leftish New York daily *P.M.* lambasted "the Little Brain at Albany." On the other hand, voters were in no mood to complain about a governor so suspicious of malfeasance that he rejected anonymous campaign contributions and insisted on investigating the motives of large contributors unknown to him personally. In 1946, New Yorkers reelected Dewey by nearly seven hundred thousand votes. In conventional times, so potent a record of political and administrative success would earn a man—especially if he happened to be governor of New York—the White House. Yet in 1948 Dewey proved too cautious, too confident, and, finally, too rational for an electoral game whose rules had been reinvented by his nemesis, FDR.

The scourge of racketeers had risked his life to end the criminal careers of Dutch Schultz and Lucky Luciano, but in Albany and on the campaign trail the one thing Dewey wouldn't risk was his dignity. Long after his stunning defeat at Truman's hands made him an elder statesman at forty-six, Dewey put it all in perspective. "Everything came too early for me," he said ruefully. By then, the impossibly youthful Gangbuster was too old to obtain more than the wisdom or wealth he already had.

Joseph Burstyn fought film censorship all the way to the U.S. Supreme Court. Credit: Courtesy of the Museum of Modern Art.

50

Freedom of the Screen

Joseph Burstyn and *The Miracle*

Laura Wittern-Keller

In 1915, when the film industry seemed to pose a threat to morality, the Supreme Court denied that films deserved the First Amendment free speech and press guarantees that we take for granted today. That case, *Mutual Films v. Ohio*, stood as precedent for thirty-seven years. But 2002 marks the fiftieth anniversary of another landmark Supreme Court decision that turned the tide of film censorship in America.

Joseph Burstyn, a Polish immigrant and film importer, was an unintentional yet unrelenting advocate of freedom of the screen who took on the seemingly indestructible *Mutual* precedent. I first came across Burstyn's story at the New York State Archives while researching New York's film censorship bureaucracy. From 1921 until 1965, New York State censored all films shown commercially. (One of the largest film script collections in the world is at the New York State Archives in Albany. Stored there are case files for seventy-three thousand films that the Motion Picture Division reviewed for licensing between 1921 and 1965, including fifty-three thousand movie scripts.) The censorship was done by the Motion Picture Division, which became a part of the State Education Department in 1927. On average, the state banned six to eight films per year and ordered another 10 percent changed before granting licenses. While Joseph Burstyn's name appears in several of the division's archives as the importer of such acclaimed films as *Paisan*, *The Bicycle Thief*, and *Open City*, the film that would

This essay first appeared in spring 2002, volume 1, number 4.

make him a civil libertarian was *The Miracle*, a forty-minute Italian drama about man's inhumanity to man. In this short film directed by Roberto Rossellini, Anna Magnani plays a Catholic peasant who believes that St. Joseph has fathered her child.

Packaging *The Miracle* with two other short films, Burstyn submitted the trilogy, called *Ways of Love*, to the New York censors in 1950, received an exhibition license, and prepared for a profitable run in New York City. However, City License Commissioner Edward T. McCaffrey, prodded by the Catholic Legion of Decency (the film-rating and -censoring agency of the Church), objected to the movie, calling it "officially and personally blasphemous." He threatened the theater's license unless it dropped *The Miracle*. Burstyn, who passionately believed in the value of the film, decided to challenge the license commissioner's authority in court.

The American Civil Liberties Union, which had been waiting for a film censorship test case and was a frequent adversary of the Legion of Decency, sensed promise in *The Miracle* and offered legal assistance. The New York Supreme Court agreed with Burstyn that the license commissioner had overstepped his bounds and granted an injunction, opening the screens of New York to *The Miracle*.

Just two days after the film's reinstatement, the immensely powerful Francis Cardinal Spellman proscribed all American Catholics from viewing *The Miracle* and activated the Legion of Decency's most potent weapon, a boycott. That evening pickets barricaded the theater with signs reading "Don't enter that cesspool!" and "Don't look at that filth!" The situation grew uglier each night, as the picketers grew to two hundred strong. The Board of Regents, reporting "hundreds" of complaints about *The Miracle* and facing immense political pressure, revoked the film's license.

The ACLU was ready for a showdown, and *The Miracle* seemed the perfect test case. First, it was an artistic film, named by the New York City Film Critics as the best foreign film of 1950 and backed by a well-respected importer. Second, threatening legislation had recently been introduced in Congress that would certify all film actors, producers, and directors with licenses that were rescindable for "moral turpitude," so time was growing short for a decisive judicial curb on the censors. Third, a test in New York presented maximum potential, since many other states without censors followed New York's pronouncements. Florida, for example, refused exhibition, at least by statute, to any film that had not passed either the National Board of Review or New York's Motion Picture Division. Fourth, the Supreme Court had dropped a hint in an antitrust case against Paramount two years before that it might be ready to revisit the film censorship issue.

Finally, *The Miracle* presented two solid constitutional issues: freedom of speech and—because it had been censored as "sacrilegious"—separation of church and state. It was the right case to test the constitutionality of censorship: a fine film, with a principled distributor and a highly publicized confrontation in the background, and a healthy dose of church-state controversy thrown in for good measure.

Burstyn lost in both the New York Supreme Court and the Court of Appeals. The state successfully argued that *The Miracle* was "sacrilegious" and that "everyone knows what is meant by this term." Despite what seems to be, by today's standards, a strong case by Burstyn that censorship of *The Miracle* violated the First Amendment, state courts in 1951 were reluctant to overturn administrative decisions of state agencies. And New York courts preferred to avoid constitutional questions altogether.

Burstyn's last recourse was the Supreme Court. To convince the justices to hear the case, Burstyn's lawyer, Ephraim London, successfully asserted that New York's statute was too vague, violated due process, and breached separation of church and state. The long-anticipated showdown between the ACLU and the Legion of Decency was finally at hand.

The result was a unanimous decision in 1952 that reversed the tide of film censorship by overturning the thirty-seven-year stranglehold of the *Mutual* decision. For the first time, the court extended "free speech and free press guaranty of the First and Fourteenth Amendments" to films. However, the decision also stated that "since the term 'sacrilegious' is the sole standard under attack here, it is not necessary for us to decide whether a state may censor motion pictures under a clearly drawn statute." Thus, contemporary commentators and historians tend to see *Burstyn v. Wilson* as a letdown, since the court refused to throw the knockout blow that would have overturned censorship once and for all. However, it is not unusual for the Supreme Court to decide cases on the narrowest constitutional grounds, and historians have overlooked a significant part of the opinion: the *Burstyn* decision completely reversed the direction of censorship by placing the burden on the censors to prove the necessity of any limitation imposed. By extending First Amendment rights to film, the decision opened the door for further challenges. And it signaled the beginning of the end of the Legion of Decency's influence on the film industry.

Why would an independent film importer take on the censorship system of the 1950s? Burstyn explained at a victory party shortly after the decision that "every time I had to submit a film for censorship, I felt that I was in an illegitimate business and that being in this business was a crime . . . it was about time to try to restore a little dignity." The ACLU gave Burstyn full credit for the victory, saying that "the motion picture industry with all its money couldn't accomplish what [he] . . . did."

Sadly, Burstyn did not live to see film censorship ended in New York. He died the year after his Supreme Court victory. His friend, the film critic Bosley Crowther, eulogized him in the *New York Times:* "Though Mr. Burstyn is no longer here to see it done, the case he singly and bravely carried . . . may yet spearhead full freedom for the screen." It did. By 1965, succeeding Supreme Court decisions based on *Burstyn v. Wilson* had so emasculated film censorship statutes that every censoring state finally surrendered.

Floating baths were segregated by gender. The girls here are being taught how to swim on "Ladies Day," when this public bath at West 51st Street and Hudson River was restricted to women and girls. Credit: Museum of the City of New York, the Jacob A. Riis Collection.

51

Awash in New York

A Chronicle of the City's Floating Baths

Ann L. Buttenwieser

A century ago, and fewer than ten blocks from today's South Street Seaport, the delighted shrieks of several hundred wet New Yorkers echoed from the Grand Street Floating Bath, one of almost two dozen seasonally movable pools berthed in the middle of the economic life of the city. These floating saltwater baths, resembling giant houseboats with inner courtyards of seawater, offered their patrons exercise, relaxation, and—coincidentally—a place to wash.

As early as 1817, Edmund March Blunt's *Stranger's Guide to New York* advertised two privately owned marine baths, located on Manhattan's West Side near the Battery. By 1830, the baths had become elegant, private, saltwater floating pools. Upon payment of a fee, fashionable New Yorkers could enter the baths through frame buildings erected on both sides of Castle Garden, the stage for singer Jenny Lind.

Public Baths a Necessity for a Crowded City of Immigrants

After the Civil War, public health advocates and temperance societies made cleanliness a public obsession. Citing the bathing practices of the Greeks and Romans, nineteenth-century reformers believed that a clean body ensured a sound mind, whereas clogged skin caused such societal evils as ill-temper, business failure, divorce, immorality, and

This essay first appeared in summer 2002, volume 2, number 1. This is a modified and updated version of an article that first appeared in the spring/summer 1984 issue of *Seaport* magazine.

criminal behavior. They clamored for legislation to institute municipally owned "free floating baths."

By 1870, when New York's population had reached 1.4 million and an average of two thousand new immigrants arrived each month, public baths came to be regarded as a necessity rather than a novelty. Newcomers, crowded into tenement districts that lacked basic facilities such as showers or tubs, gravitated to Manhattan's greatest natural resource, its rivers. On the wharves that rimmed the city, the *New York Times* reported that people "exposed their naked persons at all hours." Such adventurers offended the sensibilities of commuters and workers who used the rivers for daily commerce and travel, so New York's first free baths were opened in June 1870 by William Marcy ("Boss") Tweed, commissioner of public works. Reformers applauded the public river baths as one way to accommodate what the *Times* called "the pressing needs of the great unwashed" in a contained, supervised setting.

Pontoons Support Pools Built of Pine Slats

Initially a pair, and growing to a fleet of fifteen by 1890, the pools were novel constructions. Afloat on eight pontoons, a single-story wood structure surrounded a rectangular atrium that contained the outdoor pool. A decorative tin-roofed cupola in the center of one wing capped a small second-story apartment that provided year-round office space and living quarters for one bath attendant. Patrons entered the bath from the pier or bulkhead by way of a portable gangway and were ushered by a "keeper" to one of several dozen tiny dressing cubicles that opened onto a narrow deck that girdled the pool. The cubicles were outfitted with hooks for belongings and latchless doors for ease of supervision. The absence of locks, however, also encouraged thievery, often forcing swimmers to walk home stark naked, shielded by helpful friends.

The swimming area—an open well, typically ninety by sixty feet—was lined with pine slats. These were attached far enough apart to allow river water to circulate, yet close enough to safely contain the swimmers. The depth of the water could reach a man's armpits, depending on the amount of air in the pontoons. Adjacent to one side was a narrow and shallow "aquatic kindergarten" that separated children from the adult swimming area.

On a steamy summer day, several hundred people often packed into a single pool. A policeman was stationed outside to control the crowds, who often stood in line for hours for a twenty-minute turn in the brackish river water. To keep order inside, each bath had a staff of two men and two women who acted as lifeguards, traffic directors, and aquatic janitors, but who were often both the brunt and cause of disorder. One rescued a drowning boy, only to find that his pocket had been picked as a reward. Some augmented their meager salaries—$13 a week for women and slightly more for men—through graft, charging admission to impatient, well-off patrons who miraculously appeared at the head of the line.

Men and Women Swim Separately

The pools, which were open from the end of June to October, were rigidly segregated by gender. Although male patrons outnumbered females two to one, the pools were equally accessible to both men and women. On "Ladies Days"—Mondays, Wednesdays, and Fridays from dawn to dusk, and a half-day on Sundays—women and girls could learn to swim. A fashionable woman's swimsuit was a below-the-knee dress whose sleeves had been cut off and whose skirt had been split and sewn down the center to form "legs." The remainder of the week the pools were open to men and boys, for whom nude swimming was the height of fashion.

As more pools were constructed, municipal and private facilities were often stationed within the same block. There was a distinction in clientele, however, based on the ability to pay. Uptown businessmen, clerks, and housewives visited the private baths and were charged 25¢ a visit, or $7 for the season, while the free public facilities were patronized mostly by working-class families who could not afford carfare for a beach outing. Thus to survive financially, the public baths were forced to fight for space with other city industries. Williams and Guion, a top shipping firm, obstructed the berthing of a pool at West 11th Street because it threatened the safety of their merchandise. In an impassioned remonstrance to the Dock Department in 1876, the company described the "young men and half grown boys" who ignited three fires on the pier with their "careless use of Segars."

Polluted Waters Continue to Attract Millions

Nevertheless, by the summer of 1895 fifteen public baths were operating at the edges of Manhattan. Attendance exceeded four million, since the pools were stationed at waterfronts contiguous to the most crowded residential sections of the city. They were not immune to vandalism; Bath Number 3 at Pike Street ended one season submerged in the East River because nearby residents, angry at being turned away, deflated its pontoons. Nor were people deterred by the pollution that plagued New York's rivers, even though the Board of Health questioned whether the baths were sanitary, describing the river water that flooded through them as "saturated with animal and vegetable matter in a state of decomposition."

Health Concerns Force Cleanup

By the turn of the century, as raw sewage poured into the rivers through new sewer outlets located at the ends of most streets, a second generation of reformers began a campaign to abolish the floating baths altogether. Jacob Riis and the Association for the Improvement of the Condition of the Poor (AICP) saw the baths as unsanitary rather than polluted and pressed for permanent structures to replace the seasonal pools. The Merchants Association of the City of New York published a study that enumerated the flies on sewage and decayed fish, described open manure dumps on piers adjacent to the pools, and stated that the waterfront at the East 96th Street Bath contained "swimming children with masses of filth collected on their heads and shoulders." The Metropolitan Sewage Commission laid to rest any doubts about contamination in the pools when investigators injected dye into a sewer at Rutgers Street and watched the water in the bath at Pier 33 turn bright red.

By 1910, one bath had been beached and three others were stationed in purer waters in the outer boroughs. By 1916, with the help of AICP, permanent in-ground bathhouses had been constructed, and the Board of Health refused to allow any floating pools near sewers. Wells were made watertight and were continuously filled with fresh water, which was beginning to flow abundantly from the new Catskill aqueduct. As insurance against contamination, lime was added to the pools, and dozens of showers were installed at every possible entry. Patrons complained of stinging eyes and cold water; some sidestepped these improvements altogether by using the side of the bath as a springboard into the river. In all, eight floating pools were refurbished for service and were soon praised as models to be emulated by other waterfront cities.

Alternatives to Floating Baths

Ironically, just as the baths' problems were overcome, alternative facilities became available. A seemingly endless supply of aqueduct water allowed the city to add indoor pools, open all year, to existing bathhouses. In summer, municipal parks turned on sprinklers, and showerheads were placed on hydrants in play streets. In 1936, the Parks Department opened ten huge in-ground swimming pools—and a year later, when the floating baths began the annual journey from their winter headquarters in Claussens Point, Queens, to their summer berths in Manhattan, only four baths remained. Age, winter storms, skirmishes with river traffic, and the new swimming pools had taken their toll. It was left to the vision of Parks Commissioner Robert Moses to try to modernize the half-century-old floating baths into a twentieth-century beach complex.

In February 1938, the Parks Department, now formally in charge of municipal swimming facilities, previewed the summer opening of a "modern swimming hole" at the unlikely location of 96th Street and the Henry Hudson Parkway. Three old barges were reconstructed with federal relief funds, and two outdoor pools floated on either side of a buoyant bathhouse. The floating baths once again became a public attraction, and crowds of would-be swimmers waited in line on the banks of the Hudson.

That July, Robert Moses sought city funds to operate the new pool complex. But, as he wrote, "The City did not fund them . . . the barges fell apart and there was no money to repair them." The baths were beached and continued to decay. In 1942, the War Department wrote their epitaph: "The baths are adrift, hazardous to the waterways of New York."

Twenty-First Century Floating Baths a Possibility

Since then, recreation of the floating baths has been proposed several times without success. In the 1960s, the Lindsay administration commissioned a study for a portable floating pool on a renovated Liberty Ship that would travel the waterfronts contiguous to low-income neighborhoods. In the 1980s, a consortium of city officials solicited reactions to a "floating beach club" to be berthed at the South Street Seaport, where barges would house a pool, a sundeck, dressing rooms, and dining and shopping facilities. But the lure of the waterfront remains strong. The Neptune Foundation has recently obtained funds to build a prototypical, twenty-first-century floating swimming pool, designed by architects Jonathan Kirschenfeld and Charles Cushing. Look for it soon, in the waterways of New York.

Built in 1893, the amphitheater is the heart of the Chautauqua Institution, a not-for-profit, 750-acre educational center beside Chautauqua Lake in southwestern New York. Today, 150,000 people visit Chautauqua every summer. Credit: Chautauqua Institution Archives, Oliver Archives Center, Chautauqua, New York.

52

The Endless Summers of Chautauqua

Marilyn Mathews Bendiksen

It began with two men who shared common values, complementary resources, and a vision to create "a place, an ideal, and a force." In 1874, their vision became reality: a summer community dedicated to education, religion, science, and the arts. One hundred and twenty-eight years later, the Chautauqua Institution still embodies that vision and the ideals of American education.

Lewis Miller, a successful manufacturer of farm equipment for the developing Midwest, was a devout member of the Methodist Episcopal Church and superintendent of the Sunday school at his church in Akron, Ohio. He was also a member of the Sunday School Union, an organization that directed development of the Church's Sunday schools. Miller's unique concept was to divide group Sunday school instruction into grades, and he designed a new building to accomplish this. He invited his friend John Heyl Vincent to speak at the building's dedication in 1868. Vincent, from New Jersey, was a Methodist minister who counted among his friends members of the clergy, bishops, and college presidents. He was also secretary of the Sunday School Union and editor of its journal.

The two men discussed how they might establish a community where, during the summer, Sunday school teachers of all denominations could both improve their knowledge of the Bible and have an opportunity to broaden their education in literature and the new field of science. Vincent thought that a growing urban environment would be a promising setting for their summer experiment, but Miller preferred the grounds of the Chautauqua Lake Camp Meeting Association (of which he was a trustee), located on the shores of Chautauqua Lake in western New York State.

This essay first appeared in summer 2002, volume 2, number 1.

A Summer Experiment

"Camp" or summer meetings were begun early in the century by Methodists and Presbyterians as places to hold evangelistic services. They were often interdenominational, and wooded areas were the location of choice when crowds grew too large to fit into a single church building. The week-long Methodist camp meetings were known for their fervor, and Miller and Vincent saw the possibility of extending the length of such a program, reducing its emotionalism, and instead focusing on the importance of a broad-based religious education to sustain the commitment of new converts.

Miller's instinct for the countryside prevailed, and the two men leased the wooded Chautauqua Lake Camp Meeting grounds, already laid out with "streets" named after bishops and others who had shaped American Methodism. A central outdoor "auditorium" for group meetings and lessons was surrounded by rows of numbered thirty-by-fifty-foot lots that could be used either for building small cottages or for renting family-sized canvas tents.

Thousands Flock to First Assembly

The first Chautauqua Lake Sunday School Assembly attracted about 2,500 participants for a two-week meeting in August 1874. It was rugged instruction. Participants sat on wooden plank benches in the outdoor auditorium; on an upper plateau, a large tent provided shelter during rainy weather. As superintendent of instruction, Vincent arranged for construction of a scale model of the Holy Land—Chautauqua Lake represented the Mediterranean Sea—as a visual aid to make Bible stories come alive for the first Sunday school teacher-training class. The several hundred participants who were successful in completing a written examination at the end of the course received a diploma attesting to their new level of knowledge.

As plans for the third assembly in 1876 took shape, the Philadelphia Exposition, with its advertised demonstrations of new inventions, threatened to draw off the New Yorkers. But Miller and Vincent added science demonstrations to the upcoming program so that attendees could experience yet another component of the "amazing universe." There was no reason, the two men felt, to separate science and religion; there was room for both in the schedule.

Star Power

President Ulysses S. Grant, once a parishioner of Vincent's in Galena, Illinois, was the star attraction at the 1875 assembly. Despite competition from the Philadelphia

Exposition, attendance increased significantly. Grant's appearance launched Chautauqua as a place where people of significance could be seen and heard by the general public, and as a forum for new ideas to reach large audiences. Susan B. Anthony; Jane Addams; Presidents McKinley, Garfield, and Theodore and Franklin Roosevelt; Amelia Earhart; John Philip Sousa; Marian Anderson; the New York Symphony; Eleanor Roosevelt; Peter Martin; Judy Collins, Sandra Day O'Connor; Mark Russell—the list of notable speakers continues to this day, having drawn thousands for each of Chautauqua's 128 summers.

Chautauqua Literary and Scientific Circle

In 1876, the entire Chautauqua Lake Camp Meeting Association formally became the Chautauqua Lake Sunday School Assembly. At the 1878 assembly, Miller and Vincent decided to expand their vision of adult education by announcing a new program, the Chautauqua Literary and Scientific Circle (CLSC). Vincent said he hoped that at least ten people from the assembly would "seed" the new offering. But because public higher education, in the form of high school or college, was unavailable to the majority of people at the time, there was a groundswell of interest. The CLSC course required four years: reading a prescribed set of books on history, culture, science, and literature; completing study guides; and meeting in small circles for discussion. A member was then entitled to graduate during the August assembly. There were 1,800 graduates in the first "pioneer class" of 1882; by the end of the century, over 100,000 would enroll in the CLSC and pay their membership dues of fifty cents per year.

Pioneer of Public Education

In addition to the CLSC, Vincent and Miller established two specialty schools: a school for ministers to learn biblical languages and a school of pedagogy, which set the stage for modern summer school courses for teachers. In 1883 the men combined the programs of the Schools of Pedagogy and Languages, the summer assembly, and the CLSC with the Chautauqua Press to create Chautauqua University, a year-round, degree-granting institution responsive to the growing need for universal adult education at a time when public universities were just getting underway. Here were the seeds for the now-familiar correspondence courses, as well as extension and nontraditional education. In 1892, the university was abandoned in favor of the focus on summer learning, but by then Chautauqua itself had been redefined as a process, the "Chautauqua System of Popular Education."

Starting as early as Chautauqua's second summer, traveling "tent chautauquas" began to spring up throughout the United States, Canada, and other countries as a result of the inspiration—and often the direct assistance—of Vincent and Miller. These represented yet a third level of development of the Chautauqua Movement: totally independent entities that carried on the institution's dream of universal adult education.

In 1900, Melvil Dewey, librarian for the State of New York, conducted a summer course at Chautauqua to train school and community librarians. Syracuse University, New York University, and the State University of New York at Fredonia followed over the years, holding credit programs for adults on Chautauqua's grounds. In 1902, the organization was formally chartered as the Chautauqua Institution, and since the 1950s Chautauqua itself has sponsored a unique program of studies that promote lifelong learning.

A Wealth of Programs

From its inception to the present, Chautauqua's reputation has arisen from the excellence of the programs held in the large outdoor amphitheater. The arts in particular have always played a central role. A small band of wind instrumentalists and vocal groups, formed in the early days, led to the formation of the Chautauqua Symphony Orchestra, a school of music, an opera company, and a ballet company.

A school of fine and performing arts and a theater company have also nourished talent and provided top-quality performances through the years. Children's programs have always existed at Chautauqua. Original classes included the Bible, obedience, and "good manners"; a kindergarten was then established as a demonstration program that drew many preschool education students in the 1880s. The Children's School, directed by John Dewey in 1900, is still influenced by his philosophy. Chautauqua also established the first known day camp, and by 1902 both the Boys' and Girls' Clubs had their own buildings on the grounds.

Even physical education has a history at Chautauqua. Many of the earliest instructional models for physical education were taught in the summer courses. Tennis courts were constructed after Vincent saw the game played in England. There were roque (croquet) courts, and lawn bowling is still played. Chautauqua Lake attracted sailing and other water sports enthusiasts, including, at one time, a rowing team.

Chautauqua's architecture has become another treasure. Early in the twentieth century, architects from Buffalo, Chicago, and Washington were engaged to design many of the large public buildings. Now inclusive of tent sites, small wooden houses, hotels, boarding houses, and winterized year-round homes, the entire Chautauqua Institution is a National Historic Landmark. Generous private gifts have recently made it possible to restore and/or update these structures.

John Heyl Vincent and Lewis Miller's vision continues at Chautauqua. Set apart from the frenetic pace of modern life, this legendary summer community still provides a forum for learning, discussion, and reflection to help twenty-first-century Americans define values and a philosophy of learning at the intersections of religion, education, recreation, and the arts.

Poolside at the Evans Kiamesha Hotel, Kiamesha Lake, New York. Credit: Catskills Institute.

53

Under New Management

The Legacy of the Jewish Catskills

Phil Brown

Since the turn of the century, Ulster, Sullivan, and southern Greene Counties, plus a sliver of southeastern Delaware County, have been known as the Jewish Catskills. Today their remnants are like an archeological treasure-house that covers hundreds of square miles, where no one has to dig to find the ruins.

In 1993, when I started my research on the Jewish Catskills, I made field trips to nearly all the resorts at which my parents or I had worked. I was amazed to find that virtually all of them are still standing and in use, given the area's overwhelming number of burned, decayed, fallen in, and now-demolished hotels. Of course, the most spectacular for me is still my parents' hotel (from 1946 to 1952), Brown's Royal in White Lake, now the Bradstan. In Accord, Chait's was Su Casa, since taken over by Elat Chayim, a Jewish Renewal center. The Karmel in Loch Sheldrake is now Stage Door Manor, a renowned children's theater camp. In Swan Lake, the Fieldston Hotel is now Camp B'nai Yaakov; Paul's Hotel is Daytop Village, a drug treatment center; and the Stevensville has reopened as the Swan Lake Resort. In Parkville, the Grand Hotel is another Daytop Village facility. In Kiamesha Lake, the Evans Kiamesha is a housing development and a Jewish day school. The Cherry Hill in Greenfield Park (where I first bussed tables in 1962, the year of my bar mitzvah) is Or Shraga, an Orthodox camp. These old hotels, given new lives under new management, are nevertheless reminders of the way the Catskills used to look, when you could drive forever and see nothing but hotels or bungalow colonies, one after the other.

This essay first appeared in summer 2002, volume 2, number 1. Peter Goodman contributed to this essay.

Sometimes I feel as if I've been called back to these places to document their history and the lives of their inhabitants. I've rambled through many old Catskills buildings, revisited the tiny rooms that guests would occupy for weeks at a time, examined rusted waiters' trays in crumbling kitchens, viewed rows of folding wooden chairs from which people watched shows in the humble casinos. I've even walked, with a miner's lamp on my head, through structures abandoned so thoroughly that light no longer enters. And I've enjoyed the luxury of visiting the few remaining hotels operating as such, accepting the owners' generous insistence that I stay for lunch and watching guests still living the old Catskills resort life. At the Mayflower Hotel in South Fallsburg, every resort building still remains in place, less than a decade after its successor, the Bethel Sunshine Camp, folded. You can walk the grounds and take in the whole daily routine.

If you give even a casual glance to the many buildings, including my parents' hotel, that fit the description of a classic Catskills hotel, you'll see that, architecturally speaking, the buildings are smiling. The arrangement of the small stuccoed "Main House" windowed gables on top, two side rooms on either side of the porch, a canopy over the central entrance, a broad staircase descending to a walkway, stone gateposts by the roadside as a frame to the decorative fencing—you can see it today in the "smile" of the still-operating Rainbow Hotel. The walkway is lined with benches that held a multitude of conversations as guests strolled up to the entrance of their summer Eden. This was the Yiddish promenade, the boulevard of the Jews.

Jewish Farmers Offer Summer Respite to City Cousins

The history of Jews in the Catskills began in the 1890s, with immigrants descended from peasant stock seeking farmland. But close to New York City the best farmland was already occupied, so Jews looking for soil and trees were forced farther north, onto mountainous land where growing crops was difficult. They turned instead to dairy and chicken farms; at one time, Sullivan County was the state's largest egg-producing county.

However, farms were not profitable for most, so the farmers took in boarders. They first used their own houses, converting them into *kuchalayns* (pronounced *cookh-uh-lanes*, Yiddish for "cook for yourself"), consisting of rented rooms and shared cooking and dining facilities. The *kuchalayns* grew into "bungalow colonies," tiny cottages equipped with a bedroom and a kitchen. Some even grew into large hotels. The boarders were Jewish families fleeing the summer heat and smells of Delancey Street and Brownsville, who jammed their belongings into and onto taxis ("hacks") and later their own cars and who headed upstate to the forests, mountains, and brooks where the air was fragrant and nearly everyone was just like them.

Thus, the Jewish Catskills were born.

From Kuchalayns to Bungalows to Hotels

The essence of these summer colonies was in the communality of the *kuchalayns*, the home-like boardinghouses, the bungalow colonies where vacationing families might live together for the season (although fathers came mostly on weekends), and the hotels where guests would stay from two to four weeks, often returning to the same place each year. The atmosphere was that of an extended family, intimate and convivial; thousands made year-round and then lifelong friends in the Catskills.

By the 1950s, few *kuchalayns* remained. But the small (50–250 guests) and medium-sized (250–500 guests) hotels retained that intimacy. The owners, often a pair of in-law couples, were always present, working in various capacities. They mingled with the guests, many of whom were relatives and friends. Even in large hotels with five hundred to nine hundred guests, often owners, staff, and guests all knew each other from years of vacationing and working in the same resorts. At a time when most American resorts and hotels were "restricted"—euphemistic for "no Jews allowed"—in the Catskills the food was kosher and abundant, the language was Yiddish, and the entertainment was down-home.

Strong Sense of Community Develops

During the 1950s and 1960s, about five hundred colonies and five hundred and fifty hotels were open, drawing an estimated one million vacationers each year. The four-county area seemed like one huge neighborhood. Catskills hotelkeepers pioneered the all-inclusive vacation: three meals a day, an evening tea room, nightly entertainment, sports and activities, and eventually day camps. Hotels developed a local culture and cachet. As guests returned year after year, day campers grew into junior counselors, then perhaps into busboys and waiters, and ultimately into guests with their own families.

Many of the workers, too, were closely tied to the area. Staff shared the community for the summer, frequently working for years in the same resort. Staff-guest romances, similar to those depicted in the films *Dirty Dancing*, *Sweet Lorraine*, and *A Walk on the Moon*, added to the closeness. People in their teens and twenties found summer jobs and an opportunity to work their way through college and professional or graduate school, making the Catskills a core element of Jewish upward mobility. And all summer people entered a larger community as they shopped in town, walked past other resorts, and visited friends and relatives.

Summer Resorts Not Just for the Rich

The resorts, like the cities the guests had temporarily escaped, housed people of all classes and occupations. While there was class stratification due to the range of costs in different resorts, even some of the more expensive places were accessible—if you knew someone, or even if you didn't. Bungalow dwellers sneaked into hotel casinos (nightclubs, not gambling casinos), guests at small hotels sneaked into larger ones, and workers swarmed from place to place like bees. Guests in some colonies provided their own entertainment: movies projected on rickety screens, weekend "socials," skits and talent shows that included the famous "mock weddings." Children were often organized into teams that competed all season in athletics and other activities.

In the mountains, Jews could become Americans while preserving their Jewishness. American Jewish humor grew up in the Catskills, where generations of comedians from Henny Youngman to Billy Crystal got their start. Eventually "Borscht Belt humor"—broad, genial, self-deprecating, and with that distinctive accent—spread throughout the country.

Jewish Catskills Transformed

Today, Yoga ashrams, Zen meditation centers, drug treatment programs, mental health facilities, and homes for the developmentally disabled have taken over the shells of many old resorts, and perhaps only a dozen functioning hotels remain. Once-crowded towns are subdued and lined with vacant storefronts. But Kutsher's Country Club and the Raleigh look, feel, and taste familiar to Catskills veterans, as does the Homowack, now ultra-Orthodox. Smaller places like the South Wind in Woodbourne, the Grand Mountain in Greenfield Park, and the Rainbow Hotel in Ulster Heights are still captivating, their original appearance untouched even by the renovation craze of the 1950s. Many bungalow colonies survive, most Orthodox and Hasidic, although more are secular than is popularly believed.

There is the promise of a renaissance. The Concord and Grossinger's, both owned by the same developer, Capelli Enterprises, will reopen in stages over the next five years. With state approval, Kutsher's has arranged with the St. Regis Mohawk Indians to open a gambling casino next door to the hotel. No one expects a resurgence of the past, but the Catskills remain a powerful draw. Many former guests have bought summer homes, including condos developed from bungalow colonies and the old Brown's Hotel (now Grandview Palace). Orthodox Jews keep the Catskills a distinctively Jewish location through their network of colonies, camps, and yeshivas. Yet if you look just beneath the surface, the houses of the old resorts still stand upright and secure, as in their heyday, smiling and offering the haven of their lobbies for schmoozing, the endless food of their dining rooms for sustenance.

Martha Matilda Harper used her "crowning glory"—her own luxurious mane of floor-length chestnut hair—as a means to extricate herself from the confines of class and poverty. Along the way she changed the way the world did business, affirmed the right of women to control their economic destinies, and, not coincidentally, altered the way society looked at female beauty. Yet by the end of the century, the story of this extraordinary businesswoman had been forgotten by all but a devoted few. Credit: Courtesy of Jane Plitt, Harper biographer.

54

Martha Matilda Harper

The Business of Beauty

Sally Parker

If Horatio Alger had written stories for girls, she could have been his heroine. Tough, smart, and possessed of uncommon business acumen, Martha Matilda Harper entered the world of work at the age of seven. Half a century later, at the height of her Rochester-based career, she presided over a global beauty salon business that counted the rich and powerful among its devoted clientele. At its apex in the early 1930s, the Harper Method, a health-based beauty regimen, was offered in more than five hundred salons in cities worldwide, including New York, Chicago, San Francisco, London, and Paris. Among Harper's most notable clients were Woodrow Wilson, Grace and Calvin Coolidge, Eleanor Roosevelt, Jacqueline Kennedy, Lady Bird Johnson, and Helen Hayes. Even foreign dignitaries were customers: the Queen of England, Kaiser Wilhelm of Germany, British prime minister Anthony Eden.

Harper used her "crowning glory"—her own luxurious mane of floor-length chestnut hair—as a means to extricate herself from the confines of class and poverty. Along the way she changed the way the world did business, affirmed the right of women to control their economic destiny, and, not coincidentally, altered the way society looked at female beauty. Yet by the end of the century, the story of this extraordinary businesswoman had been forgotten by all but a devoted few.

This essay first appeared in fall 2002, volume 2, number 2.

An American Success Story

Martha Matilda Harper's story was rediscovered in 1994 when biographer Jane Plitt was doing business research. She went on to write the entrepreneur's first biography, *Martha Matilda Harper and the American Dream* (Syracuse University Press 2000). Says Plitt, "When I started researching this, I never imagined that the Harper Method was as significant an international enterprise as it turned out to be. This was a huge, huge enterprise."

Born in 1857 in Ontario, Canada, Harper was bonded out by her parents at age seven as a household servant to her aunt and uncle. Later she went to work for a kindly physician interested in the physiology of hair who invented a secret formula to promote its growth. Appreciating Harper's interest (and probably her hair), he shared his knowledge, and eventually his formula, with her.

In 1882, twenty-five years old and still a domestic servant, Harper moved to Rochester to work for a wealthy family who lived in an East Main Street mansion (where the Auditorium Theater now stands). Although the family left her behind when they moved, Harper continued to work fourteen-hour days for the next homeowners. At the same time, she experimented with the hair tonic formula, and an idea for a business began to form.

Using her entire lifetime savings of $360, Harper opened her first hair salon in 1888 in the swanky Powers Building in downtown Rochester after convincing the landlord that her business would not attract women of ill repute. The salon offered customer comforts: private and serene surroundings, calm attendants, reclining shampoo chairs with neck supports (which she invented), and all-natural beauty products that would be at home in today's trendiest salons. This elegant environment allowed her to coax wealthy Victorian women out of their homes to have their hair done—she was the first to do so—since the prevailing custom was to have a stylist call on them at home. Then, building on her initial success, Harper originated the beauty regimen that would make her both rich and famous.

The Harper Method

The Harper Method was a health-focused salon experience. Using scientific methods and applications, stylists sought to bring out the "inner beauty" of customers by promoting healthy skin and hair and by reducing the stress of everyday living. Neck, shoulder, and head massages were part of the package. The focus on pampering clients, both men and women, would eventually create customers for life and become the industry standard.

When she sought to expand her business from a solo shop, Harper invented—more than half a century before Ray Kroc would launch the McDonald's franchise—a system of satellite operations that duplicated in every respect the original shop, products, and training. But once again, Harper's genius was to operate counter to the custom of the times: every satellite franchise was, by design, owned and operated by a *woman*, most importantly a woman from Harper's own working-class background. Shortly after arriving in Rochester, Harper had become a Christian Scientist; it was this belief system, which embraced women as strong, equal members of society, that was the underpinning of her personal and business philosophy. Throughout her career, Harper believed that women could achieve whatever they wanted if they were willing to work hard. She preached this repeatedly in her company newsletter as the network of salons grew into the hundreds.

"With a charisma equal to any magnetic leader, Martha enlarged her organization by converting ordinary women into proud businesswomen," Jane Plitt writes. Harper accomplished this transformation by means of idea-sharing, production and performance incentives, and spirited reunions. Her own early experiences set the bar for her franchise owners, and she never forgot her working-class roots, giving attendants time off during the day to take care of responsibilities outside of work—unheard of at the time.

Empowering Women

Harper recruits were required to go through training in the company's popular schools. Once they finished, they were eagerly sought out by competitors. But the success of the company hinged on these recruits' pioneering spirit, their desire for a better life, and their willingness to work hard to get it, wherever that work would take them. Many "Harperites" opened salons in distant cities where they knew no one. A New York City salon owner during the 1930s wrote,

> We started for the big city with . . . determination (which no one thought I had). At last our first customer entered. She was sent by Miss Farquhar of Chicago. Such joy! . . . Let [Miss Harper's] heart rejoice, knowing her girls love her and appreciate what she has done for womanhood.

Just how strongly Harper believed in helping women succeed comes through in a message to salon operators in a 1926 company newsletter: "I believe that the Great Achievement of the Harper Method does not consist of the large number of our shops—though the sun never sets on them. . . . The Great Achievement of the Harper empire is the women it has made." Not surprisingly, suffragists applauded her vision and frequented her salons, including Rochesterian Susan B. Anthony.

A Company in Decline

Harper's salons were successful when she was at the helm, but she made two critical mistakes, Plitt says. One was her failure to patent the reclining shampoo chair that she invented, now a fixture in salons worldwide. The other was creation of a faulty succession plan that failed to recognize the key ingredient in the Harper Method: its commitment to its employees. When Harper retired and passed the reins to her husband, Captain Robert MacBain, the thirty-nine-year-old man she married at the age of sixty-three, the company lost that commitment. Subsequently the Captain, and those he left in charge, abandoned the Harper Method's science-based, healthful image in favor of the beauty-in-a-jar approach of 1950s competitors. Before long, Harper Method products were lost in the crowded beauty market.

Harper died before that happened, in 1950 at ninety-three. She is buried in Rochester's Riverside Cemetery. After the Captain died in 1965, the business continued for seven years under a variety of owners. Then a wily competitor bought the training academy and shut its doors, closing off the network's only source of talent and ensuring the company's demise by attrition. Amazingly, two salons still remain open today, although only one of them, the Harper Method Founder's Shop in Rochester, takes new customers.

The formulas for Harper's original products are in the hands of Niagara Mist Marketing Ltd., a Niagara Falls, Ontario, business owned by the former manager of the Harper manufacturing center. Plitt believes that an enterprising individual could look into buying the rights to the formulas, relaunch the shops, and bring back the Harper name, twenty-first-century style.

Posthumous Recognition

Yet after her biography was published, Martha Matilda Harper has once again received recognition—although this time for her genius in business, not beauty. She was given a posthumous Bonny LeVine Award from the International Franchise Association. She will be inducted into the Rochester Business Hall of Fame this fall. State and federal lawmakers are calling for a postage stamp in her honor. And her story will be included in a major exhibition organized by the Schlesinger Library at Harvard

University. "Enterprising Women: 250 Years of American Business" will open at the National Heritage Museum in October before traveling to six cities over two years.

Jane Plitt still gets phone calls from people eager to share their memories of Martha Matilda Harper and her salons; the loyalty that Harperites had for their leader still runs deep. One Midwestern woman said she stores Harper's letters in a locked wooden box that she whisks to the basement whenever a tornado threatens. A couple from Wisconsin took several boxes of Harper Method documents with them each of the four times they moved. Another woman tenderly recalled childhood visits to a local Harper salon with her mother. And a gentleman from Pittsford, New York, told of his great-aunt who had run a London shop and who counted among her customers the playwright George Bernard Shaw. "It just never ends," Plitt says. "I have been overwhelmed by people who are still sharing their stories."

Patients huddled in blankets in sub-zero temperatures as part of the fresh-air treatment for their tuberculosis. Credit: Adirondack Collection, Saranac Lake Free Library, Saranac Lake, New York.

55

Curación en el Norte ("The Cure" in the North)

Amy Catania

In the summer of 1936, Mercedes Andino left her comfortable life as a government clerk in Cuba and traveled 1,500 miles north to Saranac Lake in upstate New York. But it was not for a vacation. Like many wealthy Latin Americans who had been coming to the heart of the Adirondack Mountains since the turn of the century, Mercedes made the long, grueling trip in search of a cure for her tuberculosis.

One man's experience in the North Country in the 1870s had made Saranac Lake world-famous among physicians and wealthy TB patients. In 1873, Dr. Edward Livingston Trudeau arrived in the Adirondacks to die—or so he thought. But the clean mountain air, the pristine climate, and plenty of hearty food sent his tuberculosis into retreat, and Dr. Trudeau soon settled in Saranac Lake, determined to share his "cure" with other health seekers. As news of the long-term, fresh-air treatment spread, consumptives from all over the world began coming to Saranac Lake. The village quickly grew to meet their needs—and became rich, famous, and international in the bargain.

Like the thousands of patients from all over Latin America who came for "the cure" and then returned home, Mercedes Andino left behind few traces of her activities. But by researching health records and old newspaper and magazine articles, and by recording local residents' memories in oral histories and interviews, a picture gradually emerges of cultural and daily life for these "relocated" Latinos in the little village in New York's last wilderness.

This essay first appeared in winter 2003, volume 2, number 3.

Home Away from the Homeland

By 1900, tuberculosis was a tremendous health problem in Latin America, even among the wealthy, spreading rapidly in regions with underdeveloped sanitation and few public health infrastructures. Many Latin American doctors visited Saranac Lake to study the latest medical procedures at the Trudeau Sanatorium or to cure their own cases of TB, a common hazard of the job. Although nearly two-thirds of Saranac Lake's Latino patients came from Puerto Rico or Cuba, health records show that the remainder came from virtually every country in the Americas. TB was famous for striking people in the prime of their lives, and the Latino patients were mostly young adults in their twenties and thirties. Some came alone; others traveled with family members, friends, or entire households with servants. While the peak years for Latinos were the mid-1930s, Saranac Lake hosted a steady population of Spanish-speaking patients through the entire first half of the twentieth century.

In 1936, Mercedes Andino's personal physician in Cuba probably referred her to the village based on personal knowledge of the town and its facilities and most likely arranged for her to "cure" at the only Spanish-speaking "cure cottage" in town, 80 Park Avenue, run by Alfredo and Alicia Gonzalez. Thanks to them, over the next five years Mercedes would not only recuperate from TB, she would also learn English, make friends with local residents and other patients, and participate in community life.

The dashing and gregarious Alfredo no doubt met Mercedes in person at the train station. Once she was registered by local health officials, Mercedes settled in at her room—not a cottage by ordinary standards, but an elegant three-story building with eighteen cure porches. She must have passed a winter unlike any other in her memory, wrapped in blankets outside on her porch as temperatures dipped past thirty below zero. But she probably found comfort in the familiar food, language, and company of the other Latino patients, some of whom may have been friends or relations from back home.

Only about a quarter of the Latino patients stayed in the Gonzalez' hostel; the rest lived scattered throughout the village. A sample of 184 patients with Spanish surnames turned up eighty separate homes that hosted them. Along with other international patients, Latinos mixed into the daily life of the village, adding to an atmosphere that was both small-town friendly and cosmopolitan. At the Gonzalez' hostel, Mercedes spoke Spanish, ate Latin American cuisine, and listened to Latin music. As soon as she was well enough, Alfredo Gonzalez invited her to participate in community life.

A Man for All Seasons

Alfredo Gonzalez was born in San Juan, Puerto Rico, in 1903. Stricken by TB as a young college student, he came to Saranac Lake in 1920 seeking a cure. He found it in thoracoplasty, a radical operation in which ribs were removed in order to collapse and thus provide rest for the diseased lung. In 1926, Alfredo met and married a visitor from Havana, Alicia Milanes del Prado, a short, stout, soft-spoken woman twenty years his senior. The couple soon opened their first "cure cottage" catering to Latin American patients; over the next forty years they would operate several such cottages in Saranac Lake, the largest and longest-running one at 80 Park Avenue. From the 1930s to the 1950s, Alfredo also inaugurated a number of community projects, including the annual Harvest Hop dance at the Hotel Saranac from 1942 to 1952. The first hop was a gala affair with a Latin American theme; the Pan-American Union in Washington, D.C., loaned a set of large flags representing the twenty-one Latin republics to decorate the hotel ballroom. The event included a Latin dance contest; a beauty pageant with each female contestant representing a different Latin American country; a New York City band, Señor Uvanni and His Caballeros; and the singer Louisa Paván Hennessey.

Several local Latin American families helped Alfredo with the organization and planning of 1948's hop, retitled the Fiesta Hop. Events included a costume ball; a samba exhibition by Mr. and Mrs. P. J. Serrales (of the wealthy Don Q. Rum family); and entertainment by Benito Collada, owner of the El Chico Nightclub in New York; famous singer and dancer Rosita Ríos; and Raúl Barragan's five-piece orchestra. Local photographer Bernard Acosta of Costa Rica recorded the festivities. The Fiesta Hop also showcased one of Alfredo's most prestigious guests, Lieutenant Colonel Mario Vargas, the Venezuelan war hero and chief of the armed forces. Many old-timers in Saranac Lake still remember the general's heavily medaled uniform, as well as the two Venezuelan presidents, Rómulo Gallegos and Romulo Bentancourt, who came to visit him in town.

The Communities Mingle

The Harvest Hop was the main fundraiser for the Study and Craft Guild, an organization that provided TB patients with occupational therapy and diversion from the long, boring hours on the cure porch. Alfredo Gonzalez served on the guild's board of directors for many years, helped start an Americanization English Class, and was one of its most popular teachers of Spanish. Both locals and patients clamored to sign up for his classes. He taught as many as one hundred students a week, meeting with students at five local sanatoria. To make the classes more accessible to bedridden patients, Alfredo helped arrange for a popular *Time* magazine radio series, *Let Us Learn Spanish*, to be broadcast on a local radio station.

Alfredo also tapped into his students' interest-by-proximity in the language and culture of Latin America by starting a Spanish Club, which met on a regular basis through the 1940s and 1950s. These monthly meetings were an opportunity for non-Hispanic community members and patients to experience Latino culture and to converse in Spanish. Records show that Mercedes Andino helped serve refreshments at a Spanish Club party in November 1941.

At this and other community events, Mercedes socialized with local Latin American patients and their families. Some were new acquaintances, but others, like Pilar Benero, were old friends from Cuba. Pilar (née Gordon), from a family of physicians, had accompanied her sister who was ill with TB to Saranac Lake in 1925. There she met Manolo Benero, who had left Puerto Rico in 1917 seeking the cure. Manolo and Pilar soon married and settled down in the village to raise two sons.

The Benero Family

For many Latino patients, their humdrum, often difficult existence in Saranac Lake must have contrasted starkly with the wealthy lives of leisure they had led back home. This was particularly true for Pilar Benero, who came from one of Cuba's wealthiest and most prominent families but who settled in Saranac Lake to live out a middle-class life in a small brick house. While the Beneros mingled happily with the townspeople, they also socialized with the wealthy elite of Cuba and Latin America. Pilar taught Spanish classes to local children and held piano recitals with her close friend Dita, wife of the composer Béla Bartók, one of Saranac Lake's "famous" TB patients. Manolo, host to a stream of Latin American guests, also worked in the office of a local laundry and was a member of the Lions, Rotary, and Fish and Game Clubs. Their sons Joseph and Manny played hockey and grew up speaking English with the slightly Canadian twang of a North Country accent, although at home they spoke Spanish with family and visitors. The Beneros lived the rest of their lives in Saranac Lake; today their headstones stand out in the Catholic cemetery, the only ones with Spanish surnames.

The End of an Era

With the development of antibiotics following World War II, the TB "cure industry" began a steep decline. By the mid-1950s, wealthy Latino patients were no longer making the journey to Saranac Lake; their absence, both culturally and financially, was keenly felt. Alfredo and Alicia Gonzalez moved to New York City in 1962, where they died in 1965. And like so many children born and raised at the end of the boom times of the TB era, Joseph and Manny Benero left Saranac Lake after their high school graduation in the forties. With their departure, the village lost its only two native-born Spanish speakers.

In recent years, Saranac Lake, proud of its vibrant and colorful past as a world-famous health resort, has experienced a renewal. Many of the old cure cottages, as well as the train station, have been restored to their original state, and tourist money has fueled a revival of interest in the town's unique history. The Latin Americans, whose circumstances took them far from their homelands during the cure years, make up an important part of that history.

Governor Al Smith cooling off at a Democratic picnic in Poughkeepsie, an ice cream sandwich in one hand and a glass of soda (and his ubiquitous cigar) in the other. Credit: From the collections of the New York State Library, Manuscripts and Special Collections, Albany, New York.

56

Made in New York

Robert A. Slayton

Al Smith, the quintessential New Yorker who rose from the tenements of Manhattan to the Executive Mansion in Albany, had an impact on how New Yorkers live their lives . . . and it endures to this day.

His name means little to most Americans today, but at one time Alfred Emanuel Smith was among the most famous political figures in the nation. A New Yorker all his life, Al Smith was not only New York City writ large. He was also the state's ambassador to the world beyond the Hudson.

Al was born in a tenement on December 30, 1873, in the middle of one of Manhattan's most crowded neighborhoods, just north of the present-day South Street Seaport. Census figures show the diversity of this neighborhood: immigrants from Mexico, France, Sweden, Spain, Greece, and Canada. Al's paternal grandparents came from Italy and Germany, while his mother was Irish—an ethnic identity he adopted fully. From the windows of his apartment, Al watched the Brooklyn Bridge being built and then went down to the docks to play, shimmying up the rigging of masted schooners. For education and moral guidance, his family turned to the Roman Catholic Church. Al attended classes at St. James, where he was a good student. But it was clear from the beginning that he possessed a politician's attributes. Old-timers in the neighborhood remembered him as a "smiling child" and recalled how he would talk his way out of fights or entertain local toughs with a song or dance, story or joke.

His education did not last long. When his father died in 1886, thirteen-year-old Al had to quit school and go to work. Thus, all of his future accomplishments would be backed by a mere seventh-grade education; he never received even a grade school diploma.

This essay first appeared in spring 2003, volume 2, number 4.

None of Al's subsequent jobs were particularly distinguished or interesting, but one did provide some ballast for his future career in politics: he would turn stories of his work at the legendary Fulton Fish Market into part of his own mythology.

A Natural Politician

As a young man, Al began to use some of his natural talents as a politician on behalf of local candidates, and Tammany Hall's ruling political machine, which had branches in every neighborhood, began to offer rewards. His first job as a process server was modest enough, but in 1903 local ward leaders decided that he had something on the ball and ran him for state assembly. In Al's East Side community, Tammany's endorsement was second only to the Lord's, and maybe not even that. To no one's surprise, he won.

Albany's two legislative chambers were ruled by tradition and by gentlemen farmers and lawyers from upstate. Al, just a Tammany hack in those years, would vote how he was told to vote and then dutifully return to Manhattan on weekends to take care of individual constituents' problems and needs. Yet he chafed at his limited role, and considered going back to New York City and taking a job in local government.

Self-Taught Legislator

But he made a decision that would change his life: he would stay in Albany and become the best assemblyman he could be. Thus, he began a remarkable process that would take him several years to accomplish. Every night, often until two or three in the morning, he sat up and read each bill that had come before him. If he did not know a word, he looked it up. If a proposed law was an amendment to some other part of the civic code, he looked up the precedent. If he needed more information, he haunted the legislative library for facts and figures.

When this self-imposed education was complete, Al's mastery of governmental detail, combined with his natural charm, made him one of the most outstanding members the assembly had ever seen. He could stop anyone mid-track with what he knew of the state's operations, but he always added humor so the person he interrupted would laugh as Al made his point. On one occasion, when gentlemen legislators stopped an important floor debate to discuss their respective alma maters' sports teams, Al casually mentioned that he was a graduate of FFM. What did that stand for? someone demanded. "The Fulton Fish Market," Al replied, and only after the hearty laugh subsided in the assembly did he allow legislators to resume their business.

The Triangle Shirtwaist Fire

Al was clearly becoming a leader, and in 1911 he had an opportunity to use his abilities for the good of New York and the nation. On March 25, fire broke out at the Triangle Shirtwaist Company in Manhattan, a sweatshop that manufactured blouses and that employed mostly women. Inside the tall, narrow tenement building were long worktables bolted to the wall at each end, so that some workers had to travel seventy-five feet before they got to an aisle leading to a door. Positioned every few feet along the tables were sewing machines, whose highly flammable lubricants dripped onto the discarded piles of lint and fabric underneath each worker's station.

Within seconds, the factory was an inferno. Women plunged from tenth-story windows as they faced the choice of jumping or being burned alive. Within less than half an hour, 146 people had died. Prior to September 11, 2001, the fire was New York's worst high-rise tragedy.

A horrified legislature appointed a Factory Investigating Commission to probe the disaster. Chaired by future U.S. senator and father of Social Security Robert Wagner, and with Al serving as vice-chair, the committee investigated fire safety in New York's sweatshops and then went on to examine factory work in general, producing the first detailed, comprehensive study in the nation of industrial conditions.

Safety Reforms

As leaders of the state assembly and senate, respectively, Smith and Wagner engineered a complete overhaul of New York's fire codes—and their reforms are still in force. They had discovered at Triangle, for example, that workers could not find the exits; today every public venue, even those that must stay dark, like movie theaters or fashionable restaurants, has red signs showing where to exit in an emergency. Panicked workers at Triangle had also been unable to turn superheated doorknobs or, with so many people stampeding to get out, to open doors that pulled inward. Under the leadership of Wagner and Smith, the state passed a bill that fire doors must have what is now known as a panic bar, and they had to open outward. First implemented in New York, these and other safety procedures and devices were adopted throughout the United States.

An Accomplished Governor

In 1915, Al distinguished himself at New York's Constitutional Convention with his extensive knowledge of state operations, and state leaders began looking to him to lead the battle for good government. Three years later, in 1918, he was elected governor of New York. Although he lost in the 1920 Republican landslide, he would win the two-year term again in 1922, 1924, and 1926, making him one of only a handful of governors to be elected four times. In the twentieth century, only Nelson Rockefeller beat Al's record.

Al immediately distinguished himself as a social reformer, building parks and hospitals and creating housing for the poor. His greatest accomplishments, however, came in the field of education—not surprising, given his background. Al once told an audience that the state could sideline many of its obligations, "but the process of education must always be kept at one hundred percent of efficiency . . . because time lost cannot be regained by the children who are injured by the state's failure to make adequate provision for their education." Under his leadership, New York's spending on education jumped from $7 million in 1918–1919 to $70 million in 1926–1927—an astonishing tenfold increase. Salaries for teachers doubled, as did enrollments in high schools. How was this accomplished? Quality education, Al said, took only two things: "money and nerve."

An Administrative Genius

What is less well known is that Al was also the state's premier administrative reformer, creating the governmental system that guides New Yorkers to this day. When he first became governor in 1918, there were 187 different state departments, commissions, and committees operating on equal status, some of them duplicative, with no overall plan of organization between them. Al was determined to reform New York's government and turn it into a functioning administrative entity. By the time he left office in 1928, he had created a cabinet system of clearly designated departments, with all subsidiary bodies folded into the structure. And for the first time, an executive budget was drawn up, instead of allowing the legislature to cobble together disbursements to satisfy 187 separate requests. These two administrative reforms have become the tools that all governors have since used to run the state.

Running for President

But what Al gave the nation as a whole was as important as governmental reform. The twenties were years of great change for America, an era when the Ku Klux Klan came to power as a national organization and boasted millions of members, when John Scopes was tried in a criminal court because he taught evolution, when Nicola Sacco and Bartolomeo Vanzetti went to the electric chair because they were Italian anarchists. Amid these fears, no politician stood taller than Al Smith in the fight for dignity and pluralism. Repeatedly, he told the people of New York and the country that its immigrants—those whose ancestors had arrived three years and not three centuries ago—had the same right to be called Americans as anyone else.

In 1928, New York's governor Alfred E. Smith, graduate of FFM, earned the Democratic nomination for president. Al ran against Herbert Hoover, a self-made man like himself and—at least in those days—something of a reformer whose views were not all that different from his own. But Hoover had come from a small town in Iowa, had descended from old stock, and was dry on Prohibition—the ultimate wedge issue at the time.

A Campaign of Hate

The 1928 presidential contest was the worst example of cultural war in U.S. history. It was conducted not by debates over policies and programs but by rants over prejudices and fears. Millions of Americans learned that if a Catholic were elected president, all Protestant marriages would be annulled and their offspring rendered illegitimate on the spot. In Daytona Beach, Florida, the school board sent every child home with a note to parents that read, "If [Al Smith] is elected president, you will not be allowed to have or read a Bible." Bigots pasted up thousands of nasty cartoons that portrayed "A Cabinet Meeting" in a Smith-occupied White House, with the Pope presiding at a table populated with priests and monsignors and Al standing off to the side in a bellboy's outfit, offering a jug of whiskey. Others captioned actual photos of the Holland Tunnel's construction as the secret passageway being built between Washington and Rome to bring the pope to America.

Capturing the Future

In the end, the 1928 campaign became a landslide of hate that no one person could reverse. Al lost his presidential bid, but he captured the future. The nation's twelve largest cities had all gone Republican in 1920, but eight years later every one of them joined the Democratic Party and stayed there, forming the core of the New Deal Coalition.

More importantly, Al Smith had reminded the nation of its core values, insisting on the necessity for decency and the acceptance of diversity. Even when it was not easy or smart to do so, this hardscrabble, heroic son of New York used wisdom and courage borne of experience throughout his years of public service to lead both the state and the nation to a greater understanding of what it meant to be an American.

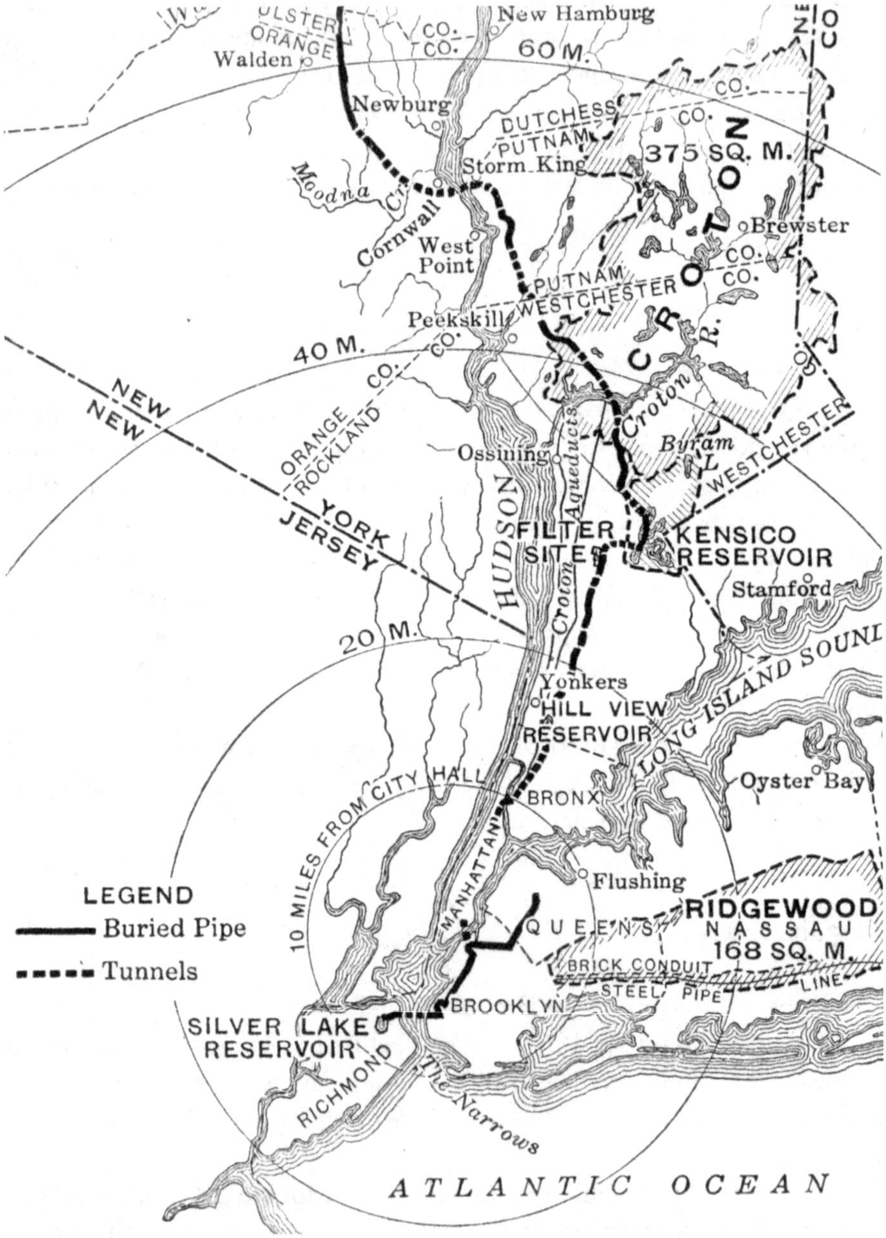

Southern section of the New York City water supply, from J. R. Smith's *Human Geography*, ca. 1920. Credit: New York State Archives, Albany, New York.

57

Water and War

David Stradling

In August 1940, with war raging in Europe and Asia and tensions rising in the United States, New York City mayor Fiorello LaGuardia wrote to Governor Herbert Lehman asking him to declare a state of emergency in New York. LaGuardia wanted the governor to make the declaration so the city could take extraordinary steps to safeguard its water supply. Anticipating that the city's upstate reservoirs would become targets of saboteurs if the United States were drawn into the war, LaGuardia specifically requested that the city be allowed to deny fishermen access to these waters, noting that "one case of abuse of this privilege" would make the policy of continued licensing of sportsmen "look ridiculous." Just seven days after his letter to Lehman, LaGuardia made an official and public application for declaration of an emergency. This led to a month of rigorous debate within the state.

State law guaranteed citizens access to city reservoirs for certain purposes, including fishing. The numerous upstate reservoirs and their tributaries had long been important recreation spots, particularly in Westchester County where the city owned so much water. But with escalating fears of war, the state legislature had passed a law earlier in 1940 allowing the governor to grant the city greater power over its own water supply during a national emergency. Indeed, the entire nation had been put on alert after a popular engineering journal ran an article entitled "Sabotage and Water Service," which suggested a number of steps municipalities should take to protect their supplies, including a ban on fishing in sensitive areas. The State Department of Health had subsequently issued a letter to all waterworks officials in the state concerning the security of water supplies, particularly since water was essential to "war industries."

This essay first appeared in spring 2003, volume 2, number 4.

In addition to possible destruction of supply structures, including dams, intakes, and aqueducts, the letter warned against the introduction of "pathogenic organisms."

Alarms Then and Now

This was not the first time that international conflict had sounded an alarm for water supply safety. During World War I, New York City had stepped up patrols around its reservoirs and restricted access to strategic areas. And in our own time, similar concern about possible terrorist acts after September 11, 2001, led the city to once again restrict access and increase patrols; these measures continue to the present day. In each instance, recreational fishermen faced reminders that their favored waters could be placed off limits and their rights could be limited by calls for security. Each time, upstate residents generally met these new restrictions with support and understanding, despite the inconveniences many faced because of the heightened security. But reservoir restrictions also served as stark reminders of the city's power over its upstate neighbors and touched on a larger national issue: the often contentious relationship between large cities and the smaller communities from which they get their water.

Despite the eventual acceptance of restrictions during World War II, as Governor Lehman debated whether or not to declare a state of emergency, both upstate and downstate residents lobbied to keep the reservoirs open. Since the law required Lehman to hold a public hearing on the issue, one was convened in Albany on September 27, 1940, allowing many citizens to voice their concerns about limiting reservoir access. At the same time, dozens of sportsmen launched a letter-writing campaign to the governor. The campaign garnered most of its support from Westchester County, especially Yonkers.

Letters Urge Access

In the letters, several individuals pleaded for Lehman to keep city waters open on the basis of economic fairness, saying that for fishermen of moderate means reservoirs were among the most accessible fishing spots. But most letters raised other points, one of which was that no state of emergency existed at the moment, since the nation was not at war. Another theme was that preventing access by fishermen would not only fail to increase reservoir security but might actually jeopardize it. For example, Joseph Capillo of Tarrytown argued that his local rod and gun club "consists largely of Volunteer firemen and fire police," and that "in granting us the privilege of using these properties, we are in a better position and are willing to keep anyone from performing subversive activities on or about these properties"—in other words, just by their presence fishermen would be able to report any suspicious behavior and thus discourage sabotage.

Yet another theme focused on the beneficial qualities of fishing itself. One sportsman from Haines Falls echoed the old argument that contact with nature made men strong: "To discourage fishing and hunting is, indeed, to discourage the development of certain rugged qualities that would be of greatest value to our nation when need for defense arises." Fishing also encouraged patriotism, he argued, since love of the streams and lakes of "his native land" would only strengthen a sportsman's love of country.

Several residents of the Catskills region wrote Lehman, including Emery Kelder, Jr., of the Hurley Gun Club. In a brief but articulate note, Kelder argued that the Ashokan Reservoir should be kept open. "We as sportsmen have suffered much at the hands of New York City," he claimed. Going well beyond the issue at hand, Kelder noted that the city had "ruined the fishing on the Esopus with the aid of the Gilboa Tunnel and no matter how much money is appropriated by the State for stocking this stream there will never be good fishing until New York City controls the flow of water." Clearly, the proposed closure of the Ashokan Reservoir to fishing was just one item on a list of grievances Kelder held against the city's management of its Catskills water supply.

Upstate Residents Have a Stake

In a less emotional letter, the Rosendale Township Association argued on economic grounds for continued recreational access. "Our principal source of livelihood is the business of our hotels and resorts regulated by our ability to attract increasing numbers of New York City people to this area for weekends and vacations," noted Louise Rossler, the association's secretary. Echoing arguments made from Westchester, Rossler also asserted that the "men and women holding permits allowing access to these waters constitute a body of law-abiding and patriotic citizens. Their very presence would furnish added protection to the water supply of New York City and would deter activities of anyone desiring its destruction." Rossler's letter suggested that upstate residents also had much at stake in the security of the reservoirs, and that they too were eager to see them safe.

In the end, the letter-writing campaign failed to prevent Lehman from declaring an emergency, which he did on September 29, 1940. The governor expressed his sorrow in disappointing the fishermen of the state, but he argued that security needs were simply too pressing. A day later, LaGuardia revoked all licenses issued for access to

New York City reservoir waters and prohibited all public use. But the letter-writing campaign may have had some impact on new rules announced by the city just two weeks later: the city would issue new permits, through a process that required photographs and fingerprints, and most New York City waters would be opened once again to fishing, except areas nearest dams—not an extreme restriction. The issuance of these new permits, combined with U.S. entry into the war after the Pearl Harbor attack in December 1941, muted complaints among upstate residents.

Unlikely Targets

With restricted access and added patrols in place, New York City's water supply remained secure throughout World War II, just as it does today. But the water supply may never have been an attractive target for either saboteurs or terrorists at all. The large earthen dams that surround most of the city's large reservoirs are not particularly vulnerable to explosives, and chlorination makes successful biological contamination unlikely. As for nonbiological toxic contamination, the sheer size of the reservoir system, capable of delivering up to 1.8 billion gallons per day to New York City, offers its own best defense through dilution.

Yet city Department of Environmental Protection patrol cars now stationed around upstate dams, as well as new "Keep Out" signs, do more than remind residents of the tragic events of September 11 and the ongoing threat of terrorism. They also remind us of the power a metropolis will always have over the communities that supply it with water.

A ride in a goat cart was just one of the many ways that people could "laugh, enjoy themselves, and . . . spend money while being amused." Credit: Library of Congress.

58

The Biggest Playground on Earth

Woody Register

Travel to just about any corner of the globe and you'll find a seaside carnival, urban "fun fair," or arcade with deafening video games called "Luna Park." In Argentina, Japan, France, Saudi Arabia, Italy, Australia, Israel, Cyprus, South Korea, Hungary, Turkey—anywhere, that is, except the United States—Luna Park is *lingua franca* for the screaming pleasure of roller coasters, the crazy driving of bumper cars, the giddy sky-scraping of Ferris wheels that anyone of any age would recognize as an amusement park.

Ironically, although that singular name has now all but disappeared from our language, for the first half of the twentieth century Luna Park was part and parcel of our American vernacular. In 1903 a pair of showmen, Fred Thompson and Elmer "Skip" Dundy, opened a twenty-two-acre amusement park at Coney Island in Brooklyn-by-the-sea. They named the resort after Dundy's sister, and Luna Park subsequently became the most popular summer destination on the North American continent.

Today, near the park's original location on Surf Avenue, only a saloon, furniture store, and housing complex bear the appellation. There's no amusement park anymore: it closed in the mid-1940s after a series of devastating fires. But a hundred years after it opened, the idea of Luna Park—and its vision of how life should be—is still very much with us.

Pleasure Palaces

Luna Park did not invent Coney Island; that "great breathing space by the sea" had been luring metropolitan crowds to its seashore, its resort hotels, and its raucous amusement

This essay first appeared in summer 2003, volume 3, number 1.

thoroughfare called the Bowery since the 1880s. By 1903, Coney Island had become a bustling summertime destination for millions of pleasure-seeking New Yorkers. Most of its diversions were respectable, although a few of them, like gambling and prostitution, were not. But the concept of pleasure that Thompson and Dundy introduced to Coney Island on the night of May 16 was unlike anything New Yorkers (or anyone else) had ever seen before: an exotic city-within-a-city crowded with brilliant white palaces and ornamented with showering fountains, onion domes, glittering towers, minarets. It seems unlikely that any amusement park today could move us as much as Luna Park stirred New Yorkers on that first night and for the rest of its first season.

At precisely 8 p.m. on May 16 the electrical switches were thrown, and against the early evening darkness the outlines of Luna Park's fantastic buildings burst into view, lit by more than two hundred thousand small incandescent bulbs. The *New York Times* reported that forty-five thousand people "rubbed their eyes and stood in wonder and pinched themselves to see if there was not something wrong somewhere." Electric illumination was already commonplace in New York City, but the sheer intensity of the spectacle was not meant to cast light or eliminate darkness. It was intended to jolt the imagination. As a bedazzled *Brooklyn Eagle* reporter observed, "It seemed that a huge mantle of light had been let down from the sky to disclose the domain of an unknown world."

After paying a dime and passing through a massive arch that spelled out "The Heart of Coney Island" in such lights, the opening night crowd beheld a world that was a combination of circus, dime museum, and carnival midway. There was a dance hall, Wormwood's Monkey Theater (featuring variety acts by animals), an outdoor circus, Venetian canals, and a nursery of premature babies warmed in glass-enclosed incubators and overseen by licensed nurses and doctors. For another fee, patrons could take "A Trip to the Moon" or to "20,000 Leagues Under the Sea to the North Pole," or watch a spectacle called "War of the Worlds."

A World Removed

There had been amusement parks before, like Coney Island's own Steeplechase Park, a bazaar of funhouse pranks and entertainments that gave people license to shed their workaday composure. But Steeplechase was a disorderly version of the everyday world that operated according to its own antic rules, and it seemed dingy and unspectacular in comparison with Luna Park, an architecturally unified and exotic garden of enchantment. Although built out of flimsy and inexpensive plaster, it appeared extravagantly luxurious and monumental—a vision of what the new twentieth century could or should be. As a popular writer of the time observed,

Luna Park seemed "a world removed—shut away from the sordid clatter and turmoil of the streets." Everywhere there "was life—a pageant of happy people; and everywhere was color—a wide harmony of orange and white and gold." It was billed as "The Biggest Playground on Earth," and its existence both asked and answered the question, *Shouldn't life always be this way, full of joy and color, without toil or pain or sacrifice?*

Fred Thompson certainly thought so; Luna Park was his design. A self-styled architect and visionary, Thompson was one of the builders of America's turn-of-the-century consumer and leisure economy. In an era when the nation's productive technologies and exploding industrial capacity flooded markets with new things to buy, Thompson and others like him retooled the machines to manufacture and sell the most sought-after items of all: pleasure and play. His ventures were just one dimension of a national revolution in urban commercial amusements that catered to the rapidly expanding middle class. Thompson's publicist called this new amusement economy "the billion-dollar smile" and declared that "it is spread to-day from Seattle to New York, from Bangor to the Gulf." It was true: American cities large and small offered low-priced theaters and vaudeville houses, opera companies, dance halls, restaurants, amusement parks, ballparks, nickelodeons, and picture palaces.

Showman Extraordinaire

Born in Ohio in 1873 but raised in Tennessee, Thompson had staked his initial claim on the business of smiles by building shows for the amusement midways of the era's great world's fairs. Moody, quixotic, given to alcoholic binges, he was an outsized figure even for the day. The spectacle of his failures would eventually overwhelm the wonder of his successes. But for a decade, with the debut of Luna Park (and later his mammoth New York Hippodrome in Manhattan, the largest theater in the world at the time), Thompson reigned as one of the early twentieth century's premiere showmen.

Thompson explained that Luna Park was a playground, dreamed up by a man who cared little about making a lot of money: what he really wanted was to have fun. And Luna was a place where grown-ups could forget their responsibilities—including the kids. Having "too much work and too little play," adults suffered from what Thompson called "tuberculosis of the heart," for which Luna was the antidote, an oasis of make-believe where "play was everything" and "responsibility had never been dreamed of." He prohibited right angles and rectilinear edges in his architecture because they reminded him of church sermons, fashioning instead "Oriental" cities of sinuous curves that would make people "laugh, enjoy themselves, and . . . spend money while being amused." At Luna Park, a man got to be a kid again.

Sensational Attendance

Thompson had struck gold with this idea at Buffalo's 1901 Pan-American International Exposition. His fantasy twenty-minute "Trip to the Moon" was the sensation of the fair, convincingly executed with theatrical tricks and illusions. After a lecture on the "great secret of anti-gravitation and aërial flight," passengers boarded a cigar-shaped winged vessel and soared to the moon, where the Lilliputian natives treated them to bites of green cheese and a dance performance by shapely moon maidens. The following summer, Thompson, now partnered with Skip Dundy, reopened "Trip" at Coney Island's Steeplechase Park, where it was a hit again. In 1903 they made it the centerpiece of Luna Park, where it continued to make money over the next decade. Since then, no major amusement park has operated without a similar attraction: anyone who embarked on Disneyland's 1955 "Rocket to the Moon," or who has joined E.T. on his bicycle at Universal Studios' Orlando Theme Park, has experienced the same thrilling illusion of antigravitational flight.

Luna Park's turnstiles suggested Thompson was on to something. The park counted an attendance of five million in 1906, a number equal to half of New York State's population, and in 1909 Coney Island logged twenty million visitors. Indeed, the island had gotten so crowded that the ordinarily grave *New York Times* quipped that year, "Who ever goes nowadays except everybody?"

Dreamlands and Wonderlands

"Everybody" included entrepreneurs from across the nation and around the world who hustled to duplicate Luna Park's success. It's not hard to see why: several million people, multiplied by a dime or any smaller coin, amounted by definition to a bonanza. In the fall of 1903, an alliance of businessmen and politicians had already broken ground at Coney Island for Dreamland, which promised to be bigger and better than Luna in every way. It was bigger, but never as popular as its rival. By 1910, the American urban landscape glimmered with hundreds of amusement parks—Dreamlands, White Cities, Electric Parks, Sans Soucis, Wonderlands, Fairylands, Playlands—nineteen of which were named for the Coney Island original. Luna Parks also arose in Berlin, Buenos Aires, Rome, Sydney, and Melbourne. At a time when American industrialists were focused on domestic markets, Luna Park, with its vision of a magical world, was perhaps the nation's most dazzling and desired cultural export.

But by 1912, Fred Thompson was financially bankrupt and physically broken, undone by extravagance and alcoholism. Luna itself passed into new hands, and Thompson's death in 1919 coincided with the expiration of the Luna Park phase both of Coney Island and of amusement parks in general. In 1920, the five-cent subway came to Coney Island, and the summertime crowds, most of them from the city's immigrant-based working-class neighborhoods, swelled again. Yet even though new landmarks like the Cyclone roller coaster dominated the skyline, by the 1940s the vast numbers of visitors—forty-six million in 1943 alone—came for the surf and beaches, not the parks. At Coney Island and elsewhere, amusement parks were dropping their prices and retooling their attractions to appeal to children and families, while middle-class Americans turned more and more to movies and automobiles for escape and diversion.

The Good Life Lives On

Still, anyone who has visited the capitals of the Mickey Mouse Empire in the years since World War II can recognize the promise of a return to childhood as an essential selling point of the Disney theme parks and movies. "There's a place where magic lives," Disney's current ad campaign assures us, reminding us by default of the un-magical circumstances of our everyday lives. All ages are urged to have fun together at the various Disney destinations, which include not only the vast American sites but also mini-cities in Paris, Tokyo, and, soon, Hong Kong. It seems the vision of the Good Life has changed little since the turn of the twentieth century, when Luna Park existed as a haven "for grown-ups and Peter Pans who will never grow up." It's just that now the kids can come along.

At age nineteen, Elinor Smith was named the best female pilot in the country. Credit: Cradle of Aviation Museum, Garden City, New York.

59

Island of the Skies

George DeWan

If aviation was born on a wind-blown, sandy hill near Kitty Hawk, North Carolina, it was raised and nurtured on the flatlands of Long Island's Hempstead Plains.

Not to take anything away from Orville and Wilbur Wright's magnificent flying adventure just one hundred years ago this December 17. (Or from an amazed teenage witness named Johnny Moore, who raced into town shouting, "They done it! Damned if they ain't flew!") Or from the multitude of adventurous, seat-of-the-pants fliers from around the world who took to the air over the next three decades to push aviation from infancy to adulthood.

But in the early days of manned flight, Long Island was where much of the action was. It was the scene of a number of firsts—the first air mail; the first solo flight across the Atlantic Ocean; the first "blind" flight, in which the pilot took off and landed by instruments; the first nonstop flight across the United States; the first American designed and built monoplane; the first wireless radio transmission from an aircraft; the first American woman to pilot an airplane—to name just a few.

Speed, altitude, and endurance records were routinely set and broken. Pioneering flights regularly began or ended on Long Island, the most memorable being the 1927 flight to Paris of Charles Lindbergh in the *Spirit of St. Louis*. Starry-eyed airplane builders set up shop and tested new designs. Daring young barnstorming pilots in their fragile flying machines thrilled huge crowds with their aerial exploits.

Fiery crashes were always part of the story. On hand to document the excitement with graphic photos and blaring headlines were the circulation-hungry New York newspapers.

This essay first appeared in fall 2003, volume 3, number 2.

The Magical Kingdom of the Air

Many a youngster who got a $10 plane ride was converted for life into a true believer in the magic kingdom of the air. Frank Harris, born in Jamaica, Queens, in 1906, got his first airplane ride a dozen years later at Hazelhurst Field in Mineola, Nassau County. He was hooked. Once he got his own pilot's license, Harris became a barnstormer himself in the heady days of the 1920s. "We would fly around until we found a lot big enough to fly out of," Harris later told an interviewer. "We would land there and start carrying passengers for $10. If we couldn't get $10 we would take $5. That is, if we were hungry enough . . . We went all over the Island."

Then there was Elinor Smith, who grew up in Freeport, five miles south of Mineola. In the summer of 1917, when she was six, she took the first of many $5 plane rides with a hotshot French flyer named Louis Gaubert, who had parked his Farman biplane in an abandoned Hicksville potato field. Smith, who thirteen years later would be named the best female pilot in the country, described her first flight in her autobiography, *Aviatrix*:

> That never-to-be-forgotten summer of flying with Gaubert shaped my life. I remember so vividly my first time aloft that I can still hear the wind sing in the wires as we glided down . . . I knew my future in airplanes and flying was as inevitable as the freckles on my nose.

Acting on a dare on a quiet Sunday morning in the fall of 1928, just three months after getting her pilot's license, seventeen-year-old Elinor Smith screwed up her courage and did something no one had ever done before (or since): she flew an airplane under all four East River bridges in New York. By nightfall, newsreels of the stunt were in all the Broadway theaters, and the next day's newspapers were hysterical in their coverage of this teenage wonder. Smith was named Female Pilot of the Year in 1929 (beating out Amelia Earhart!). But Smith was only one of a number of women aviators who took to the air from the fields on and around the Hempstead Plains.

Early Women Aviators

Women fliers were unusual in the early days of aviation. The year 1929 also marked the formation of The Ninety-Nines at Curtiss Field in Valley Stream, a group of ninety-nine women (including Smith and Earhart, the first president) devoted to promoting women in aviation.

In 1911, the year Smith was born, a strikingly beautiful New York theater critic and photojournalist named Harriet Quimby flashed across the firmament. She learned to fly at the Hempstead Plains Aerodrome, became the first American woman to get a pilot's license, and later was the first woman to fly the English Channel. But within a year of that achievement, Quimby was dead at age thirty-seven, thrown from a plane near Boston.

In 1910, Bessica Raiche of Mineola was the first American woman to fly solo. Many years later, in the midst of World War II, Grumman employed three female test pilots: Barbara Jayne, Elizabeth Hooker, and Cecil (Teddy) Kenyon. The latter, who got her pilot's license at Roosevelt Field in 1929, once said that flying was the "sanest, safest and most comfortable way to travel."

"You Will Fly Tomorrow . . ."

Those were the days when an impromptu airplane ride was irresistible for the strong of heart. In the late twenties, summertime motorists in their Model A Fords heading south on Cross Bay Boulevard in search of sun and sand at Rockaway Beach were enticed by a large sign painted on the side of a roadside airplane hangar at the end of a sandy airstrip: YOU WILL FLY TOMORROW—WHY NOT TODAY? Jammed into the sand was another sign: PASSENGER RIDES $5. OVER N.Y. CITY AND THE STATUE OF LIBERTY $10 AND $15.

An unidentified local newspaper writer later reported:

> Anyone who has not taken his first airplane ride has something in store for him . . . Passengers are not strapped in their seats, nor are parachutes fastened to their backs, any more than they would be if the ride was being taken in an automobile. As far as the actual flying is concerned, it is different from any other sensation. There is nothing of the roller coaster's breathtaking dive. It is more like soaring and the only sensation of speed is that caused by the wind whistling by.

Flying was more than just a show, however, and more than just a thrilling ride in the sky. As Joshua Stoff, curator of the Cradle of Aviation Museum at Mitchel Field, has written, Long Island was a natural airfield, especially the area in central Nassau County known historically as the Hempstead Plains, a flat, treeless prairie formed by the outwash of the glacier that sculpted Long Island. Running from Queens almost to the Suffolk County border, the sixty-thousand-acre plain was the only true prairie east of the Mississippi River, ideal in colonial days for cattle grazing. But by the beginning of the twentieth century, the cattle were gone and airfields covered the landscape. The roaring engines, combined with the smell of oil, gasoline, and the pungent odor of banana oil lacquer, or "dope"—which was applied to tighten and strengthen airplane fabric—was a heady mixture for young people who dreamed of flying.

Pilots and Plane-Makers

One of these was a teenager named George Dade, who arrived from Wisconsin in 1921 with his father, Jesse, a woodworker attracted to a job with the new Curtiss Engineering Co. in Garden City. Dade was overwhelmed with what he saw, as he later wrote (with journalist George Vecsey) in *Getting Off the Ground*. "In our way, we were joining the brigade of pioneers—the inventors, mechanics, kids off the farm, veterans from World War One, people willing to risk their lives to be pilots," wrote Dade, who in 1929, at age seventeen, became one of the youngest people in the country to earn a pilot's license. "They were flocking to an airfield Glenn Curtiss had developed on the Hempstead Plains. He came down to New York City, looking for a flat place, and when he came to Long Island he must have felt like Brigham Young when he crossed the last mountain and said, 'This is the place.'"

Not for nothing has Long Island become known as the "cradle of aviation." The great Hammondsport, New York, plane-maker Glenn Curtiss—whose Buffalo plant produced the World War I workhorse Jenny biplane—moved downstate in 1917 to Garden City, a new town built in the barren flatlands of central Nassau County. His company was the first facility devoted solely to airplane research and development, and he bought the western section of nearby Roosevelt Field, rechristening it Curtiss Field. Out of this venture came the first flying boat, and in 1919 the Curtiss-built NC-4 became the first airplane to cross the Atlantic.

Museum director Stoff refers to the period through the mid-thirties as Long Island's "Golden Age of Aviation." "During the Golden Age," Stoff wrote in his book, *The Aerospace Heritage of Long Island*, "there were more aviation manufacturers on Long Island than in any other area of the country."

Fields of Dreams

There have been at least eighty airfields, large and small, scattered about Long Island, from Queens County in the west to Montauk Point in the east. The 1910 International Aviation Meet was held at Belmont Park in nearby Elmont; a year later, a second meet was held in Garden City. At this meet, pilot Earle Ovington, designated as U.S. Mail Pilot #1, made the nation's first official airmail flight, a six-mile jaunt to Mineola, where he dropped a mailbag onto the small Mineola airfield.

But one airfield stands out in historical memory: Roosevelt Field, once the largest aviation field in the world. Originally called the Hempstead Plains Aerodrome (1911–1917), the airfield was renamed Hazelhurst Field, then in 1919 renamed again, this time for Theodore Roosevelt's youngest son, Quentin, who had died in France as a World War I aviator.

Roosevelt Field: where historic flights began or ended, where new planes were tested, where the country's first civilian flying school opened in 1911, where fliers looking for prize money or fame came to attack the record book, and where thousands of spectators would gather to watch the latest in daredevil aerobatics. (And where, half a century later, tens of thousands of shoppers would gather for the opening of a Macy's branch in the fabulous new shrine to consumerism, the Roosevelt Field Shopping Center.)

But a new era was beginning as the "Golden Age" was dying. The 1930s saw the groundwork being laid for development of the airplanes that would help win World War II: the Wildcat and Hellcat, built by the Grumman Aircraft Engineering Corporation in Bethpage, and the P-47 Thunderbolt, built by the Republic Aviation Corporation in Farmingdale.

Fast forward to July 20, 1969. That is when astronaut Neil Armstrong stepped off the spidery, Grumman-built lunar module and took "one giant leap for mankind" onto the moon. Although Hempstead Plains was by then a distant memory, Long Island proudly roared its approval of another splendid moment in its aviation history.

Margaret Sanger. Credit: Sophia Smith Collection, Smith College, Northampton, Massachusetts.

60

"A Remarkable Woman"

Peter C. Engelman

> What a remarkable woman—what imagination, what pertinacity of purpose—And how lovely—There are so few really distinguished women—I should say people—in the world & she certainly was one of them.

We were reminded of these words with the passing of Katharine Hepburn last summer at the age of ninety-five, for surely this tribute describes the strong-minded, patrician actress who redefined the role of "leading woman." But the tribute was written not for, but by, Katharine Hepburn herself in September 1966 upon the death of her friend Margaret Sanger—who perhaps was a model for the kind of independent woman Hepburn symbolized and the equally independent actress she became.

Margaret Sanger watched Katharine Hepburn flourish as a young actress on the New York stage and in Hollywood films, a career that Margaret had once envisioned for herself. Her interest was deepened by her close association with Hepburn's mother.

Childhood Friends

Katharine Houghton Hepburn (or "Kit," as she was known to friends) and Margaret Sanger had known each other as children. Kit, a year older than Margaret, frequently visited family in Corning, New York (also Sanger's birthplace), where Hepburn's

This essay first appeared in spring 2004, volume 3, number 4. It was excerpted from the fall 2003 newsletter of the Margaret Sanger Papers Project at New York University.

grandfather had founded the Corning Glass Works. Several of Margaret's brothers worked in the glass factory, and her older sister, Mary, worked as a domestic in Corning for Kit's aunt and uncle.

A longtime suffrage leader, Katharine Houghton Hepburn turned to the issue of birth control (as did a number of prominent suffragists) following the passage of the Nineteenth Amendment in 1920. She helped found the Connecticut Birth Control League in 1923 and subsequently served in two organizations that Sanger founded: on the board of directors of the American Birth Control League and as legislative chair of the National Committee on Federal Legislation for Birth Control in Washington, D.C. Both were forerunner organizations of the Planned Parenthood Federation of America.

Margaret and the young Katharine Hepburn probably met during one of Margaret's frequent trips to Hartford, Connecticut, in the 1920s, and she thereafter expressed an aunt-like devotion to young "Kate." Working side by side with Kit in Washington in the early 1930s to lobby for a bill to legalize the circulation of birth control, Margaret felt in close proximity to Kate's sudden fame.

In 1932, Katharine Hepburn became a stage and screen sensation with her first critical success on Broadway in *The Warrior's Husband*, which led to her screen debut later that year in *A Bill of Divorcement*, opposite John Barrymore. She followed with a string of movie hits in the mid-1930s, including *Morning Glory* (for which she won her first Academy Award) and *Little Women* in 1933, *Spitfire* and *The Little Minister* in 1934, *Alice Adams* in 1935, *Mary of Scotland* and *A Woman Rebels* in 1936, *Quality Street* and *Stage Door* in 1937, and *Bringing Up Baby* and *Holiday* in 1938.

Worlds Collide

But the worlds of mother and daughter collided in January 1934. Kit Hepburn was in the news after an exchange with Congressman John C. Lehr at hearings on a birth control bill. When Lehr, who opposed the legislation, claimed there had never been a contraceptive in his home and that he had six children, Hepburn quipped, "Well I have six children, too." Kate, hounded by reporters to comment on her mother's work, publicly supported the efforts of her mother and Margaret Sanger to legalize birth control. She also expressed irritation at how the press had referred to Kit as the "mother of the actress," asserting that it was really her mother who was the important one.

In a series of letters, Kit asked Margaret to write to Kate "thanking her," since "it means a good deal of sacrifice for [her] to stand openly with us." Margaret then wrote to Kate on January 25:

> I hope that this battle for Birth Control, where your glorious mother stood out so valiantly for her opinions is not going to get you in bad. You Hepburns have such courage, are such straight shooters, and are so straightforward in your thinking that I know it will be difficult for you to think of your public—especially your Catholic public, if you have such a thing. I do not say that you should—I only want to tell you that I adore your mother and I think she is wonderful to come and make the splendid fight beside us dreading all the time to get you mixed in the affair. I am not afraid that anything that your mother says will in any way hurt you. You have won your reputation by your own ability and talent, and through those qualities alone you will win or lose.

Unsure whether she had accomplished what Kit had requested of her, Sanger then wrote to Kit:

> Now, as to your daughter Kate, I wrote her but for the life of me I could not tell that wonderful creature to do anything against her own divine inspiration. I believe it is the [don'ts] and the do's of the elders constantly tugging at our young people that give them complexes and disturbs a very definite, inspired flare that a few of them have. Your Katharine is in that group and I believe that her public loves and adores her for her spirit and undaunted courage that she expresses in every part she has played so far. To be less than herself in considering a mythical public would . . . be damping down a flame that must have air and room to send out its light. The whole thing will die down in a few days and I hope you will feel that whatever she does when it expresses her innate feeling, is the right thing to do.

Somehow Margaret had misconstrued Kit's intentions, believing mother had wanted to "tone down" daughter. Kit wrote back in the margins of Sanger's letter:

> What did you think I said? All I wanted was for you to write and say you were pleased at her coming out for us as I knew that her studio would protest. She admires you & I thought that it would please her. Of course she did the right thing—I'd have spanked her if she hadn't.

Kate was characteristically nonchalant about this media episode, telling Margaret: "Don't worry about me, it's much too important for that—When they ask me what I think I say that I stand back of every thing that Mother & you say on the subject."

"The Daughter of Your Mother"

Margaret and Kit saw each other less frequently after the dissolution of the National Committee in 1937. But Margaret kept up with Kate's career, noting in her calendars when she saw the newest Hepburn film or Broadway production. Margaret tried to get Kate to speak at a Birth Control Federation of America annual meeting in 1941 (the organization changed its name to Planned Parenthood a year later), remembering her words of support for the movement in 1934: "Your words were what one would expect from the daughter of your mother, and I hope that you had no cause to regret your courage, integrity and forthrightness on the occasion of which I speak." But Kate, who had just filmed *Woman of the Year* with Spencer Tracy, was too busy to accept the invitation.

In 1951, Margaret received news of Katharine Houghton Hepburn's sudden death from a cerebral hemorrhage. She wrote Kate immediately and received in return a long letter that described the death scene:

> M[other] went up to nap & Dad & I drove to Fenwick—We got back at 5:30. Dad went up to get M. as tea was waiting. When she did not answer—he found what had happened—Apparently she had got up about 5—gone in to bathe & fix her hair—She'd taken off a wooly robe she always wrapped in, hung it up, & was fixing her hair when she must have suddenly felt dizzy—went straight back to bed & pulled the covers up & with a sweet smile closed her eyes—Dad says she could not have know[n] what it was—& she looked so relaxed that she could not have suffered or been too frightened—It is dreadful not to have her—but thank God if it had to be—it was as it was—She loved you very much—was always so proud of you—.

One of Hepburn's biographers, Barbara Leaming, later claimed that this death scene had been sanitized by Kate, with all signs of suffering removed or veiled after her father's initial discovery so he could revisit the room and see the peaceful resolution Kate had described in her letter to Sanger. The Hepburn family, however, still vehemently denies this and stands by Kate's initial description.

A Powerful Advocate

After Margaret Sanger's death in 1966, Katharine Hepburn involved herself more directly in the reproductive rights movement. She added her name to Planned Parenthood's endeavors, narrated a film about Sanger, and became a member of the board of advocates of the Planned Parenthood Federation of America and honorary chair of PPFA's National Leadership Committee to Keep Abortion Safe and Legal. Speaking about Sanger in 1981, Hepburn said, "It is imperative that I join Planned Parenthood because sadly even today there are those who would completely destroy all of her tireless work and deprive all of us of our right to plan our families."

Just two weeks before Hepburn's death, her niece, the actress Katharine Houghton, appeared on CNN's *Larry King Live* to discuss her aunt. In response to a question about recent visits with Katharine, Houghton replied, "I had a letter just before the holidays from New York University, asking for permission to publish a letter that she had written to Margaret Sanger . . . So I said to my aunt, 'Do you remember Margaret Sanger?' "

Houghton went on to relate the rest of the conversation between them as dialogue:

"Yes."

"What did you think of her?"

"She was a remarkable woman."

The American Expeditionary Forces in World War I had never seen an entertainer like Elsie Janis, and they loved her. The feeling was mutual. Credit: Author's Collection.

61

The Sweetheart of the A.E.F.

William F. Howard

Nearly thirty years before Bob Hope traveled to the front lines of World War II, a young vaudeville star abandoned the stages of New York and London and made her way to the battlefields of France. Elsie Janis performed there as a private citizen without pay, exposing herself to the dangers of war, because she believed it was her mission to bring cheer to the British and American soldiers of World War I. While many women left their homes and families to provide aid and comfort to the soldiers as nurses and civilian service workers in France during World War I, the soldiers loved Elsie Janis, the "Sweetheart of the A.E.F.," best of all. Her lilting voice and acrobatic dance routines brought culture and a bit of home to the battlefield, and she, in turn, established a lifelong attachment to the men who fought the war, even after her career as an entertainer had faded.

"The Rage of London"

Janis was born in Columbus, Ohio, on March 16, 1889. Coached by her mother, Janis performed in local church benefits at the age of two and was in stock theater by age seven, already intensely driven toward fame. She changed her surname from Bierbower at the suggestion of a New York photographer, who thought that Janis (a play on Jane, her middle name) would sound better to the New York theater crowd. At age ten she was invited to entertain President William McKinley at the White House. By fourteen, she was performing on the Broadway stage, and by seventeen she was the star of the

---

This essay first appeared in winter 2005, volume 4, number 3.

play *The Vanderbilt Cup*, which enjoyed a two-year run. The *New York Times* noted her seventeenth birthday and found humor in reporting that a group of Yale students celebrated it by sitting in the front row of the Broadway Theater and throwing violets onto the stage at the end of the last act. Janis subsequently appeared in *The Hoyden*, *The Fair Co-Ed*, and *The Slim Princess*, and she starred in her own play, *A Star for a Night*, when she was just twenty-two. She left for London early in 1914 and performed to rave reviews in two editions of *The Passing Snow*. By the start of World War I, she was "the rage of London" and the most popular American actress on the British stage, a talented vaudeville performer who combined comedy, dance, and impersonations in her act. Her impressions of the great actress Sarah Bernhardt won recognition from the "Divine Sarah" herself, who cabled the young Janis in London and told her to continue.

To the Front

But at the height of her fame, Janis left the London stage to travel to the military camps surrounding the city to entertain the British troops who were departing for France. One of those soldiers was her fellow actor Basil Hallam, who had won her heart both on and off stage. Janis described their parting in her memoir *So Far, So Good!*, published in 1932:

> [I] left him standing on the platform of Euston Station, chin up, blue eyes clear and fearless. In my hand I held a photograph he had posed for at the last moment in uniform and on it he wrote, "If we still love those we lose, can we ever quite lose those we love?"

Tragically, like so many of his generation, Basil Hallam died in France. Janis never quite recovered from his death, but she renewed her commitment to travel to the front and provide entertainment to the troops. She wrote,

> I was never really happy again until April 6, 1917, when America slipped in to take her share of the burden and the glory of the world. From that time on I had but one idea, and that was to get to France and do for our boys what I had done for the others—for I thought, if the Tommies liked me in their own land and were surrounded by their families, what would our boys feel, three thousand miles away from home?

Janis and her mother, who accompanied her to France, spent six months at the Western Front, often within artillery range of the Germans. She was the first female entertainer ever permitted on a military base, and she began an exhausting schedule of shows, traveling from camp to camp, hospital to headquarters. She sometimes performed up to nine forty-five-minute shows a day, always beginning with her cheery question "Are we downhearted?," to which thousands of soldiers would shout, "No!" She became a fixture at the front and was even allowed to pull the lanyard on one of the big guns—dubbed "Elsie" in her honor—that was pointed at the German lines. General John J. Pershing, commander of the American Expeditionary Forces, was so impressed with her impact on troop morale that he assigned her a car and driver. An American officer wrote, "The British give their men rum before a battle, the French cognac, and we give ours Janis."

Visiting an Allied hospital in Nevilly, France, Janis described her efforts in simple terms:

> I went into the wards and tried to make them forget that they had wounds. I could write pages of the bravery of our men, not under fire because that goes without saying, but under real and terrible pain. Whether they had lost one leg or two, whether they would perhaps never see again, the smile was always there for me and my little jokes . . . I sang sometimes in as many as fifteen wards in a day. I usually had a good cry when I got home, but my reward was in the fact that the boys wanted me.

The War Ends

During her time in France, Janis was exposed to a new form of music that she heard played by the African American soldiers whom she encountered at the front. Although she often laced her performances with racial caricatures and skits that are embarrassing today, Janis was impressed with the music of the black bandsmen and sought to bring the jagged, improvisational sound of jazz back to London and New York. She later incorporated it into a successful London revue titled *Hullo, America!*, starring herself and a young actor named Maurice Chevalier.

Although she had given up her extraordinary stage career to go to the Western Front, Janis never regretted her decision. But when the war ended in November 1918, she was left with mixed feelings. She had never felt as alive and purposeful as she did when she visited the soldiers in France, yet reflecting on the end of the war, she lamented,

> From that time on, things were not quite the same to me; something seemed to have snapped somewhere in the region up where my heart would have

> been if I had not left it in France. I still went to the hospitals and camps, still sang of taking my jazz band to the Fatherland, but not with the same vim, because I knew that the biggest thing in my life had gone out of it, never again would I sing to and cheer two or three thousand of our wonderful boys, and send them from me singing into the unknown. I was glad that their battles were over, but I was selfish enough to be sorry that my work which gave me such indescribable and infinite joy was ended.

Janis returned to New York in 1919 on the Danish ship *Rotterdam*. She was met at the dock by a large crowd and by a tugboat bearing a huge sign that read "Welcome Elsie Janis." She and her mother subsequently returned to the Philipsburg Manor house near Tarrytown on the Hudson River they had called home since 1915. She loved the house that had been built as a milling and trading complex by Frederick Philipse in 1683 and enjoyed entertaining friends from the city who came north to visit. The composer Irving Berlin was a frequent guest, as were Douglas Fairbanks and Mary Pickford.

Her Bright Star Fades

During the 1920s, Janis appeared in several silent films, among them *The Imp*, and was under contract to David Selznick for $5,000 per week. She and her friends made the daily trip to the studio by sailing from the Philipse Manor Yacht Club to New York—lavish voyages made more so by famous guests and extravagant parties aboard ship. But like many vaudeville stars, Janis failed to make the transition from the stage to "talkies." Although she tried to reinvigorate her stage career by playing the lead in the Gershwins' *Oh, Kay!* on the West Coast, she found that the memories of the Great War were fading at the same pace as her career.

Janis' free-spending habits and a bank failure during the Depression took much of her fortune in the 1930s. Her finances were further depleted by a serious auto accident in 1935; she was forced to auction off her beloved Philipsburg Manor house the following year, along with most of her memorabilia and possessions. She moved to Hollywood, and as war clouds gathered once again she attempted a return to the stage in 1939. She appeared in four Sunday night patriotic concerts, although these generated little public interest, and then in *Frank Fay's Music Hall*, a sad attempt to revive vaudeville, but the show closed after suffering negative reviews. She made one last film, *Women in War*, in 1940.

"Only One Real Peak"

Elsie Janis spent her final years in retirement in Hollywood, where she died on February 26, 1956, nine days shy of her sixty-seventh birthday, with her good friend Mary Pickford at her side. The framed photograph of Basil Hallam, who had died in France so long ago, was still prominently displayed on the nightstand beside her bed. While her ambition had always pushed her forward toward the next great challenge, in her memoir she acknowledged the historical and personal importance of her career as the "Sweetheart of the A.E.F." forty years before:

> There is no doubt that with the end of the war came the death of something inside me . . . I've been pleased with work that I've done and grateful for the success I've had . . . but the war was my high spot and I think there is only one real peak in each life.

The quality of vegetables grown on mucklands was legendary. Buyers from around the state often came to Canastota to inspect and purchase whole fields. Credit: Canastota Canal Town Museum, Canastota, New York.

62

Black Beach

Tricia A. Barbagallo

Muck: to the agriculturist it's a type of farming. Geologists identify it with the bottom of a lakebed and classify it as a type of silty and poorly drained soil. Linguistically, it's American slang for thick, sticky mud. But in central New York's Madison County, muck has a cultural meaning, especially to the Italians who farmed it in Canastota. From 1900 to 1970, Canastota's two hundred muck farms were so successful that the village gained national attention and was named the Onion Capital of the World. To these Italian farmers, muck was about tradition, culture, and family, as well as labor.

Muck is composed of glacial deposit and high concentrations of deciduous plant matter and phosphorus, making it extremely fertile. Italians originally farmed what was called the Great Swamp, a low, flat, five-mile area of muck south of Oneida Lake in the towns of Lenox and Sullivan. Farmer Janet Tornatore Conner found pieces of shells in the soil of her grandparents' farm on Ditch Bank Road, marking the remains of a glacial lake that once covered the area. Other farmers found projectile points, evidence that Iroquois people had hunted or fished near the Great Swamp.

Hardworking Italians

The first European settlers in Canastota were English, Irish, and German. By the 1840s, they had dredged canals and ditches to drain the swamp and farm the wet

This essay first appeared in summer 2005, volume 5, number 1.

soil, cultivating high-quality celery and potatoes. But agriculture as an industry never progressed because there was no strong manual labor force until the 1890s, when immigrants from Linguaglossa, Sicily, settled in the village. These Italians worked on the railroads and moonlighted on the muck farms as sharecroppers. By 1915, thirty-seven Italians owned farms. Their children then bought more muck, doubling the number of farms.

They bought "virgin territory," about ten to fifteen acres of woods that they cleared by hand. Many used equipment harnessed to horses to pull up roots and weeds. Carlo Tornatore's farm was cleared faster: the men marked the trees to be removed and sent a woman off "with a stick of dynamite and a match. Then, we let her run!" By 1930, Canastota was one of the largest onion-producing regions in the country. Other major businesses in Canastota were celery-packing plants and vegetable distributors, all owned by Italians. Muck ultimately produced many more affluent Italians than Canastota natives, an economic "switch" that would change the social dynamics of the village.

By 1939, 90 percent of the Great Swamp had been drained, and the county, state, and federal governments formed a commission to engineer a ditch system to further promote agriculture. Five-foot-wide farm ditches drained fields into commission ditches, which were up to twenty feet wide. The groundwater then emptied into mains, like the thirty-foot-wide Douglas Ditch, which in turn routed water into Oneida Lake. The system was not entirely successful, however. Families still remember a major flood in the spring of 1940 when water stood in the fields for a week. As it drained, the fertile soil ran off. Another flood during a hot summer heated the floodwaters and "cooked" growing onions in the ground; the whole area smelled like boiled onions. Farmers couldn't walk in the saturated, heavy muck to harvest what they could, and cars and farm machinery sank.

A Way of Life

But muck was more than just fertile soil and farmers' livelihood: it was also a culture, a way of life. While most Canastota natives visited the popular Sylvan Beach on a summer day, Italians went to what they called Black Beach—the mucklands—to work in their onion fields. Children took their shoes off when school ended for the summer and didn't put them back on until school started in the fall. They loved digging their feet into the cool, moist muck while working on a hot day. Older residents said the period of muck's heyday, the 1930s and 1940s, was the "best time of their lives," not necessarily linking muck with farming.

Farming peaked by 1945, after World War II increased the demand for truck crops. Farmers planted lettuce, celery, and carrots, but most raised onions, Ebenezer Sets or Yellow Globes. Markets and profits were good, bringing $4.25 per one hundred bushels during the war. Planting began in early spring and was a family activity. Children used a hand scuffle to prepare the soil, and everyone planted by crawling and using their thumbs to insert seeds. They weeded between rows on their hands and knees until the August harvest, when the onions were ripe. An important tool on a muck farm was the jackknife, used for topping. This involved cutting a two-foot green sprout off the top of the onion bulb in preparation for crating and packing. Onions were pulled from the ground, topped, put in slatted crates, stacked to dry, and graded for size and quality before they were sold.

Janet Tornatore Conner remembers what it was like working in the muck. "You'd get there usually as the sun was coming up, and it would be cold and damp and wet, and then it would get really hot and dry, and tedious and monotonous, no altering of the labor." Farmers complained that humidity raised the smell of the onions, which was so intense it made their eyes burn. Rose Tianello recalls, "Everything was done as a family. We worked before school, after school, during vacations. On rainy days we had to work!" Because the farms were so important, women made special clothes so everyone could work during inclement weather: "We wore inner tubes on our legs. My mother sewed them on our blue jeans."

Women worked while they were pregnant, then balanced childcare and household duties with farming. They hired babysitters, worked the fields, and took breaks to nurse infants. Janet Tornatore Conner was literally raised in the muck. "When we were little, they would put us in an onion crate. Mother would stay very close and work fast, or have us go with her, and then we learned to work the same way. She cooked lunch. There was a lot of foraging; women did most of that." Teenagers Carol Weimer and Robert Stokes, who were not Italian, worked for pay on local farms. With their lunch, jackknives, and friends in tow, they would pile on the back of a truck and head for the muck. They worked all day, enjoyed the camaraderie, had topping contests, and bought school clothes with their earnings.

Industrious Living

A typical muck farm consisted of what Italian families called a shanty (with no electricity or heat), an outhouse, and a barn or onion crib, in addition to the muck fields. Most families also owned a house in the village for winter residence. Muck was reserved for income crops, while hardland (loam) was used for living space, gardens, and crop storage. But during the growing season, since farmers worked, on average, twelve hours a day and wanted to save time traveling from the village to their farms, families lived right on the mucklands in their shanties—an industrious living situation that used the land to optimal capacity. Wells or springs served as a water source. Rainwater was used for laundry and cleaning, and wood or coal was used for cooking and heating (for an average household of eight people). The women also managed the hardland gardens, butchered fowl for meals, and canned pheasants, other game, and farm produce.

Rose Tianello's farm was typical. Their shanty had

> [t]wo bedrooms, a kitchen-living room. An outhouse. It had two seats. We had a barn for crates, and a well. We didn't have refrigerators! It was a great big crock! My father dug out the ground and made a sturdy top for it to keep the animals out. My mother had a big strawberry patch and peas patch. My godfather brought us a goat.

The farm was the Tianellos' year-round residence for ten years. "Pearl Bush, our teacher, told my father, 'Why don't you buy a house in the village, the girls could be involved in more things?' [And he said] 'No. No. No. I want them all to be brought up virgins!' "

The elder Tianello's concern for his daughters hints at the social division in Canastota. Before 1930, village natives and Italians rarely socialized. Some Italians believed this was because they were farmers, but others felt it was because of their ethnicity. Italians described themselves as being "down" on the muck, and they called contemporary hardland farmers "uplanders." Rose Tianello remembers the segregation. "They lived on the Southside. We [Italians] lived on the Northside. Years ago we were called Black people, Italians were!" Italians were scrutinized for dating "white" girls, suggesting racial prejudice and social tension. Southsider Carol Weimer remembers, "That is the way it was. It was sad." What brought the two groups together was *La Feasta*, the Roman Catholic Feast of the Assumption of the Blessed Mother on August 15. Young people from both cultures attended this Italian street festival. During World War II, tensions lessened because all of Canastota's men enlisted in the army as "Americans," and because many Northsiders and Southsiders married.

End of an Era

The 1940s were the hardest years for farming. Storms ruined crops and floods eroded the soil, which made muck farming a financial risk. By the 1950s, Italians preferred factory jobs because they received benefits and a pension. Janet Tornatore Conner recalls that muck farming died out because of both the weather and the market: "It used to be the family, but not every family had siblings that wanted to stay in it. Every family wanted to educate their children." Some blamed the state: water drained from the newly built New York State Thruway into the farms, and flooding and road salt ruined the muck. Natives felt that the Italian farmers had overworked the soil. But farms failed for many reasons.

The muck lifestyle defined a culture and cultivated family traditions, but it was also a million-dollar American business perfected and made profitable by Italian immigrants. Muck agriculture ultimately boosted the state's economy into national significance, while at the same time changing the social structure and a community's identity. Although the muck farmsteads are now in ruins, and most of Black Beach has reverted to a wilderness, the memories of those who "grew up on muck" give a fascinating insight into the social, cultural, and economic impact of this unique twentieth-century farming technique.

Every year the holdings of the New York State Archives grow by approximately two thousand cubic feet as it accessions archival records from various state agencies. Recently, the archives acquired records from the New York State Bureau of Economic Development, including thousands of color slides that were used to promote tourism. This image of the Empire State Building is from one of those slides. Credit: New York State Archives, Albany, New York.

63

New York Masterpiece

Robert A. Slayton

After all these years, it is still a New York City landmark, and since 2001 it is once again the tallest skyscraper in Gotham. The Empire State Building celebrates its seventy-fifth birthday in 2006, but the magnificent structure has earned accolades since the day it opened on May 1, 1931.

The idea for the Empire State Building began at the end of the boom of the 1920s, when New York experienced a construction rush of unprecedented magnitude and increased its office space from 74 million to 112 million square feet, a growth of roughly 50 percent. The visionaries behind the edifice were Pierre DuPont and John Raskob of the DuPont empire. Looking around for another opportunity to increase their fortunes, they turned to real estate and came up with an interesting gamble—even though it did not look like one at first.

Prime Real Estate

The location seemed perfect. In the late twenties, the corner of 34th Street and Fifth Avenue was occupied by the Waldorf Astoria Hotel, by that time aging and slightly disheveled. DuPont and Raskob insisted that a skyscraper on that corner would be near everything: only a block from Herald Square with its department stores and subway connections, not far from Times Square and Grand Central Station, and the Flatiron Building only a short walk south. The problem, however, was that the site was *near* everything but not *next to* anything. All those landmarks were blocks away,

This essay first appeared in spring 2006, volume 5, number 4.

the corner was not particularly close to any regular foot traffic route, and although it lay *between* both East and West Side subway connections, there was no station from any line actually *on* the site.

But such details never stopped high flyers, and once they obtained a mortgage from Metropolitan Life, DuPont and Raskob began to build a dream tower. The first notice of the new building appeared on the front page of the *New York Times* on August 30, 1929, heralding the fact that the Empire State Building Corporation had begun operations by hiring a president, Alfred E. Smith, the esteemed former governor of New York and the 1928 Democratic presidential candidate. On October 1—less than a month before the stock market would crash—the old Waldorf Astoria Hotel was demolished. By September 9, 1930, Smith had set the cornerstone of the Empire State Building in place—but not until he had placed a time capsule, in the form of a copper box, inside a niche in the cornerstone. The capsule contained a brief history of the building and its origins; photos of the company officers, the architects, and the contractors; one sample of every piece of currency then in circulation, from a penny to a $100 bill; and an edition of that day's *New York Times*, printed on rag paper. Smith, an opponent of Prohibition, was the subject of the best laugh of the day when a workman yelled out, "Say Al, any chance of putting the 18th Amendment in there?"

Staggering Stats

With the Depression, costs became a major concern, so construction proceeded at a record pace. The corporation was a pioneer in on-time delivery: given the crowded streets of Manhattan, there was no supply depot and no reserve space to store materials. Instead, to move along with the mammoth job, trucks had to show up at the exact moment when their load of steel, copper, aluminum, or concrete was needed. I-beams came off the furnaces at Pittsburgh and eighty hours later were being unloaded in New York, each one carefully marked to indicate exactly where in the complex skeleton they were supposed to go. Thirty-five hundred workmen built at the unprecedented pace of a floor a day; during one ten-day period, the skyscraper grew by fourteen stories. Smith wrote in a private letter to Raskob, "We have been working on the foundation up to 1:30 in the morning" with "only one complaint about the noise from the owner of a small hotel" nearby. As a result of this schedule, construction finished forty-five days ahead of plan.

The building's statistics staggered the imagination, at least in 1931. With 102 stories and a famed mast (upon which to moor dirigibles and designed to beat out the Chrysler Building as tallest structure in the city), the Empire State Building stood 1,472 feet high on a ground footprint of 88,860 square feet and added 37 million cubic feet and 2.16 million square feet of office space to the New York market. The steel used in its construction weighed 60,000 tons (by contrast, a World War II *Essex*-class aircraft carrier weighed only 30,000 tons). There were 6,700 radiators, 51 miles of pipe, and 17 million feet of telephone cable.

A View to Die For

The elevators shocked people. New York's building code permitted elevators to travel at a speed of 700 feet per minute, but everyone knew figures like that applied only to primitive buildings—the kind that came before the Empire State Building—and had to be changed. The building's elevators whizzed passengers up and down at 1,200 feet per minute, the fastest elevator speed anywhere in the world. Doctors worried about the effect on the human ear.

The Empire State Building seemed like a dream, an extravaganza, a symbol of endless possibilities. Walter Trumbell, a local journalist who wrote a column called "New York Day by Day," saluted the monolith and enthused, "No matter how many times I pass it, I can't quite get used to the Empire State Building." The National Broadcasting Company submitted an application to the Federal Radio Commission to install equipment on the skyscraper's mast to broadcast a new and still experimental form of beam known as television.

For opening day, Al Smith arranged for his old antagonist Herbert Hoover—now president of the United States—to flick a switch in Washington that would turn on the Empire State Building's lights in Manhattan. A crowd of thousands assembled; the designated ribbon cutters were two of the Smith grandchildren, Mary and Arthur, who had trouble with the scissors until grandpa applied a helping hand. Speeches by Smith and Governor Franklin Roosevelt were carried on a nationwide radio broadcast. But most important was the view from the Observation Deck on the 86th floor. The Empire State Building rose in an age long before commercial air traffic became commonplace, so the Observation Deck was the highest point many people would ever physically attain. Looking out, visitors saw the panorama of New York unfold before their eyes, from the Statue of Liberty off the Battery to Central Park and beyond.

PR to Boost Profits

Behind these marvels, however, rested a fundamental paradox: the Empire State Building was the product of a small bubble of prosperity that had opened for the fortunate few during the Great Depression. Carol Willis, founder of the Skyscraper Museum, notes that the original plans for the structure had been financial, not architectural; the builders sought money, not beauty, even though they had constructed a tower of lasting grace. But for most of its first decade, the Empire State Building did not deliver on its financial promise. The original figures had estimated a yearly rental income of $6.8 million, but as late as the 1937–1938 fiscal year, the building had only taken in $1.8 million, or a bare 26 percent of expected revenue. Only the Observation Deck turned a profit; charging the astronomical sum of $1 for admission during the worst of the Depression, it still boasted a million visitors a year. But actual occupancy was so low that some wags began referring to it as the "Empty State Building."

Thus, Al Smith did everything he could to bring attention to his monolith, and he did so by means of an unprecedented public relations campaign. Dignitaries both high and low were beseeched to put in an appearance so that photographers could snap a shot for the tabloids. Smith greeted visitors from foreign lands: Crown Prince Olaf and Princess Martha of Norway; King Zog of Albania with his three unmarried sisters, Ruhjie, Myzejen, and Marhide (Smith greeted them by bellowing, "Hello, girls!"); even Rogoso, the "King of Cannibals" from the Solomon Islands, complete with war club and shield. Domestic visitors included the world's tallest man, members of every rodeo that played Madison Square Garden (Smith swapped his trademark derby for a ten-gallon hat for the cameras), and Fay Wray, star of the 1933 movie *King Kong*, who admitted she was scared of heights.

A Beacon of History

With the coming of World War II, the Empire State Building filled up, and since then it has generally stayed profitable. The war also provided the structure with one of its most dramatic moments. On July 28, 1945, a foggy Saturday morning, a B-25 bomber flying low in a heavy fog went off course and smacked into the seventy-eighth and seventy-ninth floors. Because it was a weekend, not many people were in the building, but fourteen people died, including the flight crew, as tons of metal sheared through the floors.

In one way, however, perhaps the Empire State Building's greatest era began on September 11, 2001, when the planes struck both towers of the World Trade Center and they fell. By that terrible afternoon, the Empire State Building was no longer New York's second-tallest building—and, as it had been in its opening days, the familiar skyscraper was no longer a structure but a symbol, this time of a city's endurance, a sign that the Big Apple's majesty, at least, was still intact.

The view from the Observation Deck is still stunning and well worth the extra security checks now in place. Best of all, on a bright day, any pedestrian—jaded resident or virgin tourist—can walk a few blocks south on Fifth Avenue, turn, and watch the sunshine play over one of the most beautiful buildings in the world. After all these years, the Empire State Building still glows.

The women who created and sustained Nancy Drew operated in a business world dominated by men. Credit: © Houghton Mifflin Harcourt, Boston, Massachusetts.

64

The Case of the Independent Women

Melanie Rehak

In the spring of 1930, just as America was plunging deep into the Depression, a brilliant, beautiful, and, most importantly, intrepid young woman appeared on the scene to lighten young America's load. Her name was Nancy Drew, and even the price of her mysterious adventures—fifty cents a book, an amount that could almost always be gotten up even in hard times—was designed to delight. Of course, there were also her soon-to-be-famous blue roadster, her doting lawyer father, her fashionable wardrobe, and her unerring sense of right and wrong to recommend her. But most of all, it was her independent, enterprising spirit that made her a hit from the very first moment she landed on bookshelves across the country.

Over the course of her first three stories, published simultaneously as a "breeder set" to ensure immediate addiction among the ranks of her readers, Nancy investigated a missing will, saved a drowning swimmer, explored a haunted mansion (discovering a secret underground tunnel in the process), and restored a stolen fortune to its rightful owner. She was also locked up in a closet, knocked unconscious several times, and forced to escape by climbing down a prickly rose trellis in a skirt and heels. *The Secret of the Old Clock*, *The Hidden Staircase*, and *The Bungalow Mystery* introduced to America the bold sleuth who would become a mainstay of juvenile reading forever after. Even now, seventy-six years later, Nancy Drew remains a symbol of self-reliance, quick thinking in perilous moments, and modish independence. "If I get through, I must depend upon my own initiative," she tells herself during an especially harrowing scene in *The Bungalow Mystery*. Trapped in a ferocious rainstorm and almost killed by a falling tree, she never loses her cool, and her moxie and charm are as appealing today as they were in 1930.

This essay first appeared in spring 2006, volume 5, number 4.

A Heroine Ahead of Her Time

How did this young detective manage to capture the imagination of American girls so quickly and hold on to it through wars, television, social upheaval, and the Internet? For one thing, she did it by being ahead of her time. She was the first teenage detective of her kind, a girl who, instead of moonlighting as a solver of mysteries while holding a day job as a traditionally feminine nurse or student, was able to devote herself fully to her own interests. She also did it by never even broaching the subject of marriage and motherhood—two topics which, it had become clear by the time she made her debut, made girls drop a series faster than a hot potato. Nancy Drew was, above all, a modern sleuth from the start.

All of this was according to plan. Her inventor was a series book mogul named Edward Stratemeyer, who, thanks to his unrivaled combination of entrepreneurial instincts and imagination, was already a millionaire when he envisioned his blonde, blue-eyed detective. As head of the Stratemeyer Syndicate, a company that produced children's book series by sending outlines to ghostwriters, each of whom wrote under a series pen name, he had dreamed up most of the major series of the previous decades, including Tom Swift (1910), the Bobbsey Twins (1904), and the Hardy Boys (1927). It was when girls began to write in about his boys' series, saying how much they liked them—as well as how much they *didn't* like the "weepy and weak" girl characters in his boys' books—that he realized it was time to give them an adventurer of their own. Stratemeyer imagined Nancy as "an up-to-date American girl at her best, bright, clever, resourceful and fully of energy," and along with her, he invented her author, Carolyn Keene.

The Women Behind the Man

The secret of Nancy's success lies in the women behind this famous pseudonym. When Stratemeyer initiated the Nancy Drew Mystery Stories, he assigned them to a young woman, Mildred Wirt, who was already writing his Ruth Fielding books (needless to say, Ruth fell by the wayside when Wirt got engaged to her longtime beau in the late 1920s). Wirt was a pithy, no-nonsense journalist from Iowa, and she invested Nancy with a good deal of her own gumption, not to mention her award-winning swimming skills and relentless energy.

A good thing, because a mere twelve days after the first three books in the series were published, Edward Stratemeyer died suddenly of pneumonia. His final creation was left in the hands of not only the feisty young ghostwriter he had handpicked, but his two daughters, Edna Stratemeyer and Harriet Stratemeyer Adams, who took over their father's company when a buyer could not be found. For Harriet, who had attended Wellesley in the years preceding suffrage, it was the opportunity of a lifetime to have the career she had desperately wanted but had been denied by her traditional parents and upper-class upbringing. Though she was married and the mother of four young children, she threw herself into professional life with zeal. As editor, Harriet helped to mold the Nancy Drew whom generations of little girls have admired and aspired to, endowing her with the graciousness and poise that are as much a part of her character as her uncanny ability to sniff out a mystery. Later on, when Mildred Wirt became a reporter at the *Toledo Times* and left her series-writing days behind, Harriet took over the writing of the Nancy Drew books and left an even greater mark on the famous sleuth.

On Their Own

Both Harriet and Mildred defied great odds when they became career women in the early part of the twentieth century. Though it was certainly not unheard of for women to work, they tended to be those who needed working-class jobs for the money more than women of Harriet and Mildred's backgrounds. Harriet became a CEO by chance, and she often faced patronizing attitudes from men in publishing who were not ready to accept her in their midst; nevertheless, she pushed on. Mildred got her lucky break in the way so many women did. When the newsroom of the *Toledo Times* was emptied of reporters by overseas deployments during World War II, the paper hired her with the promise that as soon as the men were back, she'd be gone. Instead, she stayed put for more than fifty years, proving herself time and time again.

Harriet and Mildred's letters to each other, and to their friends and colleagues in the years when their children were young (Mildred had a daughter in 1938), show the enormous strains and challenges they faced as working women, as well as the intricate mechanisms that kept the Stratemeyer Syndicate and its roster of star characters running smoothly—or sometimes not so smoothly—over the years. Without Harriet and Mildred's struggles in the real world, Nancy's fictional, sometimes fantastical, ones would not be nearly as vivid. Like her writers, the girl sleuth continually faces down conventional wisdom to get to the bottom of a conundrum, and like them she does it with elegance and verve. These letters provide a fascinating window into the development of one of America's most-loved pop icons, and they also attest to the great character and innovative spirit of the two women who shaped her, without whom the Nancy Drew we've known and loved for so long would not exist.

In 1916, Times Square was the scene of a demonstration against military drills in schools and the conscription of high school boys. Credit: Women's International League for Peace and Freedom Records, Swarthmore College Peace Collection, Swarthmore, Pennsylvania.

65

Conscience in the Classroom

Charles F. Howlett

In 1964, *Profiles in Courage*, a popular television series based on the 1956 Pulitzer Prize–winning book by John F. Kennedy, detailed the lives of historical figures who, despite public rebuke, stood by their conscience. One figure profiled in the series was Brooklyn Manual Training High School teacher Mary Stone McDowell. During World War I, McDowell refused to participate in patriotic school activities because of her Quaker beliefs, and was fired. Her case represented the first test of pacifism and academic freedom heard by a state court system in the United States.

During the First World War, passions ran so deep that General Thomas Wingate of the New York City Board of Education boldly proclaimed that "the teacher who teaches pacifism and that this country should not defend itself is a thousand times more dangerous than the teacher who gets drunk and lies in the gutter." Historian Robert K. Murray noted in his popular book *Red Scare* that many charges were brought against teachers who refused to sign loyalty oaths or teach patriotism. Other teachers left their positions before being charged. In most instances, no records were kept because there was no court trial or effort to seek judicial relief; due process was accorded only by a Board of Education hearing.

The conclusion of the war, moreover, did little to assuage teachers' fears. The period from 1919 to 1920 witnessed numerous examples of intolerance with respect to civil liberties. Concerns that bolshevism would take over American society led to intensive efforts to promote a more patriotic citizenry. Throughout the United States, efforts were made to destroy the Industrial Workers of the World, as well as crack down on worker strikes such as the Boston Police Strike, the steelworkers' strike in western

This essay first appeared in spring 2006, volume 5, number 4.

Pennsylvania, and the dockworkers' walkout in Seattle, all in the name of Americanism. Teachers were by no means immune from such pressures. As Murray noted, "New York City, with its environs, was the chief area where witch hunting for 'Red' school teachers was undertaken." Considering the circumstances, the war and subsequent fears of communism provided McDowell with little opportunity to reverse her fate.

"In Every Way the Best"

Born on March 22, 1876, in Jersey City, New Jersey, Mary McDowell was a birthright member of the New York Monthly Meeting of the Society of Friends. In 1896, she graduated Phi Beta Kappa from Swarthmore College, attended Oxford University on a fellowship, and in 1900 received a master's degree in classical languages and education from Columbia University Teachers College. In February 1905, she received a permanent appointment as a Latin teacher at Richmond Hill High School, Queens, and was subsequently transferred to the Manual Training High School in Brooklyn.

According to court documents, McDowell was "regarded as a capable and efficient teacher and her record is flawless." Her classroom control and ability to influence students in "the development of habits of honor, orderliness, self-reliance, self-control, courtesy and good physical posture" was attested to in reports by the school's principal, Dr. Horace Mann Snyder, in a report dated March 30, 1914: "In every way the best. She is not of the 2:30 type," and, "She is a Quaker and her example could not be better."

So what happened to change that opinion? Clearly America's involvement in the war, and the demands placed upon public schools to foster patriotism, clashed with McDowell's pacifism. When given a directive like signing a loyalty pledge, raising money in class to support the war effort, or teaching patriotism, she simply begged off and had another teacher stand in for her, at least on the two latter tasks. Still, the principal was ordered to report teachers who refused to comply with all measures.

On January 10, 1918, McDowell was summoned before the New York City Board of Superintendents. Her main questioner was John L. Tildsley, chairman of the Committee on High Schools and writer of the first loyalty oath for teachers in New York State. Tildsley asked, "Miss McDowell, do you *believe* this country should resist by force of arms an invasion by a hostile army?" McDowell's answer was evasive: "I can speak for myself only. Personally, I would not resist by arms invasion, at least if I can live up to what I think. Can't always tell what we might do in an emergency." Tildsley pressed, "If one was threatening, would you resort to a sword or firing arms?," to which McDowell responded, "It would depend on the circumstances. I don't think I would have a sword or gun to kill one with, I would have to trust to some different kind of method, which one cannot tell." When another superintendent asked, "Would you uphold your country in resisting invasion?," McDowell answered, "I could uphold it as being a proper act for the country, but not a proper act for me." Tildsley countered, "Are you willing to assist the Government at the present time by every means in your power in carrying on the present war?" McDowell said simply, "No."

Pacifism versus Duty

The Board of Superintendents deliberated at length and concluded that charges of "conduct unbecoming a teacher" should be brought against McDowell, since her alleged conduct challenged schools that had, in essence, become "seminaries of patriotism." As H. C. Peterson and Gilbert Fite argue in their book, *Opponents of War*, "Many [teachers] conformed because they believed in the war, some because they were used to conforming, others because they were frightened into it. After all, most teachers were, and still are, so financially dependent that economic necessity compelled them not to arouse the ire of their administrative superiors."

Based on the charges, the Board of Superintendents recommended McDowell's suspension from teaching duties "pending an investigation . . . pointing to 'disloyalty.'" It was not the board's intent to challenge her pacifism as a Quaker, but rather to show that her ability to carry out her duties as a high school teacher had been seriously affected by her conscientious objection to war.

At the Board of Education's monthly meeting on January 24, 1918, a resolution was passed recommending McDowell's suspension. Superintendent Gustave Straubenmuller stated that "Miss McDowell has refused to sign, unqualifiedly, the loyalty pledge circulated in the Public Schools." Despite Principal Snyder's comments that "[s]he is an excellent teacher" and "is a very estimable woman whose views happen to be in serious conflict with those prevailing today," the key issue of her refusal to sign the loyalty pledge was seen as insubordination. "She was asked to resign," the *New York Times* reported, "but refused to do so." On April 24, 1918, she was notified that charges of "conduct unbecoming a teacher" had been approved, and that a formal hearing before the Board of Education would be scheduled for the following month.

McDowell's hearing on May 15, 1918 on charges of "conduct unbecoming a teacher" was held before a special four-member board committee. Assistant Corporation Counsel Charles E. McIntyre led the prosecution. The defense team was headed by Austen G. Fox, an active civil libertarian, and assisted by John P. Broomell, himself a Quaker. The case received extensive news coverage. According to the *New York Evening Post*, the room was "filled to its capacity by teachers, members of the Board of Superintendents, and other persons interested in the proceedings." The defense, attempting to dramatize the event, argued that this was "one of the momentous cases in American history dealing with the right of religious freedom," and "the first time in the history of the United States that a Quaker has been put on public trial for holding that faith." The prosecution, of course, denied that the case had "any such significance."

Conscience on Trial

The proceedings began with Fox charging that "[n]o one has doubted her loyalty or her love of her country. No seditious thought, much less utterance, has been attributed to her at any time." He pounded away at the allegation "that Miss McDowell's 'belief' that all war is a denial of Christianity, as she understands Christianity, and that she can not take part in war or warlike preparation, calls for the forfeiture of her office as a teacher in the public schools." In an impassioned closing argument, Fox proclaimed: "It is far more important that freedom of conscience and tolerance should be preserved than that this lady should be removed from her position."

Upon cross-examination, McIntyre asked McDowell if she had ever been told to teach "civics." She stated that she "had tried to give some instruction in patriotism." Did she present what she was asked to teach? quizzed McIntyre, and then he attacked her loyalty: "These contributions of yours have all been made for the relief of suffering caused by war, and not to promote war?" Yes, McDowell responded. McIntyre's closing summation stated, "The defendant contends that she is not obliged to comply with the regulations laid down for teachers because she is a Quaker. We say that it is necessary for the peace and safety of the State that our schools should have teachers who are in sympathy with this war."

The hearing ended after two and a half hours, but the board deliberated for a month. Its decision on the "charge of conduct unbecoming a teacher" was upheld 4 to 0, and Mary McDowell was dismissed as a teacher in the New York City Public School System on June 19, 1918.

McDowell's defense team claimed that "her dismissal violated federal and state Constitutions by discrimination against her on account of her religion." More confident in the judicial system than in the Board of Education, they filed an application for a writ of mandamus (defined in Latin as "we command," asking the court to issue an order directing someone to do something) with the New York State Supreme Court, seeking the reinstatement of McDowell and "directing the reinstatement of the petitioner as an assistant teacher of Latin in one of the high schools under the control of the board of education from which position she was dismissed." Despite well-reasoned arguments in the respondent brief, their request was denied; as the court noted, "While the petitioner may be entitled to the greatest respect for her adherence to her faith, she cannot be permitted because of it to act in a manner inconsistent with the peace and safety of the state."

When New York State Commissioner of Education John H. Finley was asked to review the matter, he concurred: "[R]eligion had nothing to do with the situation . . . she was dismissed solely because of her attitude toward the government in war." He ruled that "[i]f a teacher asserts that she will not support the government in taking up 'arms against the foe' she should not be retained in her position."

A Change of Heart

For McDowell, the results were heartbreaking, as well as financially disastrous. But after five arduous years, her fate changed. On July 13, 1923, the Board of Education reinstated McDowell after entertaining a formal request for reconsideration by her former defense attorney John Broomell. The board stated to the press: "After full consideration of the case, the committee has decided that the punishment meted out to Miss McDowell was too severe. She was tried at a time of great public hysteria. Since then, public feeling has undergone considerable modification."

Mary McDowell continued to teach until 1943, when she officially retired from the New York City Public School System. Upon her death in 1955, a school in Brooklyn was named in her honor—her legacy to both academic freedom and the power of conscience.

THE CHINESE JEKYLL AND HYDE

Leon Ling was often described as "Americanized," but this cartoon in the *Brooklyn Daily Eagle*, labeled "The Chinese Jekyll and Hyde," casts doubt on the accuracy of that depiction. Credit: From the collections of the New York State Library, Manuscripts and Special Collections, Albany, New York.

66

Murder in Chinatown

Mary Ting Yi Lui

On the afternoon of June 18, 1909, New York City police officer John Reardon made an unsettling discovery: the body of an unidentified young white woman inside a large trunk in a room above a "chop suey" restaurant on 782 Eighth Avenue. A piece of rope entwined around her neck suggested that she had been strangled. The room's occupant—a Chinese man, Leon Ling, also known as William L. Leon—had evidently been missing for over a week, leaving no clues to his whereabouts.

Reardon sent word of his grisly find to Captain Post, his commanding officer at the West 47th Street police station. After rushing to inspect the scene, Captain Post turned the investigation over to Captain Arthur Carey of the Homicide Bureau. By the end of the day, several police officers and detectives had inspected the crime scene, as well as the entire building and its occupants. Police arrested a number of Chinese men in the building, but they were later released because they could not provide any information about the murder. The police then began a citywide manhunt to locate the missing chief suspect, Leon Ling.

In the room, police found a number of letters addressed to Ling written by various American women. Among them were thirty-five letters signed "Elsie," which led police to suspect that the victim was nineteen-year-old Elsie Sigel of 209 Wadsworth Avenue in Washington Heights, who had been reported missing for more than a week by her family. Relatives later positively identified the body in the trunk as hers after recognizing clothes and jewelry.

Elsie Sigel had disappeared shortly after leaving her family's home around 10 a.m. on June 9. On June 8, her grandmother had sent Elsie a letter asking her to spend

This essay first appeared in spring 2006, volume 5, number 4.

the day at her home in the Bronx. When Elsie did not return home that evening, the family telephoned the grandmother's residence and learned to their surprise that Elsie had never arrived at all. The family became worried, fearing she had met with foul play. But on June 12, the family was relieved when a telegram, signed "Elsie," arrived from Washington, D.C., telling them not to worry since she would come home the next day. When Elsie did not return, her family grew even more alarmed at her prolonged absence.

Sensational deaths of young women were by no means unheard of in New York City. The same month Elsie Sigel was murdered, the *World* newspaper reported over one hundred unsolved homicides in Gotham that year. Yet New Yorkers were strangely fascinated with Elsie's case. Front-page news stories ran for at least a week after its initial reporting, and follow-up stories that detailed police and civilian attempts to find the missing murder suspect continued intermittently for several months. These news reports often elicited readers' responses as letters to the editor. The discovery of the alleged interracial romance between Leon Ling and Elsie lent even greater sensationalism to the case.

It is clear from both these letters and the newspapers' ongoing coverage of the murder investigation that New Yorkers and Americans at large were deeply disturbed by Elsie's relationship with a Chinese man. At the heart of their concerns were the shifting racial and gender geographies that allowed Chinese men and white women of all socioeconomic classes to encounter each other on New York City's streets in the course of their daily activities. Not confined to the Chinatown neighborhood of Mott, Pell, and Doyers Streets in Lower Manhattan, New York's Chinese population circulated throughout the city to pursue their livelihoods. Following construction of the city's elevated and subway lines, Chinese entrepreneurs set up hand laundries or chop suey restaurants throughout the city, bringing them into daily contact with mainstream populations. While their services were appreciated, the presence of these Chinese working-class males was often viewed with suspicion by police, social reformers, and residents. Many feared that the proliferating Chinese-owned businesses were conduits for vice activities like prostitution, opium smoking, and gambling into respectable, white middle-class neighborhoods. In significant ways, the death of Elsie Sigel signaled to the broader public the breakdown of social and geographical borders that protected white womanhood and middle-class respectability.

Reports of white female prostitutes and opium addicts working in Chinatown were common in popular depictions of Chinatown as a vice district. Police, social reformers, and journalists all commented disparagingly on these women's associations with Chinese men. Yet Elsie Sigel hardly fit the image of a prostitute or "fallen woman." She came from a respected Protestant family and was the granddaughter of Franz Sigel, a well-known Civil War general in the Union Army who later settled in New York

City and became a public servant and active member of the city's Turnverein Society, a mutual aid society for German Americans. Thus, the public revelation of her gruesome murder and secret interracial romance was all the more shocking.

From the beginning, reporters attempted to offer an explanation for Leon Ling and Elsie Sigel's relationship. Newspapers claimed that Elsie and her mother were active missionaries working among the Chinese, and that it was during the course of these activities that the two had met Leon Ling four years earlier, when he had operated a Chinese restaurant on Amsterdam Avenue near 191st Street. At that time, the Sigels resided at 188th Street, just a few blocks from the restaurant. The public responded harshly to the news of a murdered "girl missionary," calling for all churches to stop allowing white women to teach the city's Chinese population and casting doubt on the possibility for the conversion of the "heathen Chinese." Captain Arthur Carey of the Homicide Bureau, for example, declared to the press that Leon Ling must have deceived the well-intentioned missionaries with his claims to be a Christian convert, and he dismissed Ling's church-going as part of a "missionary game" to meet impressionable young white women. The negative publicity of Chinese Sunday schools and missions as vehicles for miscegenation deeply concerned the city's Protestant churches, and many went to great lengths to replace their white female teachers with older male peers.

Meanwhile, the movements of Chinese men around the city came under heavy scrutiny as police attempted to find the missing Leon Ling. They circulated descriptions of Ling and his roommate Chong Sing, who was also missing, thus making all Chinese men who fit their descriptions vulnerable to harassment. Eventually, no segment of the Chinese American population was exempt from the dragnet, as police and the general public pursued the suspects through racial profiling. Police arrested Chinese laundry workers, servants, students, and diplomats in their zealous efforts to capture Ling. Japanese and Korean men were likewise mistakenly arrested based on the racial descriptions used in police circulars and newspaper reports.

As the police met with failure, the search became national and international. Throughout the country, Americans responded to the Sigel murder by investigating and monitoring in their hometowns the same places occupied by Chinese workers—homes, Protestant missions, chop suey restaurants, hand laundries—that the New York police, reporters, and social reformers were targeting. Like their New York counterparts, these officials and lay citizens mistakenly arrested numerous Asian men through the use of racial profiling, and they were equally unsuccessful in capturing Leon Ling.

In the face of this constant police harassment, Chinese in New York and across the nation raised individual and collective protests to U.S. officials and petitioned Chinese diplomats for protection. On July 2, a small delegation of Chinatown's merchants traveled to Washington to appeal to the Chinese Legation for assistance and protection against police raids and local vigilantism. In preparation for the raucous celebrations that would accompany the Fourth of July, New York's Chinese Consolidated Benevolent Association, comprised of Chinese immigrant family, village, and district associations, issued handbills that warned residents of possible violence, urged them to take extra safety precautions, and told them not to venture outside or go to work but instead to stay home. The NYPD responded to these calls for protection by warning all captains of local precincts that "they would be held responsible for any attacks on Chinese in their districts." But the police did not believe that the city's Chinese population was in any real danger and remained focused on their efforts to question Chinese suspects and locate Leon Ling. They even cabled Scotland Yard and U.S. embassies overseas to ask for help in the search—and, as in the United States, police were directed to look specifically in Chinese immigrant neighborhoods, such as the Limehouse district in London. None these dragnets yielded Leon Ling.

These tactics worked to terrorize the nation's Chinese immigrant communities and to remind all Chinese immigrants of their peculiar status as a minority that had been barred from naturalization rights since the passage of the Chinese Exclusion Act in 1882. Legally perpetual foreigners, the Chinese were seen as being *in* New York but not *of* it. Although New York State refused to pass antimiscegenation laws against interracial marriage between whites and nonwhites, the surveillance of both Chinese male and white female populations in the city after Elsie Sigel's murder worked to undermine and deter social relations between these groups—and to reinforce and maintain the color line.

The murder convinced New Yorkers that the Chinatown neighborhood would forever remain an insular community, ridden with peculiar Chinese vices, that was *in* New York but not *of* it.

Notre Dame won the game, 35 to 13, giving Army its only loss of the season. Credit: United States Military Academy, West Point, New York.

67

Thunder on the Hudson

Charles F. Howlett

"Get 'em," said Charles Daly, the former Harvard and Army All-American player and new head football coach at West Point. "They're not a bad team and it's a fair enough price for a good win." The team he was referring to was a little-known Catholic college located in northwestern Indiana. But when the game was finally played at West Point on November 1, 1913, not only would Notre Dame be forever associated with college football, the way the game itself was played would also be changed.

It all began in 1912 when Army and Yale, two of the most powerful football teams around, decided to discontinue their annual game. As the story goes, the coaches and administrators at both schools felt that the game "was demanding too much from the players in terms of effort and emotion." In reality, as Murray Sperber notes in his popular book *Shake Down the Thunder: The Creation of Notre Dame Football*, Army had been a persistent abuser of the standard eligibility rules. Many talented athletes enrolled at West Point specifically to play football, even after completing their entire undergraduate course work at other schools. At a time when college football was far more popular than the professional game, Army was considered one of the premier football teams in America. But because it flaunted the rules, it had become a hypocrite when it came to intercollegiate athletics.

Meanwhile, Notre Dame's newly hired coach, Jesse Harper, was anxious to increase the small college's visibility. After Yale's departure from the competition, much had been made of Army's desire to fill its open game date. In those days, Army's schedule was drawn up by the team's manager, Cadet Harold Loomis, who had sent

This essay first appeared in fall 2006, volume 6, number 2.

out invitation letters to every school in the East and some in the Midwest. But it was actually Jesse Harper who had first contacted Army on December 18, 1912, not the other way around. Harper wasn't worried about Army's eligibility rules; during the course of negotiations, he was able to secure a visitor's guarantee of $1,000 despite Army's initial offer of $600. Reverend Matthew Walsh, Notre Dame's vice president and future president, was pleased with the arrangement. Harper was also pleased because it would help with recruiting in the East. Years later, Harper told *New York Times* sports columnist Red Smith, "Maybe it's true . . . that Army was looking for a Midwestern opponent that wouldn't be too tough for them, when they got my letter. But as far as I know, my letter was all there was to it."

Calm Before the Storm

The game was scheduled for the first Saturday in November 1913, on the plains at West Point. No admission was charged and no money was paid for concessions. Putting Notre Dame on the schedule barely raised an eyebrow among Eastern pundits. The team, dubbed the "Westerners" by the press, remained faceless, cannon fodder for the Black Knights of the Hudson. Even the *Times* committed a geographical error when it wrote that the visitors "were coming all the way from South Bend, *Illinois*."

When the eighteen members of the Notre Dame team got off the train at West Point, each carried "his own equipment," writes Ray Robinson in *Rockne of Notre Dame*, "in either a satchel or a paper bag. Many didn't even show up with cleats." Despite the formidable reputations of outstanding team members—the slick quarterbacking of Gus Dorais, the pounding running style of Ray Eichenlaub, and the outside speed of a skinny end named Knute Rockne—it looked like Notre Dame didn't stand a chance. Army was more than willing to give Notre Dame the money for "a good win"; after all, Army boasted four All-Americans, led by team captain Tom Hammond and quarterback Vern Pritchard.

The game attracted over five thousand spectators. Most brought their own refreshments, as was customary in those days. Among the distinguished guests in attendance was Army Chief of Staff and Spanish-American War hero General Leonard Wood. The 650 members of the Corps of Cadets were all present, looking forward to another easy Army win and undefeated season. Sitting on the Army bench was former player Dwight David Eisenhower. A member of the 1912 team, Eisenhower had badly injured his knee during a game against Tufts and was forced to give up playing. Civilians, bundled in overcoats, sat in Cullum Hall Field's circus-seat bleachers to witness the opening coin toss between Notre Dame's Rockne and

Army's Benny Hodge. Perhaps a portent of things to come was Rockne's winning the toss.

Passing Shocks

The game began badly for Notre Dame when quarterback Dorais fumbled during the opening series. But as Rockne later recounted, "After we took a terrific pounding by the Army line, and a trio of backs that charged in like locomotives, we held them on downs." Notre Dame's surprising passing attack eventually helped them take a 14–13 lead at halftime. Contrary to popular sports mythology, however, Notre Dame did not invent the forward pass (that distinction belongs to Denison University in Ohio)—although, despite Army being touted as the premier passing team in the East, Notre Dame's strategy during the game did revolutionize the way in which the forward pass was used. Prior to this game, the college football world thought passes should be thrown in desperation: as a last resort on third down, to avoid punting the ball to the other team on fourth down. But against Army, Notre Dame's offense continuously opened up the game by passing on first and second downs. Again, according to Rockne (with allowances for his literary inventiveness, mythologized in the 1940 movie *Knute Rockne, All-American*, starring Pat O'Brien and Ronald Reagan):

> Dorais, in a huddle said, "lets [*sic*] open up." It was amusing to see the Army boys huddle after a first, snappy 11-yard pass rush had been completed for a first down. Their guards and tackles went tumbling into us to stop line bucks and plunges. Instead, Dorais stepped neatly back and flipped the ball to an uncovered end or halfback.

The game's second half continued to feature Dorais hurling spirals to Rockne (a technique both had perfected the previous summer while working as lifeguards at a Cedar Point, Ohio, beach resort). Despite Lou Merillat, Army's right end, shouting, "Let's lick those Hoosiers!," and the great center, John McEwen, using forearms against his smaller, quicker opponent, Dorais' passes and Eichenlaub's long runs stunned the Army faithful. When the game ended, Dorais had completed fourteen of seventeen passes for 243 yards—an unheard-of total for that time. His forty-yard pass to Rockne was the longest pass ever completed up to that day. According to the *Times*, "The yellow leather egg was in the air half the time, with the Notre Dame team spread out in all directions over the field waiting for it." Not only did Notre Dame win convincingly, 35 to 13, giving Army its only loss of the season, but college offensive football was completely changed on the plains in front of Cullum Hall. And the way Notre Dame employed the forward pass—a legal weapon since 1906—made football history.

Never Again the Same Game

Eastern sportswriters raved about the game. The *Baltimore Sun* had a six-column headline: "Notre Dame Shows the Most Sensational Football the Nation Has Ever Seen." The *New York Evening Telegraph* ran a story after the game, observing that "[i]t took a so-called smaller college to come East and display an attack so versatile and dazzling that it may revolutionize the style of offensive play throughout this section of the country." But it was the headline in the Sunday *New York Times* that placed Notre Dame football on the map: "Notre Dame Open Play Amazes Army." One of the referees, former Princeton coach Bill Roper, was quoted as saying "that he had never seen the forward pass developed to such a state of perfection." And *Times* columnist John Kieran summed up the day's events this way: "The Dorais-to-Rockne forward passing combination wakened the East to the possibilities of the new open game on the gridiron. . . . [It] was the inspiration and example for a new system and a new spirit in football over a wide territory."

Historically, the game was important for a number of reasons, some true and some not so true. First, the Dorais-to-Rockne passing combination did indeed change college football forever—but Notre Dame did not invent the forward pass; it merely perfected it. Second, the myth that Notre Dame was no match for the elite team from the East was just that. Notre Dame had lost only one game in the previous three years and was considered by many, especially in the Midwest, to be a quality opponent. The fact is that the powerful Eastern press generally gave very little recognition to teams outside the region, and Notre Dame's victory over a seemingly invincible opponent only legitimized its football stature. "Report has the Indiana team strong," the press recounted after the game, "but no one imagined it knew so much football."

Once More, with Feeling

Third, Notre Dame's victory endeared the school and its team to millions of Irish immigrants living in New York. It became a focal point of pride for Irish Americans and led to the creation of the famous "subway alumni." Fourth, of all the great players who performed in that game, only one, Knute Rockne, would achieve lasting immortality—and not as a player but later as a coach. Finally, apart from the game itself, seven members of the 1913 Army team, as well as its manager, achieved officer rank of general.

There have been many memorable games between the two schools since that blustery, cloudy day in 1913. Perhaps none was as dramatic, or more important, than the 0–0 tie in 1946, when the game was played at Yankee Stadium and featured two undefeated teams and three current or future Heisman Trophy winners: Glen Davis and Doc Blanchard of Army, and John Lujack of Notre Dame. In 1944 and 1945, Army had been crowned national champions, but in 1946 that honor went to Notre Dame. Though the series is no longer played on a regular basis, the two teams will meet again on November 18, 2006. The month's selection is fitting: after all, it was Army's willingness ninety-three years ago to invite a relatively obscure team from the Midwest to travel east and "shake down the thunder" on the plains overlooking the Hudson River.

The Cities Census Committee charged Florence Knapp with misuse of $180,000 from the $1.2 million census budget, alleging "nonfeasance, misfeasance and malfeasance." Credit: Author's collection.

68

A Self-Made Woman

Mark Fleisher

For some women, the 1920s meant bootleg liquor, hot jazz, and bobbed hair. More serious and sober women, such as Syracuse's Florence Elizabeth Smith Knapp, saw the era as ushering in newfound freedom and opportunity: the right to vote, seek public office, and "clean house" by instituting badly needed government reforms.

New York State enacted women's suffrage in 1917. Three years later, passage of the Nineteenth Amendment extended the right to the federal level. When Florence Knapp won election as New York's secretary of state in 1924, she became the first woman to hold statewide office. But she soon became enmeshed in a scandal that ended her political career, damaged her health, and relegated her to a footnote in history.

Described as "ambitious, flawed and foolish" by Dr. Lauren Kozakiewicz, adjunct professor of history at the University at Albany, who included a chapter about Knapp in her doctoral thesis, the forty-nine-year-old Knapp possessed impeccable credentials when Republicans nominated her for secretary of state at their Rochester convention. Knapp had earned degrees at Cortland State Normal College, Syracuse University, and Columbia University and had studied at Cornell. She had pursued a successful career in education, first in the classroom, then as superintendent for several Syracuse-area districts, later becoming dean of Syracuse University's College of Home Economics. During World War I, Knapp was an assistant director of food conservation for all cities outside the greater New York City area, where she established thrift kitchens, organized farm bureaus, and developed food conservation classes. Her ancestry included Harvard University librarian Ebenezer Hancock, a brother of Declaration of Independence signer John Hancock, and her husband, Philip Schuyler Knapp, was a linear descendant of Revolutionary War hero General Philip Schuyler.

This essay first appeared in fall 2006, volume 6, number 2.

Equal—and Ambitious

Florence first dove into politics as a delegate to the 1920 Republican National Convention in Chicago, then headed a group of alternate at-large delegates at the 1924 GOP national meeting in Cleveland. After winning unanimous backing for secretary of state at the 1924 Republican state convention in Rochester, Knapp told the *Syracuse Journal*,

> This is the happiest day of my life. Republicans have given women recognition in return for their service to the party. The men have recognized us as their equal and we must get out now and prove to them that their judgment has not been mistaken. I'm happy to have won, of course, but happier about the spirit shown at the convention, one of equality in which women were given the opportunity.

But Lauren Kozakiewicz has a somewhat different view of the GOP's choice:

> Rather than respecting her, I think they were more afraid of her influence. She . . . self-engineered her campaign for the nomination and the party regulars were afraid of challenging her. Women were very effective in registering for the vote, and their influence concerned the party regulars. But when the party looked for someone to promote as women's leader, they saw that Florence had the right professions.

Knapp defeated incumbent James Hamilton of the Bronx by 133,000 votes for the two-year secretary of state post. Only Democrat Al Smith's victory for governor averted a Republican sweep of statewide races. But Knapp scored points with the new governor by successfully arranging his inauguration. *New York Evening Post* columnist Leonard Smith described her as a "gentle-faced, blue-eyed woman with a crisp way of talking and noted at the capitol for her tact." An additional public relations coup was riding through Syracuse's streets in an open car with Charles Lindbergh after "Lucky Lindy" flew the *Spirit of St. Louis* to the state fairgrounds. She also endeared herself to reformers by advocating the installation of voting machines.

Passed Over

However, two unrelated developments—the status of the secretary of state's office and questions surrounding Knapp's oversight of the state's 1925 decennial census—

contributed to her downfall. Seeking to streamline state government's administrative machinery, Governor Al Smith appointed Belle Moskowitz, a New York City reformer and personal advisor, as chief of a reorganization task force. One approved recommendation: appoint, not elect, the secretary of state.

Knapp spent much of 1926 hoping for reappointment. Instead, Smith chose thirty-eight-year-old Robert Moses, a Moskowitz protégé and chairman of the State Parks Council, who later won fame (and in some circles, infamy) as a political power broker and urban planner. Her political career blocked, Knapp returned to Syracuse University's College of Home Economics.

Then questions arose concerning her oversight of the 1925 state census. Individual cities questioned the final count. In the fall of 1927, the Cities Census Committee headed by former Knapp aide Dr. Walter Laidlaw charged her with misuse of $180,000 from the $1.2 million census budget, alleging "nonfeasance, misfeasance and malfeasance."

Attorney General Albert Ottinger and others called for Governor Smith to appoint a Moreland Act Commission to investigate. (The Moreland Act of 1907 gave the governor the power to appoint investigative bodies—commissions—to look into the activities of public bodies at all levels of government in New York.) But Ottinger's request triggered a legal question: could a Moreland inquiry probe the actions of an elected official? The governor reasoned that although he had appointed Robert Moses, the current secretary of state, at the time in question Florence Knapp had been *elected* to the post, not appointed. Thus, Smith believed that a department headed by an elected officer was not subject to subpoena or a Moreland investigation.

However, Ottinger's narrower view, in support of a Moreland investigation, persuaded the governor. Ottinger wrote that such an investigation was warranted because census records had been transferred from an elected to an appointed secretary of state. Furthermore, Ottinger said, the census lacked final certification.

Trouble with the Numbers

Moreland Commissioner Randall LeBoeuf, Jr., recommended criminal prosecution of Knapp. Albany County District Attorney Charles Herrick declined to prosecute, citing insufficient evidence. Governor Smith then ordered Ottinger to decide any further action.

The attorney general, himself an ambitious politician who would lose the 1928 governor's race to Franklin D. Roosevelt by twenty-five thousand votes, decided to try Knapp. He appointed two special prosecutors, whereupon Governor Smith convened an Extraordinary Term of State Supreme Court with Judge Stephen Callaghan of Brooklyn presiding.

The prosecutors noted that Knapp had put six relatives on the payroll, and that they had done little work for their combined $20,000 salary. The prosecution also alleged that Knapp had stolen a $2,875.06 census paycheck made out to her stepdaughter, Clara Blanche Knapp. Clara testified that she didn't know she was on the payroll and that she'd never received the check.

The trial ended in a hung jury. But a second panel found Knapp guilty of grand larceny. Her health problems—primarily a heart condition, exacerbated by the trial—prompted Judge Callaghan to reserve sentencing for three months. Newspaper editorials called for a suspended sentence and encouraged Governor Smith to show clemency. Callaghan ultimately handed down a thirty-day sentence, to be served in the home of the Albany County Jail superintendent.

Robert Moses later wrote of Knapp's plea to the governor:

> Smith tried his best to get a suspended sentence for Mrs. Knapp, a vain, silly, political accident . . . who was caught pulling chestnuts out of the fire for the Republican machine. Mrs. Knapp came to see the governor, put her hand on his and murmured, "You haven't lost faith in me, Al?" She was done in pink from head to toe and the governor remarked sympathetically, "She looked like a basket of peaches." The judge had a tough North of Ireland conscience, and Mrs. Knapp languished rather comfortably at Valatie . . . and then was heard of no more.

The Political Graveyard

Knapp bought land in Valatie (just south of Albany), but her plan to start a school failed to attract investors. She lived for a time with a sister in Bedford, Massachusetts, before returning to Syracuse to operate a tea room and share a house with another sister, Julia.

After her brother, Charles Smith, a former Hornell High School principal, died on October 19, 1949, Florence and Julia committed themselves to Marcy State Hospital (now Mohawk Valley Psychiatric Center) in Utica. A week later, on October 26, Florence died of heart failure at age seventy-five. She is buried in Syracuse's Oakwood Cemetery.

Years earlier, in the May 1925 edition of *New York State Education* magazine, Knapp had stated her motto: "Get up and dig. Advancement in any field is largely a matter of self-will and definite purpose. The only difference between a rut and a grave is the depth. Altogether too many persons literally dig their own graves by what be termed the rut route." On another occasion she wrote, "I am a great believer in keeping one's eyes open for opportunities."

For Florence Knapp, the opportunities did indeed arise—only to be lost by the same self-engineered drive that had first placed her in the public's service.

Lewis Latimer, shown here at age thirty-four, went to work as an office boy at the age of thirteen. Credit: Queens Borough Public Library Archives, Lewis H. Latimer Family Papers, Queens, New York.

69

Pioneer of Light

Rayvon Fouché

The creation of heroes has been tremendously important for American society. Heroes fulfill many needs within American culture: they help define what it means to be an American, create a positive and progressive narrative about our collective historical past, stabilize understanding of our cultural surroundings, and represent the best of what we want our culture to be. The iconic "great inventor" is one of many cultural images that enable Americans to communicate about a common American origin, identity, and purpose. Historian Wyn Wachhorst indicates that inventors represent, among other attributes, "the gospel of technological progress." This makes them especially powerful and authoritative ambassadors of American success.

The dawn of the twentieth century began an unprecedented period of technological development for America. But creating a modern technological nation not only included development of technological infrastructure, it also saw the rise of the inventor as cultural hero, icon, and ultimately myth. The triumphs of inventors and entrepreneurs like Thomas Edison and Henry Ford represented the submission of both the natural and manufactured worlds to men who possessed the desire and intellect to harness the power of science and technology. This heroic celebrity soon took on mythic proportions, and the mythology supported the understanding that through an inventor's command and control of the scientific and technological, he could design, construct, and most importantly invent modern America—and consequently the modern world. To most Americans, inventors were natural heroes. This is the backdrop against which electrical pioneer Lewis Howard Latimer began his career as an inventor.

This essay first appeared in spring 2007, volume 6, number 4.

Self-Taught Draftsman

Lewis Latimer was born in Chelsea, Massachusetts, in 1848 to George and Rebecca Latimer, two former slaves who escaped from Norfolk, Virginia, on October 4, 1842, to the freedom of the North. After serving in the Union Navy during the Civil War, Lewis began his technical career in Boston as an office boy for Crosby and Gould, patent solicitors and attorneys. Through his assiduous efforts to teach himself the art of drafting, he rose to the position of assistant draftsman and eventually, in the mid-1870s, to the position of chief draftsman. During his tenure at Crosby and Gould, he made drawings for Alexander Graham Bell's telephone. He also met Mary Wilson Lewis, a young woman from Fall River, Massachusetts. They were married on November 10, 1873, and from this union came two daughters.

In 1879, the Latimer family relocated to Bridgeport, Connecticut, where Lewis met Hiram Stevens Maxim, chief engineer of United States Electric Lighting Company, which manufactured lamps. Shortly after their first meeting, Maxim hired Latimer as his draftsman and private secretary. Latimer quickly moved up within the enterprise, and when the company moved to New York City in 1880, it placed him in charge of the production of carbon lamp filaments. From this position of authority, Latimer went on to invent products that were fundamental to the development of United States Electric Lighting Company—and to the enormous technological advances that would soon revolutionize American science and society.

In October 1880, Hiram Maxim was granted a patent for a filament whose resistance was equalized and standardized when treated with hydrocarbon vapor, allowing it to burn longer than the existing (and competing) Edison lamp filament. On January 17, 1882, however, Lewis Latimer was granted a patent for a new "Process of Manufacturing Carbons" that supported Maxim's earlier patent. This invention produced a highly resistant filament that could be shaped into an "M," which became a noted characteristic of the company's Maxim Lamp. In addition, Latimer patented other inventions, including an electric lamp and a globe support for such lamps. These further enhanced the Maxim Lamp during 1881 and 1882.

"The Electric Lighting Business"

In 1881, Latimer was dispatched to London to establish an incandescent lamp factory for the newly founded Maxim-Weston Electric Light Company. In 1882, Latimer left this company and began working for the Olmstead Electric Lighting Company of Brooklyn as its superintendent of lamp construction. It was here that he designed the Latimer Lamp. A multiple hexagonal-shaped globe made this incandescent bulb unique. He later continued his work at the Acme Electric Company of New York.

In 1885, after meeting Thomas Edison, Latimer began to work for the Edison Electric Light Company. He became affiliated with its engineering department, rose to chief engineer, and when the company's legal department was formed in 1890, Latimer's record of expert legal advice made him a requisite member of this new division. According to a brief biographical sketch written by Latimer, he was transferred to this department "as [a] draughtsman inspector and expert witness as to facts in the early stages of the electric lighting business . . . [I] traveled extensively, securing witnesses' affidavits, and early apparatus, and also testifying in a number of the basic patent cases to the advantage of my employers." His complete knowledge of electrical technology was exemplified in his work *Incandescent Electric Lighting: A Practical Description of the Edison System* (1890).

Latimer continued his position as patent investigator within the legal department when the Edison General Electric Company merged with the Thomson-Houston Company to form the General Electric Company in 1892. His knowledge of the electric industry became invaluable when the General Electric and the Westinghouse Electric companies formed the Board of Patent Control in 1896. This board was responsible for managing the cross-licensing of patents between the two companies and for prosecuting infringers. Latimer was appointed to the position of chief draftsman, although his duties went far beyond drafting. As in his earlier work, he used the vast body of knowledge he had acquired over the years to the company's benefit in its efforts to eliminate outside competition. Latimer remained in this position until the board was dissolved in 1911.

"Which Way Will He Fall?"

But by then Latimer was no longer a young man, so not surprisingly he was concerned for his own, and his family's, future. The depth of his concern was displayed in a drawing he made, entitled "Which Way Will He Fall?" In the sketch, Latimer portrays himself as balanced, by means of a drafting tool, on a ragged ruler edge between the safe "feathers" of General Electric and the "wide wide world" of work, embodied by the patent consulting firm Hammer & Schwarz. The most intriguing aspect of this sketch is the nametag affixed to the bottom of Latimer's jacket: it resembles a price tag. Was he alluding to the commodified nature of his existence within American society? He undoubtedly understood the value of his services to the host of companies that competed for his skills. Was he making a statement about how those competitors viewed him as a purchasable asset?

As a black man, Latimer must have fully understood his limited opportunities at General Electric. If he were going to move into its managerial hierarchy, that promotion would have already taken place, since similarly credentialed men had already made their way into upper management. The company would most certainly have found a position for him, but he was past his prime and had reached the glass ceiling there. Yet a token position may have looked better to him than journeying blindly into the "wide wide world."

Latimer eventually decided to join Hammer & Schwarz, which proved to be a very shrewd move. When the Board of Patent Control dissolved in 1911, most of the GE engineering department went to work for Hammer & Schwarz. Given the overt racism of engineering circles during the early twentieth century, a firm where he "was . . . liked and respected by all of his associates" was a good place for Latimer to be.

In 1918, when the Edison Pioneers were formed, Latimer was one of its twenty-eight founding members, and the only black member. This organization aimed to bring together men who had worked with Edison before 1885, to pay tribute to those pioneering days, and to perpetuate Edison's inventive legacy. However, a stroke in 1924 forced Latimer to retire, and he spent the last four years of his life engaged in two other activities that were also important to him: art and poetry. Lewis Latimer died on December 11, 1928, at his home in Flushing, New York.

The Price of Success

Latimer's success was not without cost; that cost was to obfuscate his connections with the general black population. But for him, it was a fair price to pay. The post-Reconstruction program of racial uplift and progress to which he subscribed deemed that for black citizens to advance toward civilization, they had to transform into—or at least emulate—white American society. Consequently, he felt that the only way to raise members of the black race to be strong, productive, and useful citizens was through assimilation. The union of black and white American cultures would have only lowered the standards of American society; thus, integration was not a worthy option.

Latimer's technical work also exemplified his worldview. He was neither an inventor nor an inventor-entrepreneur in the mode of Edison, Maxim, and others for whom he worked. Rather, he was a technical expert for whom the creation of technical artifacts, practices, and knowledge was not a fundamental goal. Inventing and patenting were merely credentials, useful tools for entering and solidifying his position within corporate culture and the associated social and economic order. As a result, he was able to gain access to a world closed to most black men. Lewis Latimer wanted to blend into this technical world to the point where he was no longer seen as a black man but instead as a "raceless" participant. Yet his ability to prosper despite the racial conditions of the day made him an African American inventive hero.

Donna Johs on her tricycle in Levittown, New York, ca. 1950. Credit: Fred and Dorothy Johs.

70

Salesman of the American Dream

Joshua Ruff

"Can the housing industry produce more houses and better houses, cheaper?" That was the question put to the nation's leading house builders at the Westchester Country Club on a spring day in 1948. America was coming out of a housing shortage so acute that some World War II veterans had converted chicken coops, trolley cars, and even automobiles into living spaces. William Levitt (1907–1994), builder of Levittown, Long Island, was clearly "the most aggressive member" of the panel assembled that day. "He feels that he has started a revolution," *Life* magazine reported.

Levitt was always quick to take credit for changing the housing industry. In a 1952 televised segment of *Industry on Parade*, the narrator put it this way: "The idea that came to . . . Bill Levitt was this: . . . why not mass produce the elements that go to make up a new house, just as the auto industry does with the parts that go into a new car?"

Levitt has often been described as the "Henry Ford of housing." Like Ford, he did not invent production-line techniques for his industry. But along with his brother Alfred, he did perfect them into a seamless set of tasks that made the complicated process of building a house textbook efficient. "One built every sixteen minutes," the ads insisted. And Bill—a man *Time* magazine called a "cocky, rambunctious hustler"—skillfully sold those houses, becoming the most famous American builder of his time.

Levitt's story is also reminiscent of a Greek tragedy: great rise, great hubris, great fall. "His ego made him, his ego broke him, and his ego kept him alive," says

This essay first appeared in summer 2007, volume 7, number 1.

his widow, Simone Levitt. From the heights of the 1940s and 1950s, Levitt eventually made a series of financial miscalculations that would cost him his fortune.

Criticized by civil rights activists, community planners, and critics of the new suburban "ticky-tacky" sweeping the nation, Levitt was also praised by legions of homeowners who saw him as a dream broker. "God bless Mommy and Daddy and Mister Levitt," went the bedtime prayer of one youngster in Levittown, according to Bill Levitt himself. This may have been no exaggeration: even today, he is revered throughout the community that bears his name.

Building Mania

Levitt's father, Abraham, a lawyer and rabbi's son from the Williamsburg section of Brooklyn, began the family's real estate business. He formed Levitt & Sons, Inc., during the summer before the crash of 1929. The company first sold upscale homes in their "Strathmore" developments in Rockville Centre (and later, Manhasset). "Strathmores" gave classy polish to a nouveau-riche clientele that craved it. Bill, a twenty-two-year-old NYU dropout who wanted "a big car and a lot of clothes," had a natural ability for sales. Alfred, just eighteen at the time, designed the houses.

While other builders struggled during the Depression, the Levitts continued to thrive by targeting upper-middle-class professionals less hurt by it. Their Rockville Centre homes were priced at $14,500, while Manhasset-area homes went from $9,100 to $18,000. Bill Levitt obtained mortgage money even as banks across the New York metropolitan area were closing during the dreaded Bank Holiday of 1933. In the meantime, he built the firm's first advertising connections.

One element of his marketing genius was skillful cross-pollination. A 1937 ad for Fenestra Steel window screens, graced by an illustration of one of Levitt & Sons' palatial Tudor homes, used a testimonial from Bill: "We have built 118 homes in the new Strathmore-at-Manhasset . . . the public buys these homes just as fast as they can be completed." Of course, the ad was selling not just Fenestra screens but also Levitt & Sons. Cooperative advertising quickly became a hallmark of the Levitts' success, and appliance and hardware companies lined up for product endorsements by both Bill and Alfred.

In 1941, Bill enlisted in the navy and became a lieutenant in the Seabees. His experiences during World War II were instructive. He later claimed to have seen the future through the men who served under him in Hawaii. When asked about their plans after the war, their response, he said, was invariably to get married, have kids, and settle down. Levitt knew they'd need a place to live at a price they could afford.

Houses from Potato Fields

In fact, the Levitts kept busy during wartime, honing their mass-production techniques at a navy housing project near Norfolk, Virginia. The new Federal Housing Administration gave money to developers to build new homes that veterans could then purchase with financial aid from their GI Bill benefits. It was in this climate that Levitt & Sons broke ground in 1947 on their first mass-produced housing community, Island Trees (later renamed Levittown), built on former potato farmland.

Their pace of building over seventeen thousand houses in just four years was breakneck—and they learned as they went. Above all, they cut out the middleman: when lumber couldn't be gotten fast enough, they purchased an entire forest in California. To pound all that wood into place, a factory in Belgium turned out their nails. Hundreds of non-union workers were hired to do piecework at high wages. Edward Konop, a construction superintendent who worked for Bill Levitt for seven years, remembers him being "very good to his employees and very hands on . . . I saw Bill at the job site more than anybody."

The community was finished in phases, with simple Cape Cods constructed the first year and ranch houses introduced each successive year. The appliances with which these homes were outfitted, from Bendix washing machines to General Electric refrigerators, were a godsend to new residents.

Levittown homeowner Helen Hooper fit the typical profile: young, recently married, the wife of a navy veteran from Queens. Even today, she credits Bill Levitt for "giving us everything we never had." Applying to purchase her new home, Hooper was one of the many "crazies" who waited in line all weekend to be near the front of the line on Monday morning: "We slept in the car . . . and then they took us to a big room. . . . And there were desks and typewriters and people all interviewing us. We had to have a hundred dollar deposit . . . we moved in September '49 and we were there for forty-six years."

Others were not so fortunate. Levitt denied African Americans the opportunity to buy his houses. The Levitts were among many builders with such policies, but white flight was part of their own family history: they had fled Brooklyn in the 1920s after the arrival in their neighborhood of a black assistant district attorney and his family. Black veterans were repeatedly turned away from Levittown, and although the racial bar was rescinded by 1955, the community remains less than 1 percent black to this day.

Still, Levittown was the start of better things for many new homeowners. The houses were adaptable, and soon everyone was jumping into home improvements: putting in bedrooms in the expandable upstairs attic, adding bay windows onto the front façade. By the mid-1950s, many were cashing in on their newfound equity and moving into larger homes in other communities. And like some of their customers, the Levitts too were moving on.

The Good Life

In 1954, after much squabbling, Bill and Alfred split the business. While Alfred turned to Queens apartment complexes, Bill continued to cut a very public figure as president of Levitt & Sons. By the mid-1950s, he had hired John Reagan "Tex" McCrary, Jr., the legendary public relations specialist who helped orchestrate the Nixon-Khrushchev 1959 "Kitchen Debate" and whose clients included Chris-Craft boats, Learjet, and the government of Argentina. But Bill worked hard on marketing. Every Sunday after breakfast, he went straight to his study to write ad copy that would sell houses in the following Sunday's newspapers.

His business reach soon expanded to Pennsylvania, New Jersey, Puerto Rico, and even France—Chez Levitt, some forty miles southeast of Paris on the Seine, was a project for which he would win the Légion d'honneur. He became friends with prominent men in New York society like Senator Jacob Javits, who often swam laps at Levitt's palatial "La Colline" in Mill Neck on Long Island's North Shore. A thirty-room mansion on sixty-eight acres, Bill's home was just eleven miles north of the community that had made him famous—but light years away from Levittown's early 750-square-foot floor plans.

Levitt collected artwork and filled his walls with works by Renoir, Monet, and Chagall. In early 1969, this hobby took a romantic turn when he met Simone Korchin, an art dealer. He kept coming back for purchasing visits until he told Korchin, who was still married to her first husband (as he was still married to his second wife), "I have no more wall space. I guess I'll have to marry you." Six months later, he did.

Today, Simone Levitt remembers a man certainly more endearing than the one described in his press clippings. After their marriage, Bill adopted Simone's two daughters and devoted himself to his new family. He also sent her "special delivery love letters" and named his 237-foot yacht, *La Belle Simone*, after her.

Despite his expensive tastes, Levitt's charitable work was considerable. During World War II, he led the local chapter of the United Jewish Appeal for Refugees and Overseas Needs to raise money for persecuted European Jews. After the war, he continued to support Jewish causes with substantial financial gifts to Israel. He was also instrumental as chairman of the board of North Shore Hospital for many years, establishing the Levitt Diagnostic Center.

Fame but No Fortune

Riding in an open car at the twenty-fifth anniversary celebration of Pennsylvania's Levittown, Simone Levitt remembers feeling "like the First Lady, waving to everyone from the car." But this was actually the beginning of a dark period for the master builder and his wife. In the 1970s, Levitt's fortune and business successes began to slip. His sale of the company to ITT soured when his stock options fell to about 10 percent of their original $92 million value. From the late 1970s to the mid-1980s, newspapers were filled with headlines of his latest ventures gone awry; failed developments in Florida, Nigeria, Iran, and Venezuela followed. A project near Orlando, Florida, was particularly painful: hundreds of homes had leaks, Levitt failed to return deposits to some customers, and he ran into trouble with the New York State Attorney General.

By the late 1980s, the great builder had lost most of his fortune but none of his pride in his most famous accomplishment. He often drove his Lincoln through the streets of Levittown and was greatly touched by an outpouring of love at the parade celebrating the fortieth anniversary of the community in 1987: "You know, the 60,000 people of Levittown are much more my friends than the people of Park Avenue. Oh God, yes, more than most of those I entertained on my yacht."

When he died in 1994, the newspapers swept aside many of the difficulties of Levitt's last years, remembering him as the man who had changed the nation's housing forever. Yet by then, the new suburban world he had helped create—an affordable new way of life for ex-GIs and their families—seemed to be a distant dream.

Governor Averell Harriman looks on as Chief Judge Albert Conway of the court of appeals administers the oath of office to incoming Secretary of State Carmine DeSapio, the Tammany Hall leader. Credit: New York State Archives, Albany, New York.

71

Watchdogs of the State

Philip A. Bean

The State Police raid on a gathering of nearly sixty criminals at Apalachin, near Binghamton, in November 1957 is an incident well known to those interested in the history of organized crime. Apalachin was very much a New York event: although "delegates" attended from throughout the country, 60 percent were New Yorkers, over half of whom were from communities west of the Hudson. Less familiar, however, is the political context in which Apalachin occurred, and the uneven impact the ensuing investigations of it had on New York State.

In the mid-twentieth century, the alleged relationship between urban political machines, municipal corruption, and organized crime was an increasingly important source of Democratic vulnerability. In 1950–1951, Senator Estes Kefauver, a Tennessee Democrat, chaired senate hearings on organized crime that focused on the urban North. Some Democrats hoped that voters might reward them for permitting an inquest that affected Democratic cities; nevertheless, recognizing that northern political machines did much to underpin their power in Washington, many Democrats also feared that Kefauver's hearings might play into Republican hands.

New York: Center of the Fight

Events in New York justified these concerns. Both the Republican legislature and Thomas Dewey, the "crime-busting" Manhattan Republican district attorney elected governor in 1942, recognized that exposing relationships between organized crime and

This essay first appeared in summer 2007, volume 7, number 1.

urban Democrats might prove politically advantageous, in that Republicans were still contending nationally with charges that they had favored organized wealth rather than the public interest before the Depression. Indeed, Republican efforts in New York to characterize Democrats as "soft on crime" seemed analogous to Republican charges on the national level that Democrats were "soft on Communism" and therefore unworthy of public trust.

Under Dewey, the state investigated Albany's Democratic O'Connell machine for several years to no avail; the governor and legislative Republicans instigated the unsuccessful prosecution of thirteen Utica Democrats on vote-buying charges in 1949; and Dewey made Tammany Hall, the Manhattan Democratic organization, and its ties to criminals a key issue in his tough but successful 1950 reelection bid. Although Dewey established a special Crime Commission in 1951 that investigated corruption and vice in Republican localities (notably Saratoga County) as well as in Democratic ones, he did so only after Kefauver exposed official toleration of illegal gambling in Saratoga—which the State Police had reportedly known about at least since 1947.

In his final years in office, Dewey ordered an inquest into corruption and organized crime in Democratic-controlled New York City, and the legislature approved his proposal to establish a permanent "commissioner of investigations," a gubernatorial appointee with broad latitude to investigate malfeasance statewide. However, in creating this new office, Republicans had not anticipated the election—by a razor-thin margin—of a Democrat, Averell Harriman, as Dewey's successor in 1954. Consequently, a Democrat, Irwin Shapiro, became commissioner of investigations, and after years of Dewey's investigations Democrats were ready to turn the tables on the Republicans.

The Watchdog Committee

Recognizing the potential danger Shapiro represented, only months after Harriman's inauguration the legislature established its own investigative body, the so-called "Watchdog Committee," consisting of eight Republicans and two Democrats. Republicans thus signaled that a new Democratic governor with ties to Tammany Hall—whose leader, Carmine DeSapio, was Harriman's secretary of state—could not be trusted to administer the state honestly. Republicans also put Democrats on notice that they would respond in kind if Shapiro became too aggressive.

Undeterred by the prospect of retaliatory legislative investigations, Shapiro launched well-publicized, politically embarrassing inquiries into corruption in Republican-controlled localities, notably Westchester, Putnam, Suffolk, Nassau, and Ulster Counties. In several of these, Republican voter registration had increased sharply as a result of postwar suburbanization. In Suffolk County alone, Shapiro's initiatives and those of his successor, Arthur Reuter, eventually yielded over twenty indictments, including one against a Republican assemblyman. Shapiro also investigated corruption charges against Dewey appointees, which quickly led to seventeen resignations in the State Liquor Authority.

Because Shapiro's aggressive pursuit of alleged Republican misconduct antagonized Republicans, the Watchdog Committee commenced a long, highly publicized inquest early in 1957 into charges that Harriman's administration had surreptitiously permitted Joseph "Socks" Lanza, a gangster with Tammany ties, to escape reincarceration for parole violations. And then, about six months later, the Apalachin raid occurred.

Apalachin's impact, therefore, cannot be seen exclusively or even primarily from the perspective of the outrage it elicited, or as a result of Kefauver's undeniable effect on the public consciousness. Like Shapiro, Watchdog investigators were genuinely concerned about the influence of crime and corruption on government, but they were caught in a power struggle between Democrats and Republicans who were determined to embarrass one another by uncovering alleged scandals.

Utica Takes the Heat

This is most apparent in the fate of the upstate city of Utica. While the Watchdog Committee subpoenaed Apalachin participants from throughout the state, it subjected only Utica to an inquisition in which a dozen local officials, not just criminal figures, were publicly interrogated. The singularity of Utica's treatment seems especially noteworthy in light of two facts: only three Apalachin participants came from Utica (indeed, from all of Oneida County), and Utica was the most reliably Democratic municipality of the nine upstate communities represented at Apalachin.

In contrast, the Watchdog Committee did not subpoena officials from Erie or Niagara Counties, even though together those counties produced six Apalachin delegates and investigators knew that Buffalo-area crime boss Stefano Magaddino was reportedly the only upstater on the nine-man national organized crime "Commission." In addition, Utica was singled out partly on the justification that it was supposedly odd that a city of only one hundred thousand had produced three Apalachin delegates—yet Magaddino and two Apalachin attendees lived in the same neighborhood in Lewiston, a small village in Republican-controlled Niagara County.

To some extent, this focus on Utica arose from a brief press-generated "feeding frenzy" that deflected attention from other potential targets of public interest. The fixation on Utica began with a series of sensationalistic articles in the *New York Journal American* in January 1958 that gave Utica the catchy but hyperbolic label of "The 'Sin City' of the East" just as the Watchdog hearings on Apalachin were gaining momentum. *Newsweek* published a briefer but equally overheated feature on Utica, and more evenhanded but relatively frequent reportage in the *New York Times* and the *New York Daily News* kept Utica in the headlines for well over a year.

Still, the divergent fates of Utica and metropolitan Buffalo—not to mention other communities—in the Watchdog hearings also arose from the strengths and vulnerabilities of each community's patrons. Buffalo's Walter Mahoney, the majority leader of the state senate, was one of the most powerful Republicans in New York; he was also not immune to accusations of connections to organized crime. Mahoney was alleged to have helped a visitor gain access to "Socks" Lanza at Attica Prison in the 1940s, and in January 1958 Mahoney was compelled to admit that he had provided legal counsel to a company owned by Apalachin delegate and Magaddino lieutenant John C. Montana.

Montana, the most politically active Apalachin attendee from New York State, was a former Republican member of the Buffalo City Council, an alternate delegate to the 1936 Republican National Convention, and a Republican congressional candidate in 1938. In 1956, a Buffalo police organization had named him "Man of the Year." In his testimony before the Watchdog Committee, a defiant Montana boasted publicly that he knew Richard Nixon, a claim the vice president's office angrily denied but which made national headlines. Perhaps not surprisingly, the Republican-dominated Watchdog Committee was not inclined to investigate western New York.

Consequences

The selectivity of the Watchdog Committee's work also seems apparent in the fact that public officials from heavily Republican Broome County were not called to testify, even though Broome County was home to five Apalachin delegates and several brutal gangland murders remained unsolved there. In addition, it was known that a Republican Watchdog Committee member from Broome County had tried to help Carmine Galante, later the Bonanno Family boss, out of legal difficulty in 1956, although the assemblyman maintained that he desisted in his efforts once he became aware of Galante's very significant criminal history. A similar confluence of factors—a local history of organized crime activity, supposedly disproportionate local representation at Apalachin, and the linking of local public officials with criminals—had helped make Utica the primary target of the Watchdog Committee, but somehow Broome County, like Erie and Niagara Counties, did not elicit Watchdog scrutiny.

At the same time, the "Socks" Lanza affair put Governor Harriman, presumably the natural champion of an upstate Democratic stronghold like Utica, on the defensive. Sacrificing Utica, a small city whose Democrats had reportedly differed with Harriman over patronage issues, offered a palatable way for a beleaguered Democratic governor seeking reelection to counter accusations that he was "lax" on crime and interested only in Republican wrongdoing. Harriman therefore supported efforts to investigate Utica even after he struck a deal in the spring of 1958 to replace both the commissioner of investigations and the Watchdog Committee with a bipartisan legislative State Crime Commission.

By 1959, when Utica's newspapers won a Pulitzer Prize for investigating local corruption, the press had begun shifting public attention from Apalachin to the McClellan Committee's inquest into the reported ties between Teamsters president Jimmy Hoffa and organized crime. Nevertheless, Apalachin inflicted lasting damage on Utica. Prior to Apalachin, local bankers, in league with Utica's Democrats, were replacing empty local textile mills with electronics factories, but this economic renaissance, which inspired a positive feature story in *Fortune* magazine in 1949, ended partly because of Utica's new national reputation as a uniquely corrupt, crime-ridden town. Although *Look* magazine scoffed at the suggestion that Utica was "Sin City," such skepticism could not undo the damage Utica suffered during this period.

More importantly, New York's "investigation wars" and similar congressional inquests in the 1940s and 1950s helped to legitimize the use of open-ended, politically motivated inquisitions and the characterization of political opponents as being "soft" on issues, like crime and Communism, about which the public was fearful. The inquests conducted by Dewey, the Watchdog Committee, and the commissioner of investigations and their counterparts in Washington embody the modern genesis of a type of political gamesmanship injurious to public discourse that has since become a prominent feature of American national political life. New York State seems to have been on the "cutting edge" of this less-than-praiseworthy political trend, the significance of which contemporary Americans might be well advised to ponder.

New York governor Franklin D. Roosevelt delivers a broadcast on WGY in August 1932. Credit: Museum of Innovation and Science, Schenectady, New York.

72

FDR and His Early Fireside Chats

Geoff Storm

> Just listened to your wonderful talk to the people of the state over the Radio wish I could find words to express the impression it made on me your plain words and sincere tone sure was wonderful it must be a Rosevelt characteristic to want to understand the people and have the people understand you.

This compliment from a Madison, New York, farmer might come as little surprise to those familiar with Franklin D. Roosevelt's famous Fireside Chats. During his presidency, Roosevelt periodically gave brief radio addresses in which he explained his administration's responses to the crises of the Great Depression and the Second World War. His straightforward, plain-spoken, fatherly style helped calm an anxious nation. Millions of Americans came to see Roosevelt as their friend and confidant and were inspired to respond to his Fireside Chats with letters describing their troubles, expressing their fears, and professing their admiration for and confidence in Roosevelt and his abilities. What might come as a surprise, however, is the fact that the letter was written in reaction to a broadcast Roosevelt delivered over WGY in Schenectady, New York, more than three years before he gave what is considered to be his first Fireside Chat.

Power Meets Power

Roosevelt began developing his radio technique during his two terms as governor of New York State. General Electric's WGY served as Roosevelt's primary broadcast

This essay first appeared in fall 2007, volume 7, number 2.

outlet during this period. General Electric had already wired the governor's mansion for WGY broadcasts by Roosevelt's predecessor, Alfred E. Smith, and by the time of Roosevelt's gubernatorial inauguration in 1929, WGY, in its seventh year of existence, had already established itself as an influential broadcasting pioneer. The station had been a format innovator by its introduction of radio dramas, the forerunners of popular radio features like soap operas and crime and adventure serials. More importantly, WGY was a technological leader; the station had garnered international fame through its successful experimentation in global signal relays via shortwave. In 1926, WGY became the first station in the United States permitted by the Federal Radio Commission to operate at fifty thousand watts. Moreover, WGY had created one of the earliest radio networks, establishing a chain that included stations in Syracuse, Rochester, and Buffalo. The station's reputation, extraordinarily high power, and network capabilities offered Roosevelt a practical and prestigious venue for his gubernatorial radio addresses. Roosevelt gave at least thirty-nine addresses, of which at least twenty-nine were given either exclusively over WGY or over WGY and its network, thus assuring the station a venerable place in American broadcasting history.

Roosevelt was confident that radio provided an effective means of reaching the people. He commented in a January 1929 speech: "Today at least half of the voters sitting at their own firesides listen to the actual words of the political leaders on both sides and make their decision on what they hear, rather than what they read." After he became governor later that year, Roosevelt was often motivated to use radio as a way to counter the actions of a combative Republican-dominated legislature, to respond to the criticisms of a largely Republican upstate press, and to politically educate his rural constituency, particularly in upstate areas where no daily newspaper service existed. In her memoir *F.D.R.: My Boss*, Grace Tully, Roosevelt's personal secretary, recalled:

> Fed up with the pulling and hauling of customary political bargaining, he declared curtly: "I'll take the issue to the people" . . . He did, by radio over a New York State chain, and the results were immediate. Mail came flooding into Albany, most of it in support of the Roosevelt position and most of it addressed to the working level of the legislature. It was a convincing demonstration, and from that time on F.D.R. made it a more or less regular practice to take his problems "to the people" in this manner.

Honing His Technique

The demonstration was convincing enough that Roosevelt began to include appeals to the public in many of his radio talks. In his autobiography *Working with Roosevelt*,

Samuel Rosenman, who helped prepare Roosevelt's speeches, remembered that "a flood of letters would deluge the members of the legislature after each talk, and they were the best weapon Roosevelt had in his struggles for legislation." This likely affirmed Roosevelt's faith in the value of public opinion and the power of radio. Following a victory on one such contentious issue, when he was able to make the legislature retreat in part simply because he had announced that he planned to discuss the matter on WGY, Roosevelt reminded his listeners of the strength of the "influence of Mr. And Mrs. Average Voter . . . public opinion when it understands a policy and supports it is bound to win in the long run."

In October 1930, at the height of his campaign for what would be a landslide reelection, Roosevelt delivered a series of broadcasts over WGY in response to the "many letters, telephones and telegrams asking me to keep on speaking." On October 16, an Albany *Times Union* editorial offered a behind-the-scenes glimpse of Roosevelt's technique and intentions:

> Flashing his characteristic smile with each sally, shaking his head for emphasis over a good point. . . . [Leaning] forward just a little to make a scathing jibe. . . . [Giving] a boyish smile of "that was a good one" . . . he anticipates. He keeps the air still for a second. His eyes narrow and he launches an attack. . . . When the half hour is over and incidentally [he] is pleased as a boy when he hits the broadcast time nail exactly on the head, he settles back to talk in that same smooth, musical voice radio listeners and critics have come to admire.

Listeners came to admire more than Roosevelt's voice. His delivery was also a key component of his broadcasting success. When Roosevelt was governor, radio was still in its infancy, and listeners were fascinated by the novelty of being able to eavesdrop on distant events from the privacy of their homes while simultaneously drawing comfort from a sense of community, sparked by the knowledge that they were part of a large audience sharing the same experience. Roosevelt recognized the medium's potential for intimacy. Avoiding the bombastic oratorical style that impaired his contemporaries' political broadcasts, he adopted an informal, conversational approach that Rosenman described as "simple, direct, chatty." In the process, the governor began fostering a unique personal relationship with his constituents. As a Saranac Lake resident wrote: "It seemed as if you were sitting here talking to me."

Inspired by a feeling of personal connection with Roosevelt, many New York State residents wrote directly to the governor. In their requests for financial and employment assistance, we—as Roosevelt likely did—can gain insights into conditions during the early years of the Depression. This excerpt from a 1932 letter written by a Gloversville man provides a good example: "I have read and listened to your talks and in all, you seem so plainly understood, by all, that is why I write this letter. I am a poor and almost destitute man. For the passed three years I have been very very unfortunate. I have lost my home, or all the home I had. . . . We don't want to become objects of charity. We are desperately in need and must have work if we are to live." In 1931, a Mohawk man "living on bread and coffee and have a few pattoes as this is all we can afford" wrote Roosevelt to request a loan to pay for a truck license so he could drive his sixteen-year-old son to school. The man explained, "i would like to give this boy a chance as i never had aney schooling . . . and i find it a bad handicap at getting aney work at presend." Even children penned notes to the governor, such as an eleven-year-old Phoenix, New York, girl who sent holiday greetings in 1932: "This year we are not going to have a Happy Xmas. But next year I hope we will all have a happy xmas."

Fan Letters

Despite hard times, New Yorkers also often wrote complimentary, optimistic letters, such as this note sent by a Syracuse man shortly before the 1930 gubernatorial election: "My congratulations for your very fine Radio speech of last evening. The reception was perfect your subject matter of equal value, and a delivery that carried a conviction to the heart. Indications point towards one of the biggest Democratic victories of all times, and remember that each and every one of us is ready and willing to render our share." In 1931, a Verona man waxed poetic in his expression of confidence in Roosevelt:

> Lead us out of this uncertain political strife,
> Known to be at our vitals like a two-edged knife.
> Nation needs a very strong judicial mind,
> And the people believe they've made a find.
> Roosevelt, you must regard the Nation's need,
> Franklin, we are going to ask you to take the lead.

Two years later, Roosevelt had indeed taken the lead, and with it he had taken on the burdens of the Great Depression. The broadcasting experience Roosevelt had acquired during his years in Albany served him well during his presidency, much as the relief programs he had implemented during his governorship served as rough blueprints for the New Deal. Eight days after his inauguration, on March 12, 1933, Roosevelt spoke to a national radio audience in his first presidential Fireside Chat. He explained the nation's faltering banking system and his proposed solutions so clearly that, as Will Rogers quipped, even the bankers understood. Americans responded by mail and telegram in overwhelming numbers. Having noted the potential of using such public reaction as a barometer of popular opinion, Roosevelt had additional staff brought in to organize the mail according to issue and position and to brief him on the results. Eventually, he could boast during a press conference: "I am more closely in touch with public opinion in the United States than any individual in this room. I get a better cross-section of opinion."

As he had while serving as governor of New York, Roosevelt used his presidential radio addresses to muster support for his position on important legislative questions. "All we have to do," he told an advisor, "is let the flood of mail settle on Congress . . . and the opposition will be beating a path to the White House door." But the president refined his strategy, speaking less frequently than he had while in Albany. While he gave at least thirty-nine radio addresses during his four years as governor, he delivered just thirty Fireside Chats during his twelve years in the White House. Thus, each chat became an event, an attempt to secure the largest possible audience and the most substantial reaction.

Chatting with the Nation

In his autobiography *Behind the Ballots: The Personal History of a Politician*, Roosevelt advisor James A. Farley asserted:

> Without that unrivaled medium for reaching millions of voters, the work of overcoming the false impression . . . put out by foes of the New Deal . . . might have been an impossible job. Yet no matter what was written or what was charged, the harmful effect was largely washed away as soon as the reassuring voice of the President of the United States started coming through the ether into the family living-room.

Radio—and Roosevelt's masterful broadcasting performances—transformed American politics. But Roosevelt's ability to use the medium effectively did not suddenly materialize with his "first" presidential Fireside Chat. On that evening in 1933, he had already spent four years developing his talents on WGY and confirming his belief in radio's potential for efficiency and cogency. As he later wrote, radio "cannot misrepresent nor misquote." His savvy, skillful, on-air delivery elicited voluminous reactions in which he found useful validation of his ideas. And he parlayed his Albany broadcasting experiences and successes into still greater triumphs in Washington, D.C.

Between the Pony Express and online click-and-send, there were pneumatic tubes, the mail delivery system of fin de siècle New York. John Milholland—financier, churchgoer, politician, and civil rights pioneer—was their champion. Credit: Library of Congress.

73

The Golden Tubes

Linda J. Lumsden

Beneath New York City's streets snake dozens of miles of abandoned iron tubes that once carried the mail of the late nineteenth and early twentieth centuries. Civic leaders unanimously praised these pneumatically powered underground networks, which propelled letters and packages through the tubes by means of compressed air; by 1905, they had untangled postal traffic and sped letters across five cities. *Scientific American* hyped the tubes' "instantaneous" delivery as being as revolutionary as the telephone. And John Elmer Milholland saw gold in them.

Entrepreneur, politician, civil rights pioneer—John Milholland's rise paralleled the expansion of New York into the Empire State. He was born May 31, 1860, the youngest of six children of Irish immigrants who settled in Lewis (Essex County), a hamlet hugging the eastern Adirondack Mountains. After a fire killed three-year-old John's mother and oldest sister, the family moved to Paterson, New Jersey, where Representative William Walter Phelps apparently later paid for Milholland to attend New York University. He dropped out of college, however, and worked for local newspapers before buying the *Ticonderoga Sentinel*, again most likely financed by Phelps. Milholland married schoolteacher Jean Torry in 1884, sold the *Sentinel*, and began work as a political writer for the Republican *New-York Tribune*, where he became publisher Whitelaw Reid's right-hand man in business and in national politics. This landed him a plum appointment as chief inspector of immigration for the Port of New York.

This essay first appeared in spring 2008, volume 7, number 4.

Putting Prosperity to Use

In 1892, however, Milholland's failed takeover bid for the Eleventh Assembly District from conservative Republican stalwarts cost him his post. Nonetheless, he had prospered enough by 1894 to move Jean and their three children from Brooklyn to an apartment at bustling Madison Square. That year he again reigned briefly as the "young Napoleon of ward politics" in another failed coup.

Burned by these political debacles, Milholland rechanneled his energy into the Gilded Age pursuit of wealth. He latched on to Postmaster General John Wanamaker's lucrative-sounding plan to use pneumatic tubes to unclog the city's mail. After discovering the vacuum-powered tubes in Europe, the Philadelphia department store magnate had installed them to shuttle cash around the vast acreage of his stores; Wanamaker sent off the nation's first pneumatic mail tube carrier in his hometown in 1893. The U.S. Post Office subsequently contracted with private entrepreneurs to install the subterranean tubes in New York City. This allowed the post office to both eliminate financial risk and use the pneumatic system free for a year before deciding whether to rent, purchase, or reject it.

Milholland was one of those entrepreneurs. He headed a group of Eastern venture capitalists that broke ground for a tubes line in New York at Park Row and Beekman Street on August 2, 1897. On October 7, forty seconds after railroad magnate Chauncey Depew dispatched the eight-inch-wide, two-foot-long tube containing the Milholland family Bible wrapped in an American flag from the post office on West 33rd Street, the city's first mail tube whisked into the Produce Exchange, which bordered Broadway in the Financial District. Eventually, twenty-seven miles of mail tubes linked twenty-two stations in New York. By 1900, the U.S. Post Office had indicated its intent to buy the system pending congressional approval, and the partners, already rich from the government contract, believed their big payoff was imminent. Milholland, the immigrant's son, estimated his financial worth at a half-million dollars.

Doing Good versus Living Well

The pious Presbyterian entrepreneur made two decisions on how to spend his wealth that reflected his need to do good versus his desire to live well. In 1898, he bought back the family farm in Lewis, gradually accumulating four thousand acres he called Meadowmount. He hoped to turn it into a home to train the poor in job skills, an idea borrowed from Salvation Army founder William Booth. But within a year, the Milhollands moved to London, where talk of utopia and reform flowed with the wine at elegant dinners at their four-story townhouse across from Kensington Gardens.

Financial fissures, however, cracked this façade. Instead of buying the tubes, the federal government decided to continue to rent them annually while evaluating their feasibility. As a result, Milholland constantly borrowed money, dodged loan deadlines, and paid debts with tube stocks, whose value hinged upon the government buying the tubes for at least one million dollars. As politics and changing technology conspired against sealing the deal, Milholland said he increasingly felt like a "galley slave" to the tubes. He lambasted himself for forgetting "God's way" and for squandering his fortune before getting to his "real work."

That work, as he saw it, was to banish racism. A lonely foe of lynching in the 1890s, in 1903 he led a virtual one-man entity called the Constitution League that lobbied for blacks' civil rights. Its most famous battle forced a congressional investigation of the Brownsville Affair, in which President Theodore Roosevelt discharged a battalion of black soldiers without honor. In 1909, Milholland helped plan a conference on racism, where he spoke alongside Ida Wells-Barnett and W. E. B. Du Bois. Attendees reconvened the following May to create the National Association for the Advancement of Colored People; Milholland, the organization's treasurer, recruited Du Bois to edit its magazine, *The Crisis*, in an office Milholland provided. The latter was also a driving force behind the Universal Races Congress that gathered a thousand people from fifty nations at the University of London in July of 1911.

Elsewhere, however, Milholland stumbled. The Salvation Army job training program never materialized. His marriage was strained, and it appears he had an affair with reformer Mary White Ovington. His business grew more precarious with the election of Democrat Woodrow Wilson in 1912, when the government was paying $929,460.30 a year to rent fifty-five miles of pneumatic tubes in five cities, with a daily capacity of 2.1 million letters. Milholland's defiant oldest daughter, Inez, had emerged as a suffrage celebrity who declared herself an agnostic and a Socialist, and the Republican Milholland's situation was not improved when Inez rode a white horse at the head of a spectacular suffrage parade down Pennsylvania Avenue that eclipsed Wilson's inauguration.

Speaking Truth to Power

Even worse, in 1915 Postmaster General Albert Sidney Burleson began pushing Congress to dump the mail tubes altogether. Although a joint congressional committee finally had recommended the government purchase them outright for five million dollars, Democrat Burleson established his own commission that conducted closed hearings, which Milholland likened to "star-chamber inquiries." Although not without quirks—tubes sometimes got stuck, and it was costly to dig up busy streets to repair or install them—Burleson's hostility toward them seemed excessive. It may have been personal: Milholland's stinging civil rights rhetoric surely offended the Texas cotton plantation owner, and according to Milholland family lore, years earlier he had accused Burleson of exploiting his African American cotton pickers. True or not, Burleson systematically fired, demoted, and segregated black postal workers.

Milholland further irked President Wilson when he funded militant suffragist Alice Paul's 1916 campaign against the Democrats. Inez Milholland starred in a whirlwind speaking tour of the West, but disaster struck when she collapsed onstage in Los Angeles. Her parents rushed to her bedside before she died November 25. Inez' ghost continued to haunt Wilson when suffragists began to picket the White House in her name on January 10, 1917.

Meanwhile, Congress extended the tubes' rental contract through fiscal year 1918, and the Senate Committee on Post Offices recommended buying them for $4.4 million. Burleson then penned an extraordinary protest letter to every senator. The Senate nonetheless approved the purchase 33 to 23, but the House rejected it 138 to 82. On June 28, Congress arrived at a compromise bill that authorized funds to continue tube service for another year, while the Interstate Commerce Commission investigated their physical value. That afternoon, Burleson invited President Wilson to play golf—and the next day Wilson vetoed the bill, claiming that trucks made tubes obsolete. At midnight on June 30, 1918, all mail tubes stopped running. "It means ruin," Milholland scrawled in his diary. "My enemies triumph tonight."

Civic leaders were dismayed. The *New York Times* decried Burleson's "prejudice." Milholland charged that automakers were bribing postal officials, and he spent the rest of his life attempting to reinstate the tubes. His health broken and his finances foundering, he continued to embrace lost causes, shipping a fat doe from Meadowmount to Dublin so Irish and English citizens could settle their political differences over a feast. His big heart finally broke on June 29, 1925.

However, pneumatic tubes have lived on. Today, Americans use them at bank drive-through windows, but banking is only one segment of a largely invisible vast network of pneumatic tubes in hospitals, factories, mega-stores, and the Pentagon. John Milholland no doubt would be pleased.

John Shippen, Jr. Credit: United States Golf Association Archives.

74

Shippen's Hole

Faren R. Siminoff

Until the 1890s, golf was virtually unknown in the United States. Stories abound of when and where Americans first teed up; thus, there is no single birthplace of golf in America. Instead, small informal golfing groups and rudimentary "courses" previewed at a variety of locations, mostly in the Northeast, during the nineteenth century's final decades. One such site was in Southampton on Long Island, where in 1891 the Shinnecock Hills Golf Club, the nation's first incorporated golf club, was established. To this day, it remains one of America's premier golfing institutions.

The founding of the club was sheer serendipity. By the 1890s, a vibrant summer community was comfortably ensconced in Southampton. It was considered a bucolic refuge for well-heeled New York City gentlemen and their families looking for a healthy alternative to oppressive city summers. During the spring of 1891, one of the community's residents, Samuel L. Parrish, received a letter from Duncan Cryder, another summer neighbor, who was "passing the winter at Biarritz, France." His letter described an invitation he and his companions had received and accepted from William K. Vanderbilt to witness a golf exhibition. Golf, Cryder's letter explained, was a wildly popular game both in Scotland and on the Continent, despite it being virtually unknown on this side of the Atlantic. At Biarritz, wrote Cryder, a young Scottish golf pro, Willie Dunn, who had been hired to lay out a new golf course, demonstrated the game of golf to Vanderbilt and his American companions.

Years later, Dunn remembered that meeting:

> I had nearly completed the links when I met Messrs. W.K. Vanderbilt, Edward S. Mead and Duncan Cryder from the United States. They showed

This essay first appeared in spring 2008, volume 7, number 4.

real interest in the game from the beginning and requested me to give a golf demonstration. I chose the famous chasm hole, 125 yards long and featured by a deep ravine, which was to be carried with a drive. I teed up several balls and laid them all on the green, some of them close to the flag. Mr. Vanderbilt turned to his friends and said, "Gentlemen, this beats rifle shooting for distance and accuracy. It is a game I think would go in our country."

American Links

Ironically, it was not Cryder who became the force behind the introduction of golf at Southampton, but Samuel Parrish—who, through this simple written description of the game, became both a convert and the powerhouse behind the founding of the Shinnecock Hills Golf Club. Almost immediately after receiving Cryder's letter, Parrish decided to import golf to America. He asked fellow summer resident Charles L. Atterbury, who happened to be on his way to Montreal, to stop by the Royal Montreal Golf Club (founded in 1873) and ask for its assistance in setting up a course in Southampton. The Montreal club responded by sending its golf pro, Scotsman Willie Davis, to assist the would-be golfers. Davis arrived during the summer of 1891 and designed and built the first nine holes of the twelve-hole course on the Shinnecock Hills in Southampton. Once it was completed, Parrish began to recruit a wider swath of his fellow "cottagers" to join him in the game. He sent out a simple letter:

> Dear Sir:
>
> Several gentlemen of Southampton having become interested in the game of golf, engaged a professional player connected with the Montreal Golf Club to come here and lay out a golf course. Many of those who practiced the game while he was here, became interested, and are desirous of forming a club. The plan . . . is to lease for five years . . . a tract on Shinnecock Hills and to erect thereon, a small clubhouse. . . . You are invited. . . . Shares will be $100 each.

The Southampton summer community greeted this idea with enthusiasm. By fall, the Shinnecock Hills Golf Club had been organized and incorporated, and sufficient funds had been collected to begin building its first clubhouse. Stanford White, the well-known architect, was selected for the job. The choice is not surprising: White was already quite familiar both with Southampton and its summer residents, since he had assisted with the design of several Southampton summer cottages and moved in the same social circles in New York City with their owners.

Within two years of Parrish being bitten by the golf bug, the Shinnecock club was an established fact of Southampton life. Golf quickly became associated with the wealthy and powerful, and the club itself proved instrumental to the game's taking root in American soil.

Americans Stake Their Claim

However, the land used for the golf course had been in possession of, and used by, the Shinnecock Indians until 1859. In that year, and over their vigorous protests, the tribe's rights to the hills had been extinguished by an act of the New York State Legislature. Ironically, it was through the golf club that was built thirty-two years later that the Shinnecock maintained and exercised some of their traditional connection to their land.

Some of the labor used to build the club was supplied by men from the reservation. More significantly, the Shinnecock became groundskeepers, caddies, and amateur golfers. The club's first caddy master was Shinnecock Joshua Kellis (1841–1916), and until recently, all of the club's head greenskeepers have come from the tribe. Consequently, the development of golf at America's first incorporated club was not only linked to the privileged classes but also to the nation's Native Americans.

Another significant figure in the development of golf in America was John Shippen, Jr. He was neither a summer resident of Southampton, a Native American, nor a local but rather a member of the first generation of African Americans born free during the first decades following the end of the Civil War. According to Shippen family history, the surname was acquired by John's father, John Shippen, Sr., who was born a slave at Violet Bank, a Virginia plantation, in 1849. There he met a visiting white doctor from Philadelphia, William Shippen III, who was exceptionally kind to the young slave, prompting the latter to ask if he could use the doctor's surname as his own. The doctor assented.

A number of facts support this story. Dr. William Shippen III (1792–1867) did indeed exist; he was a member of the prominent Pennsylvania Shippen family that migrated from England to Boston in 1668, and from there to Philadelphia. In 1817, Dr. Shippen married a Virginia woman, Mary Louise Shore (1798–1879), from Violet Bank plantation. Federal census records, letters, and numerous other documents confirm that Dr. Shippen was present at Violet Bank before, during, and after the American Civil War. In addition, Dr. Shippen often gave medical care to both freemen and slaves in the area, increasing the likelihood that the two Shippens not only could have but would have met. This family history, combined with what can be verified about Dr. Shippen's movements, solidifies the original connection between the two Shippen families.

Shippen's Hole

Sometime after the Civil War ended, John Shippen, Sr., now a freeman, married. Then he migrated in a straight line north from the Violet Bank area, finally settling with his growing family in Washington, D.C., where he attended Howard University and became a teacher. Later he became an ordained Presbyterian minister. In 1888, he was sent by the Presbyterians to Southampton to minister to the Shinnecock Indians. He took his family with him, including John Shippen, Jr., who was born in Washington, D.C., in 1879.

According to the Shippen family, young John was immediately fascinated by the Shinnecock Hills golf course. His first substantive contact with it was as a casual laborer when the course was expanded in 1893; later he became a caddy and a player. Barely a teenager, he attracted the attention of Willie Dunn, the Scottish pro who had originally taught the game to the Americans in France and who had been hired by the club in 1893. Dunn recognized John's talent for golf and groomed him to become a professional in the Scottish tradition. This meant that John was expected to be not only an excellent golfer but also proficient in all tasks related to the game, from giving lessons to repairing clubs to assisting the groundskeepers to caddying. Much to his father's chagrin, John became a devoted student of the game and the art of golf.

By 1896, just seventeen years old and having played golf for only three years, John was so gifted and well thought of at the club that he was encouraged to enter the second United States Golf Open, scheduled to be played that year at Shinnecock Hills. The pros that John would play against were all foreign born, since the United States had not yet produced its own. Some of these men objected to playing with "a Negro," but they were summarily overruled by Theodore Havemeyer, president of the recently formed United States Golfing Association, who reportedly told them, "Gentlemen, you can leave or stay as you please. We are going to play this tournament tomorrow—with or without you." They stayed and played.

Shippen played extraordinarily well, and by the afternoon of the Open's first day it looked as though he might walk away with the win. But at the thirteenth hole—one of the easiest holes on what was an otherwise challenging course—he overshot, and his ball landed on a nearby road. It took him eleven strokes to complete "unlucky thirteen," and with them went any hope of winning. Much to his disappointment, he tied for fifth place.

Despite this loss, the gentlemen golfers present all acknowledged Shippen's enormous talent and his remarkable performance in the Open. It ultimately earned him an appointment as the golf pro at the nearby Maidstone Golf Club. During his long career, Shippen went on to play in four more U.S. Opens, and he ended his career as the pro at the African American–owned Shady Rest Golf and Country Club in New Jersey. He retired from that club in 1960 after nearly thirty years of service and died eight years later.

Unfortunately, more was lost on that unlucky "Shippen's Hole" at the second U.S. Open than the win: Shippen's place in sports history as one of America's golfing pioneers has been virtually ignored until now. John Shippen, Jr., was not only the nation's first African American professional golfer, he was also the first American-born golf professional.

The original video game, *Tennis for Two*, set up for the annual visitor's day at Brookhaven National Laboratory in 1958. Credit: Brookhaven National Laboratory, Upton, New York.

75

The World's First Video Game

Mona S. Rowe

Just over fifty years ago, William Higinbotham came up with an idea for entertaining visitors at Brookhaven National Laboratory in Upton, Long Island. He never imagined that his tennis game of 1958, displayed on a small oscilloscope and played with simple controls, would inspire a new industry: in the United States alone, total sales of video game hardware, software, and peripherals topped $22 billion in 2008, according to the Entertainment Software Association.

Brookhaven—taxpayer supported, with funding initially from the Atomic Energy Commission and later from the Department of Energy—has always been open to the public through various visitor programs. In earlier years, Brookhaven had annual "visitors' days" in the fall, when thousands of people came to tour the lab and see exhibits set up in the gymnasium. Mostly the lab displayed dry posters about its basic research in the physical and life sciences. "Willy" Higinbotham, who was then head of the lab's instrumentation division, knew from past visitors' days that people were not much interested in static exhibits. So he decided to create something with more punch to it—a hands-on video tennis game.

I first interviewed Willy back in 1981 for an article in the *Brookhaven Bulletin*, the lab's employee newspaper. A small man with a friendly smile and quickness in his manner, Willy came across as someone who loved life and lived it with zest. He chuckled as he told me about the long line of people snaking around the gym, all eager to play *Tennis for Two*, as he had dubbed the game. *Tennis for Two* was part of the division's exhibit for two years, and it was a real crowd-pleaser. "If I had realized just how significant it was," Willy joked, "I would have taken out a patent and the U.S. government would own it!"

This essay first appeared in spring 2009, volume 8, number 4.

Public recognition for Willy's game came late. Prior to the 1981 article, the only mention of Brookhaven's novel exhibit was in the introduction to a book titled *Basic Computer Games* by David Ahl, later the publisher/editor of *Creative Computing* magazine, who wrote that Brookhaven might have been where video games started. Ahl had gone to high school on Long Island, and he toured the lab in 1958. He wrote that he knew about computer gaming done at MIT and at a small company in Cambridge, Massachusetts, as early as 1961, but he was not aware of it being done anywhere else prior to 1958, the year in which he spotted the video tennis game at Brookhaven.

Willy Higinbotham's Brookhaven colleague David Potter added another strand to the historical thread. Writing on the occasion of Willy's eightieth birthday celebration in 1990, Potter recalled a high school boy who was especially interested in the tennis game: "He wanted schematics and really wanted to know how it worked. I believe that Willy sent him prints of it. Years later we learned that this boy had become the president of one of the first companies to market the product commercially."

Basic Electronics

Willy's 1958 game had essentially the same basic features found in today's video games. Simulated on a screen was a vertical side view of a tennis court showing the edge of a floor with the edge of the net perpendicular to it. Each player had a knob and a button. Rotating the knob changed the angle of the ball, and a press of the button sent the ball toward the opposite side of the court. If the ball hit the net, it rebounded at an expected angle. If the ball went over the net but was not hit back, it would hit the floor and bounce again at a natural angle. If it disappeared off the screen, a reset button could be pressed, causing the ball to reappear and remain stationary until a hit button was pressed.

The game was run by an analog computer hooked up to an oscilloscope. "It was simple to design," remembered Willy. "Back then, analog computers were used to work out all kinds of mechanical problems. They didn't have the accuracy of digital computers, which were very crude at the time, but then you didn't need a great deal of precision to play TV games." Willy said it took about three weeks to put the game together. It was actually built by Robert V. Dvorak, a technician in the instrumentation division. Willy said the two of them worked collaboratively.

Based on Willy's drawings, official lab blueprints were done by Alexander Elia, a design engineer in the same division. Willy said the blueprints showed a few relay contacts in the wrong position, but the game worked beautifully, so they must have been fixed in the actual circuit.

The electronics consisted mostly of resistors, capacitors, and relays, but where fast switching was needed—when the ball was in play—transistor switches were used. As Willy pointed out in 1981, "These days, this sort of simulation is done with solid-state switches, not with relays. Where I needed it, I took a step in the right direction."

For the game's debut, the oscilloscope display was only five inches in diameter. The next year saw improvements: the display jumped to seventeen inches in diameter, and players could choose to play tennis either on the moon (with low gravity) or on Jupiter (with high gravity). After the exhibit was dismantled, the computer and oscilloscope were separated and used for other jobs.

The Legal Side

Was Willy's game the first? *Tennis for Two* was actually preceded by three other inventions—one in the late 1940s and two in the early 1950s. What was special about Willy's game was that he had created a unique way to alternate among the computer's outputs with the transistor-switching circuit, creating the image of a tennis court and allowing players to control a movable ball that was seen on a screen, just like a modern video game.

Here's what Willy knew about the legal side of the question. Sanders Associates applied for the first video game patent in 1964. The patent was purchased by Magnavox, which put out the first simple game in 1971. Magnavox then sued all other entrants to the field, the first in a continuing series of lawsuits and countersuits involving other giants like Atari and Nintendo.

Around 1976, a competitor's lawyer discovered David Ahl, who had played *Tennis for Two* at Brookhaven. Through Ahl, the lawyer tracked down Willy, who had the 1958 blueprints to prove the game's date of creation. Other lawyers followed.

In February 1982, Willy made a deposition in the first lawyer's office before the Magnavox lawyers and others. In June, Willy, David Potter, and Seymour Rankowitz, another Brookhaven colleague, were scheduled to testify at a trial in Chicago to break the Magnavox patent. The case was settled out of court before going to trial.

History-Making Science

Willy died in 1994, well aware of how wildly popular video games had become. He told me once that one of his daughters liked to play them, but he himself had never gotten hooked. He was more concerned about being remembered for his work with the Federation of American Scientists, founded in 1945 as the Federation of Atomic Scientists by himself and others who had worked on the Manhattan Project. They realized that nuclear proliferation was inevitable and that other countries would soon be able to develop nuclear weapons, leading to a nuclear arms race. They were convinced that the solution was to maintain transparency in nuclear research and international control of nuclear materials. The organization lobbied hard—and successfully—for federal legislation that established civilian control over atomic energy.

Willy joined Brookhaven National Laboratory in 1947, its first year of operation, and retired in 1984 after thirty-seven years there. Two years later, Brookhaven's historian interviewed him as part of an oral history series that included leading scientists at the lab. But in seventeen pages of transcribed text, he never once mentions the video game he invented to entertain visitors, though he talks about playing his accordion in square-dance bands, organizing bartenders for lively parties when the lab was starting up, and singing Christmas carols at an "old folks'" home in nearby Yaphank. Mostly he recounts the how and why of the world-class science that developed over the decades at Brookhaven.

Willy ends the interview with these sentiments: "Did I anticipate that I was going to stay? The answer is no, certainly not. Did I anticipate it was going to become as fruitful and constructive as it has been? The answer is, I really wouldn't have guessed that. I just thought well, it looks exciting, and we'll see how it happens, and we certainly have had a lot of fun."

FDR's "Ambassador Extraordinary" Myron C. Taylor and his wife, Anabel, prepare for an audience with Pope Pius XII in 1940. Credit: Author's collection.

76

The Man Nobody Knew

C. Evan Stewart

In his day, Myron Charles Taylor, born in 1874, was America's leading industrialist: czar of the textile industry, and later, in the 1920s and 1930s, head of U.S. Steel. But because of his prominence, he also became a key diplomatic participant in some of the most important geopolitical events of the World War II era. Taylor is little remembered today, however, in large part because of his intense personal distaste for publicity; for much of his business career, the national media called him "the man nobody knows."

Although Taylor would later own a seventy-room mansion in New York City, a fabled villa in Tuscany, and a baronial country estate on Long Island, he was born and grew up in the small upstate town of Lyons (Wayne County), just south of Lake Ontario, where his father owned and operated a tannery business. Young Myron dreamed of becoming a lawyer; that dream took him to Ithaca and Cornell Law School, where he earned a Bachelor of Laws degree in 1894. He returned to Lyons and, for a time, struggled to establish a small-town law practice.

Textile Czar

In the course of litigation he handled for his father's tannery, Taylor bid for and won a U.S. government contract to manufacture mail pouches and related products. As the company expanded rapidly beyond tannery products to cotton, Taylor began to acquire struggling mills, transforming their labor practices and modernizing their

This essay first appeared in summer 2009, volume 9, number 1.

technology; this *modus operandi* later became known as the "Taylor Formula." Blessed with an uncanny sense of timing, able to apply the formula with great discipline, and demonstrating remarkable skills in corporate finance, Taylor soon consolidated and eventually dominated the textile industry.

By the 1920s, Taylor was an extremely wealthy man. Having foreseen the boom-bust cycle in the commodities market, he had gotten out of the textile industry altogether, anticipating a blissful retirement and plenty of world travel with his wife, Anabel. But then his friend J. P. Morgan persuaded him to get involved with and ultimately take over the reins of the world's largest industrial company, U.S. Steel. Taylor was reluctant, but he agreed to do it.

After studying the company's struggling operations for nearly two years, Taylor identified the first priority: reduce U.S. Steel's existing indebtedness, which totaled a staggering $400 million. Just before the stock market crash in October 1929, he retired $340 million in debt, saving U.S. Steel approximately $31 million in annual debt-servicing costs (and, as J. P. Morgan noted, also saving the company from being "busted permanently"). During the depths of the Depression, when U.S. Steel was operating at 17 percent capacity, Taylor refused to fire employees. Instead, he instituted a share-the-work program whereby at least seventy-five thousand workers kept their jobs (and thus their income). During this difficult period, Taylor also applied the "Taylor Formula," reorganizing U.S. Steel's operations and upgrading its technology.

He also took another major step. In 1937, as "all America gasped," Taylor struck a deal with John L. Lewis, then head of the Committee for Industrial Organization (CIO). U.S. Steel agreed to recognize a CIO subsidiary that would represent and organize the company's workers, becoming the first major industrial company in America to reach an accord with organized labor. Although many captains of industry blasted Taylor as a traitor, in J. P. Morgan's view "[Myron's] was the finest performance I have ever known."

"Ambassador Extraordinary"

Although Taylor literally saved U.S. Steel during the Depression and restored it to robust health, he relinquished the position of CEO in April 1938. Once again, he hoped to enter a "sabbatical period of life" with his wife Anabel—but this time yet another friend, President Franklin Delano Roosevelt, called upon Taylor to undertake critical diplomatic duties as the president's "Ambassador Extraordinary and Plenipotentiary." Taylor's first assignment from FDR was to help solve the deepening crisis of Jewish refugees who were attempting to flee persecution in Hitler's Germany. Taylor's efforts actually led to a deal with Hitler and Goering: the Nazis agreed to permit

150,000 "able-bodied" Jews to emigrate, with their dependents allowed to follow later. Undersecretary of State Sumner Welles told the president it was "better than we hoped for." Unfortunately, because of the Nazi takeover of Czechoslovakia and Poland and the onset of World War II, those efforts achieved no tangible results.

On Christmas Eve 1939, FDR asked Taylor to be his personal representative to Pope Pius XII. This very controversial move, which in many ways represented the crafty and purposeful FDR at his best, led to what was termed the "Taylor Mission" and Taylor's critical involvement in such matters as ensuring that Lend-Lease aid (approximately $8 billion in 1941 dollars) got to the Soviet Union, which at that point was about to be overrun by the German Army. Taylor also brought the first documented proof of the Holocaust to the pope and his senior advisors, convinced Generalissimo Franco of Spain not to join the war on the side of the Axis powers, and lobbied Prime Minister Salazar of Portugal to permit an Allied airbase in that neutral country. Taylor also helped broker Italy's surrender and Mussolini's departure, ensured that the Catholic Church did not break from the Allies' policy of unconditional surrender, and almost single-handedly provided the mechanism and means for Italy's postwar recovery.

During the war, when Taylor was based in Washington and unable to travel to Rome, FDR asked him to undertake a number of planning efforts. For example, Taylor chaired the economic committee whose work resulted in the Bretton Woods Agreement, and he was crucial to the planning and ultimate success of the United Nations. To avoid Woodrow Wilson's fatal mistake of political isolationism with the League of Nations after World War I, one of Taylor's principal assignments from FDR was to round up key Republicans to support the UN. Taylor also served on the State Department's Subcommittee on Territorial Problems under the leadership of Dr. Isaiah Bowman, then president of Johns Hopkins University. The group focused on the massive refugee population (approximately twenty million) that was being created as a result of the war's devastation.

A Fateful Prophecy

A priority for the Bowman group was to figure out what to do regarding the issue of Palestine. With the formation of the League of Arab States, encouraged by Britain, as background, on March 14, 1944, Taylor wrote to Secretary of State Cordell Hull about his concern over efforts "to encourage a consolidation of the Arab world," stating that such a plan "is filled with dangers of many sorts." Among Taylor's worries was the fact that "we in this country know all too little about [the Arab world]." He added, with amazing prescience,

> Perhaps one thing the world has to fear in the future is that strong aggregation of people bound by ties of blood and religion, especially those who are almost fanatical, now separated into groups and tribes and states, may join themselves together to oppose . . . the relatively smaller numbers of the Anglo-Saxon world.

When I found and read this memorandum in a collection of Taylor's papers at the Library of Congress, I wondered what Secretary Hull's response had been to Taylor's prediction of future conflict with the Arab world. On my next trip to consult the main body of Taylor's papers in the Olin Library at Cornell University, I found Hull's response in a memorandum dated April 1, 1944. Hull was clearly influenced in his thinking by British foreign secretary Anthony Eden, citing at length a 1941 speech by Eden: "It seems to me both natural and right that cultural and economic ties between the Arab countries, yes, and the political ties too, should be strengthened. His Majesty's government for their part will give their full support to any scheme that commands general approval." Hull then went on to pooh-pooh Taylor's concerns, opining that "the difficulties existing to Arab unity are far from negligible, and the initial steps in that direction would in all probability be only cultural and economic lines."

Unfortunately, Hull (and Eden) were proven to be wrong. The year 1945 saw the implementation of the Arab League Pact, which later that year boycotted Jewish businesses in Palestine to oppose the formation of Israel. And in 1947, the British withdrew support for its Mandate of Palestine, stating that it was unable to find a solution acceptable to both the Jews and the Arabs. Later that same year, the UN approved the partition of Palestine into two states—one Jewish, one Arab—with Israel declaring independence in 1948. Most historians agree that the contemporary roots of the Arab-Israeli conflict, and probably Muslim extremism, stem from this post–World War II period. Taylor continued to press President Truman with his geopolitical concerns on this front, but his and others' views, notably those of Secretary of State George Marshall and Undersecretary of State Robert Lovett, were overruled after a bitter intra-administration debate initiated by Truman and buttressed by his principal domestic advisor, Clark Clifford.

"A Useful Life"

After World War II, President Truman asked Taylor to continue on in his ambassadorial capacity to the Vatican, but with the advent of the Cold War the Taylor Mission morphed into a different model, more oriented to visiting church officials (and others) throughout Europe, particularly in Russian-dominated areas of Central and Eastern

Europe. Taylor's new mission was primarily designed to gather Cold War information to which no other Westerner had access, and to shore up opposition by the Catholic Church to the Soviet Union in fragile postwar Europe. By all measures, he succeeded on both scores.

In 1948, the pope named Taylor a Knight of the Order of Pius IX, First Degree, and on December 20 President Truman awarded Taylor the Presidential Medal for Merit. Truman praised Taylor for having "earned the accolades of his countrymen whom he has served faithfully and well wherever duty called him." Shortly thereafter, Taylor informed both the pope and the president that he would finally be retiring—a decision made public in January 1950.

Myron Taylor quietly lived out the remainder of his life. He did not publish his memoirs or seek public accolades. His beloved Anabel died on December 12, 1958, and Taylor died five months later, on May 6, 1959. The *New York Times*, reviewing his "extraordinary abilities" and his multifaceted career, employed considerable understatement when it concluded that "[h]is was, indeed, a useful life."

Anarchists rally in New York City in 1913. Credit: Library of Congress.

77

"Sympathy for Revolutionaries"

Frank Donegan

The era of the Great War confronted Americans with many of the political and ethical questions that would surface with regularity throughout the rest of the twentieth century and into our own: What is the nature of patriotism? Is there such a thing as a moral war? Should a military draft be resisted? How much should the government intrude into private life? How free is "free" speech? The public struggle to answer such questions gave birth to the American Civil Liberties Union (ACLU), which was founded in 1920 but whose origins were intimately bound to World War I and the "Red Scare" that followed it.

The run-up to war, and America's entry into it on April 6, 1917, were accompanied by a surge of patriotism—often of a jingoistic and xenophobic nature. Many questioned whether Americans with recent roots in, say, Germany or Ireland could be trusted to support Britain and France, U.S. allies. Alternatively, there was a committed antiwar movement, many of whose members felt the war would yield little benefit for the working classes no matter who won.

The Espionage and Sedition Act, passed by Congress in June 1917, provided the legal foundation for government action against war critics. Victor L. Berger of Wisconsin, the first Socialist elected to Congress, was convicted for his antiwar views. Eugene V. Debs, founder of the Socialist Party and its presidential candidate, was sentenced to ten years in prison after a June 1918 speech in Canton, Ohio, in which he criticized war but steered clear of indicting the current one. Vigilante-style groups such as the American Protective League (APL) were supported by the Department of Justice and conducted "slacker raids," searching bars and boardinghouses for young

This essay first appeared in summer 2009, volume 9, number 1.

men who had not registered for the draft; in a single raid in September 1918, APL members seized more than twenty thousand men in New York City. College professors and teachers risked their jobs for opposition to the war. Filmmaker Robert Goldstein was prosecuted because his movie about the American Revolution, *The Spirit of '76*, was considered too anti-British. Nebraska outlawed teaching any foreign language in its schools.

Peace Turns to Anarchy

Social strife did not abate with the Armistice in November 1918. There was worry (or hope, depending on where one stood on the issue) that the country was headed for a Socialist or Communist revolution. After all, Bolsheviks were solidifying their revolution in Russia, and two U.S. Communist parties were founded in 1919.

Others saw the war as a catastrophe for workers. Demobilization had led to a surge in unemployment and inflation crippled low-wage earners. Since 1914, food prices had increased 84 percent, furniture 125 percent, and clothing 114 percent. In 1919, 3,600 strikes affected four million workers.

A series of bombings and unsuccessful bomb plots in the months following the armistice fed the hysteria. On December 31, 1918, bombs exploded at the homes of three Pennsylvania government officials. Another bomb exploded at the Atlanta home of former senator Thomas Hardwick, blowing off his maid's hands. In New York, postal inspectors discovered thirty-four small packages marked "Novelty—A Sample" with a return address of the Gimbel Brothers department store. All contained bombs. Addressees included, among others, John D. Rockefeller, J. P. Morgan, Supreme Court Justice Oliver Wendell Holmes, and U.S. Attorney General A. Mitchell Palmer. The rash of bombings led to the infamous Palmer raids, in which thousands of people around the country were rounded up, often without warrants, and frequently confined without access to counsel. Illegal searches and physical intimidation were common. But the government's efforts amounted to little: the bombers were never discovered, and most of the arrested "radicals" were not charged, although some eight hundred were deported.

Enforcers of the State

At the height of this "Red Scare," the New York State Legislature appropriated $30,000 to investigate radicals in the Empire State, while at the same time it expelled five legally elected Socialist assemblymen. The committee it appointed—commonly called the Lusk Committee after Clayton R. Lusk, the freshman state senator from Cortland County who chaired it—made national headlines. Its informal headquarters was the Murray Hill Hotel in New York City and most of its hearings were held at City Hall, the first on June 12, 1919. More than a dozen hearings followed, including ones in Buffalo, Rochester, and Utica, cities where the Joint Legislative Committee to Investigate Seditious Activities—its official name—found "considerable well-organized revolutionary radical activity." Committee agents raided more than seventy-five offices of left-wing "radical" groups, some five hundred people were arrested, and tens of thousands of documents were seized, including financial records and membership lists. These were circulated among the state's district attorneys, who arrested many of those named as criminal anarchists, although very few were ever found guilty.

The committee's tactics were questionable. When its agents seized the files of the Soviet representative in New York, they obtained their subpoena from a local traffic court judge. Journalist Walter Lippmann said the committee violated "every principle of fair play" and condemned it for smearing reputations and manipulating the media. Jimmy Walker, then state senate minority leader, called Lusk a "political juggler and sleight of hand man."

A principal target of the Lusk Committee was the ACLU and its leader, Roger Nash Baldwin (1884–1981), who would head the organization for thirty years, until 1950. The committee's final report accused the ACLU of "working up sympathy for revolutionaries, influencing public opinion and generally spreading subversive propaganda."

The ACLU had descended from two earlier organizations: the Civil Liberties Bureau of the American Union Against Militarism (AUAM) and the National Civil Liberties Bureau (NCLB). The AUAM was formed to oppose U.S. involvement in World War I and was one of the largest peace groups of the period. When the draft was instituted, the AUAM's Civil Liberties Bureau, with Baldwin at its head, became a major conduit for advising young men opposed to the war. Later the AUAM spun off the bureau as a separate organization, the NCLB. In an October 6, 1917, letter, Baldwin told a supporter that the split arose because the bureau's work was more radical "than some of our conservative friends in the American Union committee are willing to stand for." Antipathy toward conscientious objectors had reached a fever pitch; Theodore Roosevelt condemned them as "a whole raft of sexless creatures," while the Lusk Committee report criticized the NCLB for "encouraging naturally timid boys to register as conscientious objectors."

The Justice Department held that any war criticism could be construed as a violation of the Espionage Act because it might encourage men to refuse induction—but by fall 1917, NCLB attorneys were handling 125 conscientious objector cases a week. In the summer of 1918, the Justice Department began tapping NCLB phones, and on August 31 agents raided the group's office and seized files. Lusk Committee files are replete with letters on NCLB letterhead to and from objectors in thirty-two states and twelve army camps. There are also many letters from Baldwin to local attorneys around the country asking them to cooperate "without fee."

Attending to the Constitution

Baldwin was, by all accounts, a charismatic organizer and fundraiser. The Lusk Committee described him as being "a charming, well-bred liberal, of good American stock and traditions, [but] in reality a radical to the very bone." He was a Mayflower descendant from a well-off family in Wellesley Hills, Massachusetts. He went to Harvard, became interested in social issues, then followed the advice of his father's lawyer, Louis D. Brandeis, and went to the Midwest, where he became a social worker in St. Louis. To many, he was a prototypical "parlor pink": at any given time, he might be orchestrating support for indicted members of the Industrial Workers of the World, yet he could also mix socially with Morgans and Rockefellers. In 1909, he had created a furor when he invited two black school principals to address his social work class at Washington University; in 1912 he led a protest when police shut down a Margaret Sanger birth control lecture. During the war, he had been jailed for refusing induction. He was friends with such legendary leftists as John Reed, Bill Haywood, and Max Eastman and corresponded for decades with Emma Goldman, but he also had a Greenwich Village townhouse, a gentleman's farm in New Jersey, and an estate on Martha's Vineyard.

After the war, Baldwin and a group of similarly inclined notables decided to retool the NCLB as an organization that would address a broad range of constitutional issues. The founding committee comprised some sixty people, including Jane Addams, Felix Frankfurter, Helen Keller, Norman Thomas, and Scott Nearing (who would achieve iconic status in the 1960s for his back-to-the-land philosophy but was at that time a college professor who had been fired for his views). In January 1920, the name change to American Civil Liberties Union became official, and the ACLU settled into its headquarters on the first floor of a three-story red brick townhouse on West 13th Street in New York.

Baldwin told the Lusk Committee that a principal reason for the name change was "that the character of the organization had changed from a bureau of legal services to a propaganda organization in the interest of civil liberty." He said the ACLU's new strategy would be "to test the constitutionality of local ordinances and state laws which are assumed to be in conflict with constitutional guarantees." Its 1920 annual report, *The Fight for Free Speech*, summed up its guiding principle: "There should be no control whatever in advance over what any person may say [and] the right to meet and speak freely without permit should be unquestioned."

Rights of Any Variety

The "Red Scare" never resulted in the conviction of major revolutionary plotters, and public interest in subversion waned in the face of Jazz Age distractions. In 1924, Clayton Lusk retired in disgrace after his wife received what the *New York Times* described as a "handsome chest of silver[ware] worth at least $1,000" from Tiffany's, from detectives whose salaries had been increased as the result of a bill Lusk shepherded through the legislature. Lusk was also suspected of taking a $10,000 bribe for voting against a movie censorship bill that he himself had introduced. Ironically, he had once written how important it was that New Yorkers elect those "who have sufficient moral, physical, and political courage, and the necessary energy to enforce our laws."

Meanwhile, the ACLU began to mix popular protest with legal challenges, and its doctrinal devotion to absolute free speech drew fire from across the political spectrum. During the early 1920s, the ACLU worked closely with the NAACP but also spoke out for the rights of the Ku Klux Klan to hold public demonstrations. United Mineworkers' chief John L. Lewis called the ACLU "communistic," yet the organization also defended the right of Henry Ford's newspaper, the *Dearborn Independent*, to publish vicious anti-Semitic articles.

Taking the lead role in the Scopes "Monkey Trial" in 1925, which upheld the teaching of evolution in public schools, established the ACLU's national image and was a fundraising boon to its fragile finances. By the end of its first decade, the organization had also broadened its reach by intervening in cases that involved sexuality and censorship in the entertainment industry. The ACLU was still losing more cases than it was winning, but the foundation for an organization that viewed itself as a protector of constitutional rights of any variety had been firmly established—in the postwar battleground of New York.

Sulzer had a distinguished career in Congress before he became governor. Credit: Library of Congress.

78

The Impeachment of Governor Sulzer

Matthew L. Lifflander

William Sulzer was elected governor of New York in November 1912, inaugurated on January 1, 1913—and by October he was impeached and removed from office. This forgotten incident is one of the most intriguing, dramatic, and colorful stories in the history of American politics. It embodies issues that continue until this day, including pervasive questions about money in politics.

With the support of the powerful Tammany political machine led by the infamous Richard Crocker, Sulzer had been elected to the state assembly from New York's Lower East Side in 1889 at age twenty-seven; three years later he became the youngest man in history to be elected assembly speaker. In 1894 he went to Congress and served with considerable distinction for eighteen years as an innovative legislator, a Tammany stalwart, and a great orator, rising to become chairman of the House Committee on Foreign Affairs.

Although Tammany expected absolute, unwavering, and total loyalty from its candidates, its influence was sublimated during Sulzer's New York gubernatorial campaign. "Plain Bill" Sulzer was presented to the people as an independent who would stand up to "invisible government," even though his nomination received a necessary nod from Tammany chieftain Charles F. Murphy and the theme of the campaign was Sulzer's proud pronouncement that he was totally free of boss control. However, based on the long history of his relationship with Tammany (especially as a Richard Crocker man in the assembly and his early years in Congress), the state's political leaders accepted this campaign rhetoric as good politics for a candidate from New York City seeking statewide support. Well aware of upstaters who considered the Tammany machine anathema, they nevertheless enthusiastically supported Sulzer

This essay first appeared in spring 2010, volume 9, number 4.

because, despite years of Tammany endorsements, he had a superb record of standing for progressive legislation and of eloquently articulating his beliefs. Sulzer's winning plurality of 205,000 votes was the largest in New York's history.

In eight years as Tammany's chief, Charles Murphy had grasped unprecedented power as the leader of the Democratic Party in both New York City and the state. Murphy, a saloon keeper, made a good living by running Tammany Hall, selecting winning candidates, and influencing government in New York City and Albany. When Sulzer was elected governor in November 1912, Democrats also carried New York for Woodrow Wilson as president and won a solid Democratic majority in both houses of the state legislature—whose leaders were loyal Tammany men destined to ascend to the highest rungs of the Democratic ladder: Alfred E. Smith of Manhattan was the new assembly speaker and Robert F. Wagner of Manhattan was senate majority leader. Both were very much beholden to Murphy.

Turmoil in Albany

On Inauguration Day, Sulzer initiated unprecedented turmoil. First, he began the process of ingratiating himself to political reporters at the Capitol by telling them he would always be available to them. This went hand in hand with the brand of populism he was trying to bring to his new administration. He also announced that he "belonged to no man," renamed the Executive Mansion "The People's House," held a public reception for all who wanted to attend, and abolished the traditional inaugural military parade and twenty-one-gun salute. For the inaugural festivities, Sulzer wore his battered fedora instead of a top hat and rejected the traditional horse-drawn carriage, instead walking to the Capitol and up the steps to the second floor.

On the second day of his term, Sulzer challenged Tammany's complete control of political patronage and began investigating corruption in state government—battles that would have far-reaching consequences. He started by inviting reporters for official briefings twice a day. As they gathered around him, Sulzer endeared himself to them by having chairs brought into the chamber. It was not lost on the reporters that Theodore Roosevelt had been the last governor to offer them seats, thirteen years ago. They were delighted with the governor's availability and most were justifiably flattered by his attention, especially when he started asking for their advice on issues.

During the late afternoon, when Sulzer, intending to alert the press to his plans for instilling honesty, efficiency, and economy in his administration, met again with the reporters, a newspaperman asked, half in jest, "Have you received the O.K. of Charles F. Murphy, Tammany leader, on your plans?" Until that moment, Sulzer had been seated among the reporters, talking on an off-the-record basis—a clear understanding in exchange for candor. But suddenly he stood up. "I knew that question would come up sooner or later, and it's just as well that we have an understanding on this subject right now, and then we will never refer to it again," he said. The governor then asked that his remarks go on the record:

> I am the Democratic leader of the State of New York. The people decreed it at the polls, and I stand on their verdict. I cannot succeed in doing what I want to do as Governor unless I am the leader. If any Democrat wants to challenge that, let him come out in the open and the people will decide.

Another reporter asked, "Does that mean that if Mr. Murphy wants to see you, he will have to come to the Executive Chamber?"

"This is the place," the governor answered with a determined nod.

One of the reporters who was stunned by the governor's challenge to Murphy's leadership said, "Those are the most comforting words I have heard in this room since Governor Hughes left" (referring to Charles Evan Hughes, whose administration ended in 1910). To which Sulzer replied, "Well, you are likely to hear plenty like it if occasion should arise. I am not afraid of Murphy, I am afraid of no man. No political boss can make me do anything I don't think I ought to do."

The governor had declared war on Tammany.

The Battle Is Joined

While the press could not get any direct reaction from Murphy himself, several Tammany district leaders (who were guaranteed anonymity) predicted that the "Chief" would take up the governor's gauntlet and make the challenge to his leadership the fight of his life. The essence of what Sulzer was trying to accomplish was captured in the headline of the *New York Times*' lead story on January 3, 1913: "Sulzer Invites Murphy to Fight for Leadership, Proclaims That He Is Democratic Chief in the State by Decree of the People."

Later in the year, when Sulzer rejected Murphy's most reliable allies for key positions regulating railroads and distributing highway construction contracts, Murphy finally realized he was being thwarted: a candidate whom he had supported was leaving the Tammany reservation. In a confrontation, Murphy called the governor an "ingrate" and let him know that his refusal to designate James E. Gaffney, a Murphy business partner, as state highway commissioner indeed meant "war."

Sulzer ultimately told his side of the story. According to his account, which I found in a draft of a never-published partial autobiography in the governor's personal files at Cornell University,

> Just prior to taking office as Governor, I spent an afternoon with Mr. Murphy, at his request, at his private room in Delmonico's. . . . He said he was my friend . . . and that he wished to help me out.
>
> To my astonishment he informed me that he knew I was heavily in debt. Then he offered me money to pay my debts, and have enough left to take things easy while Governor. . . .
>
> He said that nobody would know anything about it; that I could pay what I owed, and go to Albany feeling easy financially. . . .
>
> I declined Mr. Murphy's offer, saying that I was paying off my debts gradually; that my creditors were friends and would not press me; that I was economical; and that I would try to get along on my salary as Governor.

A Bridge Too Far

The second battle of Sulzer's war also began on the second day of his term. In his inaugural address, Sulzer had signaled his intention to review state government for the purpose of eliminating useless expenditures, abolishing sinecures, and promoting honesty and efficiency for the taxpayers' benefit. On Day 2, he announced the creation of a three-man Commission on Inquiry with the broad power to investigate all of the state's departments. The commission quickly initiated investigations of state officials involved with the awarding of lucrative prison, highway, and canal contracts—many of whom were Tammany's close friends from the previous administration of Governor John Dix, an upstate Tammany man who was not reelectable.

This would prove too much for Tammany. In August, an assembly investigating committee appointed by Speaker Al Smith recommended Sulzer's impeachment for a variety of offenses, primarily challenging the accuracy of the governor's reports on the money contributed and expended in his gubernatorial campaign—reports that had been filed before he took office. The committee alleged that Sulzer had pocketed large amounts of cash for his own use and invested it in Wall Street. After an all-night telephone session, orchestrated by Charles Murphy, between Murphy at his Long Island retreat and Smith in Albany, the assembly shocked everyone—especially Sulzer—by voting to impeach Sulzer at a special legislative session that he had called to consider his direct primary bill, which challenged the power of political bosses to select statewide candidates.

Sulzer's month-long impeachment trial before the state senate involved the state's best lawyers and a parade of prominent real estate developers, industrialists, and financiers who described their campaign contributions as personal gifts to Sulzer, for whatever purpose he wanted to use them. Some of them involved very large sums of cash that proved embarrassing to the people's governor.

The trial drew daily nationwide attention, and on October 17, 1913, the Court on Impeachment found Sulzer guilty on three of eight Articles of Impeachment and removed him from office. However, the court did not exercise its power to bar him from ever holding public office again.

A Political Survivor—Temporarily

The next morning Sulzer took a train to New York City, where thousands of enthusiastic supporters greeted him and took him in a motorcade from Grand Central Station to his old Lower East Side assembly district. A month later, after speaking at many receptions populated by huge crowds demanding Tammany's punishment, Sulzer was reelected to his old assembly seat by his biggest majority ever. In the same November election, the Democratic assembly majority was lost to the Republicans, and many of the Tammany senators who voted to remove Sulzer lost their seats. Tammany also lost the New York City mayor's office, mainly due to Sulzer's campaigning.

Tammany's influence was severely set back for several years. Sulzer was reelected to the assembly in 1914, where he served without distinction. He mounted an ineffective independent campaign to regain the governorship in 1914 and an unsuccessful effort to gain the Prohibition Party nomination for president in 1916—and was never heard from again politically.

NEW YORK
archives
Volume 1 · Number 1 · SUMMER 2001

NEW YORK
archives
Volume 1 · Number 2 · FALL 2001

NEW YORK
archives
Volume 1 · Number 3 · WINTER 2002

NEW YORK
archives
Volume 1 • Number 4 • SPRING 2002

NEW YORK
archives
Volume 2 · Number 1 · SUMMER 2002
AWARD-WINNING PUBLICATION
New York Archives
NORI Award
Magazine Design
Albany Ad Club
Association of Professional Communicators
1st Prize
Magazine Design
American Association of Musuems

NEW YORK
archives
Volume 2 • Number 2 • FALL 2002
242-6

NEW YORK
archives
Volume 2 • Number 3 • Winter 2003

NEW YORK
archives
Volume 2 · Number 4 · Spring 2003

WHIP
Volume 3 · Number 1 · Summer 2003
NEW YORK
archives

NEW YORK archives Volume 3 • Number 2 • FALL 2003

Celebrate
New York Archives Week
OCTOBER 12–18

Check these websites for events in your community:
www.archives.nysed.gov/a/newsroom/
www.nycarchivists.org

NEW YORK
archives
Volume 3 • Number 3 • Winter 2004

NEW YORK
archives
Volume 3 • Number 4 • Spring 2004

NEW YORK
archives
Volume 4 · Number 1 · SUMMER 2004

NEW YORK
archives
Volume 4 · Number 2 · Fall 2004

NEW YORK archives

Volume 4 • Number 3 • Winter 2005

NEW YORK archives

Volume 4 · Number 4 · SPRING 2005

NEW YORK archives

Volume 5 • Number 1
SUMMER 2005

NEW YORK archives

Volume 5 • Number 2
FALL 2005

NEW YORK archives

Volume 5 • Number 3
WINTER 2006

SPECIAL SECTION: 2004–2005 Annual Report of the Archives Partnership Trust

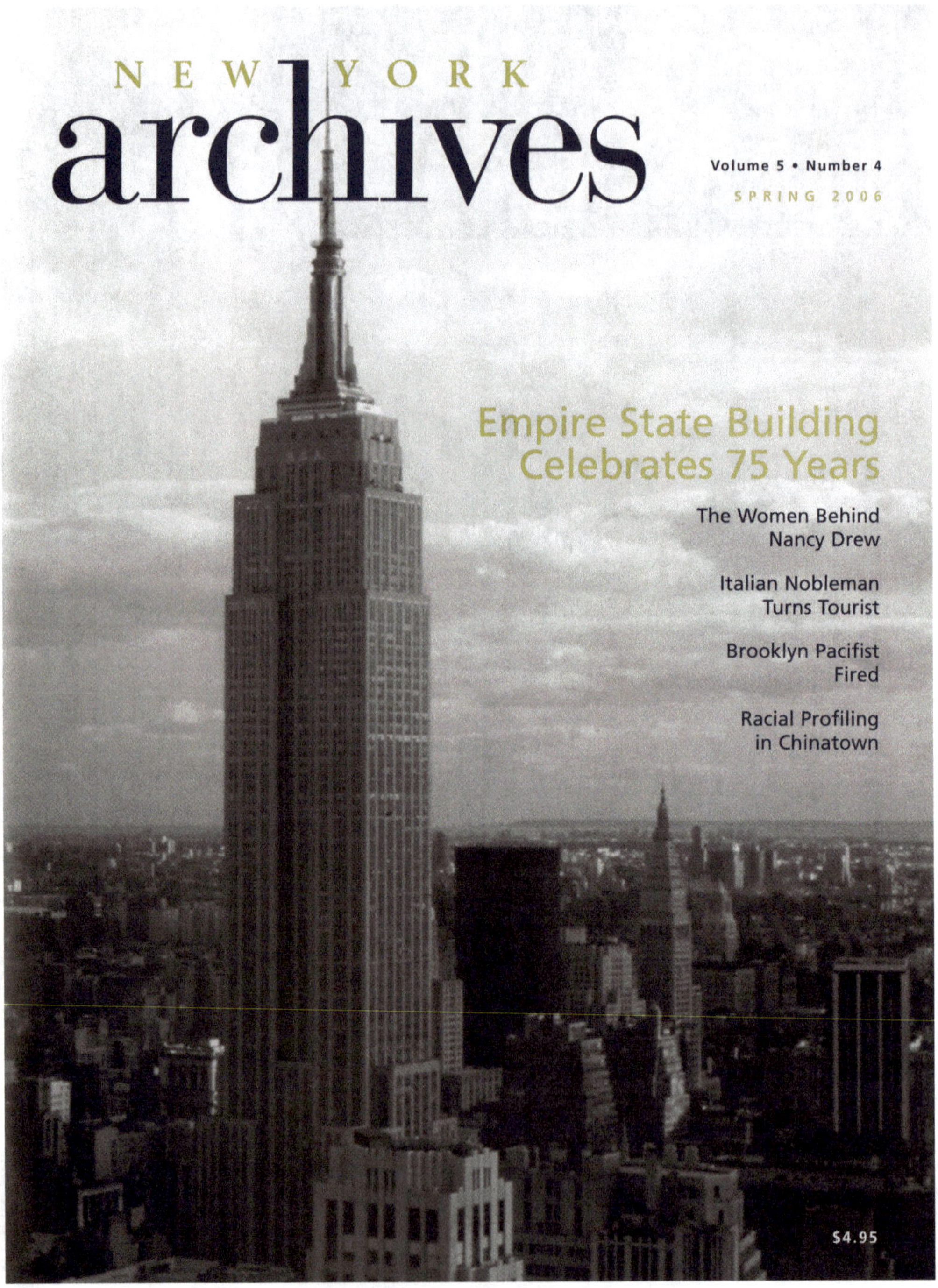
NEW YORK
archives
Volume 5 • Number 4
SPRING 2006
Empire State Building Celebrates 75 Years
The Women Behind Nancy Drew
Italian Nobleman Turns Tourist
Brooklyn Pacifist Fired
Racial Profiling in Chinatown
$4.95

NEW YORK
archives
Volume 6 • Number 1
SUMMER 2006
Albany Observatory Maps the Heavens
Thomas Jefferson Goes Shopping in Queens
A Dying President Says Thank You
Japanese Crowds Welcome Helen Keller
Westchester Prompts Heated Debate in Congress
$4.95

NEW YORK archives

Volume 6 • Number 2
FALL 2006

Making Beer Better

West Point Cadets Trounced by Unknown "Westerners"

Scandal Topples First Woman To Hold Statewide Office

The Yiddish Press in America

Teacher's Diary Details Life in Rural New York

$4.95

NEW YORK

archives

Volume 6 • Number 3

WINTER 2007

$4.95

Train Delivers Immigrants to the Poorhouse

Cameras Capture Civil War Soldiers

Oneidas Sell Land for Pittance, Peace and Protection

Murder and More Revealed in Westchester Trial

Daughters Go Onstage for Families

SPECIAL SECTION:

2005–2006 Annual Report of the Archives Partnership Trust | page 33

NEW YORK archives

Volume 6 • Number 4
SPRING 2007
$4.95

New York's "Paul Revere" Was a Girl

Richest Woman in New York • Lewis Latimer's Legacy of Inventions • Armories that Guarded the State • Child Soldier Killed by Stray Bullet • Rochester Builds a Subway

NEW YORK
archives
Volume 7 • Number 1
SUMMER 2007
$4.95
From Potato Farm
to Suburban Dream
Welch's Grape Juice, Not Wine
Canal Vandalism
as Economic Development
Politicians Spill Blood
on Albany Streets
After the Gangster Barbecue

NEW YORK
archives
Volume 7 • Number 2
FALL 2007
$4.95
STRIKE
War Protests
Cause Turmoil on
Syracuse Campus
Governor FDR Debuts
Fireside Chats on WGY
Borden's Condensed Milk
Transforms Central New York
Women Against Women Voting
Private Turnpike Promises
a Way to Get Rich Quick

NEW YORK
archives

Volume 7 • Number 3
WINTER 2008
$4.95

Mohicans
in New York

Long Islanders Protest
Government Order

History of an
Adirondack Paper Mill

The Golden Age
of Whaling

Teachers Join Forces
to Make Changes

Edward Rulloff,
Scholar and Criminal

NEW YORK
archives

Volume 7 • Number 4
SPRING 2008
$4.95

Heartbreak on the 13th Hole

Whisking the Mail Through Underground Tubes

William Livingston, Catalyst of the Constitution

Mixed Welcome for Holocaust Survivors

Meetinghouse Hosts Caldron of Reform

Pro-Slavery Sentiment in Central New York

NEW YORK

archives

Volume 8 • Number 1
SUMMER 2008
$4.95

Disaster on Cayuga Lake Claims Eight Lives

NEW YORK archives

Volume 8 • Number 2
FALL 2008
$4.95

New York Hotels: Icons at the Cosmopolitan Crossroads

Mothers Abandon Babies on the Streets

Voting to Deny Black Men the Vote

Harriet Tubman's Biographer

WPA Fails Domestics

Jewish Criminals Behind Bars

NEW YORK

archives

Volume 8 • Number 3

WINTER 2009

$4.95

SPECIAL ISSUE

LINCOLN AND NEW YORK

WITH GUEST EDITOR HAROLD HOLZER

WILLIAM KENNEDY · JAMES M. McPHERSON · CRAIG L. SYMONDS · CATHERINE CLINTON · FRANK J. WILLIAMS · JAMES OLIVER HORTON · HANS L. TREFOUSSE

NEW YORK archives

Volume 8 • Number 4
SPRING 2009
$4.95

Ethel Merman, Queen of Broadway

Giants Heed Call to Go West • Before There Was Pong • A Short Line for Shopping
Canadian Capital in Flames • Archives Inspire Hudson Valley Novel

NEW YORK
archives
Volume 9 • Number 1
SUMMER 2009
$4.95
Myron Taylor, Man with a Mission
The World's First Cancer Center • Champlain Meets the Mohawks
New York City's Slave Trade • America Ducks and Covers • The ACLU Is Born

NEW YORK
archives

Volume 9 • Number 2
FALL 2009
$4.95

Bringing Down Benedict Arnold

Confederate Prisoners Speak • The Photography of Berenice Abbott
New York Cleans Up Its Streets • Seaway Celebrates Fifty Years

NEW YORK
archives
Volume 10 • Number 1
SUMMER 2010
$4.95
Secrets of Niagara Falls
Inconvenienced by General Washington
Troy Riot Liberates Captured Slave
Misbehavior in Saratoga
The Rise and Fall of the Jewish Deli
DO NOT THROW STONES OVER THE CLIFF.

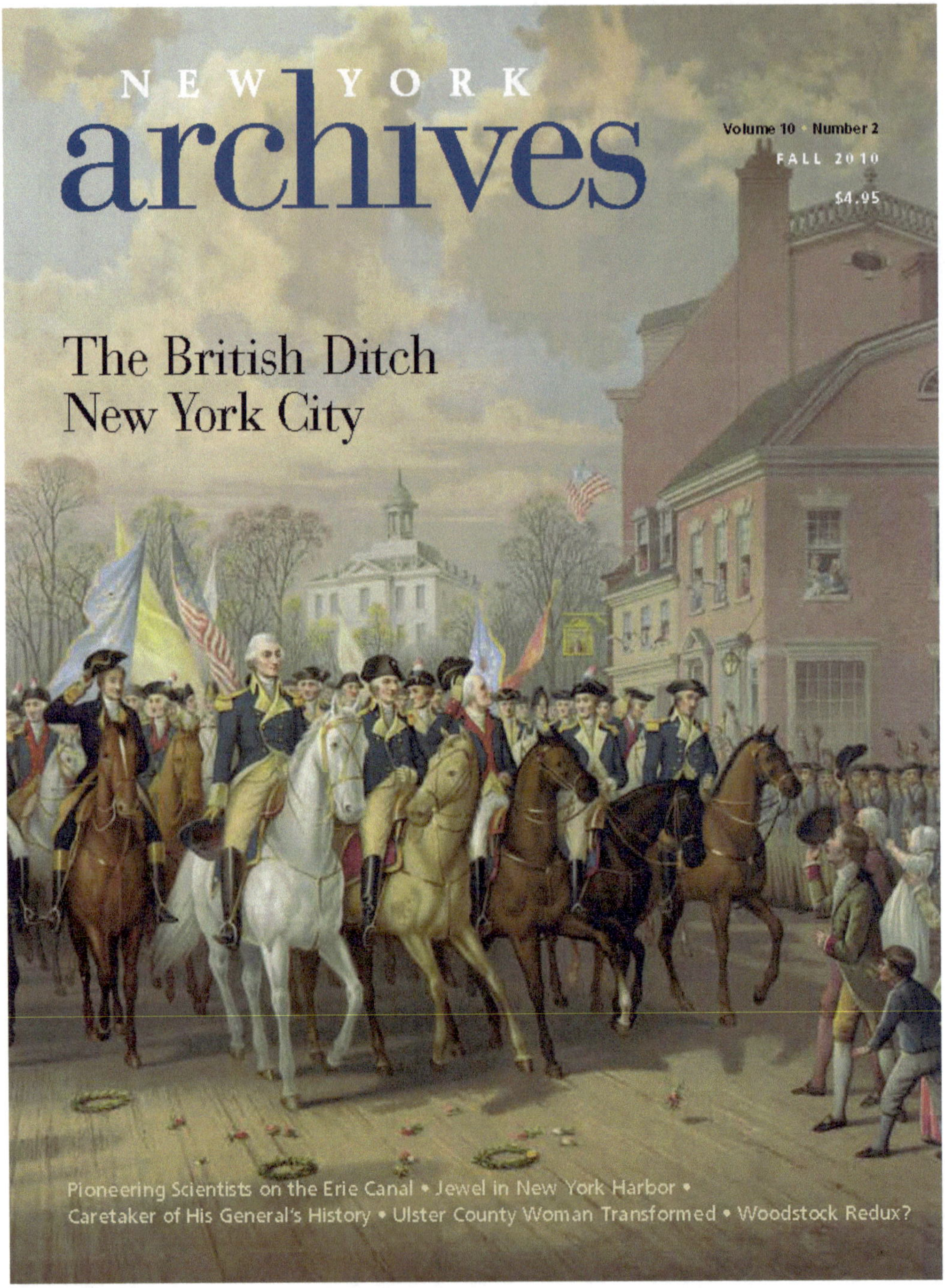
NEW YORK
archives

Volume 10 · Number 2
FALL 2010
$4.95

The British Ditch
New York City

Pioneering Scientists on the Erie Canal • Jewel in New York Harbor •
Caretaker of His General's History • Ulster County Woman Transformed • Woodstock Redux?

NEW YORK
archives
Volume 10 • Number 3
WINTER 2011
$4.95
Huck Finn
Born in
New York
Boy Soldiers on the Front Lines
Muslims in New York City
Fatal Plane Crash Saves Many
The House That Westinghouse Built
Hunting for Communists in the Classroom

Index